Warning!

Horror, Monsters, Violence & the Supernatural

The *fictional* world of Nightbane® contains subject matter that deals with the supernatural, monsters, conspiracy theories, the paranormal, magic, war and extreme violence.

The setting is our modern world taken over by demonic creatures from another world and their legion of nightmarish henchmen. Even the heroic Nighbane must turn into monstrous beings and use magic and strange powers to battle the supernatural invaders.

Some parents may find the subject matter, violence, magic and supernatural elements of the game inappropriate for young readers/players. Furthermore, the realistic manner in which the fictional horror material is presented *may* be disturbing for some young readers.

WE STRONGLY SUGGEST PARENTAL DISCRETION.

Please note that none of us at Palladium Books® condone or encourage the occult, the practice of magic, the use of drugs, vigilantism or violence.

Nightbane® Dark Designs™ **is a sourcebook for the** *Nightbane®* **role-playing game.**

Dedication

This one is for the fans. Those of you who have patiently waited through the long night. I hope you enjoy this book, because there are more where it came from.

Mark Oberle ~ 2017

The cover, by *Charles Walton II* and *Eduardo Dominguez S.*, depicts a band of Nightbane on the move and ready for action.

First Printing – August 2017

Palladium Online: **www.palladiumbooks.com** – also visit us at **facebook.com/PalladiumBooks**

Nightbane® Dark Designs™ Sourcebook is published by Palladium Books Inc., 39074 Webb Court, Westland, MI 48185-7606. Printed in the USA by McNaughton & Gunn.

Palladium Books® Presents:

Dark Designs™

A guide to creating & playing the Nightbane®

Written by: **Mark Oberle**

Additional writing and ideas: **Kevin Siembieda**

Editors: **Alex Marciniszyn**
Kevin Siembieda
Wayne Smith

Proofreader: **Julius Rosenstein**

Cover Painting: **Charles Walton** and **Eduardo Dominguez S.**

Interior Artists:
Charles Ferguson-Avery

Border Art:
Charles Walton II
Kevin Siembieda

Art Direction: **Kevin Siembieda**
Typography and Layout: **Wayne Smith**

RPG rules by **Kevin Siembieda**
Nightbane® RPG setting created by **C.J. Carella**

   Special Thanks to *Mark Oberle* for writing and compiling this comprehensive Nightbane® resource. To Chuck and Eduardo for an evocative and moody cover, to Charles Avery-Ferguson for his wicked interior art, and to the heroes of the secret war on this side of the Mirror Wall at Palladium Books, *Wayne, Kathy, Alex, Julius, Chuck, Ben, Gwen* and *Scott*.

– Kevin Siembieda, Publisher, 2017

Contents

Dark Designs **6**
The Monster Within 6
Life after the Becoming .8
The Becoming **10**
Facade to Morphus Transitions 10
   Transformation Effects 11
Anatomy of a Morphus 13
Nightbane Morphus Tables **15**
Nightbane Appearance Table (Updated) 15
Characteristics Table (Updated) 16
Appearance Table (Comprehensive) 16
Characteristics Table (Comprehensive) 17
New Morphus Tables **18**
Ancient Warrior Table 18
Animal Form Table 20
Insectoid Table II 21
Primate Table 23
Artisan Table 25
Athlete Table 28
Clown Table 29
   Clown Gags 31
Gear-Head Table 33
Hobbyist Table 35
   Video Games (powers) 36
Mythical Creature Table 37
Nightmare Table 40
Occupation Table 43
Pestilence Table 45
Plant Life Table II 47
   Types of Mushrooms 49
Sci-Fi Table 50
   Personal Scanner/Sensors 52
Modern Soldier Table 53
   Weapons 55
Substance Abuse Table 55
   Pill Descriptions 56
Superbeing Table 58
   Gadgets 60
New Common Talents **62**
All-Nighter 62
Ashes to Ashes 63
Blast Wave 64
Bomb-Maker 64
Bookworm 64
Brain Freeze 65
Bypass 65
Chain Lightning 66
Channel Speed 66
Channel Strength 66
Chronosphere 66
Darkblast 67
Dark Edge 67
Darkmetal Infusion 67
Death-Grip 67
Down the Drain 68
Dust in the Wind 68
Earthworks 69
Eavesdrop 69

Encryption 70
Fear No Evil 70
Flurry 70
Form-Lock 70
Frightener 71
Ghost Tag 71
Gunslinger 72
Hotwire 72
Hound Leash 73
Hyper-Awareness 73
Ignorance is Bliss 73
Inferno Fist 74
Iron Will 75
Jam Senses 75
Killing Spree 75
Launch 76
Leap 76
Leave No Trace 77
Livewire 77
Mage Siphon 77
Mass Transit 78
Mimic Spell 78
Mimic Talent 79
Mirror Sense 79
Mirror Shield 79
Nega 80
Open Channel 80
Phantom Limb 80
Pipe Bomb 81
Pocket Change 81
Raven Wings 81
Reality Mooring 82
Skill Stealer 82
Sky Writer 82
Solar Flare 83
Switchboard Operator 83
Trap Shadow 84
Ultra-Vision 84
Wall Runner 85
Wall Whisperer 85
Witch-Hunter's Sight 85
New Elite Talents **86**
Beguiling Beauty 86
Beyond the Call 87
Choke 87
Contortionist 87
Corrupting Influence 88
Dark Dreams 88
Dark Fathom 89
Diamond-Hide 90
Divine Wrath 90
Epic Proportions 90
Fan Club 90
Ghost Ship 91
Hatred's Mirror 91
Hysterical 92
Legionnaire 92
Living Nightmare 93
Master Stroke 93
Mystic Amplifier 94

Nature's Fury 94
Necrosis 95
No Rest 96
Overdrive 97
Pariah's Mantle 97
Passing the Torch 98
Payday 98
Rallying Cry 99
Revolting Spit 99
Rigor Mortis 100
Seedling 100
Shadows of Despair 101
Shadow Swarm 102
Share the Needle 102
Sideshow 103
Summoner 103
The Ties that Bind 104
Too Much Stereo 106
Urban Golem 106
War Cry 107
Talent Creation and Conversion **108**
A Game Designer's Advice 108
To Convert or Create? 108
Creating and Altering Talents 109
Step #1: Select One or More Base Effects 110
Damage 110
Step #2: Modify the Base Cost 110
Duration 111
Step #3: Wrapping Up 112
Ancient Nightbane **113**
Creating an Ancient Nightbane 115
Ancient Nightbane R.C.C. Stats 118
Ancient Nightbane Experience Table 121
Plot Hooks for Ancient Nightbane 120
Questions and Answers **121**
Morphus Appendix **124**
Unearthly Beauty 126
Animal Form 126
Arachnid 127
Avian/Bird 128
Bat 128
Canine 129
Equine/Bovine/Deer 130
Feline 130
Insectoid 131
Reptilian 132
Rodent 132
Snake 133
Stigmata Table I 133
Facial Features 134
Alien Shape 135
Unnatural Limbs 136
Biomechanical I 137
Morphus Tables: Between the Shadows **138**
Bear Form 138
Amphibian 138
Biomechanical II 139
Stigmata Table II 140
Morphus Tables: Nightlands Sourcebook **140**
Mineral Table 140

Plant Life 141
Appendix Talents **142**
Common Talents from the Nightbane® RPG **143**
Anti-Arcane 143
Borrow Morphus 143
Darksong 143
Darkwhip 143
Doorway 143
Infectious Control 144
Lightening Rider 144
Mirror Sight 144
Mirror Search 144
Nightbringer 145
Premonition 145
Reshape Facade 145
See Truth 145
Shadow Blast 146
Shadow Shield 146
Sharing the Flesh 146
The Shroud 146
Shadow Slide 146
Soul Shield 146
Splittin' Image 147
Storm Maker 147
Elite Talents from Nightbane® RPG **147**
Bloodbath 147
Deus Ex Machina 148
Lord/Lady of the Wild 148
Swarm Self 148
Talents from Between the Shadows **149**
Air Grab 149
Astral Self 149
Darkwave 149
Dervish Dance 150
Dreamer 150
Piece Work 150
Common Talents from Survival Guide **151**
Air Swim 151
Fire Breather 151
Heal Facade 151
Severance 151
Shadow Pockets 151
Shadow Weapon 152
Speed Darkling 152
Elite Talents from Survival Guide **152**
A Face in the Crowd 152
Abduction 152
Commanding Presence 153
Forbidding Woods 153
Gorgon's Touch 153
Guardian Angel 153
Kill Switch 154
Lend a Hand 154
Nightshade 154
Spelljack 154
The Taint 155
True Reflection 155
Vicious Cycle 156
Voice of the Beast 156
Zombie Master 156

Dark Designs

A guide to creating the Nightbane®

The Monster Within

Imagine waking up in the morning, looking in the mirror and seeing a monster like something out of a nightmare staring back at you. Now imagine what you would feel when you realize the creature is *you*.

In comic books and film, when you wake up one morning miraculously gifted with inhuman powers it is a thrilling and joyous event. You throw on a mask and a pair of tights and go out into the world to fight crime and protect the innocent. People quickly accept you and all is good.

Real life is much more complicated.

First comes the horror and fear. There is nothing joyous about this unexpected and unwanted manifestation. It is earth-shattering and soul-crushing. You have Supernatural Strength and these powers, but to use them you must turn into something else. Something inhuman. Monstrous. It makes no sense. Even those whose inhuman self is beautiful and exotic are left in shock, and likely to lock themselves indoors and cry for a week. Maybe even consider suicide.

You can't help but to question, *what are you?* Was the life you've always known all a lie? A dream? Only to awake to this living nightmare? It feels like it.

We human beings are conditioned by our homogenous nature and commonality to each other, so that becoming something else – something entirely inhuman, even part of the time, is devastating and horrifying. It shakes you to your very core. You feel isolated and ostracized. Alone with this terrible, terrible new truth. This desperate secret.

Your knee-jerk reaction is to hide and shut out the rest of the world. Your mind reeling, you begin to question what you are and what you have ever been. Suddenly, the world is a different place and you are the outsider. The *Frankenstein monster* that doesn't fit in. Everything you thought you knew is a lie. Nothing makes sense. You question *everything* and realize you don't know anything anymore.

Who do you turn to? The authorities? Hell no. Friends? Family? No, how can you? They'll think you are insane when you tell them about your condition. And when you show them proof by becoming something else, something not human, they'll be shocked and horrified. Can you face such a reaction and the rejection that will certainly follow? It is too terrible to consider. Every possible scenario swirls through your thoughts. None of them any good.

So you are alone to face the unspeakable truth that you are a monster or demon or alien of some kind. An inhuman creature that has been hiding inside of you all this time. Hiding inside a human shell waiting to come out and ... do what?! Kill? Invade? Eat babies? How could you not know this thing was inside of you? Is this where bad thoughts come from? Is this the proverbial demon said to haunt people? Are you evil? Do you give in to the dark impulses or fight them?

For days there is nothing but questions, tears and a painful fury of terror, doubt and self-loathing. You wonder if you are hu-

SIEMBIEDA 2017

man. Were you ever human? You beg God – any god – to make it stop. To take it away, but your prayers go unanswered and the torrent of questions start again. "How do I stop this? Can I get back to normal? What did I do to deserve this?! Who will love me now? Accept me? I am a freak! A monster! How can I live like this? What am I going to do? What does this mean? Who can I turn to for answers? Turn to for help? Can I hide this horrible ... thing ... that I am?

The answer to the last question is a quick, yes.

And no.

As you and others like you soon discover, a **Nightbane** – as they are called online – can switch from human Facade to Nightbane Morphus at will. A fact that provides great comfort for Nightbane immediately after their *Becoming*. They are quick to hide under the human Facade that everyone knows and hide the beast within them. Bury it deep and try to forget, except once a person has *Become*, it is impossible to bury those traumatic memories. This is where the "no" part of the answer comes into play. Once the proverbial genie has been released from the bottle, it is impossible to forget the experience. The truth cannot be forgotten, not even when the genie is stuffed back inside the bottle. You know what's there, lurking inside. Waiting for release.

Moreover, Nightbane can sense other Nightbane. It's not like a neon sign or glowing aura, or anything like that, but one Nightbane, even in his or her human Facade, will notice and sense something strange about another human being who is also a Nightbane under his Facade. The awareness of others like you manifests as a strong hunch or feeling that the mousy woman or young skateboarder on the corner is like you. A fellow Nightbane. The closer the proximity or the greater the frequency of exposure to the person, the stronger that suspicion becomes. However, the Nightbane can never be certain until the suspect reveals his or her true Morphus.

Second, comes the denial. "This can't be happening to me. Okay, it's over. I'm back to normal! No, it's happening again. God, I can make it happen whenever I want it to. That's fine. I can control it. Nobody has to know. Not ever. Nothing has changed. I'm not that ... that thing. I'm the same person I've always been. It's okay. Everything will be okay."

Nightbane in denial try their utmost to put the Becoming behind them and ignore the manifestation of special abilities, and any unwanted transformations that might occur as a response to fear, anger or self-defense. They also try to ignore the growing awareness that the world is not right. That it has not been right since *Dark Day,* and that monsters, demons and the supernatural are real. Much too real.

Some make an effort to ignore news reports and discussions on the topic of strange happenings and the growing number of disappearances and violence since Dark Day. Others study such news reports, rumors and speculation with intense interest and dread. The Internet is, of course, a hotbed for widespread speculation, rumors, innuendo and hearsay on such matters. It is there you are likely to first hear the word, *Nightbane,* as well as hear about dark conspiracies, government cover-ups and monsters instigated by the terrifying event dubbed **Dark Day**. New Nightbane gathering such information do so in the hopes that they can find a "cure" or some evidence that their "condition" will improve and go back to normal. The problem is, there is no normal in the world since Dark Day, that much is clear, and there is more cause for concern than peace of mind to be found.

Despite all this, most Nightbane in denial desperately try to go about their day to day routine as if nothing has changed. Under this pretense of normalcy, the Nightbane in denial is probably a seething mess of conflicting thoughts and emotions, driven by fear, and constantly on edge. Work performance is likely to drop 1D6x10%, and the individual keeps to himself and worries about what comes next.

Third, anger. "What am I!? Why me?! What did I do? How do I get back to normal? I don't deserve this! What if I can't ever return to normal?! (They can't.) Am I stuck like this forever?! (Yes.)"

The angry Nightbane is irritable, tense and quick to anger. Constantly afraid they will lose control and reveal the monster within, many are ticking time bombs. And they know it. Their greatest fear: what then? That is the million dollar question and the real terror that haunts the newly risen Nightbane. What happens if someone uncovers the truth about them? Already angry about what is happening to them, this makes the Nightbane extremely self-aware and hyper-sensitive. Anger may manifest as surly or argumentative behavior, moody avoidance, sudden outbursts (angry shouting or tears), and even acts of physical violence. ("What are you looking at? Mind your own business!")

If bullied or threatened, the individual may assume his Nightbane Morphus as a response and fight back. This is when some Nightbane discover they enjoy their newfound inhuman powers. Others become even more frightened of themselves and the power they wield. And if unleashing a new ability or even just assuming the frightening Morphus causes an innocent person or loved one to be injured or killed, the newborn Nightbane may now carry the weight of guilt on his shoulders and become all the more convinced he or she is a dangerous monster. And another reason to shun people and hide.

Fourth, depression and introspection. At this stage, most newly awakened Nightbane fall into a depressed state and engage in a strange flirtation with their "monstrous" or "dark side." This involves practicing the transformation from Facade to Morphus, studying the Morphus in the mirror, discovering and experimenting with special abilities available in Morphus, thinking about the Morphus (and why that form?), and trying to come to terms with it all. It is a time of serious questions and self-discovery. I have these wings, can I fly? What else can I do? There must be a reason for this, what is it? How can I use this to my benefit or to help others?

It is also around this time that most begin to wonder if there are others like themselves. And if so, how do they find them? Should they try to find them? Do they hold the answers they seek?

This is a dangerous phase, because the Nightbane may decide he or she is, indeed, an evil monster or hell-spawned demon, and respond accordingly. Such thoughts may lead to attempts at suicide or acts of violence. Those who believe themselves to be evil or uncontrolled monsters may use their Morphus and the powers that come with it for acts of terror and violence. They may seek vengeance upon enemies, rivals and people they believe are out to get them, or may turn to crime. Others deliver violence upon others to test themselves or just to vent their emotions. The most ashamed or despondent turn violence on themselves. Putting themselves in situations where they suffer attacks and grievous bodily harm to punish themselves for whatever perceived "sins" they must have committed to have become this monster.

The majority of new Nightbane going through this phase isolate themselves, shunning friends and family, and keep to themselves. Tormented by the fear and self-loathing already discussed, for a time, some may turn to alcohol or drugs to find relief. This often makes matters worse, causing the individuals to feel more depressed, out of control and irrational.

Others study themselves like a lab rat, and test themselves and their mysterious Morphus abilities behind closed doors or in their basements or attics, or in an abandoned building or a deserted stretch of country. Most tests and experimentation take place at night when few people are around and the Nightbane is less likely to be seen. Unable to hide from themselves, new Nightbane are drawn to explore the dimensions of their new, other self. Making this time of depression also one of reflection and self-discovery.

It is a difficult transition. A small percentage kill themselves rather than live as a monster. Some go mad. Others try to hide among the wash of humanity and wait for a sign to do more, or for a clear direction to take hold. A small percentage become a force for evil or adopt a self-serving agenda.

Fifth, acceptance. In the end, whether it takes days, weeks or months, there is no denying or escaping the fact they now straddle the line between human and something else. Something supernatural and/or magical. This acceptance changes the way the Nightbane see themselves and the world.

It helps if the Nightbane can find someone to confide in. Someone who can help carry the burden of their terrible secret and offer a shoulder to cry on and a sounding board on how to move forward. This confidante may be a close friend or family member, or a fellow Nightbane. After all, who but another like you can truly understand what you are going through?

The vast majority eventually come to accept their transformation and seek to find purpose. For them, questions become a search for answers. The Internet and rumor mills are swollen with eyewitness and third party accounts of strange occurrences, monster sightings, supermen, demons and, yes, Nightbane. The word *Nightbane* is found all over the web. Some

talk about the Nightbane as superhuman protectors of humanity — heroes who are kind and courageous. Others say the 'Bane are monsters or demons, and dangerous. While still others, including most government websites, insist the so-called Nightbane are nothing more than urban myth and mass hysteria rekindled after the strangeness of Dark Day. Conspiracy theories abound, some of which claim the government knows all about the Nightbane and is keeping their existence a secret to avoid widespread panic and rioting. Or because the Nightbane are the creation of a secret government operation gone terribly wrong (Dark Day, too), and they don't want people to know. There are all kinds of rumors and conspiracy theories like these. In fact, such conspiracy theories claim that the NSB (National Security Bureau) was created specifically to hunt the Nightbane down, cover up their existence, and bring them into government custody for further study and extermination. Some even say the NSB and most of the governments of the world have been infiltrated and taken over by shadowy demons who are the enemies of humankind and Nightbane alike. And some on the Internet even claim to be *Nightbane* themselves, with offers to help others like them.

It is hard to tell what is true and what is not. And it is especially difficult to determine what a Nightbane should do with his newfound abilities. Some self-proclaimed Nightbane and groups offer to meet and help novice Nightbane to find their way. But can they be trusted? Are they really Nightbane or is it a trap set by haters, the government, or worse?

Finding *the right* Nightbane or group of Nightbane can change everything for those looking for answers and direction, but even the most well-intended can only offer so much guidance. The path a Nightbane must ultimately follow is left to each individual and it is fraught with peril and difficult life choices.

The last step for a newly revealed Nightbane, is finding peace with what he is, and a way to go on. Finding a way to accept what you have become is important, but it is just the beginning. For Nightbane, the Becoming is the start of a hard, unforgiving existence. Some Nightbane do their best to hide from that life and avoid conflict, but most accept what seems to be their fate, or are thrust into it when conflict finds them.

Life after the Becoming

All of this is traumatic and difficult enough, but there is more. None of it good.

Nightbane soon learn they are hunted, kidnaped, interrogated, caged and slaughtered without mercy. And they are most vulnerable after the Becoming when they are scared, confused and searching for answers.

A secret campaign of genocide is taking place in the shadows of every city on Earth. Here the Nightbane are hunted and slaughtered without mercy by their own governments and police agencies under the control of the real monsters pulling the strings.

SIEMBIEDA 2017

As talk about the Nightbane becomes increasingly prolific on the web, so are the rumors about demonic beings called **the Nightlords** and their unholy minions. The Nightlords are said to be evil demonic beings from a twisted, alternate Earth dimension known as the *Nightlands*. A place of eternal twilight and evil.

The Nightlords, their Princes, Princesses and minions are all various sorts of demons who became able to cross into our world when the dimensional wall between Earth and their mirrored twilight Earth was weakened during the **Dark Day** event.

According to some websites and self-proclaimed supporters of the Nightbane (or enemies of the Nightlords), the Nightlords and their minions have infiltrated all corners of the world's governments via shape-shifters and human-looking Doppelgangers in the service of their Nightlands masters. Moreover, the Nightlords can make themselves appear completely human. Thus, they and their demonic minions have managed to quietly replace their human counterparts on Earth. This has enabled the Nightlords to seize control of most of the world governments and security agencies without the public knowing it. A global invasion without anyone – but the Nightbane – being the wiser. One day the president or prime minister is fine, the next he is different. A bit more bombastic, extreme, selfish and sadistic, or cruel and manipulative. A personalty change, whether subtle or extreme, accepted without anyone suspecting the man or woman is not the same person at all, but a wicked, demonic duplicate.

The invasion continues as more wicked denizens of the Nightlands manage to trade places with their Earth counterparts. Swapping places from one dimension to the other. As more humans in high places are replaced with Nightlords, Night Princes, Night Princesses and Doppelgangers, more Nightbane come into existence to challenge them.

As the invaders knew they would.

According to popular rumors, the Nightbane are hunted because they can see through the demons' false human face and possess the power to destroy them. They recognize the evil denizens of the Nightlands even when they are in human guise, seeing them for what they are, and instinctively knowing they are evil and must be destroyed. Moreover, the very essence and Talents of the Nightbane give them the power to fight and destroy supernatural evil, whether they be from the Nightlands or some other hellish dimension.

As a preemptive measure, the forces of darkness taking control of the human world strike first. Trying to discredit, slay and imprison Nightbane to prevent them from interfering with their invasion of the planet. The Nightlords replace innocent people within the government, military, law enforcement and in positions of influence, with wicked Doppelgangers and Night Princes, while the innocent are sent to live in the nightmarish **Nightlands** in their place. The Nightlords' ultimate goal, to make Earth their playground. A new conquest to be transformed into a hellish world of chaos, violence, and torment. The Nightbane trapped in the role of the tragic hero.

There have been tales of the "chosen ones" throughout the ages. It is quite another thing to actually be the "chosen ones" in real life, which is where the **Nightbane** find themselves. They are the antithesis to the Nightlords. The yang to the Nightlord's yin. The Nightbane representing light, positive energy and humanity, while the Nightlords and their minions (yin) represent the dark, the negative and the demonic.

Why them? Why are the Nightbane the *Chosen?* A very good question to which there may never be a definitive answer. Some legends and rumors suggest they are *fallen angels*. To redeem themselves, they live among humans until the day comes when they are needed once again, and are given the opportunity to stand on the side of goodness and light in the face of a great darkness. Others speculate the Nightbane have always existed and are some sort of reincarnated or immortal *eternal champions*. Still others have suggested there is a *recessive gene* or latent ability found in some (all?) humans. When it is triggered, it turns ordinary people into Nightbane to protect humanity as a whole against the supernatural evil that has hunted and tormented humans since the beginning of time. That gene or demon-slaying ability remains dormant until a spectacular event like *Dark Day,* and the mass invasion of supernatural evil, occurs. Then, like *antibodies* found inside of our own human bodies, the Nightbane manifest to battle the invading infection of evil. And fight to destroy the darkness that threatens to consume humanity like a cancer.

Whatever the reason, the Nightbane do seem uniquely empowered to deal with supernatural evil of all types and guises.

Nightbane, the Chosen Ones, are born human, and though some believe otherwise, they are human in every way that counts. They are gifted (or cursed) humans with the ability to see supernatural evil even when it (and the Nightbane) is cloaked in the flesh of humanity. Nightbane see the truth, recognize the demonic enemy as if by instinct, and intuitively know they possess the power to destroy such monsters. Thus, the hunted become the hunters in the dark corners of our modern world. The Nightbane's Morphus is much like a supernatural suit of living armor, like the knights of old, worn into battle against a wicked and demonic enemy. The so-called *Talents* and *magic* serving as the Nightbane's sword and lance with which to slay the monsters that threaten the innocent.

Evil is cowardly, so the wicked beings from the Nightlands hide under the face and flesh of humanity. There, they hope to remain unnoticed among the masses. Quietly (and not so quietly) nudging innocent people and unwitting henchmen to fight their battles and slay the Nightbane for them. This is in addition to a legion of demonic monsters and shape-changers who also hunt the 'Bane at night and from the shadows.

Matters for the Nightbane are made worse by the fact that their Morphus clearly marks them for what they are, and they must morph to use their full range of powers. There is no disguising the Nightbane when they transform from human Facade to their true, warrior Morphus. Each a tortured visage that terrifies the

very people they are trying to protect from evil. The Nightlords in power have made certain that the public knows nothing of the shadow war between the Nightbane and their human allies against the Nightlords and the government agencies they control. So it is that people not aligned to the invading darkness inadvertently help the forces of evil every time they call the authorities to report a strange occurrence or sounds of battle. Some may even call with the impossible story that their friend or acquaintance turned into a monster before their very eyes. Mistaking the Nightbane as the danger, not the heroes, the innocent and frightened help the forces of evil destroy the very beings trying to protect them. Such are the cunning and twisted ways of the Nightlords. Sightings of monsters are covered up as hysteria, claims of lights and shadows playing tricks on the eyes, swamp gas, and flat-out lies.

So it is that creatures of darkness disguised as humans walk among us unnoticed and as welcomed friends and loved ones; while the Nightbane must figure all this out on their own and hunt the Nightlords even as they themselves are hunted.

It is a lot to accept.

For the Nightbane who find their footing as the "chosen ones" – heroes preordained to fight for the soul of humanity – their path and purpose become clear over time, but not any easier. All forces are aligned against them.

The authorities are either infiltrated by the enemy or manipulated by them, or both. The enemy, secured in positions of power and unrecognized by the masses, are free to do as they please with minimal constraint. They manipulate the law, the media, and the government to do as they please and corrupt all around them. Keeping their own demonic existence, along with the Nightbane, concealed. Shielded in lies, unsubstantiated rumor and disinformation.

Upon death, the Nightbane turn back into their human Facade, leaving no trace of their supernatural nature. Another reason for their enemies to kill them upon sight and claim them to be criminals, madmen, rioters or members of a terrorist cell. While the Nightlords and their minions choose to live in secrecy, the Nightbane are forced to do so for their own survival. Never knowing who they can trust. Battling against a supernatural foe that most humans don't even know exists.

The Becoming

"The Becoming" is the common name for the first time a Nightbane shifts into the Morphus form, but it is may also be used to describe every other shift from Facade to Morphus and vice versa. This process, like the Morphus form itself, is highly individual.

The Becoming can appear in almost any number of ways. While a Nightbane with stigmata features might tear through the skin of the Facade's current form to reveal the other beneath, a Nightbane with fantasy features might disappear in a puff of smoke or swirl of energy and reappear in his or her Morphus form.

Despite the many possible appearances of a Nightbane's Morphus (no two Nightbane are identical), all transformations from Facade to Morphus, and vice versa, function the same way.

After that very first Becoming, the Nightbane can transform at will, making the shift from Facade to Morphus with a thought, and it can be started or stopped at any point. That means if a Nightbane were to fail the Mental Endurance save and face a full melee round of transformation, the player may choose to cancel the change and stay in the current form. It does, however, take a single melee attack (3 seconds) to return fully to the starting form. The transformation can easily be a moment of comparative weakness, and must not be entered into lightly. That's why Nightbane expecting trouble will usually try to find a secluded place to "morph out" before a fight, rather than risk being stuck in Facade form in the middle of a battle, or transform into their Nightbane Morphus (or human Facades) in front of eyewitnesses or cameras that may be used to identify and track them down in their human identities. Remember, the Nightlords and their minions cannot recognize a Nightbane in his or her human Facade, so the human identity is greatly valued and carefully protected.

Facade to Morphus Transitions

If a Nightbane is forced to change forms during melee combat, there are three possible outcomes. First, the character succeeds the Mental Endurance roll and rapidly shifts. Second, the character fails and cancels the Becoming to avoid being caught between forms for a full 15 seconds (one melee round). Third, the character is between forms for an entire melee round (15 seconds) before the change is complete. That third scenario has lacked description until now. See below.

While undergoing the transformation between Facade and Morphus, or vice versa, Nightbane are physically in flux, but can typically still function and take action. All stats and bonuses – whether they are for combat or otherwise – stay those of the starting form until the transformation is complete. This means that a Nightbane changing from Facade to Morphus uses the Facade's bonuses for as long as the transformation flux lasts, and uses the Morphus's bonuses when transitioning from Morphus to Facade.

There are a few areas of exception to this rule. S.D.C., Hit Points, rate of healing, and saving throws all operate a bit differently. Any time the Nightbane is changing forms and sustains damage, it is subtracted from the Hit Points and S.D.C. of the *Morphus* form. Likewise, the rate of healing is that of the Morphus. The same logic applies for any saving throws such as those against psionics or magic spells; use the Morphus form's bonuses when in transition and ignore those of the Facade.

SIEMBIEDA 2017

One major weakness, though, is that Talents are completely unavailable when undergoing the transition between forms. Likewise, skill performance may or may not make sense (G.M.s, use your discretion).

Transformation Effects

(New and Optional)

What follows is a table that can help further describe a Nightbane character by detailing the appearance of that character's Becoming and subsequent transitions from one form to the other. Entries may be selected by players or G.M.s to suit a specific character, or rolled randomly. Each category has specific benefits listed with it which are entirely *optional*, but intended to help defray the disadvantages of transforming during combat. Even if the bonuses are ignored, this table can still be interesting to add a bit more color to Nightbane characters.

01-07% Binary Code/Pixelated: The physical form of the character turns into rows of ones and zeroes, tiny colored dots, or even the "snow" of an untuned analog television channel. This digitized mass then rearranges into the alternate form. In some cases, sounds such as computerized beeping or hissing static can be heard during the transformation. **Bonuses:** While undergoing the Becoming, the Nightbane is immune to any physical attacks such as punches, kicks, and bullets. +1 bonus to Becoming speed (the M.E. saving throw that determines how long the Becoming takes). **Penalties:** If hit with any electrical attacks while transforming, the attack deals double damage and cancels the Becoming.

08-14% Disintegration & Reconstruction: The body of the Nightbane actually breaks down at the start of this Becoming or transition from one form to the other. Examples of this include shattering into shards of glass, rapidly decomposing, and burning to ash. The remnants of the body then reassemble to become the alternate form. **Bonuses:** All damage done to the Nightbane while undergoing the transition/Becoming is reduced by half. This transformation also has a Horror Factor of 1D4+8 to any spectators unfamiliar with it. **Penalties:** Minimum length of the Becoming is two attacks (6-7 seconds) rather than one on a successful Becoming speed roll, and movement speed is halved for the duration of the shift. Skill performance is likely to be impossible during these seconds of flux.

15-21% Dimensional Hideaway: This character's Becoming is a freak dimensional anomaly some think is related to the Nightbane's affinity with the *Mirror Wall*. At the start of the transformation, the Nightbane appears to step through an invisible door and disappear. Actually, the character has disappeared into a tiny pocket dimension where the transformation takes place. Once it is completed, seconds later, the altered form steps back out, transformed, at the exact same location he disappeared from. **Bonuses:** During the Becoming this character is completely removed from reality and thus cannot be targeted for attack or even detected for those seconds of transformation! **Penalties:** The Becoming always takes a full melee round regardless of the outcome of any Becoming speed roll. Also, the Nightbane is completely unaware of anything that happens in his or her absence. Permanently reduce the Nightbane's P.P.E. base by 10 points at the time of his first Becoming.

22-28% Double Negative: For the duration of the Becoming, the Nightbane appears to be two beings occupying the same physical space. The visual effect is similar to a photography term called a "double exposure" where one image is overlaid upon another. This is difficult for the perceptual systems of most beings to reconcile, giving them pause to try and figure out exactly what is being seen; the features of both blurred and unrecognizable. **Bonuses:** Opponents viewing this Becoming must roll a saving throw using any bonuses from an exceptional M.E. attribute. If the roll is not 15 or greater, the opponent loses his next attack/melee action and is -5 to strike the character while between forms. **Penalties:** -4 to any Perception Rolls and -50% to all Communications skills (including *Language*) while undergoing the Becoming.

29-35% Energy Shift: To start with, the Nightbane begins to crackle or glow with energy. This could be anything from light, to fire, and even electricity. This intensifies until the character appears to be made of this energy with an intensity that is blinding. The shape then changes to that of the new form before the energy fades away. **Bonuses:** Anyone viewing this Becoming without eye protection (sunglasses, tinted goggles, etc.) must roll to save vs temporary blindness (needs to roll a 17 or higher to save). A failed roll means the character is blinded for 1D4 melee rounds (15-60 seconds); -10 to all combat rolls, and skills requiring sight are impossible. Anything within three feet (0.9 m) of the energy transformation suffers 3D6 damage from the intense energies and heat. **Penalties:** The possible penalties and damage are dealt indiscriminately, which may harm allies or innocent bystanders or damage property.

36-42% Gargoyle: The Nightbane momentarily freezes and takes on an earthen hue and seems to turn into a stone statue. A moment later, the thin, stone outer crust fractures and falls away to reveal the new form (human or Nightbane) waiting underneath. Nightbane whose Morphus causes them to grow in size or bulk may seem to erupt from the stone statue. **Bonuses:** During this Becoming transition, the Nightbane has a Natural A.R. of 17. The character can also choose to burst forth from the stone shell, causing a small blast of fragments that inflict 1D6 damage to a 6 foot (1.8 m) radius. **Penalties:** The Nightbane is completely unable to move or take any actions while transforming from Facade to Morphus and vice versa, not even in self-defense.

43-50% Gory Rebirth: During this transition, the alternate form seems to tear out of, or burst through, the other form. This creates a bloody, gory affair often accompanied by the sounds of tearing flesh (and possibly the screams of the character), mak-

ing this a gruesome transformation that leaves behind blood and gore. Ironically, none of it with any identifiable DNA markers other than "probably human." Many Nightbane with stigmata or nightmare features have Becomings like this. **Bonuses:** This transformation has a Horror Factor of 1D4+13. Anyone failing to save against Horror Factor is unable to attack the character during his transformation. Instead, they watch, transfixed by the gruesome scene. **Penalties:** The transformation is painful for the Nightbane, imposing -2 on all combat rolls for the first melee round (15 seconds) after the Becoming/transformation.

51-57% Maelstrom: The Nightbane becomes a flurry of physical activity. The movement is so fast, in fact, that all physical features, tattoos, etc. are a blur. This transformation can take the form of spinning like a top, vibrating like a humanoid jackhammer, or even appearing like an old cartoon fight with limbs and face appearing randomly from a chaotic swirl or blur of movement. **Bonuses:** All opponents are -3 to strike the Nightbane during this transformation. Anyone who comes within arm's reach is struck hard (1D6+1 damage), knocked back 10 feet (3 m), probably onto their backside, and loses two melee attacks/actions. **Penalties:** The Nightbane is -4 on Perception Rolls and is unable to attack or perform skills while transforming (but may still attempt to parry or dodge incoming attacks without penalty).

58-64% Obfuscation: Something gathers or swirls around the Nightbane, obscuring the individual from view. This might be smoke, ash, mist, dust, sawdust, feathers, leaves, ice particles/snowflakes, or even a cloud of insects. Whatever the material, it swirls around to cover and obscure the individual inside, falling away only when the transformation stops. An alternative might be that the features of the character blur and distort as if viewed through a poorly focused lens that continuously distorts what is seen. Whatever the specifics are, the function is the same, with a 5 foot (1.5 m) area around the transforming Nightbane affected. Features are indistinct and the exact location of the Nightbane within the cloud is difficult to discern. **Bonuses:** All opponents are -5 to strike the Nightbane during this Becoming/transformation. **Penalties:** The Nightbane is -6 on Perception Rolls involving sight and sound for the short duration of the transformation, as well as unable to attack or perform skills while transforming (but may still attempt to parry or dodge incoming attacks without penalty).

65-72% Overlay/Cocoon: Some material, be it webbing/silk, resin capsule, crystalline encasement, ice, paper, rags, dust, twigs, mud, concrete, or an army of tiny machines or particles rush at the transforming Nightbane as if he were a magnet. Only they don't stick to him or swirl around him, rather they form a hard shell around him like a cocoon. When the transition from one form to the other is complete, the material all falls apart and drops to the ground. **Bonuses:** For the duration of this Becoming transformation, the character gets an additional 100 S.D.C. that absorbs any damage directed at it, protecting the character inside. Furthermore, the Nightbane's healing rate is temporarily

increased to 10 S.D.C./H.P. per melee attack/action rather than melee round. **Penalties:** Reduce movement speed and all Physical skills by half while transforming.

73-82% Physical Shift: This is the classic monster transformation, like that of werewolves in any number of movies. Features distort, stretching or contracting. The character might sprout or lose hair, or produce spikes or other protrusions. The body might enlarge or shrink, and so on. There is little to no blood and gore associated with this change, and while it might look and even sound painful, there is little discomfort to the Nightbane. **Bonuses:** +3 bonus to Becoming speed. **Penalties:** -10 to Spd attribute while transforming, -2 on all combat rolls, and -20% to all skills while changing form.

83-90% Shadow Shift: The Nightbane's starting form dims and darkens to the point it appears to be composed entirely of solid shadows. Then, the physical shape of the dark shadow seems to be absorbed or fade into the desired form (Facade or Morphus). **Bonuses:** +2 bonus to Becoming speed and any physical damage inflicted during the transformation does only 30% its usual amount. **Penalties:** While transforming, bright light actually damages the Nightbane. High-powered flashlights inflict 1D6 damage, vehicle high-beams or floodlights do 2D6 damage, large searchlights deal 4D6 damage, and being outside on a sunny day or in a brightly lit room inflicts 1D4x10 damage.

91-95% Vanishing Act: Quite simply, the Nightbane disappears and then reappears in the form shifted into. The 'Bane is still present, just invisible to the naked eye (identical to the effects of the Invisibility: Simple incantation on page 131 of the Nightbane rule book). The invisibility only lasts for as long as the transformation takes, however. **Bonuses:** A difficult Perception Roll is needed just to detect the presence of the character, and even then opponents are -8 to strike the invisible Nightbane. **Penalties:** Permanently reduce the Nightbane's P.P.E. base by 15 points.

96-00% Melt, or Other: This is by no means meant to be an exhaustive list, so players and G.M.s are encouraged to develop their own unique Becoming sequences. Simply use the table above as a guide and remember that as a rule, any bonuses or penalties associated with the Becoming transformation should be short-lived (a few seconds to one full melee round/15 seconds). Alternatively, the player can choose to simply re-roll on this table or has a Melting transition.

Melting transformation: The character seems to melt like a human-sized candle into a pillar of goo, before it reforms into the identity (Facade or Morphus) desired. **Bonuses:** Any attacks leveled at the character during the melting transition inflict half damage and all who witness the event must roll to save vs Horror Factor 1D4+13. A failed Horror Factor save means the character simply stands and watches the transformation, and is incapable of attacking (but can defend himself) until the transformation is complete. **Penalties:** The Nightbane is -5 on Perception Rolls involving sight and sound for the duration of the transformation,

SIEMBIEDA 2017

as well as unable to attack or perform skills while melting and reforming (but may still attempt to parry or dodge incoming attacks without penalty).

Anatomy of a Morphus

Reprinted from Nightbane® Survival Guide

The appearances of Morphus forms are as unique as the individual Nightbane who wear them. Despite how bizarre and frightening the inhuman form can appear, the looks and abilities of the Morphus are hardly random. Even the smallest of details about the the Morphus is a reflection of the Nightbane and determined by the psyche of each individual. Therefore, the appearance of a Morphus is affected by the Nightbane's personality, how he sees the world and his place in it, his darkest fears, insecurities, deepest hatred, strongest desires, wildest dreams, personal aspirations, interests, and the people, places and things that affect/touch him in some way. That may include a particularly vivid childhood memory or impression, a spiritual belief, a favorite animal or person, or how he thinks of himself (or wishes he was), or how he

fears others think of him, or even a fictional character, image, sentiment, or aspiration inspired by a movie, TV show, book, comic book, video game, song, or anything that had a profound impact on the individual's life.

While strong elements of the Nightbane's personality determine the appearance of his Morphus, not every factor dictates his appearance, just the elements that had a significant and profound impact on the individual, and not even all of them. For example, if a Nightbane simply had a pet cat while growing up, that doesn't mean he or she has feline characteristics for the Morphus Form. On the other hand, if the person had a deep fondness for the cat, or more to the point, felt he could relate to cats, wished he was a cat, or felt he was a cat in a past life, then that Nightbane might have a feline Morphus Form. However, there are many other contributing factors, so that feline Morphus might be thin, sensual and agile, or bulky, powerfully built and armed with large claws and fangs. Likewise, the feline might have machine parts or weapon limbs, or wings or . . . just about anything, all representing some subconscious aspect of the individual.

All of us have a lot going on in our *subconscious* of which we are unaware. Strong subconscious feelings, desires, fears, etc. can have a large impact on the appearance of the Morphus. This means oftentimes even the Nightbane themselves can't explain why they look the way they do! Body armor, for example, could represent power and strength, or insecurity and the need for a protective shell.

Although the initial shock of the Becoming is usually terrifying, most Nightbane quickly become comfortable in their Morphus skin. Monstrous or not, a character's Morphus soon feels right. Many Nightbane actually come to think of their inhuman looking *Morphus* as their "true self." This is likely due to the fact that the Morphus is indeed a reflection of the person's inner self; that which is often kept hidden and locked up, but is as real and as important (maybe even more so) as the outward Facade we all let the rest of the world see. Consequently, a short while after the Becoming, most Nightbane do not see themselves or other 'Bane as monstrous, ugly or frightening.

Of all the questions, shocking revelations and life changing transitions, the three questions that a Nightbane is likely to struggle with the most go to the core of human identity: *Who or what am I? What is my purpose and place in the world? How do I fit in?* This is why Nightbane wonder which is the real them: Their human Facade or their monstrous Morphus? Are they human or Nightbane? Depending on the individual person, they may regard their human self or their inhuman Morphus as the "real" them. Ironically, *both* are the real them; different sides of the same coin.

Likewise, there is much debate over whether the Nightbane are human or supernatural. That question seems more difficult to answer, as they are born ordinary humans, raised as humans, and think and behave as humans. When they Become a Nightbane, their physical form is clearly more than human and they wield

supernatural abilities. However, they are the same person inside, and isn't that person human? Again, the question really seems to come down to appearance, emotional trauma and personal perception as to whether a Nightbane chooses to think of himself as *human* or *inhuman*. To make the matter worse, the Nightlords and their minions try to divide the Nightbane's ranks and create confusion and emotional turmoil by raising the question of their humanity and whether a supernatural being or monster has any loyalty to the human masses. Of course, making the Nightbane feel separate and ostracized by the rest of humanity works in their favor and weakens their Nightbane enemies. It's psychological warfare, and the masters of lies are very good at it.

Finding meaning behind a Morphus

In a game context, players are encouraged to explore the possible meanings behind their Nightbane's Morphus as an exercise to develop their character's personality, hopes, dreams and back story. It can add a lot of depth to the personality of the character.

One way to develop meaning and personality around a Morphus. This is just a suggestion, but it has worked for one of the authors in creating Nightbane characters.

Step 1: Roll one four-sided die and add two to the total. This determines the number of Nightbane Characteristics that are clearly reflected in the Morphus.

Step 2: Determine personality elements equal to the number rolled. These may include fears, goals, interests, experiences, beliefs, and the like, but they have to play a part in who the character is and his personality.

Step 3: Look over the Morphus tables and pick a particular Morphus characteristic or table that relates to each personality element, roll on the tables (re-roll if duplicate rolls result), and assign them to your Nightbane character.

Step 4: Obtain the G.M.'s approval of the Morphus to make sure the relationships make sense and the powers will not unbalance the game. You now have a Morphus Form that relates directly to the character.

For example, Nadine is a fourteen year-old girl who lost her parents in an automobile accident a year ago. Before that, she always tried to change how she looked and acted to fit in with the "cool kids" at school. Recently, she has taken up bird-watching as she has always found birds beautiful and wishes she had wings so she could fly away somewhere.

When Nadine undergoes her *Becoming*, she finds her Morphus to be an elegant humanoid with no face (since she sacrificed her identity to fit in), bird wings (to fly away with), broken glass imbedded in her skin (from the car accident), and four arms (because though she was unaware of it, she has been feeling overwhelmed by the amount of work she has to do in school).

Behold, a Morphus Form that makes sense. To further the concept, Nadine might start with a Nightbane Talent such as *The Shroud*, allowing her to hide her true self.

Another example is Charlie, a seventeen year-old high school student who is a bit of a science fiction geek. He is sensitive and caring which, in concert with his sci-fi nerdiness, gets him picked on every day at school. He never seems to stand up for himself, or fight back physically, leading even his father to think of him as a "wimp." However, Charlie deliberately draws the bullies' attention away from the younger kids and upon himself to save them the torment he's known all his life. Deep down he knows that he is meant for something greater, he just doesn't know what.

His greater purpose manifests in his Morphus as a thick metal exoskeleton (from both his sci-fi interests and to represent the "inner emotional armor" with which he defends himself against the bullies and the disappointment of his own father), he is tall and powerfully built to heroic proportions (because he's always wanted to prove to his father and those who laughed at him that he isn't a wimp), and an inner light (representing the nobility and kind heart that most don't see) glows from within. He would also likely have a starting Nightbane Talent that deals with defense, such as *Shadow Shield*.

In the alternative, roll up a Nightbane character using or picking from the usual tables, and/or the new ones in this book, and then build the personality traits around the appearance of your fictional character. In other words, figure out the personality, fears, emotions, etc. based on the Morphus traits randomly rolled or selected.

A Game Master & Player Note: Flexibility and imagination are key to enjoying this game. It is fun to allow a player to roll a lot of inhuman characteristics for his Morphus. The more combinations to the appearance, the more horrific, weird and fun it is to play. However, multiple Morphus characteristics also mean multiple bonuses, powers, and penalties.

Too many bonuses are likely to create a ridiculously powerful character. C.J.'s original advice was for the G.M. to "put a cap on the number of attribute and S.D.C. bonuses if the Game Master felt the players were just trying to stack bonuses for the sake of power." It was also stated, "don't let rolls rule the game; be imaginative and have fun." While we agree with this statement, the new tables offer a great many multiple selections and bonus stacking, so we felt it necessary to drop in some formal guidelines.

If you want (and if the G.M. allows) truly superhuman Nightbane with incredible power, let all bonuses (and penalties) be cumulative, and you are done.

However, if you allow the bonuses for characters who roll on 4, 5, 6 or more Morphus characteristics tables, you are likely to have a character with bonuses to strike, parry, dodge, etc., in the range of +12 and greater. That can take away from game balance and even game play. If the character is, say, +18 to strike, where is the fun in that? Dice represent luck and happenstance. If the bonus modifiers are too high, it removes the element of chance, and makes the game much less exciting. Here is Kevin Siembieda's solution:

SIEMBIEDA 2017

Morphus Attribute Bonuses: Add the Morphus bonuses for each individual attribute together. For Example: Three of your character's four Morphuses provided a different P.S. bonus. Add all three of those P.S. bonuses together. Before you add that total to the character's P.S. attribute, you may have to adjust the number. If the total bonus is greater than 6, divide the bonus number by half. Round up in the case of fractions, and add the halved number to the character's attribute. Thus, if the character has P.S. attribute bonuses that add up to +9, divide by half. Half is +4.5, but round it up to +5. The +5 bonus is added to the P.S. attribute, not the original +9 number.

Do this for EACH attribute. The only exception is Spd. Let Spd bonuses add up and apply the bonus unchanged.

If the total bonus is 6 or less, it gets added to the attribute without modification. As always, high attributes provide greater bonuses to strike, parry, dodge, etc.

Morphus Combat Bonuses: In addition to attribute bonuses, a character often also enjoys *combat bonuses* for things like *Perception Rolls, initiative, strike, parry, dodge, pull punch,* etc., as well as *Horror Factor.*

In this case, add the bonuses for each of the different combat moves (i.e. bonuses to strike, then parry, etc.) and divide the total for *each by half* and round down. Thus, if the combined Morphus bonuses were say, +14 to strike, +10 to parry, +9 to dodge, +6 to Perception Rolls, and +9 to Horror Factor, the number actually given to the character is HALF *rounded down.* Using the example above, the bonuses given to the character would be +7 to strike, +5 to parry, +4 to dodge, +3 to Perception Rolls, and +4 to Horror Factor. This is in addition to bonuses from high attributes and skills, so the character is still a powerhouse.

Morphus S.D.C. Bonuses: If the total bonus is 180 S.D.C. or less, I say let it stand. After all, Nightbane are, a) monsters, b) supernatural in Morphus form, and c) superheroes. If the S.D.C. is more than 180 points, reduce by half or bring it down to 180 S.D.C., whichever is greater. For example, if the bonus S.D.C. amount was 90, 100 or 134, the character gets that number because it is under 180. However, if a character had a combined S.D.C. of 220, the S.D.C. bonus would be reduced from 220 to 180. If it was, say 430 S.D.C., dividing it in half would make the S.D.C. bonus 215 because the number after division was greater than 180. In this example, even after division it is higher than 180, but that's okay, some Nightbane are tough as steel. Moreover, if the Game Master is running a high-powered campaign, he may, at his or her discretion, allow Nightbane with very high amounts of S.D.C. that numbers into the several hundreds. Have fun.

Nightbane Morphus Tables

The following tables are split into two distinct sections. **The first set of tables** combine the new material in this sourcebook with the **Nightbane® RPG** core rule book. If you *don't* have the **Nightbane® Survival Guide™** or other sourcebooks at your disposal, use the first set of tables to make your character. **Publisher Note:** We have tried to include all Morphus tables from those titles in the Appendix section at the back of this book.

The second set of tables are more comprehensive, and reference tables included in the **Nightbane® Survival Guide™** and other supplements. If you have those other titles on hand, use the Comprehensive tables.

All of it is presented to help Nightbane players and Game Masters roll up and create Nightbane characters more quickly and with more nuance.

In all cases, these tables are intended to be guidelines and food for thought. Feel free to incorporate *your own* ideas, designs, appearances and Morphus variants.

Nightbane Appearance Table (Updated)

Roll percentile for a random determination, or select one.

01-10% Almost Human: The Nightbane's Morphus is almost totally human, except for one inhuman trait. If lucky, that one Nightbane trait *might be* easily disguised with makeup or concealed with clothing, a hat/headwear, or other type of covering. That said, the not so lucky get one trait that is monstrous enough to give away the character's true supernatural nature. This could be massive size, a third eye in the middle of the forehead (or in the back of the head, or in the palms of the hands), small horns, monstrous claws for hands, an animal-like feature (fin, fur, or fangs, or snake tongue, cat's eyes), and so on.

Roll only ONCE on the *Characteristics Table* below to determine the unusual characteristic. If the result asks for more than one characteristic, ignore it and reroll.

11-20% Inhuman but Beautiful: The Nightbane combine a beautiful appearance with rolls on the *Unearthly Beauty Table* and the *Characteristics Table.*

21-30% Marred Beauty: The character has a beautiful True Shape, but it is marred by a gruesome stigmata. Make rolls on the *Unearthly Beauty Table,* the *Stigmata Table,* and the *Characteristics Table.*

31-39% Mundane: While this Morphus is still bizarre, it combines elements of everyday life. Roll 1D4 times total, on any combination of the *Occupation, Hobbyist, Athlete,* and *Gear-Head* tables.

40-45% Starving Artist: This Nightbane's Morphus reflects his or her artistic side. Roll once on the *Artisan* or *Clown/Jester Table* and once on the *Characteristics Table*.

46-50% Historical: Whether the 'Bane is a modern history-buff or actually an Ancient Nightbane from a bygone era, this Morphus reflects an age long-since passed. Roll once on the *Ancient Warrior Table* and once on the *Characteristics Table*.

51-56% Super-Soldier: The character has a Morphus that seems tailor-made for waging war. Roll once on the *Superbeing, Soldier,* and *Sci-Fi Tables*.

57-65% Lycanthrope: The Nightbane's Morphus is a mixture of animal and humanoid traits. Roll once on the *Animal Form Table*.

66-73% Monstrous Lycanthrope: Not only is the Morphus form animal-like, it has hideous deformities that give it a terrifying appearance. Roll on the *Animal Form, Nightmare* or *Stigmata,* and *Characteristics* tables.

74-78% Fabled: The Nightbane looks to be something straight out of a twisted fairy tale. Roll once on the *Mythical Creature Table* and once on the *Characteristics Table*.

79-83% Carnifern: This Morphus appears to be a walking, talking plant come to life. Roll once on the *Plant Life Table II* and the *Characteristics Table*.

84-88% Inhuman Shape: The Nightbane's True Shape is a gruesome mockery of humanity. Roll on the *Stigmata* or *Nightmare Table* and once on the *Characteristics Table*.

89-92% Bizarre: Roll once each on the *Nightbane Characteristics, Unearthly Beauty, Animal Form,* and *Stigmata* tables. Then exercise your imagination to combine the alien result.

93-96% The Sickness: This Morphus type is common amongst those who view being a Nightbane as a disease or disorder and those who were coping with an illness at the time of the Becoming. Roll once on the *Pestilence* or *Substance Abuse Table,* once on the *Stigmata* or *Nightmare Table,* and once on the *Characteristics Table*.

97-00% Xenomorph: The character's Morphus form flies in the face of biology and anatomy. Roll once each on the *Alien Shape, Animal Form, Plant Life Table II,* and the *Biomechanical* or *Gear-Head* tables.

Characteristics Table (Updated)

When rolling on the following table, if the roll is 91% or higher, any subsequent rolls on this table are rerolled if that result is also 91% or higher. In other words, only one roll that provides multiple characteristics is allowed.

01-10% Comic Book: Roll on the *Sci-Fi* or *Superbeing Table*.

11-20% Unusual Facial Features: Roll on the *Unusual Facial Features Table*.

21-30% Macho: Roll on the *Athlete* or *Soldier Table*.

31-40% Biomechanical: Roll on the *Biomechanical* or *Gear Head Table*.

41-50% Performer: Roll on the *Artisan* or *Clown/Jester Table*.

51-60% Alien Creature: Roll on the *Alien Shape Table*.

61-70% Workaday: Roll on the *Hobbyist* or *Occupation Table*.

71-80% Unnatural Limbs: Roll on the *Unnatural Limbs Table*.

81-90% Wretch: Roll on the *Pestilence* or *Substance Abuse Table*.

91-95% Two Characteristics: Roll or select two categories.

96-98% Three Characteristics: Roll or select three categories.

99-00% Four Characteristics!: Roll or select four categories.

Appearance Table (Comprehensive)

This comprehensive appearance table includes not only the **Nightbane® core rule book,** but also Morphus tables from **Nightbane® World Book 1: Between the Shadows™, World Book 2: Nightlands™,** and the **Nightbane® Survival Guide™.** Roll or select one.

01-07% Almost Human: The Nightbane's Morphus is almost totally human, except for one inhuman trait that might be disguised or concealed – although sometimes that one trait is inhuman enough to give away the character's true supernatural nature. Roll once on the *Characteristics Table* below to determine unusual characteristics. If the result asks for more than one characteristic, ignore it and reroll.

08-12% Inhuman but Beautiful: The Nightbane's Morphus combines a beautiful appearance with a touch of the inhuman. Roll once on the *Unearthly Beauty Table* and the *Characteristics Table*.

13-18% Mundane: While this Morphus is still bizarre, it combines elements of everyday life. Roll 1D4 times on any combination of the *Occupation, Hobbyist, Athlete,* and *Gear-Head* tables.

19-21% Marred Beauty: The character has a beautiful Morphus, but it is marred by a gruesome stigmata. Make rolls on the *Unearthly Beauty Table,* the *Stigmata Table,* and the *Characteristics Table*.

22-26% Starving Artist: This Nightbane's Morphus reflects his or her artistic side. Roll once on the *Artisan* or *Clown/Jester Table* and once on the *Characteristics Table*.

27-29% Gladiator: Nightbane often have to fight for survival and this character is especially well-suited for it. Roll once on the *Athlete* or *Ancient Warrior Table, Sci-Fi* or *Fantasy Table,* and *Animal Form* or *Characteristics Table*.

30-32% Dimensional Traveler: A blending of science and magic, this 'Bane appears to be something from an alien dimension. Roll 1D4 times on any combination of the following: *Animal Form, Extraterrestrial, Characteristics, Stigmata,* and *Un-*

dead Tables. Ignore and reroll any result that calls for multiple rolls. Also roll once on the *Biomechanical Table* and once on the *Fantasy* or *Sci-Fi Table.*

33-37% Super-Soldier: The character has a Morphus that seems tailor-made for waging war. Roll once each on the *Superbeing, Soldier,* and *Sci-Fi Tables.*

38-43% Lycanthrope: The Nightbane's Morphus is a mixture of animal and humanoid traits. Roll once on the *Animal Form Table.*

44-46% Anthromorph: The Nightbane's Morphus is an odd blend of human and animal characteristics that borders on caricature. Roll once each on the *Unearthly Beauty* or *Angelic, Animal Form,* and *Characteristics* tables.

47-49% Monstrous Lycanthrope: Not only is the Morphus animal-like, it has hideous deformities that give it a terrifying appearance. Roll on the *Animal Form, Nightmare* or *Stigmata,* and *Characteristics* tables.

50-54% Carnifern: This Morphus appears to be a walking, talking plant come to life. Roll once on the *Plant Life Table* and the *Characteristics Table.*

55-57% Inorganic: The Nightbane's Morphus has little in common with humanity, and is generally not even made from flesh and bone: Roll once each on the *Mineral* or *Artificial Appearance Table, Biomechanical* or *Gear-Head Table,* and the *Characteristics Table.*

58-62% Inhuman Shape: The Nightbane's True Shape is a gruesome mockery of humanity. Roll on the *Stigmata* or *Nightmare Table* and once on the *Characteristics Table.*

63-64% Patchwork Horror: The Nightbane's Morphus appears to be stitched together as if made from spare parts that did not quite match. Roll once each on *Unusual Facial Features, Disproportion, Unnatural Limbs,* and *Stigmata* tables. Additionally, all the limbs are connected to the torso by some form of artificial attachment, such as large staples, heavy stitches or even reams of duct tape. Add 2 to Horror Factor.

65-68% Amalgam: Ever play the game of trying to guess whether something is animal, vegetable or mineral? Well this Morphus falls under the category of "All of the Above." Roll once each on the *Animal Form, Plant Life,* and *Mineral* tables.

69-72% Morbid: This 'Bane has some kind of connection with the darker side of life. Roll once each on the *Infernal, Stigmata,* and *Undead* tables.

73-74% Bizarre: Roll on the *Unearthly Beauty, Characteristics, Animal Form,* and *Stigmata* tables. Then exercise your imagination to combine the alien result.

75-77% Chosen One: This Nightbane's Morphus appears as though his power comes from on-high and he may see himself as a righteous crusader or even a spirit of good. Roll 1D4 times on any combination of the *Animal Form, Mythical Creature, Mineral, Superbeing,* and *Characteristics* table. If the table asks for more than one characteristic, ignore the result and reroll. Also

roll once on the *Unearthly Beauty Table* and once on the *Angelic Table.*

78-80% Condemned: Believing themselves to be the victim of a dark curse or evil pact, these Nightbane often feel that they are a product of evil or demonic forces. Roll 1D4 times on any combination of the following: *Animal Form, Alien Shape, Biomechanical, Nightmare, Pestilence, Stigmata, Undead, Unearthly Beauty, Unnatural Limbs,* and *Unusual Facial Features* tables. If the table asks for more than one characteristic, ignore the result and reroll. Also roll <u>twice</u> on the *Infernal Table.*

81-85% Dino Freak: This 'Bane is a blend of human and dinosaur attributes. Roll on the *Dinosaur Form Table* and the *Characteristics Table.*

86-90% Victim: This Nightbane bears deep psychological and/or emotional scars from some trauma which has manifested in his Morphus form. Roll 1D4 times on any combination of the following: *Substance Abuse, Nightmare, Unearthly Beauty, Characteristics,* and *Stigmata* tables. Ignore and reroll any result that calls for multiple rolls. Roll once on the *Victim Table.*

91-94% The Drowned: This Nightbane looks like a nightmarish monstrosity from the ocean depths. Roll once on the *Aquatic Animal Form Table,* once on the *Biomechanical* or *Aquatic Biomech Table,* and once on the *Undead Table.*

95-97% Living Myth: Everything about this Nightbane's Morphus seems derived from fantasy and/or pop culture mythology. Roll once on the *Unearthly Beauty, Fantasy* or *Mythical Creature,* and *Extraterrestrial* tables. Also, roll once on either the *Angelic* (1-50%) or *Infernal* (51-00%) tables.

98-00% Apocalyptic: The character has a Morphus form that looks like something out of a prophecy of the end of days. Roll once each on the *Infernal* or *Angelic, Nightmare* or *Stigmata, Pestilence,* and *Undead* tables.

Characteristics Table (Comprehensive)

This comprehensive characteristics table includes not only the **Nightbane® core rule book,** but also Morphus tables from **Nightbane® World Book 1: Between the Shadows™, World Book 2: Nightlands™,** and the **Nightbane® Survival Guide™.** Roll or select one Characteristic for your Nightbane.

01-05% Comic Book: Roll on the *Sci-Fi* or *Superbeing Table.*

06-10% Geo-Creature: Roll on the *Mineral Table.*

11-18% Unusual Facial Features: Roll on the *Unusual Facial Features Table.*

19-23% Facsimile: Roll on the *Artificial Appearance Table.*

24-28% Macho: Roll on the *Athlete* or *Soldier Table.*

29-36% Biomechanical: Roll on the *Biomechanical Table, Gear-Head,* or *Aquatic Biomech Table.*

37-41% Dinosaur: Roll on the *Dinosaur Form Table.*

42-46% Performer: Roll on the *Artisan* or *Clown/Jester Table.*

47-54% Alien Creature: Roll on either the *Alien Shape Table* or *Extraterrestrial Table*.

55-62% Disproportional: Roll on the *Disproportion Table*.

63-66% Workaday: Roll on the *Hobbyist* or *Occupation Table*.

67-72% Unnatural Limbs: Roll on the *Unnatural Limbs Table*.

73-80% Medieval Fantasy: Roll on the *Fantasy, Mythical Creature,* or *Ancient Warrior Table*.

81-85% Botanical: Roll on the *Plant Life Table*.

86-90% Wretch: Roll on the *Pestilence, Substance Abuse,* or *Victim Table*.

91-95% Two Characteristics: Roll or select two categories, ignoring and rerolling any result above 90%.

96-98% Three Characteristics: Roll or select three categories, ignoring and rerolling any result above 90%.

99-00% Four Characteristics: Roll or select four categories, ignoring and rerolling any result above 90%.

New Morphus Tables

Ancient Warrior Table
Animal Form Table
Insectoid Table II
Primate Table
Artisan Table
Athlete Table
Clown/Jester Table
Gear-Head Table
Hobbyist Table
Mythical Creature Table
Nightmare Table
Occupation Table
Pestilence Table
Plant Life Table II
Sci-Fi Table
Soldier Table (Modern)
Substance Abuse Table
Superbeing Table

Ancient Warrior Table

From Stone-Age hunters, to Sikh swordsmen, to the Japanese ninja, mankind has a long and brutal history of conflict. Given this, it should be no surprise that some Nightbane have ended up with elements of their Morphus forms reflecting aspects of ancient warfare and foreign cultures. Features from this table are most common among *Ancient Nightbane* who are 150 years old or older. Modern Nightbane, however, may have one or more Ancient Warrior features as well, due to the influence of books, comic books, movies, television, video games, manga, anime,

education and the Internet. For example, perhaps this Nightbane feels he was born in the wrong age and longs for a simpler time. Strongly identifying with a particular code of conduct or outlook, such as chivalry or bushido originating from a warrior caste leads to the manifestation of Morphus features from another time and culture. Or maybe his favorite heroes from a comic book, anime or video game with such historical weapons, costumes and values inspire or resonate with the individual in some way. The Morphus is, after all, a reflection or manifestation of something inside of the Nightbane, whether it is an ideal, fear or desire buried in his psyche or something that resonates with him on some other powerful level. That can be something that sparks his imagination or strikes a nerve that makes him want to be a hero of old. Humans tend to hold their emotions inside, so the Morphus may be a reflection of that inner torment, hidden goodness, fear, sense of nobility or heroics, darkness, light, pain, love, hate, etc.

Whatever the case, those with features from the Ancient Warrior Table tend to be more aggressive and combative, whether they are protecting the innocent or fighting to take what they want or believe they deserve. Such warlike Nightbane are more likely to join or be recruited by groups like **the Resistance** or **War-**

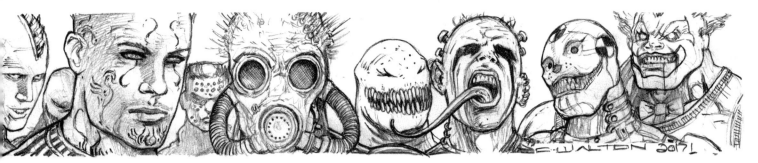

lords. Combat Note: These Nightbane are also more willing to engage enemies in close-quarters combat, which grants them *one* additional Ancient Weapon Proficiency.

Roll percentile dice once for random determination, or pick one.

01-15% Ancient Infantry/Foot Soldier: The backbone of almost any ancient military force was its infantry. While not as glorified as warriors such as knights or archers, these steadfast and brave souls were often required to march for hundreds of miles and engage enemies in brutal melee combat. On more than one occasion, "infantry" included simple peasants using their farming implements or scavenged weaponry.

Nightbane warriors are dressed in simple clothing, perhaps even as little as a loincloth, that may or may not match that of an ancient society. They may also have other small distinguishing features such as the piercings of a Zulu warrior or face paint of a Viking or Native American. Armor and helmet or uniform/iconic imagery may be Babylonian, Egyptian, Greek, Roman, Norman, French Musketeer, Samurai, American Civil War, and countless others. A single two-handed melee weapon or pair of one-handed weapons (see the **Nightbane® Main Book**, pages 204-209 for some options) rounds out *the warrior*. Note that one-handed weapons may also include shields, and almost every infantry soldier throughout time had a helmet or headdress of some kind that protected the head and identified the fighting force. The helmet may be something worn or horns or bone in the shape of the helmet for the infantry of the appropriate era and country.

Damage inflicted by each ancient weapon is the same as its mundane equivalent though it can never be broken and he blade never dulls. Of course, it also cannot be separated from the Nightbane which means it either stays in the hand (cannot be disarmed) or somehow secured to the character. **Bonuses:** +1D4 to the P.S. attribute, +1D4 to P.E., and +1D6 to Spd. +1D6x10 S.D.C. +1 to strike and parry with a melee weapon. +1 to Awe/Horror Factor. **Penalties:** -1 to the M.E. attribute, -1 to M.A., and -2 to P.B.

16-30% Archer: The snipers and marksmen of their day, archers were typically meant to rain death upon enemies from afar. Primarily deployed in ranks behind other units, on defensive structures, or in ambush positions, archers were almost never intended to engage the enemy in close quarters except as a last resort. Of course, exceptions such as Comanche braves, Russian Cossacks, Mongolian horsemen, and Japanese samurai, all excellent horsemen skilled at firing a bow from horseback at full gallop, did exist. Amazon warrior women, though the stuff of myth, my also be an element in a Nightbane's Morphus.

Nightbane archers may be dressed according to the garb of an ancient civilization or a fictitious equivalent, or something more gothic. While the dress of Nightbane archers can vary from individual to individual, every Nightbane archer has at least one thing in common: Each has a bow of some kind and quiver of arrows or bolts when in Morphus form. This can be a short bow (1D6 damage, 340 feet/104 m range), longbow (2D6 damage, 640 foot/195

m range), modern crossbow (2D6 damage, 470 foot/143 m range), modern crossbow pistol (probably one for each hand/arm; 1D6 damage, 120 feet/36.6 m range), or heavy modern crossbow (3D6 damage, 600 foot/183 m range), whichever weapon seems the most appropriate. The number of attacks per melee that can be made with this weapon is equal to the number of hand to hand attacks using a bow, and half that for a crossbow. The quiver NEVER runs out of ammunition. **Bonuses:** +1 to the M.E. attribute, +1 to P.S., +1 to P.P., and +1 to Perception Rolls. Also +1 one attack per melee round and +2 to strike, but ONLY when using a bow and arrow or a crossbow. **Penalties:** -1 to the P.E. attribute and -1D6 S.D.C. Also tends to be uncomfortable in confined spaces.

31-45% Assassin: Clandestine warriors whose job it was to infiltrate enemy camps or cities and eliminate high-value targets, assassins used a number of tactics to accomplish their missions. From the ubiquitous ninja clans of ancient Japan to lesser known varieties, these trained killers were often widely feared. Then again they were just as often shunned for doing the dirty work so few would undertake.

This Morphus is dressed in dark clothing that has numerous folds and pockets or pouches suitable for concealing weapons and tools. The Nightbane also always appears tense and on edge as if danger lurks around every corner. Two small weapons such as daggers are always hidden somewhere on his person, along with 2D4 small throwing weapons such as darts, spikes, or shuriken. These weapons deal the same damage as their mundane counterparts, but disappear after striking the target and reappear on the Nightbane after a single melee round (15 seconds). **Bonuses:** +1 to the M.E. attribute, +1 to P.S., and +1D4 to P.P., +4D6 to S.D.C., +1 to all Perception Rolls, +1 to Awe/Horror Factor, +1 to strike with melee weapons, bow, and thrown weapons, and +10% to the Prowl skill. **Penalties:** -1D4 to the M.A. attribute. Their appearance makes other leery, making *Invoke Trust* impossible.

46-55% Cavalry: Cavalry soldiers are mounted warriors trained to fight while astride powerful steeds and used to punch holes in enemy lines or flank around them. The cavalry were the battle-tanks of their day. Superior height and momentum gave them a decided advantage against unmounted opponents, and speed allowed cavalry to adapt quickly to changing battlefield conditions and harry enemy forces with hit-and-run tactics. Dress can vary widely among those Nightbane with this feature. From richly colored robes to simple animal skins or furs, the appearance can reflect real warriors such as the Cossacks, Samurai or Sioux horsemen, to imaginary or fictional types. Whatever the garb, the thing that distinguishes these Nightbane is that they always appear in Morphus with a horse, or may be Centaur-like themselves, with the lower body of a horse.

The horse can be of any color or breed, and may look absolutely ordinary, beautiful, emaciated, monstrous in some way, partially armored or demonic, but it is always a horse. While

the mount may look like a separate creature, it is actually a part of the Nightbane and fully under his or her complete control. A large weapon meant for mounted combat, such as a lance (1D8 damage) or flail (2D6 damage), or long, curved cavalry sword (2D6 damage) rounds out the appearance. Though the "rider" can dismount, the two must remain in physical contact, even if it is leading the horse portion by the reins. The only exception is when one or the other is destroyed. If this happens, restoring the destroyed half requires transforming to *Facade* and back to Morphus which splits the remaining Hit Points/S.D.C. between the two. **Bonuses:** Humanoid: +1D4 to the P.S. and +1D6 to Spd attributes; +2D6x10 S.D.C. and +6D6 Hit Points. Horse: +2D6 to P.S., +2 to P.E., +1D4 to P.B. and 1D6x10+20 to Spd; the horse can also pull 10 times the normal carrying weight and jump 10 feet (3 m) high and 20 feet (6.1 m) lengthwise. Mounted Combat Bonuses (Nightbane is on his horse): +2 attacks per melee, +1 on initiative, +2 to parry and dodge, and +6 to damage. **Penalties:** The "mount/horse" has half of the Nightbane's S.D.C. and Hit Points while the rider has the other half, making the two halves easier to destroy when targeted separately. Each portion heals 5 Hit Points/S.D.C. per melee round, and both must be destroyed to kill the Nightbane. **Note:** When dismounted the Nightbane has half the normal number of attacks and combat bonuses.

56-60% War-Chief/Warlord: The Nightbane looks like a nobleman, warlord, or chieftain outfitted for battle. Any garb worn is of the highest quality and an ornate headdress or helm denoting a commanding rank. If armor is a part of the Morphus, via another feature, it will be richly decorated or gilded and adds 50% more S.D.C. The same goes for the three high-quality ancient weapons that are also part of this feature. Typically, these consist of a large, two-handed weapon, a sword or dagger as a backup, and a ranged weapon such as a bow, spear or javelin. Each of these weapons inflicts 50% more damage than its real world equivalent. For example, a warlord's battle-axe would deal 3D6 damage rather than the normal 2D6. **Bonuses:** +1 to I.Q., +2 to M.A., +1D4 to P.S., +2 to P.P. and P.E., and +1D4 to P.B. +1D4x10 to S.D.C., Natural A.R. 9, +2 to strike, +1 to parry and disarm with melee weapons, and +1 to Awe/Horror Factor. **Penalties:** The appearance of a warlord is meant to inspire friendly forces and intimidate enemies, not to make it easy to hide in shadowy alleys, so the Nightbane is -20% to Prowl and any enemies are +2 on Perception Rolls to notice the actions of this character. Looking like a leader also tends to make one a target in battle.

61-75% Light Armor: The Nightbane appears to be wearing some kind of light armor such as studded leather armor or a half-suit of chain mail and a helmet. This armor was favored not just because it was much cheaper to produce and maintain. Light armor was also much easier than heavier types to wear and move in while still offering a measure of protection against melee and missile weapons. The type and look of the armor is left up to the

player and does not affect the bonuses gained. This armor cannot be removed. It is a part of the character. **Bonuses:** Increase the character's base Natural A.R. to 11 and +1D4x10+40 to S.D.C. **Penalties:** -1 to the P.E. attribute, -10% to the final Spd attribute, and -10% to the performance of Physical skills such as *Swimming, Prowl, Climbing* and *Acrobatics*.

76-90% Heavy Armor: From the plate mail of Eastern Europe to the lacquered armor of Japanese samurai, a number of ancient cultures sought to protect their warriors from harm as best they could. A Nightbane with the Heavy Armor feature is clad in some kind of heavy armor. Appearance and styling of the armor is up to the player, but it looks like an ancient suit of armor rather than anything modern. The armor is full body, including some sort of helmet that may or may not cover the face. It is a part of the Morphus and cannot be removed like normal armor. **Bonuses:** Increase the base Natural A.R. to 13. +1D6x10+100 to S.D.C. **Penalties:** -2 to P.P. and P.E. attributes, -20% to the final Spd attribute, and -20% to the performance of Physical skills such as *Swimming, Prowl, Climbing* and *Acrobatics*.

91-00% Color Standard: A standard is some kind of flag, banner, or symbol representing a military force. In ancient warfare they were used to identify different armies or army units on a battlefield. Standards served as a rallying point and as morale boosters, so if the carrier was slain the standard would be picked up by another soldier and hoisted once more.

The Nightbane possesses such a standard while in Morphus form. It might be carried or mounted somewhere onto the body, but whatever the case, it is displayed prominently for all to see. The exact symbol, colors, design or flag is up to the player and can be historically accurate or completely made-up as long as it holds some kind of meaning for the Nightbane character. If handheld, the standard can be used as a blunt weapon, like a staff that does 1D6 damage in addition to that of the Nightbane's Supernatural Strength. **Bonuses:** +1 to the M.E. attribute, +1D4+1 to M.A., +1 to P.S., and +1 to P.B. +4D6+6 S.D.C., +1 to parry and disarm if the standard is handheld, and +1 to Awe/Horror Factor. **Penalties:** -1D4 to the Spd attribute, -1 attack per melee, and -1 to dodge.

New Animal Form Table

All animal forms are capable of *full human speech*. The words may be raspy, guttural or more like a growl, depending on the Nightbane's inhuman shape, or they could be perfectly human-like (player's choice). Hearing words coming from an animal adds +1 to the Horror Factor of the creature the first few times, until the person gets accustomed to it.

Roll percentile dice once for random determination, or pick one.

01-07% Bear: All large ursinoids. Roll on the *Bear Table*. (See **Between the Shadows,** page 130, or the Appendix in this book).

52-59% Snake: All crawling, no-legged, scaly creatures, from the huge anaconda or boa constrictor to rattlesnakes and vipers, to the tiniest garden snake. Roll on the *Snake Table.*

60-67% Avian: Any bird species can be selected, however, Nightbane tend to lean toward predatory raptors like eagles, hawks, falcons and owls, or scavenging birds, vultures, ravens, etc. Roll on the *Avian Table.*

68-75% Canine: Any variety of dog to their wild cousins, wolves, coyotes, foxes, dingos, and so on. Roll on the *Canine Table.*

76-83% Reptilian: Lizards – as in reptiles with legs – from geckos, ignuanas or chameleons to alligators, crocodiles, komodo dragons, and many, many others. Most lizards are predators even if they prey upon insects. Roll on the *Reptilian Table.* (**Note:** Snakes are not included as they have their own table.)

84-90% Equine/Bovine/Deer: Includes not only horses and cows, but all kinds of hoofed plant-eaters such as deer, antelope, zebras, bulls, water buffalo, cows, goats, sheep, etc. Roll on the *Equine/Bovine/Deer Table.*

91-96% Primate: Covers humanity's closest cousins from monkeys to great apes. Roll on the *Primate* Table.

97-99% Combination of Two: Roll twice on this table (ignore and reroll any result of 97% or higher), and combine the elements from the two animals. To decide which bonuses apply, roll 1D6; 1-3 means use the bonuses and penalties (if any) of the first animal, 4-6 means use the bonuses and penalties from the second one. **Example:** A Nightbane has snake and equine characteristics. The player decides the character is a centaur with a were-snake upper body. When selecting P.S. bonuses, the player rolls 1D6, and on a roll of 1-3, he gets the snake bonuses; on a roll of 4-6 he gets the horse bonuses.

100% Combination of Three: Roll three times (ignore and reroll any result of 97% or higher) and combine elements from the three animals. To decide which bonuses apply to each attribute, roll 1D6: 1-2 means use the bonues and penalties (if any) of the first animal, 3-4 means the second one applies, and 5-6 means use the bonuses of the third selection.

Insectoid Table II

Those Nightbane with insect features typically "have a thing for bugs," collecting, studying, and reading about them on a regular basis, and maybe even eating them! Of course, there are some Nightbane who view themselves as social outcasts having more in common with insects than human beings and may keep them as pets/friends, and/or respect them more than people.

01-10% Mantis Arms: One pair of arms is replaced by long, slender, chitinous limbs with sharpened barbs that line the inner edges. These limbs are much longer than equivalent human-like arms and fold inward toward the body of the Nightbane. This enables the character to grab and hold opponents just like the prey of a mantis. The grip is powerful and requires a Supernatural P.S.

08-14% Amphibian: Mostly frogs and toads. Roll on the *Amphibian Table.* (See **Between the Shadows** page 131, or the Appendix in this book).

15-20% Insect: All types of insects, from beautiful butterflies to disgusting dung beetles or centipedes. Roll on the *Insectoid Table* or *Insectoid Table II.*

21-27% Rodent: Rats, mice, squirrels, beavers, and similar creatures. City-bred Nightbane tend to favor rats, while those who grew up in the country or suburbs are more likely to transform into wilderness varieties like rabbits, squirrels, moles, etc. Roll on the *Rodent Table.*

28-35% Arachnid: Spiders and scorpions. Roll on the *Arachnid Table.*

36-43% Bat: All varieties of pointy-eared flying mammals, including vampire bats, fox-bats, fruit bats and others. Roll on the *Bat Table.*

44-51% Feline: All cats, from the big, exotic predators like the tiger, African Lion, panther, cheetah, etc., to the cougar, puma, lynx, and even varieties of house cats. Roll on the *Feline Table.*

greater than the Mantis Nightbane's own (see below) to break free. **Bonuses:** +5 to the P.S. attribute, +2 to strike, +2 to pull punch, +4 to entangle, +2 to Horror Factor, +15% to Climbing/ Rappelling, and any target successfully *entangled* by the Nightbane needs a Supernatural P.S. twice that of the Nightbane to break free. A slash with the barbed arms inflicts damage equal to Supernatural P.S. punch damage +1D6+3. **Penalties:** Without digits or opposable thumbs, most skills requiring manual dexterity are difficult in the extreme, -60% skill penalty to perform. The use of tools and simple melee weapons is impossible – cannot be held or used properly – though keyboards, steering wheels, door-knobs, large buttons, light switches and levers can be used with a little effort and care.

11-20% Spiracles: In place of lungs, the Nightbane has several small holes located all over the abdomen, back and neck through which he breathes. These spiracles are often concealed and hard to spot (a Perception Roll of 18 or better is needed to notice them with casual inspection). **Bonuses:** +3D6 Hit Points and +2D6 S.D.C. Cannot be choked or strangled by cutting off air in the neck/throat. Al spiracles would need to be blocked to choke this Nightbane, such as burying him up to his chin. **Penal-**

ties: The Nightbane cannot speak or smell. Holding one's breath is also impossible without lungs.

21-30% Proboscis: In the place of a mouth, a long, needle-like protrusion or flexible tube allows the Nightbane to ingest only liquids similar to drinking through a long straw, only this straw is part of his body. **Bonuses:** +1 to Horror Factor. A needle-like proboscis can be jabbed into soft targets to inflict one point of damage. On a successful strike roll of 16 or higher, this attack can then be used to draw out vital fluids like blood from the victim. For each attack spent draining the target, 1D6 damage is dealt directly to Hit Points! **Penalties:** -4 to the P.B. attribute and the proboscis only has two S.D.C. per 20 S.D.C. of the Nightbane, but will regrow completely in a matter of 5D6 minutes if severed, damaged or destroyed.

31-40% Stinger: A retractable stinger is housed somewhere in the Nightbane's body. This could be a scorpion tail-like appendage or the stinger could extend from the forearm or wrist like a long knitting needle or spike. The stinger inflicts 2D6 damage (2D6+2 if barbed) for a stabbing attack and an additional 1D4 damage if the victim fails to save versus non-lethal poison (needs 16 or higher to save), and is affected by the poison the stinger releases. Poison: Victims are -2 on all combat rolls for 1D6 melee rounds due to swelling and muscle pain and a bit of a woozy sensation. A barbed stinger lodges in the victim and tears free from the Nightbane, doing 1D6 damage direct to the Nightbane's own Hit Points. However, the stinger inside its victim continues to excrete its poison for 1D4 minutes or until removed. Poison does 3D6 damage per melee round and removal of a barbed stinger by anyone other than a surgeon does an additional 3D6 damage. The Nightbane re-grows any lost stinger in 8 hours. **Bonuses:** +2D6 S.D.C., +1 to strike and parry with the stinger, +2 to save vs poison and drugs, and the Nightbane gets a +1 to his Horror Factor when the stinger is extended. **Penalties:** -1 to the P.E. and P.B. attributes.

41-45% Bombardier Chamber: Separate internal glands house two different chemicals that, when combined in a protected chamber inside the body, produce a volatile reaction similar to expelling napalm. This stream of viscous, superheated fluid deals 5D6 damage to anyone in a 30 degree cone of effect up to 50 feet (15.2 m) away. Body armor only absorbs half this damage unless it is made to protect against hazardous chemicals, in which case protection is 100%. Those without natural armor struck by this attack must save vs pain at 15 or higher, including any bonuses for a high M.E. attribute. Failure to save causes the victim to drop to the ground and writhe in agony for the next 1D4+1 melee rounds. During this time they can do nothing except defend themselves against other incoming attacks and crawl at a speed of 3. **Note:** The chemical "payload" is limited to one attack per every 4 P.E. points of the Morphus. It regenerates at a rate of one attack's worth every hour. **Bonuses:** +2 to strike and the chemical may be expelled from the Nightbane's mouth or from an opening in his wrist (pick one). **Penalties:** The Nightbane is a potential time

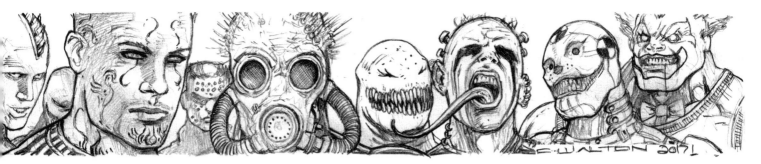

bomb! Any single attack that does more than 40% of the Morphus's Hit Points has a 25% chance of breaching the chemical glands and causing the character to explode. The explosion does half the damage the remaining bombardier attacks would have inflicted to a 20 foot (6.1 m) radius. Under most circumstances the Nightbane is killed, though individual G.M.s can decide if some feature of the Morphus (like a plasmoid form) may prevent this or a split-second healing spell, activation of a Talent (like Swarm Self), or shift to Facade form might prevent the explosion.

46-55% Goo Glands: This Morphus has a number of exterior glands that are capable of secreting a sticky, foul-smelling substance that functions similar to tear gas. Anyone other than the Nightbane within 10 feet (3 m) of just a handful of this goo must roll to save vs non-lethal poison (16 or higher to save), to keep their eyes from tearing up and themselves from gagging. Those who fail lose one melee attack and are -3 on initiative and -4 to strike, parry, and dodge for 1D6+1 melee rounds. If at any time someone ingests this substance, they immediately lose all attacks for the entire round (15 seconds) to violent vomiting. The substance is also extremely difficult to wash off. The Nightbane can secrete up to 12 handfuls of goo per hour. However, the stuff only retains its irritant properties for 5 minutes. After that, it just smells bad, no penalties. **Bonuses:** The Nightbane is +4 to save vs tear gas and any other chemical irritant. **Penalties:** After this ability is used even once, the Nightbane smells terrible until he switches back to Facade form. This prevents any attempt to hide or Prowl within 30 feet (9 m) of anything with a nose. The smell does not win any friends, causing a temporary -5 to the M.A. attribute.

56-65% Climbing Filaments: Tiny, needle-like hairs cover the Nightbane's palms and soles. This improves climbing ability and even allows the Morphus to cling to sheer surfaces as long as it is not completely smooth and featureless, like glass windows or polished chrome. **Bonuses:** +20% to the *Climbing/Rappelling* skill. Also, assailants are -2 to disarm the Nightbane as long as the weapon or object he holds is something the filaments can grip onto, like wood, leather, soft rubber, rope, etc.

66-75% Bioluminescence: One or more sections of the body glow with a soft light when in Morphus. While green, light blue and violet are the most common colors, any color is theoretically possible. Just like a firefly, this light is internally produced and can be controlled by the Nightbane to shine with different intensities and rhythms.

This Morphus feature can be used to illuminate a space for himself or others, see details in darkness, flash as a signal, attract prey, cause a distraction, and even flash Morse code messages. Perhaps most amazing of all is that, by temporarily sacrificing one Hit Point per melee round, the Nightbane can radiate the equivalent of *magical sunlight* like that from the spell Globe of Daylight. This drives vampires and other creatures vulnerable to sunlight out of the area filled with light produced by the bioluminescence. The maximum radius for such light is 5 feet (1.5 m) per level of the Nightbane. While no one is sure how the light can have this effect, some theorize that since it's biologically created, the light symbolizes life and thus hurts and drives undead away the same as sunlight. This bright light completely illuminates the area enough to read a book or map, or see details on walls, doors, etc. **Bonuses:** +2D6 to S.D.C., +2 to the P.B. and M.A. attributes. **Penalties:** Unless covered in some way, the glow makes Prowling in dark environs difficult; -30% to the *Prowl* skill in such instances.

76-85% Danger Markings: In normal insects, these markings consist of brightly colored patterns that serve to warn predators away from trying to eat them. As part of a Nightbane Morphus, the markings are likely to be things that make the character seem scarier, stranger and more dangerous. Such as traditional bands and marks that look like lightning bolts or tiger stripes, false eyes, fangs, mandibles, horns, claw marks, claws, dark shadows to emphasize sunken or empty eye sockets or give the Nightbane an animalistic or skeletal appearance, etc. However, these markings can also take the form of recognized danger symbols like those for biohazard or radiation, black on yellow caution markings, racing stripes, a death's head/skull/death mask, clenched fist, spider shape(s), barbed wire, and so on. Whatever the form or color, the message is the same: "Back off, pal. Don't mess with me. I'm trouble." **Bonuses:** +2 to Horror Factor and any creature with an animal I.Q. will avoid attacking the Nightbane unless attacked first, otherwise agitated or threatened, or commanded to do so by its master or leader. **Penalties:** Unless covered in some way, the markings may scare and intimidate potential allies and associates; -1D4 to M.A. and P.B. attributes and the Nightbane finds it difficult to blend in with ordinary looking people or disguise himself.

86-95% Camouflage Markings: These markings are designed to help the insect to blend in with its surroundings to hide from predators. While for normal insects this benefit is usually only for a certain number of environments, for the Nightbane the markings somehow seem to function equally well in most outdoor settings, actually changing and adjusting to fit his current environment. **Bonuses:** +10% to *Prowl* skill and ability to hide unseen when outdoors among forest and vegetation, rocks and desert and other natural environments. **Penalties:** The markings are a bit odd-looking, -1 to M.A. and P.B. attributes.

96-00% Other: Roll instead on the original Insectoid Table (**Nightbane® RPG**, page 98, and in the Appendix at the back of this book).

Primate Table

Humanity's closest cousins, primates are some of the most intelligent animals on Earth. With the wide variety found in the size, shape, and abilities of primates, there are a great number of things to admire about them. Reasons behind a Nightbane's primate features could be as simple as having a Capuchin as a

Reduce the total S.D.C. (but not Hit Points) by half when in the Morphus form.

15-26% Baboon: While baboons are technically monkeys, their unique appearance, non-prehensile tail, large fangs and different name distinguishes them from the rest of their cousins swinging through trees. Size varies between 2-3 feet (0.6-0.9 m) for the body and 1.5-2 feet (0.5-0.6 m) for the non-prehensile tail. Weight averages roughly 33-82 pounds (15-37 kg). Unlike their tree-dwelling relatives, baboons are largely terrestrial. They have small claws, large, sharp canine teeth, and may have brightly-colored facial features and buttocks. **Bonuses:** +1 to I.Q., +2 to M.E., +1D4 to P.S., +1 to P.E., and +1D4+1 to the Spd attribute. +1 attack per melee, +2 on Perception Rolls, +1 on initiative, +1 to dodge, and +1 to roll with punch/fall/impact. Bite attack deals 2D6 damage. **Penalties:** -3 to the P.B. attribute. The Spd attribute reflects the speed of the Morphus when running on all fours or jumping from perch to perch. Reduce running speed by half if trying to move in an upright position.

27-38% Chimpanzee: Next to humankind, chimps are likely the most intelligent beings on planet Earth. These close relatives of man form intricate social bonds, use tools, and have even been taught to communicate with humans on a limited basis. Chimpanzees have dark hair that covers most of the body, almost non-existent tails, and prehensile hands and feet. Standing about 4 to 5.5 feet (1.2 to 1.7 m) tall and weighing approximately 70-130 pounds (32 to 59 kg), a chimp Morphus isn't much smaller than most Facades. **Bonuses:** +2 to I.Q., +1 to M.E., +2 to M.A., and +1D6 to the P.S. attribute. +1D4x10 S.D.C. +2 on Perception rolls, +1 to strike and parry (may parry with legs/feet) and +2 to roll with punch/fall/impact, and +10% to the *Climbing* skill. Bite attack deals 2D4 damage. **Penalties:** -2 to the P.B. attribute. The Spd attribute reflects the speed of the Morphus when running on all-fours. Reduce running speed by half if trying to move in an upright position.

39-50% Orangutan: Orangutans are long-armed, largely arboreal great apes with long, reddish-brown hair covering all but the face, hands, and prehensile feet. The size of the Morphus is slightly shorter than the Facade (reduce height by 1D6 inches/2.5 to 15.2 cm) and averages between 100 and 260 lbs. (45 to 117 kg), but the arms are elongated, so add one foot (0.3 m) to the character's reach. **Bonuses:** +1 to I.Q., +1 to M.E., +1D4+2 to P.S., and +1 to the P.E. attribute. +1D4x10+25 S.D.C., +1 attack per melee, +1 on Perception Rolls, +2 to parry (+1 using the legs/feet), +2 to roll with punch/fall/impact, +1 to entangle and disarm, and +10% to the *Climbing* skill. Bite attack deals 2D4 damage. **Penalties:** -3 to the P.B. attribute. The Spd attribute reflects the speed of the Morphus when climbing and swinging from tree to tree or building to building. Short and bowed legs reduce running speed by half when moving across flat ground.

51-64% Gorilla: The largest of the great apes, gorillas are intelligent, powerfully built, and awe-inspiring. The upper body appears slightly more developed than the lower and is covered

beloved pet to as complex as an attraction to the notion of unleashing one's more primal nature or the brute force of a gorilla or the savagery of a baboon. All Nightbane with at least one of these features automatically gain the *Climbing* skill at a base ability of 50%.

Roll percentile dice once for random determination, or pick one.

01-14% Monkey: While real monkeys vary drastically in size and appearance, the common conception is what is reflected in this Morphus form. A monkey Morphus form is typically half the size and weight of the Facade, covered in fur, and the hands, feet, and tail are all prehensile. The tail is as long or longer than the body, with 3 feet (0.9 m) being the average length. **Bonuses:** +1 to I.Q., +1 to M.E. and M.A., +2 to P.P., and +1D6+2 to the Spd attributes. Can climb, jump, and swing through trees, and even dense urban settings with many poles, pipes, and ledges, at *twice the normal running speed,* and +20% to the Climbing skill. +2 to Perception Rolls, +1 on initiative, and +3 to roll with punch/fall/impact, and Auto-Dodge (use only the bonuses from the R.C.C. and high P.P. attribute). Bite attack deals 2D4 damage. **Penalties:**

in dark hair which is usually black, gray, or dark brown. Despite being primarily herbivores, gorillas do have a number of large, sharp teeth that can savage anything unfortunate enough to be on the receiving end of a bite. This Morphus is roughly the same height as the Facade, but weight is increased to 3D6x10+300 lbs (149 to 216 kg). The Nightbane can stand and walk on two legs, though running is done on all-fours in a loping fashion. **Bonuses:** +2 to I.Q., +1 to M.A., +1D6+5 to P.S., and +2 to the P.E. attribute. +1D6x10+50 S.D.C. +1 to Perception Rolls, +1 to strike, parry, and roll with punch/fall/impact. Bite attack deals 2D6+3 damage. **Penalties:** -2 to the P.B. attribute. The Spd attribute reflects the speed of the Morphus running on all fours. Reduce running speed by half if trying to move in an upright position.

65-76% Missing Link: The Nightbane appears to be a cross between one of the great apes and a Neanderthal. The body is covered in short, dark hair, the powerful arms are slightly elongated, and the Nightbane has a hunched posture even when running. Facial features are somewhat similar to normal humans, but with a pronounced brow-ridge, strong jaw, and wide nose. The canine teeth are slightly pronounced and speech is somewhat guttural. **Bonuses:** +1D4+3 to P.S., +2 to P.P., and +1 to the P.E. attribute, +2D4x10 S.D.C., +1 on initiative, +1 to strike, parry, and dodge, and +1 to roll with punch/fall/impact. **Penalties:** It's hard for most not to think of the Nightbane as a dull-witted caveman. -2 to the M.A. and P.B. attributes. -10% to all Communications skills.

77-88% Prehensile Feet: A Morphus with this feature is able to grasp objects like branches and weapons with dexterous feet similar to many primates. **Bonuses:** +1 attack per melee, +1 to parry using the legs/feet, and +10% to the *Climbing* skill. **Penalties:** Since the feet are built for dexterity instead of running, reduce the Nightbane's Spd attribute by half.

89-00% Other, but Related: Roll on the short table below for random determination or choose one of the following:

01-25% Sharp Teeth: The Nightbane has long, fang-like teeth. **Bonuses:** The character's bite inflicts 3D6 damage and +1 to Horror Factor whenever the teeth are displayed, in a smile, for example. **Penalties:** -1 M.A. and -2 to P.B., -10% to Disguise and Undercover Ops skills unless prosthetic teeth are used to cover the pointed teeth.

26-50% Prehensile Tail: The Nightbane has a prehensile tail, which can be used to grasp and carry things or help climb. **Bonuses:** The tail is very strong, and able to support the character's full body weight when suspended above the ground. However, it can only carry the equivalent of one third of the character's body weight (typically about 60 lbs/27 kg). Add +20% to Climbing and balance when the tail is used, and it adds one additional melee attack/action. **Penalties:** The character has a furry (or not) monkey tail! -1 to M.A. and -2 to P.B. attributes. Easy to conceal tucked in clothing.

51-75% Shaggy Hair: The Nightbane's body is covered by thick, shaggy hair. The hair can be any color the player desires, even unnatural colors like green or blue. The hair covers every part of the Nightbane's body except the palms of the hands and the soles of the feet. It may even cover the face and hang over the eyes unless it is moved aside, or the face may be more like an orangutan, hairy everywhere but on the face around the eyes, nose and mouth. **Bonuses:** +4D6 S.D.C., +10% to the *Concealment* skill, and +1 to Horror Factor. **Penalties:** Hair may leave clearly discernable trace evidence, -30% to Disguise and Undercover Ops skills and may get in the way from time to time.

76-00% Elongated Arms: The character has long upper and lower arms reminiscent to a gorilla or ape. The character looks out of proportion, but has an extended reach (20% longer than usual), and is +1 to parry, disarm and entangle. **Penalties:** -2 to P.B., -20% to Disguise and Undercover Ops skills and requires custom clothing for the Morphus form, otherwise shirts, jackets, etc., look too short/small in the arms.

Artisan Table

Works of art are able to transcend cultural barriers and survive for eons. Other than academic and social advances, art is quite possibly the only lasting legacy that humans can leave for future generations to appreciate. For these reasons and more, people ca-

pable of creating artwork are often considered special, talented, or gifted for their ability. Some of the best artisans can become near-mythical figures that may be idolized for hundreds or even thousands of years. Take Leonardo da Vinci or Michelangelo, for example. With the power that art can represent, many artists see their creative abilities as an integral part of their identity. As a result, artistic Nightbane and those who share a great appreciation for art may find their Morphus forms reflect this through one or more of the following features.

As a Morphus, the elements of the artist may be incorporated into his appearance. For example a painter may have a body that resembles a living painting with permanent splatters, dots, smears of paint or abstract patterns across his body, or covered in tattoos. A sculptor might have a body that resembles a statue made of marble or roughly chiseled like a Rodin statue, or be melded metal, and so on. Use your imagination.

Roll percentile dice once for random determination, or pick one.

01-15% Paint Palette: Attached to the forearm above the non-dominant hand, a wide board contains a number of daubs of different colored paints. The paint never runs out and the color and consistency of it can be altered before it is used by the Nightbane with nothing more than a thought. Accompanying this palette is a small, quiver-like container of paintbrushes of different sizes and shapes hanging from a belt or shoulder-strap.

This feature enables the Nightbane to paint images that are startlingly realistic, and can even work like optical illusions for a time. For instance, from a distance a painting of a large pothole on a road might keep someone from driving over it, or a painting of a guard next to a door might discourage others from approaching. **Note:** Only a save vs illusions or a Perception Roll of 14 or better lets observers realize the image is an illusion – a painting – without careful examination that takes at least 1D4 minutes (twice as long if examined from further than 10 feet/3 m). **Bonuses:** +15% to any Art skill involving paint and +10% to create *Camouflage*; +2 on Perception Rolls, +1 to parry using the palette like a shield and +1D4 P.P.E. **Penalties:** -1 to strike with the limb holding the palette. It also makes certain Physical skills like Acrobatics, Climbing and Swimming harder to perform, imposing a -10% penalty to such skills.

16-20% Bellows Lungs: Reflecting an interest in glassblowing or metalworking, the powerful lungs of the Nightbane's Morphus form are actually oversized bellows. Part or all of the flesh of the upper torso is replaced with a dark, leathery material that is visibly ribbed. As the Nightbane breathes the material expands outward, allowing for a much greater lung capacity than normal. **Bonuses:** +2 to the M.E. and P.E. attributes, +3D6 S.D.C. Those with this feature can hold their breath for a number of minutes equal to the P.E. attribute. Additionally, heat and fire (even the magic varieties) do half damage to the Morphus

form. **Penalties:** -2 to the P.B. attribute. The bellows increase buoyancy which makes swimming difficult, -20% to the Swimming or S.C.U.B.A. skills. Also, they make a lot more noise than normal breathing, causing a -10% penalty to the *Prowl* skill.

21-30% Drawing Table: The front of the torso folds down to reveal a flat, sturdy surface suitable for drawing anything from building plans to cartoon illustrations. Instead of organs, the chest cavity contains a variety of drawing implements and tools from a compass to a T-square as well as various pencils and pens to suit the needs of the chosen type of art. **Bonuses:** +1 to the M.E. attribute and +4D6 S.D.C.; +1 on Perception Rolls. The character gains the equivalent of the psionic power of *Total Recall* at no cost, but only for *images*, not words; however, that includes faces and tattoos as well as design elements. Normal verbal memory will likely remember key words or short phrases but not whole texts. Recalled images can then be duplicated as a detailed sketch with a successful roll under the character's Art skill. This process takes just 2D4 minutes (twice that for color images). Those Nightbane who are skilled in drafting can duplicate building plans just by having seen them or been through the building once. +10% to Art skill. **Penalties:** -1 to the P.S., P.E. and P.B. attributes, -1D4 to Spd.

31-40% Chisel Fingers: A sign of a sculptor or woodworker, the tips of each finger end in a variety of metal tools useful for chipping away at and carving wood or stone, engraving, etc. **Bonuses:** +1 to the M.E. attribute and +1 to Perception rolls. +10% to the *Whittling & Sculpting* skill while in Morphus form. The Nightbane is also able to dig/tunnel through rock and dirt at the rate of three feet (0.9 m) per melee round, and the sharpened tips function like claws, adding 1D6 to the Supernatural P.S. punch damage for any claw attack. **Penalties:** -1 to the P.B. attribute. -20% to any skills requiring a sensitive touch like Art, Computer Programming, Surgery, Forgery or Pick Pockets.

41-50% Typewriter/Keyboard: Whether it is carried or built into the body of the Morphus, the character's love of writing is represented as a computer keyboard or old-fashioned typewriter. This tool is fully functional and can be used at any time to type personal reminders, a record of events, etc. There is never a need for paper or replacement ink, either, and any finished document will either appear on the character's hand, somehow print out, or can be removed from the top of the typewriter. **Bonuses:** +1 to the M.E. attribute and +2D6 S.D.C. +10% to *Creative Writing* or *Technical Writing* skill. A final, odd effect is that a Nightbane with this feature can sometimes (5% base chance, +3% at levels 3, 6, 9, 12, and 15) gain spontaneous insight about a nagging question by taking 1D4 hours to journal about it. Such questions can include anything from the identity of a mole within a faction to the location of a lost object or the significance of a clue (G.M. discretion). Many think this is just an effect of careful contemplation, but there are some who believe the writer taps into the

collective unconscious, or an unearthly source of knowledge that enables him to recognize overlooked clues or snatch a sudden burst of insight from the aether. **Penalties:** -2 to the M.A. attribute. -1D6 base P.P.E.; Nightbane with this feature often seem to be distracted by their own thoughts.

51-60% Costumes/Outfits/Cosplay: The hallmark of an actor and cosplay costume makers (or other costume/fashion designer), is creating costumes for the characters they portray. In this case, the Nightbane Morphus manifests as one particular "outfit" *each* time he switches from Facade to Morphus. He may select the same favorite appearance as the Morphus or a completely new costume and different look each time he transforms into his Morphus. That can include a diverse range of looks and characters: cyborg, executioner, spy, ninja, executive in a suit, wizard, knight, werewolf, demon, an anime character, a super-hero, and on an on; each look typically reflecting the Nightbane's emotions or state of mind or whether he or she is trying to impress, scare or confuse his adversaries. Inevitably, the Nightbane is likely to have 2-4 favorite default "costumes" or looks that he appears in the most often, but that too can change over time. Such outfits can include small tools, gadgets, weapons, regalia and makeup that go with the costume. HOWEVER, much like *props* in acting and cosplay, any equipment is completely fake and non-functional even if it looks convincing (and cosplay creations usually look amazingly real, including faux tails, wings and claws). But that can work to the Nightbane's advantage, since his opponents don't know what's real and what's fake. **Bonuses:** +1D4+1 to the M.A. attribute, +15% to the Disguise and Impersonation skills, +5% to any other skill that might benefit from a specific outfit, such as dark-colored clothing aiding the *Prowl* skill in the dark. Special: +1 to Horror Factor and/or +10% to intimidate when trying to look scary or dangerous, or +10% to evoke trust and confidence BUT ONLY WHEN dressed for the part. +1D4 to P.B. when dressed and made up to look glamorous and sexy. The Nightbane also gains S.D.C. protection from the costume as if he was wearing a physical outfit. This is equal to the actual S.D.C. of the real costume, but remember, the armor is NOT real, but only made to look like armor, and so it offers *minimal protection.* **Special Conditions: 1.** Because it is fake, the most S.D.C. any outfit can add is 30 points. **2.** The Nightbane can only manifest costumes/appearances (including makeup) that he has actually worn or created himself. Yes, this means a cosplayer or costume designer can create new outfits, disguises, and appearances for himself, BUT they must be worn, in public, for at least 2 hours for them to become accessible as a Morphus option. **Penalties:** -1 to strike, parry, and dodge, -5% to all Physical skills like Acrobatics, Climbing, Gymnastics, Prowl and Swimming.

61-70% Iron Works: This is a sculptor who works in metal, cutting and welding metal to create abstract works of art or animals and such out of metal, or could be a blacksmith hobbyist. In either case, the Morphus is a well-muscled body that seems to be made of smooth steel (light grey) or iron (a darker, blue grey), a welder's mask (or monstrous equivalent) that can flip up to reveal the face (could be anything underneath), heavy work gloves, and an acetylene torch (2D6 damage, melee combat range) or a small sledgehammer (1D6 damage) and a large sledgehammer (2D6 damage). **Bonuses:** +2 to P.S. attribute, +1 to P.P., and +1D6x10+40 to S.D.C. Damage from weapons is in addition to his Supernatural P.S. **Penalties:** -1 to P.B., -1D6 to Spd attribute, and -10% on skills like Acrobatics, Climbing, Gymnastics, Prowl and Swimming.

71-80% Instrument/Mic Stand: Musicians of all stripes may find that they appear in Morphus form with their chosen or favorite instrument ready to play. Vocalists will have a microphone with or without its stand rather than an instrument. Without any kind of amplification, the music produced with this instrument can be heard up to a half mile to one full mile (0.8 to 1.6 km) away. This may be useful for putting on concerts, making money as a street performer or at clubs, signaling allies, confusing the enemy or creating a distraction (may even cause a crowd to gather which can add to confusion, block traffic, etc.). **Bonuses:** +1 to the M.E. and M.A. attributes, +20% to the *Play Musical Instrument* and/or *Sing* skill, whichever this feature reflects. Unlike most musical instruments, this instrument is sturdy enough to be used as a blunt weapon in combat. A small instrument like a flute or fiddle does 1D4 damage while medium-sized instruments like a saxophone, clarinet or guitar do 1D6 damage and the largest instruments like a cello or tuba do 1D6+3 damage. **Penalties:** -1D6 on base P.P.E., -1 to Horror Factor, and -5% to all Physical skills like Acrobatics, Climbing, Gymnastics, Prowl and Swimming.

81-90% Body Artist (Tattoos & Piercings): The Morphus body is covered in tattoos (player's choice of how many and what they are), or scarification (cuts to create patterns; may be aboriginal or something more modern), and/or piercings of all kinds. The fingers may also be adorned in heavy rings (+1D4 damage to punches). **Bonuses:** In combat, the tattoos or scar patterns seem to move, which is unnerving and makes opponents -1 to strike and parry, and adds +1 to the Horror Factor of the Nightbane. +1D4x10+10 to S.D.C. **Penalties:** -10% to Prowl, -50% to Disguise and Impersonate, and is impossible to look inconspicuous unless completely covered, and even then, piercings and tattoos or scarification on the face may make that difficult.

91-00% Other: Roll on or choose an entry from another table and relate it back to the character's *artistic focus.* Likely alternatives include any of the Animal tables, the Artificial Appearance Table (see Appendix), Athlete, Biomechanical (see **Nightbane® RPG**, page 105, or the Appendix in this book), and Unearthly Beauty Table (**Nightbane® RPG**, page 92, and the Appendix in this book).

Athlete Table

There are many people who enjoy rigorous physical activity on some level. Whether this is some kind of organized sport or simply for personal fitness, the level of involvement can range from an occasional game of recreational fun shooting hoops to an Olympic gymnast who trains the majority of the day, every day. Whether these Nightbane were budding young professionals, physically fit, or just hopelessly dreamed of one day becoming a pro athlete, features from this table indicate a substantial interest and/or investment in athletics of any number of styles and types.

Roll percentile dice once for random determination, or pick one.

01-11% Streamlined: Built for running, this Nightbane has a lean body with long, powerful limbs. Whether walking, jogging, running, or swimming, he or she seems to glide almost effortlessly across the ground or through the water. Of course, this also means that the body is less massive than would otherwise be the case (-20% normal weight), sacrificing strength and damage resistance for speed and endurance. **Bonuses:** The Morphus is taller than average, add one foot (0.3 m) to normal height. Nor-

mal Spd attribute is *replaced* with 2D4x10+40 (approximately 20.5 to 82 mph or 33-131 kph), and +1 to the P.P. attribute. Even running at maximum speed for hours at a time does NOT fatigue the Nightbane in any way. +1D6 to kick damage. **Penalties:** -1D6 to the P.S. attribute and reduce starting S.D.C. by 10%. If the Morphus form has an A.R., reduce it by 2 points.

12-22% Gymnast's Build: Compact, lithe, and flexible, the build of this Morphus form is perfect for feats of physical agility and strength without compromising speed of movement. While it is not always apparent that 'Bane with this build are as physically adept as they are, when they spring into action the grace of their movements is stunning. **Bonuses:** +2 to the P.S., +1D4 to P.P., +1 to P.E. and +2 to the P.B. attribute, +4D6 S.D.C., automatically gets the Gymnastics skill at 68% +4% per level of experience, and +10% to Physical skills such as Acrobatics and Climbing/Rappelling. **Penalties:** -2 to save vs poisons/toxins and -1 to Horror Factor.

23-34% Musclebound: The Morphus has musculature on par with an Olympic weightlifter or circus strongman, with a thick neck, broad shoulders and chest, and massive arms and legs. Every major muscle in the Nightbane's body is also toned and well defined. In the absence of obvious deformities, this character can enter and win bodybuilding contests hands-down. **Bonuses:** +1D6+4 to the P.S. attribute, +2 to P.E., and +1 to P.B., +1D4x10 S.D.C., +1 to Awe/Horror Factor, and the character can lift and carry twice the standard amount for their strength attribute. **Penalties:** -1 to the P.P. attribute, -1D6 to Spd, and -10% on skills like Acrobatics, Climbing, Gymnastics, Prowl and Swimming.

35-45% Team Jersey: Whether this jersey is from the character's high-school sports team, a favorite professional team, or some other athletic organization, the effects are the same. Wearing a team's colors provides a strong sense of identity and belonging that is reassuring, comforting, and a point of pride and inspiration. Interestingly, no substance like dirt, blood, or even paint soils the team logo on this jersey no matter how much covers the Nightbane. **Bonuses:** +1 to the M.E. attribute, +1 on Perception Rolls involving sports and sports teams (+2 on Perception Rolls involving the team represented on the jersey), +1 to save vs mind control and possession, +1 to save vs Horror Factor, and +1D6 S.D.C. **Penalty:** -1 to the P.E. attribute.

46-56% Skates: Ice skates, inline roller skates, or some other type of skates are attached to the feet of the Morphus form. Moving on skates is second nature to this Nightbane, allowing him to not only perform feats of speed on flat surfaces but also to move normally on surfaces not ordinarily negotiable on skates. **Bonuses:** Double the Nightbane's speed on hard, flat surfaces like ice, roller rinks, pavement, concrete, tiled flooring, etc., +1D6 to kick damage. **Penalties:** -20% to Prowl and half speed on rough, uneven or soft surfaces such as gravel, grass and mud.

57-67% Club/Stick: Several sports use a stick, club, mallet or bat. This Nightbane played or admired such a sport and so his Morphus includes the blunt item of that game be it a hockey

stick, golf club, cricket bat, baseball bat, polo mallet, etc. No matter what form it takes, this piece of gear is a blunt weapon that inflicts 1D6+3 damage in addition to the Supernatural P.S. punch damage of the character when used as a weapon. **Bonuses:** +1 to strike and parry with the club, +2 to pull punch. **Penalties:** The stick is large and unwieldy to carry, so other two-handed weapons cannot be used unless it can be slung over the back or the Nightbane has other appendages.

68-78% Protective Gear: The Morphus wears the protective gear common to the Nightbane's chosen sport(s) like American football, hockey, and so on. This protective gear may appear to be vintage, modern, or even futuristic, and may have stylistic features that fit with the overall Morphus, such as shin guards made of chitin for an insectoid Nightbane. **Bonuses:** Heavy pads and protectors like those worn by most football or hockey players over the shoulders, chest, elbows, hands, knees and thighs, as well as some sort of helmet or head protection provides an additional +2D4x10 S.D.C. and +1 to Natural A.R. **Penalties:** -3 to the Spd attribute and -15% to all Physical skills that require flexibility and movement such as Acrobatics, Climbing, Gymnastics, Prowl, Swimming, and in this case skills like Pick Locks, Pick Pockets and Disguise.

79-89% Cleats: Specialized footwear with small metal spikes built into the bottom. Worn by runners, golfers, baseball players and many other athletes who compete on dirt or turf. These shoes are meant to provide greater traction. For the Nightbane with this feature, the cleats even dig into asphalt and concrete that hasn't been reinforced. **Bonuses:** +1D4 to the Spd attribute and +3 to kick damage. Surfaces such as ice, mud, and even oil-slicked floors do not cause the Nightbane to lose his footing, slip or fall. **Penalties:** -20% to Prowl across hard surfaces where the spikes scratch, clunk and make a rackets as well as leave scuffs and scratches on the surface. The Nightbane is also easily tracked across soft and hard surfaces due to the tell-tale gouges and holes left in the ground by the cleats and scratches and pockmarks left on hard surfaces.

90-00% Game Ball/Projectile: The Nightbane's Morphus is likely to have the kind of stitching and patterns of the ball used in his sport of choice, incorporated into his body appearance. He also carries a ball, puck, Frisbee, or similar object used to play a particular sport. This ball may look like the genuine item or be styled after the Morphus, but the effects are the same. The projectile can be thrown, kicked, or otherwise propelled at tremendous speed to strike up to 300 feet (91.5 m) away and *returns to the character* after being thrown. Bank-shots are also possible, but -2 to strike, with only the final surface struck taking damage.

Anything hit by the speeding ball/projectile takes damage equal to half the Nightbane's Supernatural P.S. punch damage +1D6. There is also a chance that a victim struck by the ball is knocked off his feet, losing initiative and one melee attack. Against targets with normal strength, there is a 01-25% chance of being knocked flat, and a 01-10% chance against those with

Supernatural Strength or larger than 8 feet (2.4 m); +20% to those odds if the target is already off balance. The Nightbane may pass this projectile to another person up to 300 feet (91.5 m) away, but once dropped or thrown, it returns to the Nightbane it belongs to. **Bonuses:** +2 to strike with the projectile, +2 to catch balls or intercept thrown projectiles, and +1 to dodge projectiles. **Penalties:** -3 to base P.P.E. -20% to skills like Climbing, Swimming, and other physical activities that require the use of both hands. The ball must always be held, meaning that no two-handed weapons can be used unless the Nightbane has multiple limbs, or turns into his Facade.

Clown Table

Nightbane with features from this table might have been the "class-clown," dreamed about joining the circus, wanted to become a mime, clown or rodeo clown, or possibly even had a deathly fear of clowns and their ilk, so to them, clowns are scary and monstrous. While Nightbane with such a comical appearance might initially be disregarded or even persecuted by their breth-

ren, there is something a little more than unsettling about watching this Nightbane in combat or caving in a Hound's head with a "toy" mallet or cartwheel through a gunfight while cackling like a fool. Even the most battle-hardened warriors grudgingly accept Clown Nightbane as capable allies or foes, even if their antics can be annoying. **Note:** Nightbane with any of the features below automatically have a Horror Factor of 18 to anyone afraid of clowns.

Roll percentile dice once for random determination, or pick one.

01-10% Clown Nose: The character has a small, brightly colored rubber ball over the tip of the nose which honks when squeezed. Unlike a normal clown nose, this one is a part of the 'Bane and cannot be removed. The skin color of the Nightbane's face may be normal or pale grey or white like that of clown, or reflect the rest of his Morphus. **Bonuses:** Keen sense of smell. Track by smell equal to a bloodhound (70% +1% per level of experience; +10% to follow blood or chemical scent). As a funny prop, if the character honks the nose while smiling, laughing, behaving in a silly manner or striking a silly pose, those who see or encounter him are temporarily unaffected by the Nightbane's Horror Factor. In fact, as long as he makes no aggressive or scary moves, he seems harmless, even comical and friendly. It also gives the Nightbane a base Charm/Impress of 35% or a +10% if his P.B. attribute offers a higher than 35% chance, and double the base percentage (or +20%) when dealing with children under the age of thirteen. **Penalties:** -2 to M.A. and P.B. attributes, -3 to base P.P.E., -2 to Horror Factor and -20% to the Disguise and Impersonation skills.

11-20% Face Paint: The Morphus of the Nightbane has a white face painted in classic clown patterns in a riot of garish colors. This may be the traditional embellishment of clowns the world over or a completely original pattern that may look silly, friendly, happy, sad, or yes, frightening and monstrous. The juxtaposition of the clown motif with other monstrous or spooky elements like fangs or pointed teeth, glowing eyes, spikes, mouth sewn shut, etc. can make the clown face seem all the more menacing and creepy. **Bonuses:** +2 to M.A., +1 on initiative, +1 to Horror Factor, and can mold his face to resemble another person or monster! Mold Face (special): The Nightbane can morph his face to look like some other kind of humanoid, demon or monster or to look like a specific person (must have the person there or good reference). The transformation takes 1D4 melee rounds (15-60 seconds). If the subject being copied is in front of him, he/she can imitate the person's voice as well! This is transformation is done to confuse and freak out people as well as to impersonate them. Suddenly seeing your own face or that of a loved one looking back at you is very unnerving and frightening. Automatically gets the Disguise and Impersonation skills at 62% +2% per level of experience. **Penalties:** -2 to P.B. and M.E. attributes, -1 to save vs magic, and -3D6+10 from permanent P.P.E. base.

21-30% Clown Clothes: The clothing that appears on this Nightbane is garishly colored and may be baggy and oversized. The actual type of attire varies drastically, and can range from the denim overalls and the western shirt of a rodeo clown to multicolored outfits attributed to clowns or medieval court jesters, to suit and tie. **Bonuses:** +2D6 S.D.C. and +1 to Natural A.R. +1 to dodge and entangle. +15% to any skills used to entertain such as Performance, Sing, and Dance. +20% to the Concealment and Palming skills if hiding something on the Nightbane's person. Moreover, no body can remember the clown's face. They can describe his clothing, but his face is a blank and it is blurred out in photographs, video and film. **Penalties:** -1 to the P.P. attribute and -2 to Spd. -15% to Climbing, Prowl, and Swimming skills. Skills like Seduction and Undercover Ops are likely impossible while in this Morphus, but nobody can remember the face.

31-40% Clown Shoes: The character's Morphus is wearing brightly colored shoes that are roughly twice the normal size. These stereotypical "clown" shoes make running or sneaking more difficult, but they're good for a laugh and have a few perks. **Bonuses:** +6 to the swimming Spd only, +6 damage from kicks and stomp attacks, and *impervious to damage from falls and impact from large objects* (special) like a falling safe, car, truck, boulder, etc., as well as explosions (no damage!). Note that punches, kicks, bullets and melee weapons, including blunt weapons, do full damage to the clown. **Penalties:** -2 to the P.P. and M.E. attributes, reduce land Spd by half, -20% to Prowl, -30% to Climbing and cannot leap/jump.

41-50% Outrageous Hair and Head: The Nightbane has a painted clown face, and wild hair that could be a mohawk of any variety, shaped into spikes, frizzed up and out in one or more weird directions, a giant Afro, incredibly long or in ponytails, and in one or more bright colors. And the head is REMOVABLE! Yes, removable. This us usually done for shock value and to create fear, confusion and panic. Or the head could have some other outrage and disturbing element such as being able to split the head in half, or lift the top off like a lid to a jar to reveal his brain (momentary +2 to Horror Factor), or has fangs when he wants them to show, etc. **Bonuses:** The head is impervious to physical damage! Bullets bounce off, blows to the head hurt but do no damage, and the clown cannot be knocked out from a blow to the head. +2 to Horror Factor when the head is visibly detached from the body and held in one of the Nightbane's hands or tucked under an arm, kept inside a box, etc. The head can be removed and placed someplace inconspicuous to spy on people, removed to frighten people, kept in a box and revealed to frighten people, placed on a stick like a living scepter, or float like a balloon on a string one or two feet (0.3 or 0.6 m) above the neck and shoulders. The head holds the brains and consciousness of the Nightbane, and it still controls the body even when detached. Though detachable, the body is never more than 20 feet (6.1 m) away. If the head or body is stolen and taken more than 120 feet (36.6 m) away, it forces the Nightbane to switch from Morphus into

his Facade to reunite his body with his head. **Penalties:** -1D4 to the M.A. and P.B. attributes, -5% to Prowl and -40% to Tailing. Skills like Undercover Ops, Seduction, Disguise and Impersonation are impossible while in this Morphus.

51-60% Balloons: Tied to this Morphus on strings are 2D4+3 medium-sized helium balloons of various colors. Each floats a few feet (a meter) above the Nightbane. They never seem to tangle or otherwise impede the Nightbane's movement, though they may obscure views of anything directly above. Each balloon has only a single point of S.D.C., but they are only damaged by attacks leveled directly at them. The balloons can also be cut free and even handed out or left tied to objects. By squeezing and twisting the balloons, they can be made into balloon animals and other shapes. Balloons that are destroyed or cut loose regenerate at the rate of one every hour. **Bonuses:** As long as one balloon is still attached, the Nightbane floats down when he jumps from any height, taking 1D6 damage upon a hard landing; double damage from heights greater than 200 feet (61 m). He can also jump up to 30 feet (9.1 m) high or across as long as he has one or more balloons. When separated from the Nightbane, each balloon continues to register to any supernatural senses as that Nightbane for one hour. This can be used to create the equivalent of supernatural decoys, sending pursuers off on wild goose chases or causing them to overestimate the number of Nightbane present. **Penalties:** -6 to the Spd attribute when there are two or more balloons attached to the Nightbane (-2 if there is only one balloon attached), -3 to dodge, and the balloons are easy to spot, so -10% to Prowl and skills like Tailing, Disguise, and Undercover Ops are impossible.

61-70% Clown Gags: Part and parcel of almost any clown act are the gimmicks and gags used to garner laughs. A Nightbane with this feature may look like a clown or have subtle clown-like features along with 1D4+1 of the following gags that always appear on the Morphus. They may be worn, kept on a web-vest or inside pockets, tucked in a belt, carried in hand or slung over the shoulder in a cloth sack. However, these gimmicks are usually not concealed in any way.

Chatter Teeth: 1D4 sets of teeth (human or animal) that animate and chatter along the ground at a maximum speed of 5. They can also jump up to 8 feet (2.4 m) high to nip and bite opponents. Human-sized and smaller teeth inflict 1D6+1 bite damage while larger and sharper teeth may do up to 2D6+2 damage. Each set of chatter teeth has two attacks per melee round and is +3 to strike and +5 to dodge attacks against it.

Exploding Cigars: A package containing 1D4+3 normal looking cigars. However, five seconds after being lit these cigars explode with a loud report. Anyone in a 20 foot (6 m) radius that isn't wearing hearing protection loses one melee attack and is -2 on initiative for 1D4 melee rounds. If in someone's mouth or slipped into a pocket or bag, or held in hand, the cigar does 1D4 damage and blackens the face, hand or bag with soot. Exploding cigars are replaced at the rate of one per hour.

Extend-O-Glove: A large boxing glove at the end of an extendable armature, this odd device enables the Nightbane to deliver a punch to a target up to seven feet (2.1 m) beyond his normal reach. The Nightbane can dictate the amount of damage delivered by the glove's punch: One point of damage (a playful bop), 1D6 damage, 2D6 damage or 4D6 damage. The character's usual bonus to strike applies.

Fake Hand: This is a convincing facsimile of one of the Morphus' hands. Often used when shaking someone's hand for a laugh, the fake hand can detach to remain holding onto the person who just shook hands or grabbed the Nightbane's hand. It holds on until it can be pulled off, which takes 1D4 melee attacks to shake or pull loose. Until pulled off, the victim cannot use that hand to punch, hold a weapon or perform a skill. The fake hand can also be detached and animated to scurry over the ground or a piece of furniture to retrieve small items or to enter small spaces, slip through an open window to unlock a door, etc. The hand can crawl at a maximum speed of 7 and has a P.S. that is half that of the owner. To manipulate the fake hand, the Nightbane must be able to see it to control it with his mind. Maximum range is 60 feet (18.3 m) with a clear line of sight. The fake hand is unable to punch, strike, or use a weapon, but the hand can grasp and cling to others, distracting and often creeping opponents out. The appendage has three attacks/actions per melee round and is +2 to dodge. A lost or destroyed hand reappears after the Nightbane returns to his Facade and back into his Morphus.

Toy Horn: This is a small, metal or plastic horn that resembles a miniature trumpet or bicycle horn with a squeeze bulb to make it honk. While it can be used purely for entertainment, once per melee it can unleash a foghorn-like blare which is accompanied by a powerful blast of air. This blast is sufficient to knock down human-sized targets within 10 feet (3 m) and send lightweight objects like loose papers, dry leaves, sawdust, and magazines flying up to 20 feet (6.1 m) away. The latter is done to cause confusion or momentarily obscure the vision of an opponent. Targets must make a saving throw vs a 14 or lose initiative and one melee attack/action.

Toy Pistol: This may be a brightly colored, obviously toy gun, or a realistic-looking pistol that extends a little flag reading something like "POW!" "Boom!" or "Gotcha!" Alternatively, it might be a gun that produces a small pop and fires only confetti or streamers. That is, until the Nightbane sacrifices two Hit Points to temporarily allow the weapon to fire a real slug. This attack deals 2D6+2 damage and has a range of 120 feet (36.6 m). Each real shot requires the sacrifice of two Hit Points that heal normally. Afterwards, it reverts back to its natural toy form.

Joy Buzzer: This small electric device is concealed in one of the palms of the Nightbane in Morphus. Upon contact with another person it emits a loud buzz and a low-grade shock (does a single point of damage). Most often this is used when shaking hands with someone for the first time. The damage can be increased by the Nightbane by temporarily burning Hit Points. Up

to 3 Hit Points can be spent in this manner per attack, with each H.P. adding 1D6 damage. Furthermore, anyone hit with a "juiced up" buzzer attack is at -1 on all combat rolls for one melee round.

Pie Case: A medium-sized satchel, duffle bag, purse or crate contains shaving cream pies. These are hurled into the faces of hapless marks just for laughs. If done for fun, the pie's contents can simply be wiped or rinsed off, but the victim of a pie to the face is momentarily blinded until wiped from the eyes, and loses one melee attack. The Nightbane can elect to generate pies that cling like thick mud at the cost of one Hit Point. This forces the target to spend 1D4 attacks to clear the muck from his eyes and face. Otherwise, the victim is blinded, suffering the usual -10 penalty to strike, parry, dodge, etc. The Nightbane is +2 to strike with either type of pie, with a maximum throwing range of 20 feet (6 m). Throwing a pie in the face of a specific target requires a *Called Shot*, though it should be presumed that any pie is intended for a shot to the face.

Squeak Mallet: This looks like a large, imposing gag hammer that squeaks when it strikes and does no damage. For the most part, it is used to playfully swat others or pop them on top of the head (no damage). Each blow is accompanied by some humorous sound effect such as a squeak or honk or fart noise. At will, the Nightbane can spend two Hit Points to turn the Squeak Mallet into a weapon capable of caving in a person's skull! It remains a deadly weapon for one melee round per level of the Nightbane and each attack does 1D6+2 damage in addition to the character's own Supernatural P.S. punch damage. This can be especially deadly if the opponent is only expecting one of the playful hits.

Squirt Flower: A fake-looking plastic flower pinned to the lapel discharges a small, four ounce (118 ml) stream of water when the hidden bulb is depressed. Harmless to most (if annoying), the water does 1D6 damage to vampires and other creatures vulnerable to water. The Squirt Flower somehow never runs dry, meaning it can be used to slowly fill canteens and the like with potable drinking water in the absence of other sources. By temporarily sacrificing one Hit Point, the flower can release a 10 ounce (2957 ml) squirt of water or one of the following substances: blood (sufficient to feed a vampire with multiple uses), ink (stains most cloth, paper, etc.), inorganic acid (does 2D6 damage to metal, concrete, and other non-organic substances), kerosene (highly flammable), or mace (victim is temporarily blinded and -10 to strike, parry, and dodge for 1D4 melee rounds). **Bonuses:** See items above. **Penalties:** -3 to the Spd attribute, -2D6 base P.P.E., -15% to Invoke Trust/Intimidate, and -10% to Prowl.

71-80% Jester's Cap and Costume: The Morphus of this Nightbane is that of a jester with an odd, multi-pointed cap affixed to the head. A bell may be attached to each point of the cap, or it could have some other decorative item like charms, rings, spikes, tiny skulls, bones or fingers. The cap and costume may be multi-colored, bright or ominously dark. **Bonuses:** +5% to any single Espionage and Rogue skill (pick one from each category). **Penalties:** -1 to the M.A. and M.E. attributes.

81-90% Scepter/Baton or Bowling Pin: A scepter or baton is a short staff or rod made of anything from wood to bone, to metal, and is almost always ornate. Some even include gems, bells or ribbons for added flair. Everyone should know what a bowling pin looks like. The Nightbane is able to perform numerous tricks with the item, spinning, flipping, juggling and balancing it on end or on one finger, his head or nose. In a pinch, it can be used as a blunt weapon that deals 1D6 damage in addition to a Supernatural P.S. punch damage and can parry melee attacks. **Bonuses:** +1 attack when using only this item in combat for the entire melee round, +1 to strike in hand to hand combat or thrown, and +2 to parry and pull punch with the item. **Penalties:** -2 from permanent P.P.E. base.

91-00% Jack-in-the-Box: One of the oddest Morphus forms are those Nightbane who look like giant versions of the children's toy known as a *Jack-in-the-box*. The upper half of the character's body may look like a clown, a jester or inhuman, and has a humanoid shape with arms, neck and head. The lower body from the waist down is a giant coiled spring covered in fabric, making it resemble an accordion, and is attached to a decorative box large enough for the Nightbane to hunker down into and close the flip top lid. The box may be colorful or ominous in its design but always has a circus, carnival or freak show vibe. There is also a winding key that when cranked, causes the box to play music until the box lid pops open and the hidden Nightbane inside springs out. The Nightbane has full control over this, which means another person cannot force the handle to turn and make the box open against his will. The Nightbane is also in control of the moment he chooses to pop out, making his appearance unpredictable and startling every time.

The extendable, accordion-like leg area enables a Jack-in-the-Box Nightbane to stretch up to twice his normal height with an average of 12 feet (3.7 m). The character can also collapse to half of his normal height with an average of 3 feet (0.9) for the box, leaving little room inside for anything but the torso, a few weapons and some personal equipment. The Jack-in-the-Box Nightbane can twist his accordion-like legs attached to the inside of the box to turn 360 degrees and is so bendable that the Nightbane can invert the torso by bending in half. Movement is an interesting process, with the Jack-in-the-box having to hop like a person in a potato-sack race (reduce Spd by 70%!) or he can crawl, inch-worm fashion, dragging the box behind him.

This toy anatomy also changes the way damage is dealt with. The body from the waist up can be specifically targeted and has Hit Points and S.D.C. as you would expect, but Hit Points and S.D.C. are divided evenly between the upper body and the box, which also has a Natural A.R. of 12. If the body is severed below the waist, the torso must crawl into the box portion to reattach, which takes one full melee round (15 seconds). Otherwise the Nightbane's Morphus can only be made whole again by transforming back into the Facade, which causes the box portion to disappear. **Bonuses:** +2 to the P.P. attribute, +1D6x10+60 to

32

S.D.C., the box has a Natural A.R. of 11, +2 to Horror Factor ONLY the first melee round that the Nightbane "pops out" of the box, +2 on initiative, a surprise attack occurs on a roll of a Natural 19 or 20, double damage on a surprise attack, +1 to strike and parry, +2 to dodge, and +1 to entangle. Coil jumps are possible by compressing the trunk then rapidly extending it and can propel the Nightbane 1.5 feet (0.5 m) per point of P.S. This can also be used to perform a power strike, which works just like a power punch (counts as two attacks). **Penalties:** The Spd attribute is reduced by 70% and half that when crawling, -30% to Climbing, -50% to Dancing and Swimming, and some skills like Acrobatics, Bicycling, Disguise, Gymnastics, Prowl, Running, Tailing, Undercover Ops and driving most vehicles (no legs) are impossible in this Morphus form. Likewise, special kick attacks are impossible to perform.

Gear-Head Table

For around 100 years, people have had a special relationship with automobiles, relying on them not only for transportation but also for a livelihood, recreation, racing and even as a place to live. Nightbane with Morphus features from this table epitomize just such a bond in a new, physical way. Perhaps the character spent hours wrenching on engines with Dad or with friends, went sightseeing around the country in a motor home or family car, worked in an auto factory or design center, loved cruising on his motorcycle, is a NASCAR or other racing enthusiast, lived on the road as a traveling salesman or trucker, or just always had a love for cars. Whatever the reason, this Nightbane's Morphus now incorporates one or more features of a vehicle. **Note:** Features in this table are considered *Biomechanical* for the purposes of Talent eligibility.

Roll percentile dice once for random determination, or pick one.

01-10% Engine Block: Either replacing or built into the chest of this Nightbane is an entire engine block. This might be a miniaturized car or truck engine, a motorcycle engine, etc. When stationary, the engine constantly idles, but when the Nightbane is running or engaged in strenuous activity, it revs up just like the real thing. **Bonuses:** +3 to the P.S. attribute, +3D6+10 to Spd, +2D6x10 to S.D.C. with a base Natural A.R. of 10 (or +1 to an existing A.R. that is greater than 10), +2 to Horror Factor and +10% to all piloting skills that involve a motor. **Penalties:** -3 to the P.P. and P.B. attributes. Electrical and fire attacks inflict 50% more damage and the character will drown within 1D4+2 melee rounds if dropped into deep water in Morphus form (can't hold breath or swim, too heavy). -30% to Climbing and Tailing. Skills like Acrobatics, Disguise, Gymnastics, Prowl, and Undercover Ops are impossible in this Morphus.

11-19% Coolant Tubes/Radiator: In place of veins, this character has transparent or translucent plastic tubes filled with blue or green liquid. In truth, this is ethylene glycol (antifreeze) and water, and the tubes all connect to a central radiator that juts from the abdomen or back. This radiator has 1D4x10+20 S.D.C. and an A.R. of 9, but is a relatively small target that requires a Called Shot at -3 to hit. **Bonuses:** +2 to the P.E. attribute, +2D6+10 to S.D.C. +1 to Horror Factor, the Nightbane is impervious to poisons/toxins as well as diseases that affect the blood, his blood is toxic to vampires (4D6 damage per sip) and cold, heat and fire (even magical) do half damage. **Penalties:** -2 to the P.B. and Spd attributes, and -1D6 P.P.E. If the radiator is ever completely destroyed, it will not regenerate as normal unless the Nightbane returns to Facade form for at least 1D4 hours. Without the radiator, the Morphus form takes double damage from fire and cold-based attacks and heals at half the normal rate (usually 5 S.D.C./H.P. per melee). Also, the leaking antifreeze makes the Nightbane much easier to track (+20% bonus to those tracking him).

20-28% Exhaust Pipes: One or more metal pipes protrude from the shoulders or back of the Nightbane, releasing a steady stream of exhaust vapor. This exhaust is indistinguishable from vehicle exhaust (gas or diesel), though it contains carbon dioxide rather than carbon monoxide. The pipes themselves may look like any car, truck, or motorcycle exhaust, with or without a muffler,

and are hot to the touch. **Bonuses:** +1 to the P.E. attribute, +3D6 to S.D.C., impervious to poisonous/toxic gas or fumes, including smoke, tear gas and knockout gas, and +1 to Horror Factor. **Penalties:** The Nightbane is much easier to locate due to the smell of the exhaust, heat of the pipes, and larger visual profile; -20% to the Prowl skill. The exhaust also hampers the character's own sense of smell, so there is a -5 penalty to any Perception Rolls relying upon olfactory senses.

29-37% Nitrous Bottles: Nitrous oxide is sometimes used in amateur street-racing and thrill-ride experiences. When injected into the engine it provides a short boost of power and speed at the risk of destroying the engine. This Morphus feature adds small nitrous tanks or "bottles" to the Nightbane's back, body or upper legs to give him temporary speed boosts and the ability to leap 12 feet (3.7 m) high and up to 40 feet (12.2 m) across! **Bonuses:** Four times per hour, the character can hit the nitrous to enjoy a rocketing +70 Spd bonus (that's a bonus of 50 mph/80 km added to his usual Spd). The speed boost lasts for 1D6 minutes at a time. During this period the Nightbane is +2 on initiative, +2 to dodge, and +3 to roll with impact. **Penalties:** -2 to the P.E. attribute, -1D6 to his base P.P.E., and the character is a speed-freak and/or thrill seeker who tends to be a daredevil who likes to take risks.

38-46% Hydraulics: The Morphus has hydraulic struts attached to his limbs, which are extendable. Arms and legs can stretch an additional three feet (0.9 m). **Bonuses:** Has an extended reach, can perform power punches without using up two attacks, counts as one attack, can leap 10 feet (3 m) high or 20 feet (6.1 m) across, +1D6 to the Spd attribute, +1 to roll with impact, and +4D6 S.D.C. **Penalties:** -2 to dodge, and -20% to Acrobatics, Dance, Disguise, Gymnastics, and Undercover Ops.

47-55% Shocks & Struts: The Nightbane's legs incorporate heavy-duty automotive shocks and struts capable of reducing the impact from falls and running. For Morphus forms with *wheels* in the place of legs, they are able to handle rough terrain without any difficulty and enjoy a 10% speed bonus. **Bonuses:** +3 to the Spd attribute, can drop from heights as great as 200 feet (61 m) and land on his feet without injury (only loses two melee attacks; no penalty if the drop or fall was from 60 feet/18.3 m or shorter), and is +4 to roll with falls and impact (half damage). **Penalties:** -1 to P.P. and P.B. attributes, -15% to skills like Acrobatics, Dance, Disguise, Gymnastics, and Undercover Ops.

56-64% Air Horn: Incorporated into the character's Morphus form is a large air horn similar to those used on eighteen-wheelers and locomotives. This horn is usually visible as several flared tubes sticking out of the Nightbane's back, neck or shoulders. This horn can be heard for one mile (1.6 km) and can be used as a warning or signal. At close range, its blare is powerful enough to temporarily deafen anyone unprotected within a 25 foot (7.6 m) radius of the Nightbane). The deafness lasts for 1D4 melee rounds (15-60 seconds). Those affected are temporarily unable to hear sounds and are -4 on initiative and -2 to all combat rolls. Note that the character is unable to choose who is or isn't af-

fected. Everyone in the radius of effect is impacted; only the Nightbane himself is not affected. **Bonuses:** +1 to the P.E. attribute, +1D6 to S.D.C., impervious to loud sounds that would otherwise deafen other people. **Penalties:** -1D4 to base P.P.E., and the Nightbane is a bit hard of hearing, incurring a penalty of -3 to Perception Rolls involving sound, identifying and following/tracking sounds, and cannot hear whisper level sounds; -1 on initiative and may mishear/misunderstand something that could be important or lead to a misunderstanding/brawl or mistake on his part.

65-73% Searchlight(s): The character has 1D4 high-powered lights built into his torso, head, upper arms, or forearms near the wrist. These lights are capable of swiveling up to 30 degrees (or points where the arm points when in the forearms or where the head turns when in the head), and have the benefit of being able to penetrate even magical darkness, though at half their usual range and intensity. **Bonuses:** The searchlights can be engaged to see in the dark and through any magically created darkness as well as used to attempt to "parry" incoming Shadow or Darkness-based attacks (-3 to parry such attacks). If the parry is successful, the light completely negates them. **Penalties:** -1D6 base P.P.E. When any of the lights are on, Prowling is impossible. When off, the Nightbane is -10% to skills like Disguise and Undercover Ops.

74-82% Winch and Cable: This is a 50 foot (15 m) length of cable attached to a motorized spool, or winch. The winch may be built into the back, shoulder, or abdomen of the Nightbane Morphus or the 'Bane may have cable coiled around his arms and torso. To unleash the cable, it can be fired or released from the Nightbane's hands or wrists. Shooting out at its target as if they had a life of their own. The cable(s) automatically wrap and tie themselves to an inanimate object like a tree, lamppost, flagpole, ledge or vehicle, with the other end remaining tethered to the Nightbane. This can be used to secure himself to particular location, to pull out a vehicle or person trapped in mud or water, etc., or to climb by having the cable snare a ledge or outcropping and using the winch to pull the 'Bane to that location (or to lower him to the ground). Maximum range/length of cable is 50 feet (15.2 m) +1 foot (0.3 m) per level of experience.

Against a live opponent, the Winch and Cable Morphus enables the Nightbane to unspool a 5-10 foot (1.5 to 3 m) length of cable he can use as a whip (one in each hand even), that inflicts 2D6 damage or can be used to try to disarm an opponent. Or the 'Bane can entangle the legs or pin one or both arms of an opponent with the cables (maximum one from each hand). The cables shooting out as if they were alive. Opponents can try to parry or dodge such attacks. **Bonuses:** +2 to the P.S. attribute, +2D6+8 to S.D.C., +1 to strike with cable, +2 to disarm, entangle or pin, +15% to the *Climbing* skill. The winch is capable of pulling twice the Nightbane's maximum carry weight. **Penalties:** -1D6 to P.P.E. base, -1D6 to the Spd attribute, and -1 to dodge.

83-91% Chrome Job: A Nightbane with this Morphus feature has several metal accents incorporated into his physical

34

form. These take the shape of bolt-heads, grilles, tanks, shielding on the side of the forearms and legs, and other such details, but all are polished chrome and gleam in the light. The Nightbane might even have a chrome head (+20 S.D.C. to the head) or chrome hands (+1D4 damage and can parry melee weapons with bare hands). Whether the bits are plain, ornate, or even futuristic, the end result is the same. **Bonuses:** +2D6+10 to S.D.C., +1 to Natural A.R., +2 to roll with impact and +1 to Awe/Horror Factor. The character can also attempt to parry light-based attacks such as those from Guardians or high-tech laser weapons with only a -3 penalty to parry. **Penalties:** -10% to Prowl, -5% to Swimming, -20% to Disguise, Impersonation and Undercover Ops, and the Nightbane heals a bit slower than usual (6 S.D.C./Hit Point per melee round).

92-00% Other: Roll on or choose a Morphus Feature from one of the Biomechanical tables (**Nightbane® RPG**, page 105, **Between the Shadows**, page 131, or **Nightbane® Survival Guide**, page 83, or see the Appendix in this sourcebook).

Hobbyist Table

It seems that everyone in the developed world has a hobby of some sort. From collecting and/or reading books or comic books to hiking through the wilderness, people spend their free time pursuing thousands of different activities. For Nightbane with characteristics from the following table, so much time and energy has been spent on one or more hobbies that after the Becoming they find that their Morphus form reflects this deep interest.

Roll percentile dice once for random determination, or pick one.

01-11% Backpack: The character might be an avid outdoorsman, amateur athlete, hiker, camper or even a student or bookworm. Whatever the case, the Morphus appears with a very large, oversized backpack or duffle bag. This bag is much tougher than usual (60 S.D.C.) and can usually only be struck from behind. The large backpack, despite its size, does not seem to encumber the Nightbane too much and is somewhat larger inside than what it appears, making it capable of storing up to 120 pounds (54 kg) +10 pounds (4.5 kg) per level of experience. **Bonuses:** In addition to being able to carry a lot of gear, +1 to the P.S. and P.E. attributes and +2D6 to S.D.C. **Penalties:** -1 to P.P. and -6 to the Spd attribute, and -10% to skills like Climbing, Acrobatics, Gymnastics, and Prowl, and -30% to Disguise, Tailing and Undercover Ops in this Morphus.

12-22% Card Deck: First, the Nightbane's Morphus has a playing card motif element which may be subtle or unmistakable. This may be a classic poker card symbol – spade, club, heart, diamond or one of the face cards – emblazoned on his face or chest, arms, or the palms or tops of his hands, and similar, like a tattoo, or as a symbol on clothing, armor or a helmet. This Morphus also comes with a deck of playing cards carried in a small case, usually hooked to a belt or held in a pocket. Unlike normal cards, they

are tough and flexible enough to be used as thrown weapons. The sharp-edged cards inflict 1D6 damage each, with aces and face cards doing 2D6 damage. Throwing range is 60 feet (18.3 m). When the deck is used up, the Nightbane reaches back into his pocket or carrying case and pulls out a new deck; never runs out. **Bonuses:** +1 to I.Q. and P.P., +2 to strike with his pocker cards or any weapon designed for throwing, and does +2D6 damgae on a roll of a Natural 19 or 20. **Penalties:** -1 to the M.E. attribute and -1D6+2 from permanent P.P.E. base.

23-35% Video Games: Video games are extremely popular, especially among the adolescents and young adults most likely to become Nightbane. A fanatic about this form of electronic entertainment, this character's Morphus is likely to resemble the appearance of a character from a video game, be it a hero, villain, or creature, or may incorporate some elements of such characters like hair and armor, etc. He also wears virtual reality goggles that make everything he sees in the real world appear to be part of a video game! Thus, he feels like he is a character inside a video game. This bit of detachment from reality keeps the Nightbane cool, calm and at arm's length from what can become a frightening reality.

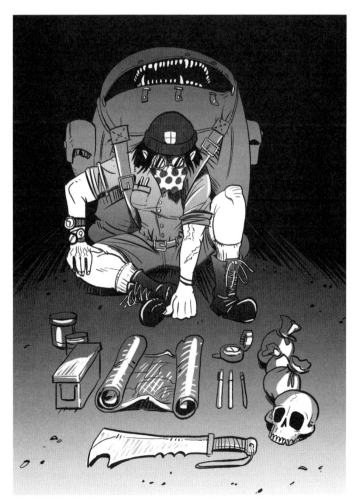

He also has a wireless video game controller or joystick that he can use to boost and alter his Morphus! With the press of a button he can bestow any one the following upon himself, with instant results in some cases like life points, or a duration of one melee round (15 seconds) for powers and special abilities. Three such video game powers, +1 per level of experience, can be activated every hour.

Demon Death Strike: With the press of a button the Nightbane's hands and any weapon he is holding glow red. His next one attack, be it from a punch, kick, melee weapon, ranged weapon/gun, Talent or spell, inflicts double damage to demons and any creature from the Nightlands, including Night Princes, Nightlords, vampires and fellow Nightbane. Applies only to one attack. Roll to strike as usual. A successful parry means the creature suffers normal damage from the Demon Death Strike, not double. A successful dodge means it avoids the attack and takes no damage whatsoever.

Float: With two quick presses of a specific button, the Nightbane can leap from any height and safely float down to the ground or a rooftop below. Can also be used to float on water or run across water.

Force Field: For one melee round the Nightbane is protected by a force field that has 60 S.D.C. +10 S.D.C. per each additional level of his experience.

Life Points: With the press of a button the Nightbane glows and instantly restores 3D6+18 Hit Points or S.D.C. to himself.

Heal Other: With the press of a different button the Nightbane can instantly restore 3D6+18 Hit Points or S.D.C. to any one person he touches.

Hyper-Combat: Hit the right button sequence and for one melee round the Nightbane has two extra melee attacks, is 20% faster, and +1 to strike, parry, dodge, and disarm.

Impervious to Fire: For one melee round the Nightbane is impervious to fire and smoke, including magic fire. Can be used to run through fire or run across burning embers or lava.

Impervious to Magic: For one melee round the Nightbane is impervious to all types of magic.

Jump: The Nightbane can jump around and over opponents. For one melee round he can leap up to 20 feet (6.1 m) high or 50 feet (15.2 m) lengthwise and is +3 to dodge.

See the Invisible: For one melee round the Nightbane is able to see the invisible; line of sight.

Special Attack: Energy Bolt: For one melee round the Nightbane can fire energy bolts from his hands; treat like a Talent. Each blast does 4D6 damage +2 per each level of the Nightbane's experience and has a range of 600 feet (183 m) +100 feet (30.5 m) per level of experience.

Special Attack: Returning Melee Weapon: For one melee round, any melee weapon the Nightbane throws does an extra 1D6 damage, has a range of 120 feet (36.6 m), and it returns right back to him so he can throw it again. This includes impromptu weapons like a frying pan, peice of pipe, a bottle or a brick.

Bonuses: +1 to I.Q., +2 to save vs insanity (but is already a little detached from reality as a coping mechanism). Penalties: -2 to the M.A. attribute, -2D6 from permanent base P.P.E., and the character tends to equate the real world with video game equivalents and analogies. Worst of all, if the Nightbane's controller/joystick is lost or destroyed, he feels powerless, loses 2D4 S.D.C. (or Hit Points if S.D.C. are gone) and is -1 attack per melee round, and -10% on the performance of all skills. To make the controller reappear, he must change back into his Facade and wait one hour before resuming his Morphus. Note: The controller has 10 S.D.C. and can only be hit if the enemy is specifically targeting it with a Called Shot.

36-44% Dice Bag: A large bag filled with multifaceted dice hangs from the Nightbane's wrist, belt, or other convenient point. The bag may be made of a number of materials from cloth to chain-mail links. Whatever the case, it is actually large and heavy enough to be used as a bludgeoning weapon in hand to hand combat, and does 1D6 damage plus Supernatural P.S. punch damage. The dice can also be removed from the bag and scattered on hard ground or floors to discourage pursuit. **Bonuses:** +1 to I.Q. and +1 to strike and parry using the dice bag as a weapon. **Penalties:** -1 to dodge and -1 to pull punch.

45-55% Display Case: One or more panes of glass are incorporated into this character's Morphus form. Underneath each one is any variety of collectible objects from toy cars to butterflies. These built-in display cases may be opened by the Nightbane and even used to carry other small objects, though they are easily seen (-30% to the Concealment skill). **Bonuses:** +1 to the P.E. attribute and +20% to the Barter skill when buying or trading for the collection. **Penalties:** -20% to Acrobatics, Camouflage, Disguise, Gymnastics, Prowl, Swimming and Undercover Ops skills.

56-66% Leather-Bound: The skin of the Nightbane is actually made of well-worn leather like that of an old book. Small belts and buckles may be incorporated as well, though things like spikes, studs, and zippers are rare. Nightbane with this feature are often avid readers/book collectors or do leatherwork as a hobby. **Bonuses:** +2 to the I.Q. or P.P. attribute, +4D6+6 to S.D.C., a Natural A.R. of 8 and +1 to Awe/Horror Factor. **Penalties:** -2 to Perception Rolls involving the sense of touch. The Nightbane also takes 50% more damage from fire-based attacks, and -10% to Acrobatics, Camouflage, Climb, Disguise, Gymnastics, Prowl, Swimming and Undercover Ops skills.

67-77% Saddle: The character is an equestrian or enjoys horseback riding or caring for the animal. In Morphus, the character may have a cowboy esthetic to his appearance and has a riding saddle either draped over one shoulder or worn on his own back, fastened to him with straps of rawhide or belts. The Nightbane's body may resemble etched leather or be covered in burns from branding irons of various designs, or he may have a long, horse-like face or mane of hair. The saddle may be made of any number of materials with a wide variety of possible appearances, but leather is most common. Any Nightbane capable of running

SIEMBIEDA 2017

on all fours can let other people ride in the saddle. **Bonuses:** +2 to the P.S. and P.E. attributes, +3D6 to S.D.C., and +10% to any Horsemanship skill. Special: Anyone riding in the saddle receives +1 to initiative, +2 to damage with melee weapon, and +1 to dodge regardless of training or experience in mounted combat. **Penalties:** -1 to M.E. attribute, -3 to roll with punch, fall, or impact, .

78-88% Telescopic or Binocular Eyes: Whether it's the result of a love of astronomy, bird-watching, or a similar hobby, the Nightbane's Morphus has a set of magnifying lenses that replace one or more of his eyes. The apparatus may be inset into the skull or protrude up to 2 feet (0.6 m) from the character's face. These optics allow the Nightbane to see objects up to 2 miles (3.2 km) away as if standing within a few feet. Characters with nightvision can see as if they have a passive nightvision scope. **Bonuses:** +2 to strike with long-range weapons like rifles or bow and arrow, +1 to Horror Factor. **Penalties:** -1 to strike, parry, and dodge in melee combat, and -15% to any skill that requires seeing fine detail up close like reading, surgery, Computer Operation, Pick Locks, etc.

89-00% Other: Roll on another random table and relate the result to the character's hobbies. The most obvious choices include Artisan, Athlete, Biomechanical, Insectoid, or Plant Life tables (see Appendix). Otherwise, re-roll on the Hobbyist table and ignore this result.

Mythical Creature

It seems that every culture the world over, has its stories about weird and wicked beings that should not exist. Modern man largely scoffed at these tales for the past couple of centuries. The minority who believe in the existence of beings like Bigfoot or Nessie are shunned as fools, the superstitious, hucksters, lunatics, or at least incredibly gullible. But since Dark Day, the world has become a place where monsters and demons are said to walk the Earth. Indeed, vampires stalk the alleys and monstrous beings from the Nightlands and other dimensions hide in human guise. Who is to say that some of the ancient stories don't have at least a grain of truth to them? How many accounts in the past resulted from Nightbane being spotted by early man? How many Nightbane end up resembling these mythical creatures because of the legends? Honestly, you might as well debate the age old chicken and egg issue. The fact is, a small number of Morphus forms uncannily match either the old stories, myths and legends, or modern reimaginings of them.

Roll percentile dice once for random determination, or pick one.

01-10% Bigfoot/Wendigo/Yeti: This Nightbane is likely be a nature lover or environmentalist, or just someone fascinated by the legends and stories about Bigfoot. The Sasquatch-type Morphus is a tall humanoid with thick, shaggy fur covering most of the body. The facial features are reminiscent to primates such as chimpanzees, as are the long, powerful limbs. The legs and feet, however, are better suited for walking and running than climbing through trees, and shaped more like a modern human's. Bigfoot Nightbane are 7-8 feet (2.1 to 2.4 m) tall and weigh 300-350 pounds (136.5 to 157.5 kg). **Bonuses:** +1D6 to the P.S. and P.E. attributes, +2D6 to Spd, +1D4x10 S.D.C., Nightvision is extended to 1,000 feet (305 m), +2 on Perception Rolls especially regarding ambushes, hiding and tracking in the wilderness, +20% to the Prowl, Camouflage and Climbing skills in wooded environments, and +10% to all Wilderness skills. Automatically starts with the *Leave No Trace Talent.* **Penalties:** -1 to I.Q. and M.A. and -2 to P.B. attributes; custom clothing is necessary to clothe these forest giants, and these Nightbane can be somewhat shy and slow to trust others. They also tend to eschew high-tech "gadgets" like cell phones and computers. -30% to Disguise, Impersonate and Undercover Ops skills in this Morphus.

11-20% Djinn: With origins in Near-Eastern mythology, the Djinn have been described as a curious combination of the substantial and insubstantial and said to be comprised of fire, smoke, or mist, and are seldom visible to humans. This Nightbane's Morphus is visible and solid, though it is surrounded by a veil of swirling mist, smoke or heat vapors that partially obscure the body from the chest down, so at a quick glance, the character appears to be fading in and out or looks insubstantial. The rough outline of the Nightbane's body can be discerned through this obscuring haze as it is darker than the surroundings, and the upper body and head are usually clearly visible, unless the Nightbane wants his face blurred out. The only details that truly stand out, however, are eyes that glow like hot coals and which brighten or dim with the character's mood. **Bonuses:** +1D4 to P.S., +2 to P.P., and +4D4 to Spd, has a Natural A.R. of 10, +1 on initiative and +10% to Prowl and Tailing skills. **Penalties:** -2 to M.A., P.E. and P.B. attributes, -10% to Prowl, and -30% to Disguise, Impersonate and Undercover Ops skills.

21-30% Dragon/Wyvern/Serpent: Many cultures believe in dragons and magical serpents, with stories passed down through the ages. Cultures as diverse as the Maya, Aztec and Native Americans to Europe, the Norse, to Japan, China and Australia, have stories of dragons, wyverns, winged serpents, and similar creatures. Dragons have since become the very essence of mythology while being popularized in art, fantasy literature, and many other mediums. Those Nightbane in awe of the power and majesty of fabled dragons may manifest a Morphus that is effectively a miniaturized version of them at 9-12 feet (2.7-3.7 m) in length from snout to tip of the tail. Wingspan usually matches or exceeds body length by an extra 1D4+2 feet (0.9 to 1.8 m). This form weighs anywhere from 500-800 lbs (225 to 360 kg) and can fly! The exact style and look of said dragon may vary based on the cultural or pop culture influences of the individual.

The Morphus usually has two to six wings, a serpentine tail, and a long, flexible neck. The body rests on all fours, though two limbs may be arms with fully articulated humanoid hands. The

digits all end in sharp talons and the long muzzle opens to reveal a wide mouth filled with crocodile-like teeth. The hide is tough and scaly, with many dragon Nightbane possessing bony plates or horns protecting key points such as the head and neck. Cosmetic details like color, shape of any crest or horns, etc., are left to the player and/or G.M. to determine. Some are more humanoid in shape and appearance, others are classic four-legged, winged dragons in miniature. **Bonuses:** +1D6x10+20 to base P.P.E. and +1 to Spell Strength if a spell caster, +1D6+6 to P.S., +1D6 to P.E., +2 Awe/Horror Factor, +3D6+4 to Hit Points, +1D6x10 S.D.C., Natural A.R. 14, bite attacks do 3D6 damage (double to Nightlords and the denizens of the Nightlands). The character does not get a breath weapon, but can select the *Fire Breather Talent* (**Nightbane® Survival Guide**, page 102) at half the normal cost and double the normal damage to Nightlords and the denizens of the Nightlands. **The wings** provide a flying speed of 1D4x10+88 (70-90 mph/112 to 144 kph), and have 1D6x10+60 S.D.C. each, regenerate at the same rate as the Nightbane, but will completely grow back in one day if destroyed. **Penalties:** -2 to dodge when not airborne. In Morphus form the character is too large to fit in ordinary vehicles and may have trouble negotiating hallways and staircases inside buildings. While in the dragon Morphus the Nightbane is -10% on the performance of all skills, -30% to Prowl and Swimming, while Acrobatics, Disguise, Gymnastics, Impersonation, and Undercover Ops are impossible. All magic and enchanted weapons, including Dark Blades, ignore the character's Natural A.R. and inflict full damage. Dragon slaying weapons do double damage.

31-40% Gorgon: This Morphus appears to be an interpretation of the fabled serpent-women of Greek mythology, the most well-known being Medusa. However, the Aztec, Indian and other cultures also have similar myths about serpentine gods, beings and monsters with multiple snake heads or who appeared to be part human, part snake, or could command snakes or change from serpent to human. This Morphus could represent any of them. The Nightbane's skin is covered in fine scales in shades of green, greyish blue, or bronze, some with red or black patterns, the eyes golden or green, the tongue forked like a snake's nestled inside a mouth filled with pointed teeth and a pair a fangs, and each finger ends in yellowed claws. Of course, the most bizarre and frightening aspect of the Gorgon visage is hair replaced by a coil of 2D6+10 writhing snakes, each three feet (0.9 m) long and able of attack and bite anyone who engages the Nightbane in melee combat or comes too close for comfort. All of this makes the Gorgon Nightbane as deadly as vipers and they are capable, often ruthless, warriors. **Bonuses:** +2 to the P.S. and P.P. attributes, +6D6 S.D.C., Natural A.R. 10, +2 to Horror Factor, claws damage equal to Supernatural P.S. punch damage +3 for claw attacks, the Gorgon's bite does 2D6 damage and has the same venom as the snakes (see Snake Attack, below), 2D6+10 snakes are attached to the Nightbane's head in place of hair. Each snake has 2D6+12 S.D.C. and will grow back in a single day if destroyed

(requires a Called Shot to hit per each snake). Attacks from behind are detected by the snakes and conveyed to the Nightbane, so surprise attacks are nearly impossible when the crown of serpents is not covered by a hood, hat or veil, and they also add +3 to initiative and +2 to parry and dodge. **Note:** Automatically starts with the *Gorgon's Touch Elite Talent* (see **Nightbane® Survival Guide**, page 104, or the Talents Appendix in this book) or select one extra Talent. **Penalties:** -1 to I.Q., -2 to M.E., -2 to M.A., and -1D4 to the P.B. attribute. Gorgon Nightbane tend to be a bit vain and jealous of anyone more attractive than themselves, which can cause strife with Barbie and Ken Morphuses, Guardians, etc. Disguise, Impersonation, and Undercover Ops are impossible in this Morphus.

Snake Attack (special): 1D4+1 snakes strike at the same target at a time, each doing 1D4 damage per bite. This ultimately provides the Nightbane an *extra five attacks per melee round*, but only against those who come within striking distance (3 feet/0.9 m). Each snake bite injects a poison that temporarily makes its victim turn ashen colored and makes muscles tighten and stiffen, which is where the myth of turning people to stone may have originated. (Or is it the other way around?) Victims must roll to

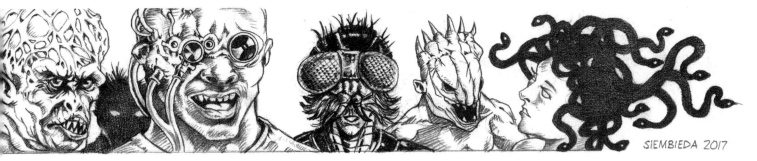

SIEMBIEDA 2017

save vs nonlethal poison (16 or greater). A successful save vs nonlethal poison means half damage and none of the penalties described below.

A failed save reduces the victim's Spd and attacks per melee round by half! Combat bonuses and the performance of skills are also reduced by half as the cramping and tight muscles make it an effort to move. Duration of the venom is two melee rounds for each failed snake bite. **Note:** Double damage and double the duration of penalties to Night Princes, Nightlords, Hounds, Hound Masters, Hunters, and other denizens of the Nightlands.

41-50% Griffin: This Morphus gives the Nightbane the head of a hawk or eagle, hands that more resemble the talons of an eagle, the mane, fur and tail of an African lion, and the wings of an eagle. The wings, chest, and forelegs are plumed while the body and hindquarters have short, tan fur. The player can decide whether the Morphus retains its humanoid body (common) or whether he becomes a four-legged creature (rare); in either case, he can speak. The Griffin Morphus is a foot (0.3 m) taller than the Nightbane's Facade, weighs 300 pounds (135 kg),and the most common colors are white and dark brown feathers and tan fur, though the colors for each are left to the player or G.M.'s imagination. **Note:** Many different cultures, from Egyptians to Russians to Asians and Native Americans, have myths about powerful and heroic avian spirits, gods and monsters, be it the winged jinn or genie, to the Anzu of Mesopotamia, and many others. This manifestation could represent any of them.

Griffins are present in several Eurasian mythologies, in which they are often said to be guardians of priceless treasure or divine figures, so Nightbane with this Morphus may be particularly protective or vigilant. They certainly make devastating foes when their powerful limbs, razor-sharp beak, slashing talons, and flight capabilities are considered. **Bonuses:** +1D4 to the P.S. attribute, +2 to P.P., +4D6 to running speed (flying speed is 1D4x10+70), +1D4x10+20 S.D.C., +20% to Prowl skill (in the air or on the ground), and +2 to Horror Factor. The wings have 1D4x10+40 S.D.C. each and regenerate at the same rate as the Nightbane. If a wing(s) is destroyed, it will grow back in one day. Nightvision is extended to 1,500 feet (457.2 m), the Nightbane has exceptional distance vision (can see a rabbit or read a sign two miles/3.2 km away), 180 degree peripheral vision, can turn his head 180 degrees, is +3 to all Perception Rolls involving sight, +1 on initiative and +2 to dodge in flight. The character can leap 20 feet (6.1 m) high or across from a standing position and 40 feet (12.2 m) with a running start without actually taking flight. Damage from the talons is +2D4 in addition to Supernatural P.S. punch damage, a beak bite or slash does +1D6 damage in addition to Supernatural P.S. punch damage. Diving/swooping attacks inflict double damage but count as two attacks. Talon and beak attacks do double damage to Nightlords and the denizens of the Nightlands. **Penalties:** In Morphus form the taloned hands/forelegs make it very difficult to use tools or weapons (-3 to strike, parry or disarm) and -20% on the performance of all skills, and Griffins

are completely unable to swim whether the Morphus is humanoid or animal shaped. Griffin Nightbane are often loyal to a fault, but can be overprotective and imperious at times. Disguise, Impersonation, Swimming and similar skills are impossible in this Morphus.

51-60% Sphinx: Similar to the Griffin, the mythological Sphinx has the body of a lion with a humanoid head and pair of feathered wings. The Sphinx Nightbane may have a humanoid form and stand erect, but his body resembles that of an African lion walking on its hind legs, or the Morphus could look just like the mythic creature and walk on all fours in the body of a lion. In either case, the head is that of a human, but it looks different than the face of the Facade, so the Morphus conceals the character's human Facade identity. Height (or length if animal form) is nine feet (2.7 m), with a majestic wingspan of 16-20 feet (4.9 to 6.1 m). In mythology, the Sphinx is a guardian of knowledge and the divine, capable of warding off evil and is associated with wisdom, knowledge, and lore-keepers. Normal speaking capabilities. **Bonuses:** +1D4 to I.Q., +2 to the M.E. and M.A. attributes, +1D6 to P.S., +1D4x10 to running speed (flying speed is 1D6x10+70), +2D6 Hit Points, +1D4x10 S.D.C., and +2 to Horror Factor. The wings have 1D6x10+40 S.D.C. each and regenerate at the same rate as the Nightbane, but will grow back in one day if destroyed. +1D4x10 to base P.P.E. and +1 to Spell Strength if a magic user. The Sphinx can leap 30 feet (9.1 m) high or across from a standing position and 60 feet (18.3 m) with a running start without actually taking flight. +2D6 damage from claw attacks in addition to Supernatural P.S. punch damage; double damage to Nightlords and all denizen of the Nightlands. Diving/swooping attacks inflict double damage but count as two melee attacks. **Penalties:** In Morphus form, the Nightbane is completely unable to use tools or weapons and is too large to fit inside most automobiles, needs a mini-van with back seats down, a van, pickup truck and similar or larger vehicles. Hates confined spaces. Skills that require hands are impossible to perform, Disguise and Undercover Ops are impossible, and the Sphinx Nightbane is -30% to Swimming. They also tend to have a penchant for acquiring and hoarding knowledge and secrets that can get them into trouble, and only trust those closest to them.

61-70% Unicorn: The body of this Nightbane Morphus a beautiful, sleek, light horse like an Arabian or Appaloosa (15 hands tall) with a single, conical horn in the middle of the horse's forehead measuring 1-2 feet (0.3 to 0.6 m) long. The horn itself appears to be made of ivory, pure white marble or a white crystal. The coloring of the fur and mane, hooves, etc., is left to the player to decide, but the hair/mane is always in contrast to the color of the body fur; which according to most myths is white or a light golden color (both a rarity in nature). It is also possible for the "unicorn" to have a centaur-like, with the body and legs of a horse and the upper body of an incredibly attractive human (+10 to P.B. attribute, male or female) with long, silky hair down to the waist, and the classic Unicorn's horn protruding from his or her

forehead. **Bonuses:** +2D6 to Hit Points, +1D6x10+20 to S.D.C., +4D6 to base P.P.E., +1D6 to the M.A. attribute, +1D6 to P.S., +1 to P.P. and P.E., +10 to P.B. attribute, and +2 to Awe/Horror Factor. +1D6x10+50 to running Spd, and the Nightbane can leap 10 feet (3 m) high and 20 feet (6.1 m) lengthwise with a running start, +10% to Swimming skill, and gains the *Auto-Dodge ability* (use only the bonuses from the R.C.C. and high P.P. attribute). Damage: +1D6 damage to kick attacks with front legs, 2D6 damage with back legs, both in addition to equivalent of Supernatural P.S. punch damage, and +3D6 damage from a stabbing/impaling horn strike or 2D6 damage with a slashing horn attack — *triple horn damage* against Nightlords, Night Princes, all denizens of the Nightlands, vampires, demons and all creatures of darkness. **Penalties:** In Morphus form the Nightbane is completely unable to use tools or weapons (unless a Unicorn Centaur) and is too large to fit inside most conventional vehicles, not even mini-vans and pickup trucks, and needs a larger vehicle or horse trailer. Moreover, the Unicorn hates confined spaces and does not like to let people ride on its back, with the exception of children and those who are gentle and innocent. Skills that require hands are impossible to perform, Disguise and Undercover Ops are also impossible. The Unicorn Nightbane is likely to be the first target of Nightlords and their minions, as well as many demons and other beings of supernatural evil that hate beauty and seek to destroy it. Many Unicorn Nightbane are idealistic dreamers which can lead to a certain level of naivety, and risk-taking, especially when it comes to helping or defending the innocent and heroic underdogs.

71-80% Fairy: This Nightbane is lithe and attractive and adorned with semi-transparent gossamer wings that resemble a dragonfly or colorful butterfly wings like those of mythical faeries. Whatever the character's Facade, he or she is beautiful, with long, delicate fingers and limbs, and a gracefulness about them. The character is 4-6 feet tall (1.2 to 1.8 m; player's choice) with a corresponding weight for a thin, agile human. The wings are iridescent or butterfly-like and provide hovering and modest flying capabilities. **Bonuses:** +1D6 to M.A., +8 to P.B., and +1D6 to running speed (flying speed is 1D4x10+20), hovering 1D4 feet (0.3 to 1.2 m) above the ground is normal for this Nightbane, +3D6 to P.P.E., +1D6 to Hit Points, +5D6 to S.D.C., +2 to all Perception Rolls, +2 to dodge, Nightvision is extended to 1,000 feet (305 m), exceptional vision (can see a rabbit or read a sign a mile/1.6 km away), +1 to Awe/Horror Factor, +10% to Acrobatics, Dance, Gymnastics, Sing, Prowl and any Wilderness skills. **Penalties:** -10% to Espionage and Rogue skills and any skills related to combat or destruction. Skills like Disguise, Impersonation, Undercover Ops and Swimming are impossible to use in Morphus form. Cannot fit inside most vehicles, because the wings are too large. **Note:** Characters with this Morphus are playful and often either quite young and innocent or naive and in denial about the Nightlords and their Minions, and the horrors in the world. They hate ugliness, cruelty, bullies and wickedness.

81-90% Cyclops/Giant: This Nightbane Morphus is that of a hulking, brutish man-monster (or giant Amazon-like woman), 10-12 feet (3 to 3.7 m) tall, muscular, barrel-chested, and with one large eye in the center of his forehead. This may not be the character's only eye, it's just that the other two are small and squinty, so they look more like folds on the face rather than eyes. Whether a single cyclopean eye or a large "third eye," the special eye provides the abilities to see the invisible and to see in darkness. (In the alternative, the eye can be in the back of the Nightbane's head. It has the same sight capabilities and bonuses, but also prevents the character from being surprised from attacks from behind.) **Bonuses:** +6 to P.S. and +2 P.E., +2D6 Hit Points and +1D6x10+20 S.D.C., Natural A.R. 10, +1D6 damage from punches and kicks in addition to Supernatural P.S. punch damage due to his strength, size and weight (700 pounds/315 kg), +3 to all Perception Rolls, Nightvision is extended to 1,000 feet (305 m), exceptional vision (can see a rabbit or read a sign a mile/1.6 km away), see the invisible, +2 to Horror Factor. **Penalties:** Using conventional modern weapons/guns and devices like cell phones and keyboards are difficult to impossible to use due to the large size of the Cyclop's hands. -2 to dodge, -25% to all skills that require a delicate touch and human-sized fingers/hands, -30% to Prowl, Acrobatics and Gymnastics, and skills like Disguise, Impersonation, Tailing and Undercover Ops are impossible to use in Morphus form. Clothing must be custom made and the large size makes fitting inside most vehicles difficult and uncomfortable to impossible. Hates confined spaces. **Note:** The Cyclops is likely to be seen as a brutish warrior or monster, but the reality is that the character may be gentle and kind, or timid and shy. The choice of a giant, bestial Morphus may be the result of his insecurity or fears, or a desire to be taken seriously or to be big and strong so as to not to be picked on by bullies.

91-00% Other: The most obvious alternatives are animal type creatures like the Minotaur, but those are generally well covered by the various *Animal Morphus Tables* (see the **Nightbane® RPG** or the Appendix in this sourcebook). With a bit of work, many animal Morphus features can be turned into mythical creatures. For example, add a stinging scorpion tail from the Arachnid Table to a Full Feline Form Morphus feature, change the color of the fur to red, and make the face more human in appearance and you have the mythological Manticore. G.M.s and players should work together to create any new features and game balance should be kept in mind, but unleash that imagination and have fun!

Nightmare Table

While Nightbane with Stigmata features are often considered the most gruesome and ghastly of the lot, a number of Morphus forms seem like something conjured from the darkest depths of the Dreamstream (see **Nightbane Sourcebook 1: Between the Shadows** for more details on this mysterious plane). Often times

such Nightbane have suffered years of vivid nightmares or night terrors. Lashing out at unseen foes and awakening to the sounds of their own blood-curdling screams in weekly, if not nightly, occurrences.

For some of these nightmare haunted souls, such unearthly horror becomes manifested in their Morphus form upon their Becoming. Some find this a remedy for their nightmares as they become that which they feared the most. Still others find themselves terrified of their new body as it is their torment given physical form. Another option is for Nightbane with Nightmare features to be incredibly emotionally and mentally disturbed. If the latter, roll for two random insanities from the tables starting on page 44 of the **Nightbane® RPG**.

Note: Nightbane with one or more features from this table can select either of the elite Talents, Bloodbath or Mark of the Nightbane as though they had a Stigmata feature.

Roll percentile dice once for random determination, or pick one.

01-10% Floating: Nightmares of falling are an almost universal human experience. As a response to this nightmare, the Nightbane floats in midair. The character is limited to a floating height of 1-3 feet (0.3 to 0.9 m) off the ground. He cannot fly but rather hovers and floats about. Maximum Spd is equal to his Spd attribute. Unlike his dreams, the Nightbane cannot fall. Dropping/falling from great heights (more than 60 feet/18.3 m) is a terrifying experience that is likely to cause the character to scream, but before hitting bottom, he suddenly begins to slow down and floats at 1-3 feet (0.3 to 0.9 m) above the ground. Impact from being struck by a vehicle or weapon does full damage. The Morphus is that of a person who looks to be in a constant state of fright, his face contorted into a grimace or scream, and his hair and clothing fluttering in the wind whether there is an actual wind or not. Moreover, the Nightbane's complexion is pale from terror, all of which gives him a rather ghostly appearance. **Bonuses:** +10% to any Intimidation rolls, +2 to roll with impact and pull punch, +1 to Horror Factor, and +20% to Prowl. Hovering and floating a few feet above the ground is his natural state of being, no damage from falls, does not leave footprints/tracks, and prevents setting off pressure plates, but he remains vulnerable to motion and heat detection. **Penalties:** -1D4 to M.E. and M.A. attributes, reduce Spd attribute by half (floating is slow), and the character has a Fear of Heights phobia plus two other phobias or random insanities. Player should pick an insanity category and make a random roll. (See **Nightbane® RPG** for Insanity Tables starting on page 44.)

11-20% Contorted Body: The body of this Nightbane is twisted far out of normal shape. The spine might be twisted so that the torso faces the opposite way, hunched over, or doubled backward so that the legs straddle the abdomen, and/or curled forward with the legs wrapping around the head, forcing the character to walk on his or her hands. Likewise, the head may be twisted around or to the side, the mouth may be extraordinarily large, the neck thick or nonexistent, the rib cage may jut out at odd angles, and so on.

Whatever the case may be, the character does not move normally. The Nightbane might waddle, crab-walk, crawl, or even tumble to get around, but he may do so with surprising speed and agility given the anatomical deformities present. This actually gives the Nightbane an advantage against opponents not used to fighting such an oddity. Just watching the character scuttle about is disconcerting for most people. **Bonuses:** +1D4 to the P.S. attribute, +1 to M.E. and P.E. and +1D6x10 to S.D.C. +1 to dodge and +2 to Horror Factor. **Penalties:** -2 to P.P. and -1D4 to the P.B. attribute, -1 to strike, parry and roll with impact, -10% to Physical skills like Prowl and Climbing, -30% to Swimming. Disguise and Undercover Ops are impossible for this Morphus.

21-30% Gnarled Limbs: Arms, legs, and any other limbs of the Morphus are deformed. The arms and legs might be juxtaposed, or elongated or too short, or twisted and deformed, or marred by odd knots, grooves, and holes. Musculature is also abnormal, with more or less muscle than normal in odd configurations. For instance, the arms might have two bicep muscles, an open gap between the bones of the forearm, large ridges of bone protruding from the shoulders, and so on. **Bonuses:** +1D4 to the P.S. attribute and +1 to P.E., and +1 point to Horror Factor. The Nightbane is also double-jointed in all of his limbs and +20% to the Escape Artist, Palming and Concealment skills. **Penalties:** -1D4 to the P.B. and Spd attributes, and -1 to strike and parry. Requires custom made clothing, -30% to skills like Acrobatics, Climbing, Gymnastics and Prowl, while Disguise, Impersonation, and Undercover Ops are impossible in this Morphus.

31-40% Spines: The Nightbane has 1D4+2 articulated spines protruding from the sides of his upper torso in addition to his arms and legs, which may be normal or slightly deformed. While not able to grasp tools or weapons, these appendages are made of bone or metal and end in very sharp points. This makes the spines suitable as close-quarters weapons useful for parrying, stabbing, raking, or bludgeoning opponents. They have a reach equal to that of the Nightbane's arms (roughly 3 feet/0.9 m on average). **Bonuses:** +1 attack per melee round, +2 to parry, +10% to the Climbing skill, +2 to Horror Factor. A slashing attack with a spine deals 1D6 damage in addition to Supernatural P.S. punch damage, while a stab deals 2D6 in addition to supernatural P.S. punch damage. The character can attack with one or two spines in a single melee attack (roll a single strike even if using two spines). Each spine has 1D4x10+20 S.D.C. and will completely regrow in an hour if destroyed. **Penalties:** -2 to the P.S. attribute, -1 to P.P., and -1 to P.B., requires custom clothing, and is -40% to Disguise, Impersonation and Undercover Ops in this Morphus (spines must be taped or otherwise strapped down).

41-50% Pulsating Skin: The skin of the Morphus is an unnatural color, or pale and mottled with dark patches of blue and purplish spider-webbed veins or large veins that seem to move like snakes or pulsate. Or the flesh may be lumpy or ordinary looking

but seems to glow and pulsate as if there were lights located under the skin. Whatever the case, the skin moves, ripples, crawls, and/or pulsates as if there is something alive and moving beneath it. This pulsating/squirming sensation is also felt when holding the Nightbane. This movement may be random or timed to a biological rhythm such as his heartbeat or respiration. Some Nightbane even have lumps that move around the body or burrowing creatures or faces that become visible at intervals beneath the flesh of the Morphus. **Bonuses:** +2 to the P.E. attribute, +5D6 to S.D.C., +2 to Horror Factor. Horror Factor must be rolled any time a new opponent wishes to grapple with the Nightbane. Failure to save means the attacker hesitates at the last second and loses that one melee attack and initiative, and he engages the Nightbane with -1 to all combat maneuvers (strike, parry, dodge, etc.), because he is distracted and grossed out by the pulsating flesh. **Penalties:** -1D4 to the M.A. and P.B. attributes, -1 on all Perception Rolls, and -20% to skills like Disguise, Impersonation, Performance, Seduction and Undercover Ops.

51-60% Straight-Jacket: The Nightbane is wrapped in what looks like a straight-jacket. The material this covering is made of may be leather, canvas, or some other resilient fabric. What is consistent is that the long sleeves and body of the jacket are fitted with belts and fasteners that restrict the movement of the arms. The arms may be held pinned at the sides or crossed over the chest or secured behind the character's back. Straight-jackets have long been associated with insanity and violent or self-destructive behavior. A leather or cage-like mask may also be part of the Morphus, obscuring the face and acting as something of a muzzle to prevent biting. **Bonuses:** +2 to the P.P. and P.E. attributes, +1D6 to Spd, +2 to dodge, +3 to roll with punch, fall and impact, +2D4x10 to S.D.C., and +1 to Horror Factor. The Nightbane's kick attacks inflict an extra 1D6 damage in addition to the usual Supernatural P.S. kick damage, and a body block/ramming attack is the same as a power punch (still counts as two attacks to perform). The bound Nightbane is surprisingly nimble and is +20% to skills like Gymnastics and Prowl, and automatically gets the Acrobatics skill with +30% bonus, enabling him to run along rooftops, walls, ledges, and taught ropes and cables with like a skilled tightrope walker and do somersaults and rolls. **Penalties:** -3 to the M.E. attribute, -2 to M.A., and -2 to P.P. The arms are immobilized, so the Nightbane is unable to use tools and weapons and cannot parry attacks, nor perform skills that require the use of hands and arms, like Climbing and Swimming. However, if the character has the Swimming skill, he is able to tread water with the legs to stay afloat.

61-70% Torture Mask: The face and head of the Morphus form is covered by a mask that may look like any number of things, from a leather covering or leather straps, to a grilled cage or metal enclosure with slits for the eyes and mouth, to being made of bone or the skin and face of another person or creature strapped over his own, to a hood or nylon making his face devoid of features, or covered in scars or burns, or melted wax, tar or

metal. What is not different from individual to individual is that the mask is intended as a torture device. From smothering black hoods, to a vice-like clamp caving in the sides of the head, to cages, such masks have been used by interrogators and torturers from ancient to modern times. The Nightbane's face may or may not be visible depending on the design of the mask. It is part of the Morphus form, though, and cannot be removed. However, the Nightbane is somehow able to see, breathe and speak through the mask as if it was not there. **Bonuses:** +1D4 to the M.E. attribute, 2D6 to S.D.C., +2 to save vs possession, +1 to Horror Factor, +1 to save vs psionics, mind control and possession, and interrogators find their Interrogation skill to be -30% when questioning this character. **Penalties:** -1D4 to M.A., -1 to P.E. and -3 to P.B.

71-80% Massive Maw: The mouth of the Nightbane becomes a giant, devouring maw unlike anything from the natural world. The exact look of the head and mouth is up to the player. Common versions include a set of insect-like multi-segmented mandibles, a maw that opens impossibly large, a widely stretching oral cavity filled with unending darkness, or a mouth filled with pointed or razor-sharp teeth that splits the cheeks back to

the hinge of the jaw. Some Nightbane even appear to have a steel bear-trap grafted to the face. Despite any difference in appearance, all function the same way. **Bonuses:** Bite attack does 4D6+5 damage, +2 to strike with a bite attack (only P.P. bonuses can be added to this attack), impervious to poison, spoiled food and disease (can eat raw and rotting meat and foods without getting ill), +1 to Horror Factor. The character can also latch onto an opponent after a successful bite attack with a bite that is like being caught in the jaws of a crocodile or vice. The target of such an attack needs a Supernatural P.S. twice that of the Nightbane to pry free, or some other means of escape such as teleportation. The Nightbane can gnaw through a wood fence, crate, door or other barrier in 1D4+2 melee rounds. **Penalties:** -1D4 to the P.B. attribute. Speech is also much more difficult, imposing a -20% on all *Language* skills. Strangely enough, this does not seem to hamper spell casting.

81-90% Gruesome Weapon: Either held in the hand or grafted to one or more limbs is a nightmarish weapon. (May have two Gruesome Weapons if they are small, such as a knife or cleaver or tomahawk size, but the +3D6 damage is divided between the two as +1D6+3 for each.) These weapons are most often unconventional and especially frightening. Examples include monstrous and gnarled claws, a bone spike or blade(s) at least the size of a short sword that extends and retracts from the forearm or are mounted onto the forearms, or pulled out (and put back into) his own body, or a handheld sword, scythe, sickle, pitchfork, cleaver, meat hook, nail-studded club, etc. Such weapons are usually rusty, dripping blood or covered in gore or slime, and/or jagged/serrated or made from bone. Whether it is grafted on as part of the Morphus' body or handheld, the Gruesome Weapon is the Nightbane's signature weapon, always with him and never lent to others. It is his. **Bonuses:** Automatically has W.P. Paired Weapons skill; +1 melee attack and +2 to strike, parry and disarm with his Gruesome Weapon ONLY, and +2 to pull punch with the weapon too; +2D6 to S.D.C. +1 to Horror Factor, and damage is equal to the 'Bane's Supernatural P.S. +3D6 damage regardless of the type or size of the weapon. **Penalties:** The Gruesome Weapon is always the Nightbane's first choice, "go-to" weapon. Other weapons can be used but are -2 to strike and parry. **Note:** The weapon itself has 45 S.D.C. +5 S.D.C. per level of the character, but only takes damage if it is targeted via Called Shot. If the S.D.C. of the Gruesome weapon is reduced to zero, it crumbles to dust and does not reappear until all of the character's personal S.D.C. are restored to full capacity. Without this weapon, the Nightbane's other combat bonuses are all reduced by half, and he is -1 attack per melee round.

91-00% Other: Random roll or choose another table and relate the result to the character's fears or nightmares. The most obvious choices include Stigmata, Pestilence, or Animal tables. Otherwise, re-roll on the Nightmare table and ignore this result.

Occupation

Most people, especially kids, grow up with one or more professions they either dream of one day becoming or plan on pursuing. Even after those kids become young adults they still tend to fantasize about that "dream career" even if they've stopped pursuing it. Jobs are a large part of a personal identity for modern men and women, and they are consequently one of the first things discussed when people meet for the first time. For Nightbane with one of the features from the following table, they identify so closely with their chosen or dream occupation that it has shown up as a permanent part of their Morphus form.

Roll percentile dice once for random determination, or pick one.

01-10% A Suit/Consummate Professional: The Nightbane is dressed in business attire. Whether that's khakis and a polo shirt, designer dress/skirt and blouse, or top quality three-piece suit, in the absence of other Morphus features the character would not look out of place on Wall Street, Silicon Valley or any cubicle farm in the business world. The 'Bane also moves with a speed and deliberateness that bespeaks a great degree of self-confidence

and sense of purpose. The character is a power-player and knows it. **Bonuses:** +1 to I.Q. and M.E., +1D4 to the M.A. attribute, +1 to P.B., and +2D6 S.D.C. **Penalties:** No Secondary Skills as the character is focused only on his career, -5% to Prowl and -5% on all skills other than Communications, Math skills and Technical skills.

11-20% Uniform/Official: The character's identity is tied to a specific service profession that is represented by its uniform. Medical professionals, firemen, police, guards, airline pilot, mechanic, and others have a highly visible style of dress that sets them apart from the public, and may be a symbol of authority, and often serves as a point of pride. The Nightbane's Morphus is dressed as one such profession, whether all the details of that uniform are accurate or even made up. **Bonuses:** +1 to the M.E., M.A., and P.B. attributes, +2D6 S.D.C., +5% to Invoke Trust/Intimidate and +2 to Perception Rolls. **Penalties:** -10% to Prowl and -10% on all Physical and Rogue skills. The Nightbane is unlikely to be fully trusted by criminals like the majority of the Warlords faction.

21-30% Hazardous Duty: The Morphus form is decked out in some kind of protective gear from one of a number of jobs. Examples of this include a bullet-proof vest, riot gear, construction (hard hat, heavy gloves and overalls), reflective clothes, Hazmat suit (full environmental), "clean" room gear (jumpsuit, hairnet, surgical gloves, surgical mask or re-breather) or even a heat-resistant "volcano" suit. Despite the wide variety of appearances possible with this feature, all provide the same bonuses. **Bonuses:** +1 to P.E., +2 to save vs disease, gases and toxins, +4D6 S.D.C. and a Natural A.R. of 8. **Penalties:** -1D4 to the P.P. attribute and -1D6 to Spd. -1 to Perception Rolls.

31-40% Communications: Simply put, the character has ear plugs or headphones or some similar device for his ears and some audio communication device such as a walkie-talkie, cell phone, electronic notepad or old-style telephone or CB radio type device built somewhere into his body and another in his pocket or in a case on his belt. This grants the Nightbane the ability to communicate with any type of wireless communications device and radios over a number of different types of networks and systems. A walkie-talkie or CB radio can be used as a short-wave, cellular, or even satellite communication device. However, the character still needs to know that the network is there and how to communicate with it (i.e. the recipient's phone number or radio frequency). This also means he has access to popular communication network systems such as the Internet, GPS, and so on. **Bonuses:** +10% to all Communications skills and the Nightbane's own communications and devices are untraceable by modern methods. And did we mention there are no roaming charges? **Penalties:** -2D4 from the character's base P.P.E. and -1D4 to Perception Rolls. This character can be detected by Hounds and other beings sensitive to the supernatural at a 50% greater range.

41-50% Tools of the Trade: The Nightbane has a handful of items when the Morphus form is assumed. These 1D4+3 items are devices or tools of critical importance to the character's chosen profession. For example, a mechanic might have a large wrench, socket set, pair of screwdrivers, pliers, a hammer and a voltmeter. A police officer or detective is likely to have a pair of handcuffs, a heavy flashlight, pepper spray, billy club/baton, a badge and a side arm. However, some of these tools may be grafted to the Nightbane's body or replace fingers and hands.

Any Tools of the Trade function and behave the same as normal, but only have 3D6 S.D.C. each and disappear for 24 hours when lost or destroyed. Those tools or devices that require batteries never run low, and ammunition or similar supplies start fully loaded and (magically?) reload/recharge every hour with a full payload. Given the wide variety of possible items, it is suggested that players and G.M.s work together to choose what Tools of the Trade are allowed. **Bonuses:** +1 to I.Q. attribute, +2D6 to S.D.C., +5% to all O.C.C. Skills that relate to the tools and the trade, like mechanical or electrical repair, maintenance, etc. Some tools may be suitable as weapons, but the vast majority only deal 1D4 to 1D6 damage. **Penalties:** -2 to the Spd attribute and -1D6 from the base P.P.E.

51-60% Time Clock or Timepiece: Built into the chest of the Morphus is a boxy device used by many employers to track the attendance of hourly workers. This might be an older "punch" device or a newer electronic scanner. Either type accurately displays the current time to the second. **Bonuses:** +2 to P.E. and Spd attributes, +2D4 S.D.C., and the character is able to accurately sense the exact time and the passage of time while in Morphus form, provides a +5% bonus to skills related to time and timing such as Demolitions, Dance, Mathematical calculations, Performance, etc., including time anomalies. **Penalties:** -2 to the M.A. and Spd attributes, -1 to Perception Rolls, -1D4 from base P.P.E., and the character is always on time, though a bit anxiety prone and overly concerned with punctuality.

61-70% Water Cooler: The Nightbane has a large, multi-gallon, plastic or glass tank incorporated into his body, usually mounted on the back. This tank is translucent, revealing water, coffee, or another drink as its contents. It is connected to a small spigot that can be used to indefinitely dispense the potable drink. In addition, the Nightbane seems to have an affable, easy-going air in casual situations and is often given to lengthy discussions or gossip. **Bonuses:** +1D4+2 to the M.A. attribute and +1 to P.E., the character does not require any hydration while in Morphus form and is never thirsty; moreover, he can unleash a blast of water (does 2D6 damage to vampires) from his hands; each blast counts as one attack, endless payload. The release of water is always in a sudden burst and cannot be neatly placed in a glass or container. The tank has 40 S.D.C. **Penalties:** -2 to P.P. and -1D4 to Spd attributes, -1 to dodge, -2 to roll with punch, fall or impact, -20% to skills like Acrobatics, Climbing, Gymnastics, Prowl and Swimming due to the weight and the sloshing from the water inside the tank (always two-thirds full and weighs 25 pounds (11 kg).

71-77% Mechanic/Mechanical: The Nightbane's profession involves making and/or repairing machines, whether it is clocks or toasters to air conditioners and automobiles/vehicle engines. This 'Bane is good with his hands and likes to build or take things apart. His Morphus has gears, springs, pulleys, nuts and bolts either built right into his body or as a sort of weird piecemeal armor bolted to parts of his body. **Bonuses:** +2 to Perception Rolls pertaining to mechanics, finding a mechanical problem and fixing it, +2 to P.S. and P.P. attributes, +1D6x10+20 S.D.C., a Natural A.R. of 10, and +10% bonus to skills related to mechanics and mechanical repair. **Penalties:** -2 on all Perception Rolls when caught up in examining or working on machines, -1 to P.B., -1D4 to the Spd attribute, and the character tends to enjoy working on machines than hanging out with people.

78-85% Electrician/Electronic Devices: The Nightbane's profession involves making and/or repairing cell phones, computers, and electronic devices, or he is an electrician who re-wires entire houses and electrical systems. This 'Bane is good with his hands and likes to build or take part electrical devices. His Morphus has wires, microchips and circuit boards built right into his body or as a sort of weird piecemeal armor attached to or coming out of his body. Eyes are probably dim LED lights. **Bonuses:** +2 to Perception Rolls pertaining to electronics and circuitry, finding electrical problems and fixing them, +2 to P.P. attribute, +4D6+6 S.D.C., a Natural A.R. of 9, electrical attacks and lightning do half damage, and +5% bonus to skills related to electronics and electrical repair and computers. **Penalties:** -3 on all Perception Rolls when caught up in examining or working on electronics or electrical devices, -1 to P.E., -1D4 to the Spd attribute, and the character tends to lose himself in electronic devices, losing track of time and the things going on around him.

86-92% Workaholic: The character's Morphus form has a haggard, disheveled look with bloodshot eyes and dark circles and bags underneath/around the eyes, a pale complexion, messy hair, and wrinkled or sweat-stained clothes, all of which speak to a long period of hard work without sleep. Males may also have a five o'clock shadow while all genders may also carry a tea or coffee mug or can of soda with them – or as the Morphus, have a device built into their body with tubes that pump caffeine into their bodies. **Bonuses:** +2 to the M.E. and P.E. attributes. The Nightbane needs only half the amount of sleep as a normal person. **Penalties:** -2 to P.B. and Spd attributes, -2 on all Perception Rolls while skills that require focus and brain power (like all Science and most Technical skills, Piloting, Demolitions and similar) suffer a -5% penalty. Physical skills that get the Nightbane moving as well as quick, easy tasks that take only a few minutes, are done without penalty. 01-50% chance of falling asleep on guard duty or as a lookout.

93-00% Other: Random roll or choose another table and relate the result to the character's actual or fantasy occupation. The most obvious choices include Biomechanical, Artificial Appearance, or Animal tables. Otherwise, re-roll on the Occupation table and ignore this result.

Pestilence & Disease Table

Despite the miracles of modern medicine rendering many maladies treatable, it is hardly an all-curing panacea. Cancers, viruses, bacteria, and fungal infections can indiscriminately maim, cripple, and kill unfortunate victims. It is for good reason, then, that many people worry about their own health and that of loved ones, or fear disease.

Nightbane with one or more Pestilence features may have been sickly in their youth, had a close friend or relative suffer with a serious disease, or even have been fighting such a disease at the time of their Becoming. Or they may just fear disease and sickness or have been a hypochondriac. On the other hand, the Nightbane might have been a doctor, nurse, pathologist or other health care professional who battled disease and looked for cures. Whatever the case, such Nightbane have a tendency to have bodies covered in pus, boils, blisters, open wounds, rashes, scaling, crust, goo, blood, and other creepy and sickly looking disfigurement on their face and bodies.

Roll percentile dice once for random determination, or pick one.

01-10% Typhoid Mary/Patient Zero: The Morphus is constantly sweaty, has sallow skin (a pasty yellow or pale brown color), rheumy eyes (rimmed in red), and raspy, labored breathing. Rattling coughs frequently rack the Nightbane's body, which may appear slightly underweight, and thick mucus dribbles from the nose. Any clothing is usually disheveled and stained with unidentifiable bodily fluids. In short, the character always appears seriously ill, but otherwise functions just fine. **Bonuses:** +2 to the M.E. and P.E. attributes, +2D6 S.D.C. +4 to save vs disease, +1 to save vs possession and insanity and +1 to Horror Factor. **Penalties:** -1 to the M.A., -2 to P.B. and Spd attributes, -10% to skills like Disguise, Impersonation, Seduction and Undercover Ops.

11-20% Ebola/Bleeding: The Morphus has a sickly pallor, hair is wet from sweat and plastered down on the head or head and neck, and blood oozes from the eyes, nose, and ears, with streams of blood that have dripped down the Nightbane's clothing or armor. When the 'Bane speaks, blood bubbles out from the corners of his mouth and makes a gurgling sound that may garble his words from time to time. **Bonuses:** +1 to M.E. attribute, +2D6 S.D.C., +3 to Perception Rolls regarding disease, blood loss and vampires, +1 to save vs possession and mind control, and +2 to Horror Factor. A character with this feature can take the *Bloodbath Elite Talent* (see **Nightbane® RPG**, page 113, or the Talent Appendix in this book) at double the range and duration and use it without taking damage. **Penalties:** -2 to M.A., P.B. and Spd attributes, -20% to skills like Disguise, Impersonation, Performance, Seduction and Undercover Ops. Vampires and other creatures that can sense and track blood by smell are +25% to track this Morphus and know the Nightbane is approaching long before he is seen. Likewise, the constantly oozing blood is likely to leave a blood trail that can be tracked (+15% to Tracking skill); the blood does NOT have the same DNA as the Facade. Some Nightbane with this Morphus develop a taste for blood and may drink the blood of their enemies.

21-25% Anthrax: The Morphus is a human covered in red and white blisters, dark scabs, and scratch marks surrounded by redness and ulcers. The skin glistens from sweat due to fever, so the character feels hot to the touch, burning up with fever. The Nightbane has a persistent cough, wheezes when physically active and has a raspy voice when he or she speaks, like he has a sore throat. **Bonuses:** +1 to P.S. attribute, +3D6 S.D.C., +3 to Perception Rolls to recognize disease, +2 to save vs fever and illusions, and +1 to Horror Factor. **Penalties:** -2 to M.A., P.B. and Spd attributes, -15% to skills like Disguise, Impersonation, Performance, Prowl, Seduction and Undercover Ops, and a penalty of -5% to all other skills.

26-35% Creeping Crud: The Morphus is fairly normal looking, though he or she may be a different gender than the Facade, and the body is covered in some sort of crusty or scabby-looking crud that covers half the face, neck, hands, arms and chest. The crusty material can be black, white, grey, red, yellow, green or just about any color, and actually provides a bit of armor-like protection. In the alternative, the crud can be a slime or goo that resembles snot/mucus that seems to either ooze from the body or from open wounds to coat part of the body. **Bonuses:** +1 to P.S. and M.E. attributes +1D6x10+30 S.D.C., resistant to fire (half damage), and +2 to Horror Factor. **Penalties:** -2 to M.A. and P.B. attributes, -20% to skills like Barter, Disguise, Impersonation, Performance, Seduction and Undercover Ops.

36-45% Pestilence/Bugs/Parasite Infestation: Half the face, neck, hands, arms, chest, back and legs are covered in maggots, worms, mites or other insects that seem to be eating through the Nightbane's skin from the inside out, or he may be partially covered in leeches or lamprey-like things and similar parasitic creatures. The Nightbane doesn't seem to notice but most people will be revolted by this Morphus. The infestation provides a bit of armor-like protection. **Bonuses:** +1 to P.S. attribute, +5D6+20 S.D.C., +2 to save vs disease/infection, is impervious to the venom of insects, and +2 to Horror Factor. **Penalties:** -3 to M.A. and P.B. attributes, -30% to skills like Barter, Disguise, Impersonation, Performance, Seduction and Undercover Ops.

46-55% Life Support/Coma Victim: The Nightbane is dressed in a hospital gown with a number of tubes and wires attached to the body of the Morphus. Some are identifiable as I.V. lines, catheters, heart monitor leads, etc. There is also an oxygen mask or breathing tube that is easily visible, but the opposite ends of these lines are not attached to any machinery, leaving them dangling or floating in midair. To make things even more eerie, the sound of the missing machinery can still be faintly heard when close to the Nightbane (requires a Perception Roll of 12 or better), beeping, whirring, and hissing away. The figure looks gaunt, and somewhat zombie-like with sunken eyes and cheeks, and poor pallor. **Bonuses:** +3D6 to Hit Points, +1D4x10 to S.D.C. +20% to save vs coma and death, +2 to roll vs impact, +1 to save vs disease, +1 to Horror Factor and the Nightbane does not need air to breathe and can swim or remain underwater indefinitely! **Penalties:** -2 to the M.A., P.B. and Spd attributes, -2D6 from base P.P.E., -10% penalty on skills like Acrobatics, Climbing, Gymnastics, and Prowl, and -20% to Disguise, Impersonation, Performance, Seduction and Undercover Ops.

56-65% Madness/Mad Cow/Brain Worm: Much more common in olden days or in countries that hold onto outdated views of mental illness, this feature occurs most often in those afraid that *madness is contagious* or caused by a parasite or disease. In modern, developed nations it may still be seen in those afraid of losing control of themselves due to illnesses such as dementia. This manifests with the Morphus having wide-open, bloodshot eyes, frazzled and unclean hair, a twitch and a generally unkempt appearance. The Nightbane foams at the mouth like a rabid dog when angry or upset, and may mutter or giggle to himself without realizing it. **Bonuses:** +1D4 to the P.S. and P.E. attributes, +1D6 to Spd, +5D6 to S.D.C., +3 to save vs insanity, and +1 to Horror

Factor. **Penalties:** -3 to the M.E. attribute, -1 to M.A. and -5% on the performance of all skills. The character may be a bit absent-minded and forgetful.

66-70% Swelling/Bloating: The Morphus' limbs, abdomen, neck, and face are severely swollen and discolored. The abdomen is so distended that it makes the character appear overweight, and the neck is almost as wide as the head. Such is the circumference of the arms and legs that they almost appear to be missing the joints. All of the swelling takes on a dark purple, brown, or yellow cast and feels squishy to the touch. **Bonuses:** +3D6+12 S.D.C. Reduce all damage from falls, punches, kicks and blunt attacks by half. +1 to save vs disease, +1 to Horror Factor. **Penalties:** -1 to the P.P. and P.B. attributes, -1D4 to Spd, and a -10% penalty on skills like Acrobatics, Climbing, Gymnastics, Disguise, Impersonation, Swimming, Tailing and Undercover Ops.

71-75% Malignant Growths: There are masses that distort the figure of the Morphus form. These may be very large, smooth lumps or clusters of smaller, irregular lumps and tumors. At least one of these masses disfigures the face while the rest are scattered over the rest of the body. These lumps may be dark brown or black melanoma-type masses or appear to be subcutaneous and just alter the shape of the body part. **Bonuses:** +1 to the M.E. attribute, +3D6 S.D.C, and +1 to Natural A.R. **Penalties:** -2 to the P.E. and P.B. attributes and -10% on Physical skills as well as Disguise, Impersonation, and Undercover Ops.

76-85% Oozing Rash: At least half of the Nightbane's body, including parts of the face, is covered with a nasty, red rash. This rash constantly seeps clear pus and/or blood and there may be patches where the skin appears to have sloughed off, revealing raw, pink flesh beneath. Though it looks as if the rash would itch like crazy, it actually does not bother the Nightbane. **Bonuses:** +2 to the M.E. attribute, impervious to infection, and +2 to Horror Factor. If an opponent attempts to grapple with the character, he must first roll to save vs a Horror Factor of 16 regardless of the standard Horror Factor of the Nightbane. If this additional roll is failed, the opponent is disgusted by the ooze, hanging flesh and open sores and cannot bring himself to touch the Nightbane. **Penalties:** -2 to the M.A. and P.B. attributes, -1 to all Perception Rolls, -5% on all skills, -20% penalty on skills like Disguise, Impersonation, Performance, Seduction and Undercover Ops.

86-90% Infected Lesions: The skin of the Morphus is dotted and crisscrossed with suppurating wounds. These are actually deep holes and splits in the skin that look to be infected to the point of being gangrenous. This means that the tissue in the wounds is a sickly yellow or greenish color and smells terrible. The immediate area around each wound is an angry red color with streaks of red following the track of veins. A small number of these lesions are severe enough to bleed continuously, and bone, cartilage, and other connective tissue may be visible at the bottom of the wound. **Bonuses:** +1 to the M.E. attribute, +1 to P.E., +2D6 to Hit Points, +2D6 S.D.C., +2 to save vs disease and poison, and +2 to Horror Factor. **Penalties:** -1 to the M.A. attri-

bute, -2 to P.S. and P.B., and -20% penalty on skills like Disguise, Impersonation, Performance, Seduction and Undercover Ops.

91-00% Buzzing Pests: A small swarm or cloud of flying insects constantly circle or enshroud the Nightbane. Most common are biting pests such as mosquitoes and horseflies that are capable of spreading diseases, but the insects could be flies, gnats, tiny moths, and flying ants or other insects. While they alight on the Nightbane and anything or anyone nearby, strangely they never seem to actually bite. Swatting or otherwise killing any number of them has no effect either, as the bodies disappear and are immediately replaced within the swarm. Opponents trying to engage the Nightbane in hand to hand combat must deal with the insects flying into their eyes, ears, nose, and open mouth, making talking difficult and imposing a -2 penalty on all combat rolls such as initiative, strike, parry, dodge, disarm, etc. 01-50% chance that trying to speak or cast a spell within a 3 foot (0.9 m) radius around the Nightbane causes the person to choke and cough on the insects that fly into the mouth, preventing the spell from being finished. No loss of P.P.E., but no spell either. **Bonuses:** +3 to the M.E. attribute, +2 to save vs disease, resistant to insect venom (half damage, penalties and duration), and +1 to Horror Factor. **Penalties:** -3 to the M.A. attribute and -1 to P.B., -2 to base P.P.E., -3 to Perception Rolls, and -10% to Prowl. Skills such as Disguise and Undercover Ops are impossible.

Plant Life Table II

A Nightbane with any of these features takes the phrase "green thumb" to a whole new level. The character may be a student of botany, an environmental activist, or just has fond memories of Grandpa's garden or camping weekends. Whatever the reasoning, some aspect of the plant kingdom is represented within the Morphus form. **Note:** As with the original *Plant Life Table* (see **Nightbane® Sourcebook 2: Nightlands** or the Morphus Appendix at the back of this sourcebook), a Nightbane with features from this table takes double damage from fire and half damage from cold. Defoliants and herbicides also act as lethal poisons if the Nightbane comes into contact with them, dealing an average of 3D6 damage direct to Hit Points per 12 fluid ounces (355 ml) on a failed save vs lethal poison (14 or higher to save); half the damage on a successful save.

Roll percentile dice once for random determination, or pick one.

01-10% Fern Fronds: Growing from the head, shoulders, and back of the Morphus form are long stems with tiny leaves. These fronds cascade down the sides of the head and the back like long, flowing hair. The most common colors are green, brown, yellow, and blue. **Bonuses:** The fronds allow the Nightbane to subsist completely on sunlight and water. As long as the character gets at least 14 hours of sunlight per week, no other food is needed. If less sunlight exposure is obtained, it must be supplemented with solid food. The foliage also makes pretty good cam-

ouflage in wooded environments, adding a +5% bonus to Prowl, and +1 to Awe/Horror Factor. **Penalties:** The character must get at least two hours of sunlight per week. Every week without it reduces the P.S. and P.E. attributes by three and the S.D.C. of the Morphus form by 30. If any of these stats reaches zero, the Morphus becomes unavailable until there is sunlight to be had. This need for sunlight does not apply while in the Nightlands. -20% on skills like Disguise, Impersonation, Performance, Seduction and Undercover Ops.

11-20% Vines: Winding around the arms, legs, and torso of the Morphus are a number of clinging vines. While not prehensile, these fibrous lengths can serve as whips, lassoes, and climbing ropes. They can even be torn off in 3-30 foot (0.9 to 9.1 m) sections to bind captives, secure cargo, use as rope, etc. Taken together, there is roughly 120 feet (36.6 m) of vines covering the character. **Bonuses:** +1 to the P.E. attribute and +3D6+6 S.D.C. The vines have 20 S.D.C. per foot (0.3 m) and regrow if removed at the rate of one foot (0.3 m) per hour. If used as a lasso, bindings, etc., the vine holds with half the Supernatural Physical Strength of the Nightbane. As a whip, the vines deal 3D6 damage with a maximum reach of 20 feet (6.1 m) and a +1 bonus to strike and disarm. +5% to the Camouflage and Climbing skills. **Penalties:** -2 to the P.S. attribute and -1D6 from base P.P.E.

21-30% Nutshell: The character is, quite literally, a tough nut to crack. The skin becomes a thick, woody shell reminiscent of a walnut or coconut. **Bonuses:** +2 to the P.E. attribute and +2D4x10+20 S.D.C. with a Natural A.R. of 12. **Penalties:** -2 to the P.P., P.B. and Spd attributes, and -5% skill penalty on those requiring delicate work or a light touch, including Art, Forgery, Palming, Pick Pockets, etc., and a -15% penalty on skills like Disguise, Impersonation, Performance, Seduction and Undercover Ops.

31-40% Itch-Weed: The skin of the Nightbane's Morphus form is green and has a waxy sheen to it. Part of this sheen is the chemical irritant constantly secreted by the character. This irritant is essentially a powerful version of the substance produced by plants such as Poison Ivy and Poison Oak. **Bonuses:** +1 to Horror Factor, resistant to poison (half damage, duration and penalties on a failed saving throw), and -15% on skills like Disguise, Impersonation, Performance, Seduction and Undercover Ops.

Poisonous Skin (special): Within 1D4 melee rounds of contact with exposed skin (and a failed save vs non-lethal poison of 16 or greater is necessary), any place an opponent has been touched by the Nightbane turns a bright red and begins to itch and burn. This causes victims to lose 2 attacks per melee round and imposes a -2 penalty on all combat rolls and a -10% penalty to all skills. These effects last for 2D6 minutes. Double the penalties and duration against the Nightlords and the denizens of the Nightlands. **Penalties:** -1 to the M.A. attribute, -2D6 S.D.C., and -1D6 base P.P.E.

41-50% Moss Monster: Growing over every part of the character is one of several varieties of moss. This clinging plant covers most if not all of the Nightbane's features, making for great natural camouflage. It even softens the sounds of movement and the appearance of the character's tracks. If standing completely still in places such as graveyards, ancient ruins, and parks, the 'Bane might even pass for an old statue. **Bonuses:** +1 to the P.S. and P.E. attributes and +4D6 to S.D.C., +1 to Horror Factor and +20% to the Prowl and Camouflage skills outdoors in fields, tall grass and woodlands. **Penalties:** -1 to the M.A. attribute, reduce Spd by half, and -20% penalty on skills like Disguise, Impersonation, Performance, Seduction and Undercover Ops.

51-60% Venus Flytrap: The Venus flytrap is a small, carnivorous plant that survives by catching insects in a wide, mouth-like opening and dissolving them for food. This Nightbane is essentially a giant version of the normal plant (think "Little Shop of Horrors"). Legs and feet are replaced by bundles of roots that form 4-8 appendages and provide locomotion. Likewise, rudimentary hands and arms are formed out of leafy vines. The body becomes a relatively thin stalk which has several leafy offshoots.

The head of the plant Morphus with its giant maw is the defining feature of this Morphus form, as it is the part that opens

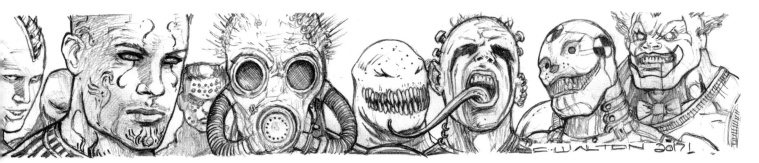

up to snap up and hold prey. When closed, the plant head is relatively thin, and appears to be two curved leaves with spiny edges that curl together to form the massive maw. The whole "head" opens up to reveal the mouth. This mouth can open 180 degrees so that the spines or "teeth" all face the same direction and is large enough to easily swallow animals as big as a large dog or wolf, a child, or half of a man. There are no visible eyes, ears, or nose, but the Nightbane is able to see, hear, and smell. In addition, the inside of the mouth is equipped with motion-sensitive fibers that are fine-tuned enough to pick up movement within 20 feet (6.1 m) of the Nightbane, so penalties for darkness/blindness are only -2 (not -10). **Bonuses:** +2 to the M.E. and P.S. attributes, +1 on initiative, +2 to strike/bite, +1 to parry and entangles with vine arms, +4 to save vs gas attacks, +2 to Horror Factor, and +1D6x10 to S.D.C. (**Note:** The giant plant head/maw/flytrap has 4D6+50 S.D.C. all by itself, and if destroyed, forces the Nightbane to turn back into his Facade. The head/flytrap regrows completely after 1D4+1 hours. The head takes damage only when targeted with a Called Shot.) Bite Attack: 3D6 damage per bite, each bite counts as one melee attack. What makes the bite attack so dangerous is that the Venus flytrap, holds its prey (or part of him) inside the maw where it secretes digestive acid to kill and dissolve it! The powerful bite holds its prey tight in a vise-like grip that requires twice the flytrap's Supernatural P.S. to pry open. (Reducing the Nightbane's Hit Points to three or less causes the flytrap head to open and release its prey.) The mouth can also hold prey, covering up to half of a human-sized target, while digestive juices inflict 2D6 damage per melee round (15 seconds)! Double damage to Nightlords and the denizens of the Nightlands. **Penalties:** -3 to the M.A. attribute, -4 to P.B., and -6 to Spd. The use of ranged weapons and most machinery is impossible and -30% to any skill requiring the use of hands (Art, Climbing, Computer Operation, Pick Locks, etc.). Skills like Acrobatics, Disguise, Impersonation, Performance, Prowl, Seduction, Undercover Ops, Piloting/driving, etc., are impossible to use in this Morphus. While the character is unable to swim as a giant plant, it does float on the surface of water indefinitely unless weighed down.

61-70% Seed/Spore Pods: Dotting the exterior of the Morphus, 2D6+2 small pods or seed clusters protrude from the skin. While seemingly innocuous, any or all of these pods can be popped or broken apart at the will of the Nightbane to fill the surrounding area with tiny spores or seeds. Wrestling with this character is also likely to break one or more of the pods (55% chance), as they only have 2 S.D.C. each. Once the particles contained within are released, they cover a 6 foot (1.8 m) radius around the character for 1D4 melee rounds. **Bonuses:** +1 to the P.E. attribute, +2D6 to S.D.C., +1 to save vs poison, and Spore Attack, below. -10% on skills like Disguise, Impersonation, Performance, Seduction and Undercover Ops. **Penalties:** -2 to the P.E. and P.B. attribute and -1D6 from base P.P.E.

Spore Attack: The spore/seed clouds impair vision and breathing as they get caught in the eyes, nose, and throat. Anyone in a seed cloud except for the Nightbane, himself, loses initiative and one attack and are -2 on all combat rolls and -10% to skill performance due to hacking and coughing. Duration 1D4 melee rounds even after leaving the cloud of spores.

71-80% Fungus/Mushrooms: A variety of small to medium-sized mushrooms grow on the back, neck, shoulders, upper arms, and perhaps on the head of the Nightbane instead of hair. Each has its own effect, which is activated by picking the fungus and getting the intended victim or recipient to consume the mushroom (or placed on a corpse). **Bonuses:** +3 to save vs poisons/toxins, +2D6 S.D.C., and mushrooms with varying effects. **Penalties:** -2 to the P.B. and Spd attributes, and reduce the permanent base P.P.E. by 2D6 points, and -20% on skills like Disguise, Impersonation, Performance, Seduction and Undercover Ops.

The Types of Mushrooms:

2D4 Decomposing Mushrooms (dark brown top, grey stem): One decomposing mushroom placed on a dead body completely devours the corpse within 1D6 melee rounds.

1D6+2 Deadly Mushrooms (red top and black underside): 3D6 damage direct to Hit Points per each mushroom eaten. Must be ingested. A successful save vs lethal poison reduces the damage by half (round down).

1D6+4 Debilitating Poison Mushrooms (white with brown highlights): Poison mushrooms taste delicious, but are poisonous when eaten. Even eating just one causes vomiting and stomach cramps (-1 attack, -2 to all combat rolls and bonuses, reduce Spd by 20%, and -15% on skill performance). Duration of penalties: 20 minutes per each mushroom eaten.

1D6+4 Edible Mushrooms (tan): One edible mushroom provides the nourishment of a single meal.

1D6+2 Medicinal Mushrooms (pale green top and stem): This small green mushroom resembles a bulbous green button. Eating one settles an upset stomach, stops vomiting, cures heartburn/acid indigestion, can help with a hangover (reduces duration by half), and restores 1D4 lost Hit Points caused by poison of any kind. In the case of curing poison, each mushroom consumed restores 1D6 Hit Points, but only damage caused by poison.

Note: Any fungus that is plucked, eaten or otherwise used or destroyed regrows in 24 hours.

81-90% Fruit-Bearing Vines: Leafy vines covers the Nightbane's body. Hanging under the arms and from vines covering the body are 6D6+10 small fruits, like berries or grapes located in clusters. These fruits can be real fruit of almost any kind, but typically berries (raspberries, blueberries, blackberries, and even small apples, small pears, plums, figs, tangerines and mangoes). They might also be completely fictional varieties but taste like one of the above. The fruit can be picked and eaten, given away as a treat, or thrown to attract attention (only the larger, harder fruit like an ap-

ple, pear, tangerine or mango do one point of damage when thrown hard). The fruit is one of the Nightbane's favorites and he regularly munches on it, but is likely to get angry with anyone who picks the fruit without asking. Fruits that are eaten, lost or destroyed regrow in 24 hours. **Bonuses:** +1 to the I.Q. and M.A. attributes, +4D6 to S.D.C. If thrown, berries only have a range of 20 feet (6.1 m) and do no damage, but splatter on impact and make a mess which could (on a Called Shot) obscure the vision of goggles, visors, camera lenses and windows until washed away with water. Fruit juice and pulp smear when simply wiped away with a hand or towel, causing a wider amount of obstruction of vision. Even if semi-transparent/semi-opaque, the smear is annoying and impairs vision (-2 to strike, parry, dodge, and disarm; -1 on Perception Rolls that require sight). Only the larger, heavier fruit do a single point of damage and have a throwing range of 100 feet (30.5 m). As a tougher fruit, they are less likely to leave behind a smear that impairs vision (01-20% chance). Eating eight berries, or one of the larger fruit like an apple, provides the equivalent nourishment of a full meal, and fruit on the Nightbane is always fresh, tasty, and edible. **Penalties:** -1 to the P.P. and Spd attributes, -1D4 from the permanent base P.P.E., and -20% on skills like Disguise, Impersonation, Performance, Seduction and Undercover Ops.

91-00% Sap: The Nightbane has a tough, brown or greenish-brown skin that feels like an onion stalk, or it may have a light bark texture to it. Rather than blood and normal body fluids, the Nightbane's Morphus bleeds a thick, sticky sap. The same sap can be produced from the mouth (half a handful per melee action, the creation of each gob counts as one melee attack) and has a variety of uses. **Bonuses:** +2 to the P.E. attribute and +6D6 S.D.C., resistant to heat and cold (half damage, but fire and magic cold do full damage), impervious to diseases, poisons, toxins and smoke that would affect humans, only poison/toxins that harm plant life hurt this Nightbane and even they only do half damage. If pierced or cut by a weapon there is a 50% chance it will become stuck in the character. For anyone but the Nightbane to free it requires a combined Supernatural P.S. of 30 and takes two attacks; the Nightbane can remove it with ease, though the blade will have sap on it which could make it stick to the next thing it touches, get stuck inside its scabbard if put away with the sap blood on it, etc. The sap can be used in place of glue to repair items, seal wounds, and to help hold onto objects and opponents (+3 to entangle and disarm an opponent, -2 for the Nightbane to be disarmed, and +15% to the Climbing and Palming skills.) The sap is also incredibly difficult to wash off so it can be used to mark a trail. To wash it off requires soap and hot (not cold or warm) water and plenty of elbow grease. **Penalties:** -1 to the P.P., P.E. and P.B. attributes, -2D4 to the permanent base P.P.E., and -10% on skills like Disguise, Impersonation, Performance, Seduction and Undercover Ops.

Science Fiction Table

While some in the academic community debate whether science fiction is even a legitimate literary genre, the public at large loves it. If anything, sci-fi and fantasy stories have only grown more popular since Dark Day as greater numbers of people seek a way to forget about a world around them that grows scarier by the day. Nightbane with a feature from this table are most likely to be avid readers, watchers, players, or even writers of sci-fi. On the other hand, the character may just be a technophile who keeps up on and is fascinated with the latest advances in technology.

Roll percentile dice once for random determination, or pick one.

01-10% Light Sci-Fi Armor: The body of the Morphus appears to be sheathed in a full suit of advanced body armor, including a helmet that fully covers the face, which may or may not be visible. This armor typically looks to be composed of overlapping plates but may incorporate form-fitting mesh, rubberized pieces, ceramic material, etc. Whatever it is, the armor looks like a high-tech, light, environmental body armor or plated spacesuit. **Bonuses:** +2D4x10+40 to S.D.C. (the armor), increase the Night-

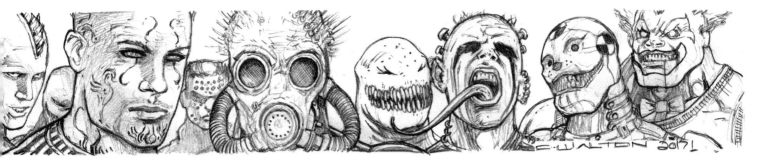

bane's Natural A.R. to 11, +1 to roll with punch/fall/impact, +1 to Awe/Horror Factor, and the armor is environmentally sealed so the 'Bane does not need air to breathe (the armored suit provides it) and he is immune to airborne irritants, toxins, and poisonous gases. **Penalties:** -1 to Perception Rolls, -1 to the P.E. attribute, -1 to save vs magic of any kind, -5% to skills that require a delicate touch or precision (like most repairs, Art, Pick Locks, Pick Pockets, etc.), and -10% to Physical skills like Acrobatics, Climbing, Prowl and Swimming due to physical encumbrance.

11-19% Heavy Sci-Fi Armor: This is a full suit of advanced, heavy body armor that covers the Morphus from head to toe. It is an environmental suit and is much heavier and bulkier than the light armor for greater protection in combat. It may have a high-tech mechanical look or may have an organic, resin or genetically engineered appearance. As a heavy armor, it is an augmentation system that slightly boosts the Nightbane's strength. **Bonuses:** +1D4 to the P.S. attribute, +2D6x10+120 to S.D.C. (the armor), increase the Nightbane's Natural A.R. to 14, +2 to roll with punch/fall/impact, kinetic attacks like punches and kicks do half damage, +1 to Awe/Horror Factor, and the environmentally sealed armor means the 'Bane does not need air to breathe (the armored suit provides it) and he is immune to airborne irritants, toxins, and poisonous gases. **Penalties:** -2 to Perception Rolls, -2 to the P.E. and Spd attributes, -3 to save vs magic of any kind, -20% to skills that require a delicate touch or precision (like most repairs, Art, Pick Locks, Pick Pockets, etc.), and -30% to Physical skills like Acrobatics, Climbing, Prowl and Swimming due to physical encumbrance.

20-28% Flight Pack/Thrusters: This feature may appear as a number of things from a flame-spewing jet pack, to a series of anti-gravity nodes built into various points of the Morphus form, to organic looking tubes growing out of the back or behind the shoulders. Regardless of the look, this feature offers the ability of high-speed, wingless flight. Maximum flight speed is 1D6x10+72 (57-90 mph/91.2 to 144 kph) with a max altitude of 10,000 feet (3,048 m). The flight system has 100 S.D.C. of its own, but is only damaged when specifically targeted via Called Shot. The Flight Pack regenerates at the same rate as the Nightbane, but takes a full day to regenerate if completely destroyed. It is inoperable while regenerating. **Bonuses:** +2 to dodge while in flight; +4 to dodge when traveling at 60 mph (96 kph). +2 to damage for every 20 mph (32 km) of speed. +1 to Awe/Horror Factor when flying. **Penalties:** -1 to the P.E. and P.B. attributes and -2D6 to running speed, -2D6 from permanent P.P.E. base, and cannot hover (built for speed).

29-37% Energy Blaster: Whether a handheld weapon or one built into the body of the Morphus form, this feature provides a long-range energy weapon. The look may vary from high-tech to organic but always looks futuristic or alien/strange. The blaster is fueled by the Nightbane's P.P.E., dealing 1D6 damage per point of P.P.E. expended with a max of 10 points able to be spent per attack. **Bonuses:** +3 to strike with an energy blast, range is 2,000 feet (610 m), +1 to Awe/Horror Factor. **Penalties:** -2D6 from the permanent base P.P.E. and reduce the number of starting Talents by one. Note that the damage inflicted by the energy blaster is NOT considered magical or supernatural in nature.

38-46% Sci-Fi Melee Weapon(s): This feature provides a futuristic melee weapon (or pair if one-handed) that can be energized to deal additional damage. The weapon itself can look like any real or imagined weapon from a knife or sword to a battle-axe or mace, but typically has artistic accents and features that set it apart from mundane versions. It may appear to be made out of alien crystal or resin, or organic, and it could have portions of it that softly glow, have an electric hum, etc. In its normal state, a small weapon does 1D6 damage while large weapons do 2D6, although if the Nightbane expends three P.P.E. per melee round for a small or six P.P.E. per melee round for a large weapon, its base damage is *doubled,* and the weapon does triple damage to Nightlords and their demonic minions. This increased power level is apparent as the weapon will hum with a high-frequency vibration, be sheathed in some form of energy, or something similar. **Bonuses:** +1 to Awe/Horror Factor when the weapon is energized to do extra damage. If not already known, the Nightbane gets the appropriate Weapon Proficiency skill for the weapon, but it is applicable only while in Morphus form. The Sci-Fi weapon(s) cannot be forcibly taken from the character or otherwise disarmed, but can be sheathed or put aside, and willingly relinquished. HOWEVER, anyone else trying to use the weapon finds it deceptively heavy and not well balanced (-6 to strike, parry and disarm). **Penalties:** -1D6 Hit Points and -1D6 from permanent P.P.E. base, and do NOT add Supernatural P.S. punch or any strength bonuses to energized weapon damage.

47-56% Universal Translator: This feature usually takes the shape of a futuristic earpiece, mask, or cell phone-like mini-computer, and sometimes what looks to be a cybernetic implant in the ear, head, or neck. It allows the Nightbane to understand and speak ALL languages with 98% fluency. Even alien languages never heard on Earth will be comprehended as long as there is no additional non-lingual component such as physical gestures or color-changing skin or lights as part of the language. In addition, this Nightbane is likely to find different cultures, people and societies very interesting. **Bonuses:** Ability to understand and speak all languages, +1 to I.Q. and M.A. attributes, +5% bonus to any Communications and Lore skills, and +10 Anthropology and Archeology skills (when applicable). **Penalties:** -1 to the P.B. attribute and -1D6 from permanent P.P.E. base.

57-66% Sci-Fi Optics: Most often appearing as a helmet, goggles, visor, or mechanical/cybernetic eye(s), this feature enables the Nightbane to see in a variety of different ways and in different spectrums of light. Infrared (heat) and ultraviolet (U.V.) spectrums are visible until they transition to radio and microwaves. The ability to see heat signatures means the Nightbane can "see" if an engine is hot or cold, see targets in smoke and through thin walls, as well as see and follow recent footsteps that

are less than 10 minutes old. Automatic light-adjusting lens and polarization protects against bright light and glare, and a virtual targeting reticule is superimposed over vision when in combat. For an expense of 3 P.P.E., the Nightbane can see the magically invisible (range 1,000 feet/305 m) for one minute per level of experience. **Bonuses:** +2 to Perception Rolls and +1 to strike with ranged weapons. +1 to Awe/Horror Factor. **Penalties:** -1 to the P.B. attribute and -1D6 from permanent P.P.E. base.

67-76% Personal Scanner/Sensors: The Morphus has a small device that is handheld or cybernetic and built into the hand, forearm, shoulder, or head. This device incorporates a variety of sensory equipment with various capabilities. **Bonuses:** +1 to Awe/Horror Factor. **Penalties:** -1 to M.A. and -1D4 from the permanent P.P.E. base per EACH scan feature selected. 1D4+1 scan features may be selected from those listed below.

Bio-Scanner: A futuristic biometric scanner that can determine body temperature, blood pressure, heart rate, respiration rate, oxygen saturation, pupil dilation, synaptic activity, etc. of the Nightbane, plus a warning system when Hit Points are being lost, blood loss, disease, etc. HOWEVER, the scanner also works on reading the biometrics of others, either by touch by the Nightbane or a scan up to 10 feet (3 m) away; line of sight required. This can be used for a host of medical and non-medical uses from pinpointing internal bleeding to respiratory function, organ failure, identifying broken bones, and to a lesser degree gauging emotional states. The latter cannot be used as a lie detector, but it will indicate if the individual seems excited/agitated, or calm/relaxed, which may offer clues as to whether the individual may be saying things contrary to his feelings, or indicate that things may not be what they seem; i.e. a capture feigning terror but the bioscan suggests he is calm and not afraid. Which, in turn, suggests this may be a trap, he is lying or more powerful or at least more confident than he is pretending to be. Which should raise the question of why? +10% to all Medical skills while in Morphus form as well as +10% to Interrogation and Intelligence skills.

EM Field Detector: A scanning tool that picks up a variety of electromagnetic radiation such as that put out by electronic devices and magnetic fields. Detection range is 50 feet (15.2 m). Add +10% to all Electrical skills while in Morphus form.

Geiger Counter: A device used to detect potentially dangerous nuclear radiation; it will deliver a warning when harmful levels are detected and indicate exactly what the level of radiation is and where the radiation increases and decreases. Detection range is 50 feet (15.2 m).

Miniature Radar: A small radar unit used to track flying objects as small as human-sized. It can isolate and track up to 20 different objects up to a range of 30 miles (48 km) with a floor of 25 feet (7.6 m). +1 on initiative and +1 to strike flying opponents, or +2 to dodge incoming attacks. Also reduce penalties in darkness and when blind by half.

Motion Detector: This sensor monitors for minute changes in air pressure that indicate moving objects. Detection range is 100 feet (30.5 m). Reduce penalties in darkness and when blinded by half, and +1 to dodge. Moreover, the 'Bane cannot be surprised by an attack that is coming in from behind or above.

Molecular Analyzer: A sophisticated tool that uses mass spectrometry to determine the exact chemical composition of anything scanned. Can detect chemical traces as low as 20 parts per million at a range of up to 25 feet (7.6 m). +10% to *Crime Scene Investigation* and all *Chemistry* skills while in Morphus form.

Sense Magic: The sensor can pick up strong, magical energy signatures such as ley lines, nexus points, and magic items and living beings who contain/possess more than 70 points of P.P.E. Detection range is 30 feet (9.1 m).

77-85% Hologram Projector: The Nightbane's Morphus form has a futuristic-looking camera built into the body (usually the head, shoulder or forearm) or carried on the person. This is actually a complex projector capable of creating holograms, 3-dimensional images made of light. Such holograms have no substance but look completely real from any angle and can even fool beings immune to *magical* illusions. Holograms may cover an area up to 10 feet x 10 feet x 10 feet (3x3x3 m) in size and projected as far as 50 feet (15.2 m) away. They can also be made to surround the Nightbane, other people, or other objects.

While these images are incredibly convincing, keep in mind that they do not fool other senses like hearing, smell or touch, nor supernatural senses like Sense Evil, Sense Magic, See Aura, or sensors such as pressure plates or thermal optic systems. Normal cameras will record the hologram, though. The projector can only operate for five minutes out of any one hour period before needing to recharge from the character's bio-kinetic energy. **Bonuses:** +1 to all Perception Rolls and +2 to save vs illusions. Automatically gets the Disguise and Camouflage skills at 80% or a bonus of +20% (whichever is higher) if using the projector for disguising his own appearance, hiding or concealment. **Penalties:** -1D6+6 from permanent P.P.E. base. -2 attacks/actions per melee round and reduce Spd 10% while the projector and holographic image are active.

86-94% Force Field Array: A series of nodes or small, electronic patches are built into the Morphus or incorporated into some kind of harness or full-body suit. This system projects a form fitting energy field that defends against a variety of attacks. The force field protects the Nightbane from poison gases and fumes, as well as kinetic and energy attacks such as punches, explosions, bullets, energy blast and even magically created energy like a fire ball or lightning bolt. It does NOT protect against Mesmerism, illusions, mind control and possession.

The force field provides an additional 1D6x10+200 S.D.C. Any damage directed at the Nightbane is subtracted from the force field first. As long as the force field has S.D.C., it regenerates from damage and restores S.D.C. at the same rate as the Nightbane normally heals. If the force field is reduced to zero S.D.C., it is down and unavailable for 6 hours. When it comes back online it is at full power. **Note:** To activate Talents or to

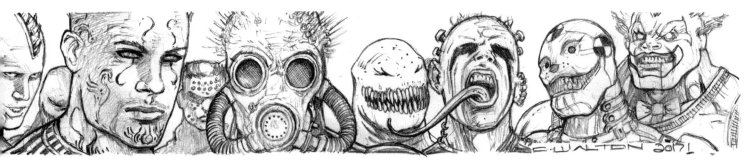

cast spells this force field must be *dropped* while the P.P.E. is expended. Raising and lowering the shield is so fast it does not require using a melee action, but does leave the Nightbane open to attack for 2D4 seconds. **Bonuses:** +1D6 to the 'Bane's Hit Points. Damage is always subtracted from this force field before the character's personal S.D.C. or Hit Points can be affected. Immune to gases, poison, and diseases while the force field is up. **Penalties:** -2D6+3 from the permanent P.P.E. base, and a Nightbane with this feature can never develop Talents such as *Shadow Shield* or *Pipe Bomb* that create a magical protective field.

95-00% Bug-Eyed Monster: The Nightbane resembles like an alien from another world. This could be the classic "Grey" alien like those depicted in the movie *Close Encounters of the Third Kind* or the *X-Files TV show*, or a *strange, scary creature* like those depicted in Grade-B sci-fi novels, comic books, films, TV or games, usually with weird, oversized eyes and/or insect or crustacean features like eye stalks, crab claws, antennae, and so on, as long as the alien is *monstrous* vs very human or attractive in appearance. For example, the Nightbane may resemble the aliens from Mars Attacks, or the Alien series of movies, or Independence Day, or a Gorn from the original Star Trek TV show, or any aliens in the Star Wars cantina scene. Be creative, or random roll or select from another table which can create a science fiction alien look. Likely alternatives include features from the Alien Shape, Biomechanical, or the Extraterrestrial table.

Modern Soldier Table

The origins for features from the Modern Soldier Table share much in common with those of the *Ancient Warrior Table,* except rather than identifying with knights, samurai, and other warriors of a bygone era, the Nightbane feels closer to the modern day equivalents. The individual may come from a military family, be a trained soldier himself, or have always wanted to serve in the armed forces, or always found the military, especially their weapons, vehicles and gear, fascinating and appealing.

Nightbane with a Morphus based on the Modern Soldier table are not necessarily more aggressive or warlike than the average Nightbane (unless you want them to be), but often prove to be slightly more resilient, with a head for modern military strategies and tactics. Weapons, helmets, armor and gas mask may be Biomechanical and a living part of the Nightbane's Morphus integrated into his physical body, head, arms, and so on. **Bonus Note:** Therefore, all Nightbane with at least one Modern Soldier feature gets an additional +1 to save vs Horror Factor, and +1 to Perception Rolls to recognize potential ambushes and booby-traps, as well as military weapons and explosive devices.

Roll percentile dice once for random determination, or pick one.

01-10% Body Armor: This 'Bane is always wearing a modern body armor of some form. Regardless of the style, it is a full suit of combat armor complete with a helmet. While it looks like the genuine article, complete with zippers and other fasteners, the armor is unable to be removed as it is part of the Morphus. The coloring is typically a matte black, dark grey, desert brown or some kind of camouflage pattern and may have multiple pockets and fasteners to store equipment. **Bonuses:** Increase the base Natural A.R. to 1D4+10, add 1D6x10+70 to S.D.C., and blunt attacks and explosions do half damage. **Penalties:** -1 to the P.E. attribute and -1D4 to Spd, -5% to skills like Acrobatics, Climbing, Gymnastics, Prowl, Swimming, Disguise and Undercover Ops. The armor provides no protection against damage from disease, gas attacks, possession, spells, Talents, magic weapons, or other supernatural powers (which ignore the armor's S.D.C. entirely).

11-20% Camouflage: This character's Morphus form is dressed from head to toe in camouflage clothing. This may be as simple as a set of modern "digital camo" fatigues and grease paint to a full-fledged ghillie suit that incorporates local foliage. Biomechanical Nightbane might have a camouflage paint job or cargo netting. Whatever form the camouflage takes, it alters every time he changes to Morphus to match the surrounding environment and/or the psyche of the Nightbane. **Bonuses:** +4D6 to S.D.C., +25% to the Camouflage skill, and +10% to Prowl and Tailing skills. Given 1D4 minutes and suitable materials, the Nightbane can prepare a personal hiding spot that is extremely difficult to detect (Perception Roll of 1D4+13 needed to spot the character). -20% to opponents' ability to Detect Concealment, Detect Ambush, Tailing, or Tracking rolls when trying to locate this Nightbane (bonus does not apply if other people are with the 'Bane). Gets automatic first initiative when ambushing an opponent from a hiding place. **Penalties:** -1D4 to Spd, -1 on initiative when not ambushing opponents, and -5% to skills like Disguise, Impersonation, and Undercover Ops.

21-30% Dress Uniform: Dress uniforms are meant for formal occasions such as military ceremonies rather than combat. Such clothing is typically replete with patches, medals, and other such ornamentation designed to look striking and impressive. This Morphus is always decked-out in such military finery which gives him an aura of authority. It may also make him look out of place. This uniform can be from any military organization that has ever existed or a fictional one like in Star Trek. Whatever the case, it is sure to attract attention. **Bonuses:** +2 to M.A., +1 to M.E., +3D6+10 to S.D.C., +2 to Awe/Horror Factor, and the Nightbane gains one Modern Weapon Proficiency of choice, but it can only be used while in Morphus form. **Penalties:** Such uniforms tend to be quite conspicuous; -10% to Prowl, and skills like Disguise, Impersonation and Undercover Ops are impossible unless impersonating a military officer in full regalia.

31-40% Gas Mask: Like the Body Armor feature, the gas mask is part of the Nightbane's Morphus and probably permanently attached to his face (Biomechanical or cybernetic). It can be any style of gas mask from WWI to modern day equivalents. This protective device was invented to shield and protect the wearer from chemical weapons on the battlefield, but this one

ter thinks of what is needed, reaches into the kit, and retrieves the supplies he was thinking of (within reason and only as it applies to first aid situations and healing, not a gun or cell phone or large equipment like an EKG machine). All conjured supplies should be basic medical supplies that you would expect to find in a large, well-equipped first aid kit. No rare and expensive drugs, no narcotics, no fancy medical devices. Also, this feature does NOT automatically create the right tool for the job. The Nightbane must visualize what is to be produced and *spend one P.P.E.* for each item (a pack of tongue depressors or band aids would still count as one item). If the Nightbane Medic has any stigmata, it is likely to be bullet holes in his body or limbs that never heal and regularly ooze blood. Likewise, this morphus may have bandages covering his head or face, even though he is the medic. **Bonuses:** +1 to M.E. and P.E. attributes, +2 to pull punch and disarm, and +20% to the First Aid, Paramedic, or Medical Doctor skills and with an expenditure of 6 P.P.E. he has a healing touch that stops bleed, causes open wound to begin to heal, start any heart that has stopped, and instantly restores 4D6 Hit Points or S.D.C.! **Penalties:** -1D6+6 from the permanent P.P.E. base and -4 to damage from this character's melee attacks.

51-60% Night Hunter/Nightvision Goggles: Though this feature may seem redundant given the Nightbane's natural nightvision, this permanent fixture increases range to 3,000 feet (914 m) and enables him to see in magical darkness and shadows at half the usual range without need of a saving throw. **Bonuses:** +2D6 to S.D.C., +2 to all Perception Rolls, never afraid of the dark, impervious to even magical blindness and his punches, kicks and melee attacks with a handheld weapon do double damage to Shadow creatures, Nightlords and all creatures from the Nightlands! **Penalties:** -2D4 from permanent P.P.E. base, dislikes bright lights/sunlight, and -3 on Perception Rolls and -5% on all skill performance in well-lit areas and in daylight.

61-70% Field Radio: The Nightbane has a military-grade field radio and/or satellite phone on hand at all times while in Morphus form, or a cybernetic equivalent. This device ranges from the size of a large cell phone to the bulky, WWII era, backpack units. This provides the Nightbane with a 50 mile (80 km) radius of radio communications that can only be jammed by magical means like the Anti-Magic Cloud or Sanctum spell. **Bonuses:** +4D6 to S.D.C., automatically gets the Radio: Basic and Cryptography skills at 80% (or +20% whichever is greater) while in Morphus form; +10% to any other Communications skills the character may possess. Double the range and halve the cost of using the *Operator Talent* if possessed by this Nightbane. Also double the range in the Nightlands. **Penalties:** -2D4 base P.P.E., and electrical attacks deal an additional 50% damage to the character.

71-80% Personal Weaponry: The Nightbane's Morphus may have a bit of a machine-like appearance and certainly wears a combat helmet and fatigues. Select one weapon from each of the following lists. These weapons always appear on the character when the Morphus form is assumed, with firearms fully

is equally useful against chemical fumes, tear gas, gas attacks of all kinds and even airborne pathogens. **Bonuses:** +2D6 to S.D.C. and +1 to Horror Factor. While in Morphus form the Nightbane is immune to any airborne chemicals, gas attacks, fumes, stench or disease that is not magical in nature. Even when it is magical, the character is +4 to save against its effects. Nuclear radiation is also ineffective against this Nightbane and will not even irradiate personal equipment kept on the character's person. **Penalties:** -1 on Perception Rolls, -1D4 to M.A. and P.B. attributes, voice is a bit muffled, -10% to all Communications skills, -60% to Disguise, Seduction and Undercover Ops.

41-50% Medic and First Aid: This Morphus is a combat medic, which means a pair of surgical gloves and surgical mask covering the mouth and nose are likely to be part of it, along with a medium-sized kit of field medical supplies. Blood pressure device, stethoscope, thermometer for taking temperature, pen flashlight, various sizes of bandages, rolls of bandages, tubes of antiseptic, quick-clotting agent, needle and thread, bottle of aspirin, pen and notepad, and various other useful medical items. However, the bag/box/kit seems too small for everything that the Nightbane can remove from it to help people. In truth, the charac-

loaded and with spare ammunition. Expended rounds are replenished every 24 hours, but additional store-bought commercial rounds (or stolen ordnance) of the same caliber may be provided by the character. Note that these may be hard to come by, especially high-damage rounds of military ordnance. All weapons have standard features common to that type (e.g. assault rifles and machine-guns can fire bursts, sniper rifles have long-range scopes, etc.), and may be Biomechanical, meaning they many be built into the Nightbane's body or limbs. **Bonuses:** +1D6 to Spd attribute, +6D6 S.D.C., and while in Morphus, the Nightbane has a bonus of +2 to strike and +1 to parry with any weapons from this feature, and all ch weapons do an extra +2D6 damage against the Nightlords, their demonic minions and all denizens of the Nightlands. **Penalties:** -2D6+6 from the permanent P.P.E. base, and -5% on the performance of all skills except W.P.s, Military, Physical and Espionage skills.

Primary Weapon

Light Assault Rifle: 4D6 damage with a 1,969 foot (600 m) range and three 50 round clips.

Heavy Assault Rifle: 5D6 damage with a 1,640 foot (500 m) range and three 30 round clips.

Light Machine-Gun: 6D6 damage with a 3,280 foot (1,000 m) range and a single 100 round belt.

Sniper Rifle: 5D6 damage with a 5,280 foot (1,609 m) range and three 10 round clips.

Shotgun: 4D6 damage with a 200 foot (61 m) range and a 7 round capacity plus two full reloads.

Submachine-Gun: 3D6 damage with a 656 foot (200 m) range and three 30 round clips.

Secondary Weapon/Side Arm

Light Pistol: 3D6 damage with a 200 foot (61 m) range and three 15 round clips.

Heavy Pistol: 4D6 damage with a 160 foot (48.8 m) range and three 9 round clips.

Machine-Pistol: 2D6 damage with a 160 foot (48.8 m) range and three 20 round clips.

Grenades (x3): Hand thrown or rifle-launched, deal 1D6x10 damage to a 15 foot (4.6 m) radius.

Survival Knife or Small Melee Weapon: Likely a knife or bayonet, deals 1D6 damage, for melee combat and may retract from a wrist or forearm housing.

Large Melee Weapon: Something like a machete, sword or large entrenching tool that inflicts 2D6 damage, for melee combat and may retract from a wrist or forearm housing

81-90% Heavy Firepower: The Nightbane's Morphus possesses heavy weaponry that by all rights shouldn't be one man-portable. This weapon might take the form of a multi-shot rocket pod, a heavy machine-gun, Gatling-gun, or even a miniaturized light artillery cannon. Whatever it is, it's big and unwieldy, but deals out devastating amounts of damage: 1D6x10 damage per melee attack! Maximum range is also impressive at 4,000 feet

(1,219 m). Any ammunition necessary is provided at a rate of three shots per melee round. Each attack with this beast counts as one attack, but there are encumbrance and size penalties. **Bonuses:** +2 to P.S. and P.E., +1D4x10 S.D.C., double the range and damage of the *Darkblast Talent* if channeled through this weapon, +1 to Horror Factor, and add an additional +10 damage against the Nightlords, their demonic minions and all denizens of the Nightlands. **Penalties:** Reduce Spd attribute by half, -3 to dodge and roll with impact, -1D6 to Hit Points, -3D6+10 from the permanent P.P.E. base, and -40% to skills like Acrobatics, Climbing, Gymnastics, Prowl, and Swimming, while skills like Disguise and Undercover Ops are impossible!

91-00% Biomechanical: The Nightbane may have tank treads for legs, or a machine-gun or other weapon or piece of equipment for an arm. Roll for or select a feature from one of the *Biomechanical tables* (including Aquatic and Gear-Head), then relate it back to modern military. For instance, a Nightbane with the Rocket Jets feature may have dreamed of being a fighter pilot while one with tank treads instead of legs might have worked on armored vehicles as an army mechanic, or loves tanks.

Substance Abuse Table

Author's Disclaimer: The following table is in no way meant to trivialize or celebrate the use/abuse of addictive and/or illicit substances. Quite the opposite. I ended my abuse of alcohol several years ago and have seen first-hand the terrible consequences of substance dependency. If you or someone you know is abusing drugs or alcohol, please seek help through resources such as Alcoholics Anonymous, Narcotics Anonymous, or a local treatment center. Those players and G.M.s who are uncomfortable dealing with substance use or abuse themes in their game should feel free to ignore this table and re-roll. – *The Author*

The unfortunate truth is that substance abuse is endemic in most of the societies of Nightbane Earth, and has only become more prevalent since *Dark Day* and the quiet invasion of the Nightlords and their demonic minions and wicked human henchmen. Substance abuse and dependency often becomes quite a large part of the abuser's identity, so it should be no surprise that there are a number of Nightbane with one or more features of their Morphus form that reflect their drugs of choice. A Nightbane with one of these features will typically (01-60%) have an addiction that corresponds with it, or a history of abusing that substance (61-80%), or a family history or fear of becoming addicted (81-00%). In the latter case, the Nightbane does not have an addiction problem himself, but has suffered the agony of watching a friend or loved one fighting addiction.

Roll percentile dice once for random determination, or pick one.

01-10% Hypodermic Quills: Hollow needles protrude from the back and shoulders, and may even continue down the back or arms of the Nightbane. These quills only add 1D6 damage to

attacks using them, but the true danger lies in the poison they can inject (whether the syringe chambers are visible or not). If the chambers are visible this poison can be seen sloshing around inside. In some cases, the substance even slowly leaks from the tips of the needles and drips to the ground.

In combat, the Nightbane can remove one or two hypodermic syringes to use like poisoned daggers or spikes for stabbing and slashing. However, the 'Bane's bite (1D6 damage) and claw slash also deliver the same toxic substance that hurts and impairs his opponents. The Nightbane does not have claws per se, but does have somewhat overgrown fingernails that can cut and gouge. The cut is not deep, but it is enough to cause bleeding (1D4 damage) and to get the poison into his opponent's system. On a successful strike that pierces an opponent's skin, the Nightbane may choose to release a dose of poison into the target. If said target fails the saving throw vs poison (needs a 14 or better), he takes an additional 2D4 damage from the poison. This damage is done directly to Hit Points! Victims of this drug are also -1 to all combat and Perception Rolls for 1D4 minutes per each failed roll up to a

maximum penalty of -5. The poison is only half as effective (1D4 damage and penalties last only one minute) against supernatural and magical creatures, including the Nightlords and their demonic minions. **Bonuses:** +1D4 to the P.E. and P.S. attributes, +6D6 to S.D.C., +2 to strike and parry with syringe only, +3 to roll with punch, fall or impact, and +2 to Horror Factor. **Penalties:** -1D4 P.B. and Spd attributes, -2D4 to Hit Points, -2D4 from the character's permanent P.P.E. base, -2 on Perception Rolls and initiative, -1 to dodge and pull punch, -10% on the performance of all skills, and skills like Disguise and Undercover Ops are impossible.

11-30% Pills: This Morphus can manifest in a number of different ways. Prescription pill bottles may be inset into various parts of the Nightbane's body, portions of the flesh replaced by the transparent plastic of pill bottles revealing medication inside; or one of the most common and horrific manifestations is pills as the heads of pimples and warts all over the face, arms, and body, the heads of the capsules and pills poking out through the skin, and the Nightbane picking at them, plucking them out and eating them like candy to get a buzz. A bit of ooze or pus coats every pill when it is removed and trickles out from the empty socket. Whatever the case may be, it is bizarre and repugnant – tablets and capsules poking out of the skin or pills heard rattling around in the containers inside the Nightbane's body as he moves. **Bonuses:** +1 on initiative, +5D6 to S.D.C. and +1 to the Nightbane's Horror Factor, and +2 to save vs Horror Factor, drugs and poison.

Pill Notes: Pill Duration: The effects and bonuses of ALL pills last 1D4+2 minutes unless stated otherwise.

After-Effects: Last for 2D4+4 minutes or as indicated in the description.

Ingested: All pills must be taken orally and ingested, with the effect kicking in within 1D4 melee rounds. Slipping a ground-up pill into food and drink makes it noticeably bitter and foul tasting, so the target is likely (01-80% chance) to throw it away and not consume enough for the pill to have any effect.

Saving Throw: 16 or higher vs non-lethal poison. No save applicable when the pill is taken willingly. A successful save means no bonuses or penalties occur in the person, unless stated otherwise. Taking more than one of the same pill has NO additional effect. Penalties and bonuses cannot be stacked via taking multiple pills. Likewise, the effects of only ONE pill at a time apply, so if a new pill is taken, it cancels out the bonuses and effects of the previous pill and *replaces them* with the effects of the new pill. HOWEVER, penalties from all pills remain in place, with new penalties occurring after the previous ones stop, in the order that the pills were taken.

Pill Quantities and Descriptions:

1D4+2 Anti-Toxin: Taking this pill settles an upset stomach, stops vomiting, cures heartburn/acid indigestion, can help with a hangover (reduce duration by half), and it also restores 1D4 lost Hit Points caused by poison of any kind.

After-Effects: None.

1D4+6 Booster Pills: This is a cocktail of chemicals to increase awareness and prevent sleep. Character is +2 on Perception Rolls, +1 on initiative, and is wide awake for 1D4+2 hours.

After-Effects When Duration Ends: -4 on Perception Rolls, -2 on initiative, and drowsiness (-20% on performance of all skills, and will doze off when things get quiet or slow down). The after-effects last for 1D6+6 hours or go away after getting seven hours of sleep.

1D4+4 Fat Pills: Kills the user's appetite. Does not feel hungry for 1D4+4 hours. On the down side, the character is not eating enough to be properly well nourished and over a long period of time, could feel sick and become malnourished and weak.

After-Effects When Duration Ends: Low energy and hungry for 1D6+4 hours: -1 on Perception Rolls and initiative, -1 on all combat rolls and -10% to Spd attribute.

2D6+3 Happy Pills: The user feels relaxed and cheerful, and is disoriented in a positive, happy manner, making him feel unafraid and calm even under duress. This is good and bad, because while +4 to save vs Horror Factor, and +5 on all skills even when under fire and dealing with life and death conditions, the character is -4 on Perception Rolls, -4 on initiative, reduce Spd by 20%, and the character would rather talk, negotiate or drink than fight.

After-Effects When Duration Ends: -1 to save vs Horror Factor, and -10% on the performance of all skills, double when facing death conditions, and the character remains -4 on Perception Rolls and initiative and reduce Spd by 20% for 1D6x10 minutes.

1D4+2 Hallucinogenic Pills: On a failed saving throw, the person suffers from strong perceptual distortions and visual hallucinations. For example, the character may see everyone around him as cartoon characters or monsters, or angels, or aliens, or as members of a favorite (or scary) TV show, and so on. Or the environment might be someplace different or reflect the setting of a favorite or feared book, game, TV show or movie. ("How did we get on the Nostromo?! Where's Ripley?") Or people may glow or the sky may be filled with changing colors, flashing lights and so on. While hallucinating, victims are -6 on Perception Rolls, -5 on initiative, -3 to strike, parry, and dodge, -4 to save vs Horror Factor and illusions, and skill performance is -30%. These effects last for 1D4 minutes.

After-Effects When Duration Ends: The character remains disoriented for the next hour, -2 on Perception Rolls and initiative (not sure what's real and what's not), -10% to the performance of all skills and -2 to save vs Horror Factor and illusions for the next hour.

1D4+1 Magic Pills: Is it a placebo or real? +1 to save vs all magic attacks, illusions, disease, poison and mind control, and +2 to save vs possession; double the bonuses to save against demons, the Nightlords, their demonic minions, any creature from the Nightlands, and other Nightbane.

After-Effects When Duration Ends: Feels emboldened and powerful or lucky, but is now really -1 to save vs all magic attacks and illusions, mind control, poison and toxins, and -2 to save vs possession and the magic or psionic attacks of the Nightlords and any creature from the Nightlands as well as demons, for the next 1D6+6 minutes.

2D4+4 Powerful Painkillers: Reduces pain and decreases any pain related penalties by half. The character can function reasonably well, but is foggy and the painkiller makes him -2 on Perception Rolls and initiative, -1 on all combat rolls and -5% on the performance of skills (in addition to any other penalties already in place from injury/pain).

After-Effects When Duration Ends: None, other than the pain returning and the full penalties from it roll back in place. Frequent use of powerful painkillers can lead to addiction.

1D4+4 Sedatives: On a failed roll to save, the recipient is incredibly groggy: Reduce attacks per melee, Spd and the performance of all skills by half, and combat bonuses to zero for 1D6+2 minutes. If the roll to save was 4 or below, the victim falls into a deep sleep.

After-Effects When Duration Ends: Remains sluggish for 1D6 minutes during which the character is -1 on all combat rolls, -10% on speed and -5% on skill performance for 2D6+2 minutes.

2D4+2 Steroids: Temporary bonuses of +1D4+4 to P.S., +2D6+10 to S.D.C. (damage comes off this first), +2 on initiative, but makes the character aggressive, quick to physical violence and prone to take risks and throw a punch rather than talk things out peacefully.

After-Effects When Duration Ends: The character's P.S. returns to normal and then is temporarily reduced by 1D6 P.S. points, S.D.C. returns to normal, -4 on initiative, reduce Spd by 20%, and the character feels tired and sluggish. Penalties last 2D4+4 minutes.

31-40% Alcohol-Soaked: The Nightbane is drenched with liquor to the point that any clothing is soaked through, the liquid drips to the ground, and its smell pervades the surrounding area. The character also moves in a stumbling manner as if permanently drunk. **Bonuses:** +1D6 Hit Points, +3D6 S.D.C., +1 to the P.S. and P.E. attributes, +5 to roll with punch, fall or impact, +3 to save vs poison and Horror Factor, never has a hangover, and interrogators suffer a -30% Interrogation skill penalty when trying to get anything useful out of this 'Bane. Cold attacks, even magical ones, only do 10% of their normal damage. **Penalties:** -2 to the I.Q. and M.E. attributes, poor memory and subject to blackouts, -3 on Perception Rolls, -2 on initiative, -30% on all Communications skills, and -10% on all other skills. The alcohol-soaked Nightbane has a 50% chance of catching fire from any fire attacks, in which case he takes an additional 3D6 damage per melee round for 1D6+4 rounds or until the fire is put out.

41-50% Branded Loyalty: 1D6+1 product names are burned into the Nightbane's skin. These may be brands of alcohol, cigarettes, prescription drug manufacturers or the names of drugs, etc. These brands are rough in appearance and always in clearly visible places like the forearms, chest, tops of hands, wrists, neck and

face. **Bonuses:** +2 to the P.E. attribute, +3D6 to S.D.C., impervious to any negative effects and disease from the products whose logo is branded into his skin, and +1 to Horror Factor. **Penalties:** -2 to the M.E., M.A. and P.B. attributes, and -40% to skills such as Disguise, Impersonation, Seduction and Undercover Ops.

51-60% Rolling Paper or Leafy Skin: The skin of the Morphus form is composed of overlapping green or brown leaves, or a paper similar to that used to hand-roll cigarettes. At various points on the body the skin may appear to be yellowing and the eyes resemble a lit, smoldering cigarette. Small wisps of smoke sometimes issue forth from the eyes, nostrils and mouth, especially when excited or agitated, and the breath smells of cigarettes. **Bonuses:** +5D6 to S.D.C. Heat and fire do half damage (even magic fire), smoke has no adverse effect while in Morphus form, and +1 to Horror Factor. **Penalties:** -3 to the M.A. and P.E. attribute, and a persistent cough imposes a -30% to Prowl, Performance and Public Speaking skills.

61-70% Pipe Throat: The throat of the Nightbane is at least partially replaced by metal or glass tubing. This has a drastic effect on the sound of the character's voice and breathing (think Darth Vader). The voice has a rasping, wheezing or even gurgling quality and the piping may or may not glow red as the Nightbane speaks or breathes. At the same time, acrid smoke regularly wafts from the mouth and nostrils and hangs about the character like a shroud. **Bonuses:** The Nightbane is immune to smoke, sulfur, tear gas and other such airborne toxins/poisons, +1 to Horror Factor, and Blowing Smoke (special): The Nightbane can blow smoke in rings for entertainment or as a signal, or can blow a gust of smoke into an opponent's face (3 foot/0.9 m range). The smoke temporarily irritates the eyes and lungs, imposing a -1 penalty to Perception Rolls and all combat rolls for one melee round (15 seconds). **Penalties:** -1D6 from the permanent P.P.E. base, bad breath, -1 to Perception Rolls, -1 to strike with ranged weapons due to the obscuring smoke and a persistent cough that also imposes a -25% penalty to Prowl and Seduction.

71-80% Rotted Teeth: Many of the teeth are brown or yellow, cracked and broken, and 1D4x10% are missing. The teeth and gums are discolored and the breath is likely rancid. **Bonuses:** Bite attack does 2D4 damage (double damage to Nightlords and their demonic minions), +2D6 S.D.C., +1 to Horror Factor, and stench. The Nightbane can blow a gust of stench into an opponent's face (4 foot/1.2 m range). Victims roll to save vs non-lethal poison (16 or greater is needed to save). A fail roll means the foul smell temporarily irritates the eyes and lungs, and causes the stomach to churn (01-30% chance of vomiting, in which case the victim loses one melee round). The rancid smell imposes a -3 penalty to Perception Rolls and -2 penalty to all combat rolls for one melee round (15 seconds). A successful save means eyes suddenly burn but only -1 on Perception Rolls for one melee round. **Penalties:** -2 to the M.A. and P.B. attributes, and -30% to skills like Disguise, Undercover Ops, Barter, Seduction and Public Speaking.

81-90% 'Roid-Rage: Every muscle in the character's body looks larger but strained at all times. Veins stand out, breathing is heavy, and the expression on the face of the Morphus is almost always one of anger or madness. This does not make the Morphus larger or stronger, but someone with this feature seems to completely ignore physical injury. **Bonuses:** The character does not feel pain, +4 to the P.E. attribute, +1D6x10+20 S.D.C., and +1 to Horror Factor. **Penalties:** Because the Nightbane does not feel pain, he takes foolish risks, fights beyond rational limits, and does not realize when his S.D.C. and Hit Points plummet toward zero; -10% to save vs coma and death. Tends to be aggressive and quick to anger and violence.

91-00% Speed Freak: The Morphus form is gaunt and unhealthy looking. Dark circles ring the eyes, cheeks are hollow, rib bones are visible beneath the skin, and the Nightbane's hand and body shake slightly with nervous energy. It is as if the character hasn't slept or eaten in days. **Bonuses:** +1 to all Perception Rolls, +3 on initiative, +1 to parry and dodge, +10% to all Piloting skills, and talks fast, lives hard, and is +2 to save vs Horror Factor. **Penalties:** -1D4 to M.A., -10% on all skills that require a delicate touch due to trembling, and takes risks and tends to be a daredevil and death defying thrill-junkie who is sometimes a danger to himself and to those around him. Loves action, danger and speed.

Superbeing Table

While the primary milieu of the Nightbane setting is one of dark supernatural horror, it must be remembered that there is something more (or less) human about the Nightbane and their comparatively awesome powers that leads to comparisons between them and the super-heroes of comic book, film, and television fame. And what adolescent or young adult in modern society could help but consider these similarities when they wake up and find themselves transformed into a monstrous or beauteous being with superhuman abilities that seem to defy reality? Mutant. Superman. Defender of the weak. Protector of the innocent. Champion against evil. All these things can be said about many Nightbane and are apparent to those Nightbane who love the super-hero genre. They identified with a particular comic book character or type of superbeing so heavily that their Morphus exhibits features common to so-called super-heroes! The appearance of such features may reflect a specific, known character, a completely unique creation but with comic theatrics and noble sensibilities, or some blending of the two.

These Nightbane are often considered a bit naïve or too idealistic and even immature by their more experienced and pragmatic brethren, but they have also been known to display higher than average conviction to their morals and extreme valor under fire, and face difficult circumstances with a positive attitude. They, more than many other Nightbane, also care about ordinary people

and try to avoid collateral damage and protect those not blessed with superpowers.

Those Nightbane who style themselves after super-villains exhibit the same comic book flair and theatrics as their super-hero counterparts, but are known to be some of the most vindictive, maniacal and scheming adversaries to deal with, and tend to be shunned even by other Nightbane.

Roll percentile dice once for random determination, or pick one.

01-10% Super-Brain: The cranium of the Nightbane may be enlarged and even have the shape of a brain, or show the enlarged brain under bulletproof glass, or perhaps the character has the stereotypical "mad scientist" look. Whatever the case, the Nightbane becomes much more intelligent than normal while in Morphus form. Some Nightbane with this feature become attached to the increased cerebral power and find any excuse to stay in Morphus form. Others like returning to "normal" and thinking about one thing at a time rather than juggling five or more concepts or tasks simultaneously. **Bonuses:** +2D4+4 to the I.Q. attribute, +1D4+1 to M.E., +3 to save vs mind control, illusions and possession, +20% to ALL skills when in Morphus and knows 1D4+3

additional skills total from one or a combination of the following: Science, Medical, Electrical or Mechanical skills (with a +30% bonus) when in Morphus. **Penalties:** -2D6 to permanent P.P.E. base, -1D4 to the M.A. and P.S. attributes, -2 to the P.E. and Spd attributes, -1 on Perception Rolls and initiative (distracted), -2 to save vs magic, and -1 to Horror Factor.

11-21% Super-Fast: The legs of the Morphus may be exceptionally strong and muscular, and surrounded by an odd energy and may have special boots, and wings or lightning bolt design elements. Biomechanical Nightbane will be beautifully streamlined and aerodynamic. However this feature manifests, the Nightbane can move with blinding speed whether running, swimming, or flying. **Bonuses:** Multiply the character's initial Spd attribute number x10 and +1 extra attack per melee round! +2 damage to physical attacks, punches, kicks, body blocks, and strikes with a melee weapon per 20 mph (32 kph) above 40 mph (64 kph) the Nightbane is traveling. Even running at maximum speed does NOT fatigue the Nightbane in any way, and +3 to roll with punch, fall or impact. **Penalties:** -2D6+6 from the permanent P.P.E. base, -3 on Perception Rolls due to moving so fast and being distracted or bored, and -2 to save vs magic and illusions. High metabolism requiring the Nightbane to eat three times more than an average human being. Without enough food, double the Perception penalty, reduce speed and S.D.C. by half, -1 melee attack, and -15% on the performance of all skills.

21-30% Super-Strong: The musculature of the Morphus form is exaggerated like many comic book heroes. The upper body may even seem slightly out of proportion to the lower body just due to the sheer muscle mass packed into the chest, shoulders, and arms. With this overabundance of brawn, the raw physical power of the Nightbane is drastically increased. Some level of comic-style physics does seem to be at work, though, as the lifting and carrying capacity skyrockets. **Bonuses:** +1D4+10 to the P.S. attribute (and resulting Supernatural P.S. damage), handsome with a square chin and thick flowing hair, and punches and physical attacks do 50% greater damage to Nightlords, their demonic minions and all denizens of the Nightlands. The hero is able to lift and carry *triple* the normal weight as well as throw objects three times farther than normal. +1D6x10 to S.D.C. and +2 to Awe/Horror Factor. **Penalties:** -1 to the P.P. attribute and -1D4+2 to Spd, -1D6 from permanent P.P.E. base, and -30% to skills like Disguise, Impersonation and Undercover Ops.

31-40% Chiseled Jaw and Physique or the Bold and the Beautiful: In Morphus, The character has the good looks of the traditional comic book hero/heroine, i.e. movie star with rugged good looks, perfect skin and beautiful hair that stays perfectly coiffed even in the most brutal battle. The face and body are well-proportioned, chiseled and sexy, and may look nothing like the Facade! In short, the ideal of the perfect human specimen without physical flaws. **Bonuses:** +1D4+1 to P.S. and P.B. attributes, +6D6+10 to S.D.C., +1 to Awe/Horror Factor, +10% (in addition to possible M.A. or P.B. attribute bonuses) to charm and impress,

or evoke trust or intimidation, and +20% to Public Speaking and Seduction skills (though no true hero would do the latter). **Penalties:** -2 to the M.E. attribute, -2D6 to the permanent P.P.E. base, -10% on the performance of all other skills, and may underestimate his opponent and overestimate his own abilities.

41-50% Super-Costume: The Morphus is clad in a dynamic costume befitting a cartoon or comic book super-hero. This might be the ubiquitous spandex body-suit that may or may not cover the head and face, and could display a host of different styles, with and without a flowing cape. A crest, symbol or emblem is likely to be worn on the chest of his costume and or belt buckle. Whatever the individual looks like, the suit marks the Nightbane as a crusading hero and typically draws attention. **Bonuses:** +2 to the M.A. and P.B. attributes, +2D4x10 to S.D.C., +2 to Natural A.R., and +1 to Awe/Horror Factor. It also completely regenerates damage at the same rate as the Nightbane heals. **Penalties:** -10% to the Prowl and -20% to skills such as Camouflage, Disguise, Impersonation, Tailing and Undercover Ops in Morphus form unless the costume can somehow be concealed.

51-60% Oversized, Flowing Cape or Cloak: The Nightbane wears an oversized cape or cloak that clasps to the shoulders and/or goes around the throat and drapes to below the knees. This garment gently billows behind the character even in the absence of a breeze. The colors and overall design of the cape or cloak are left to the player, and can be brightly colored or dark and ominous, and may bear some kind of emblem or crest that represents the Nightbane's heroic persona. The same crest or emblem is likely to be worn on the chest of his uniform or costume. The cape also represents some cool powers, described below. **Bonuses:** +1D6 to Spd attribute, the cape itself has 1D6x10+40 S.D.C. and a Natural A.R. of 14. It is large enough to completely cover the Nightbane and up to two other adults to serve as a temporary shield or shelter to protect against gunfire, explosions, falling debris, etc., +20% to the Concealment skill when hiding things in the cape. The cape enables the superbeing to hover, float and fly in the air at a speed equal to his Spd attribute (so probably not very fast, but still, he can fly!), and +2 to Awe/Horror Factor. **Penalties:** -1D4 to P.E. and -1 to P.P. attributes, -2D6 from permanent P.P.E. base, and -10% to all Physical skills, including Climbing and Prowl, as the cape gets in the way.

61-70% Energized: The Morphus is frightening because fire or energy covers or crackles around the head and conceals the face except for glowing eyes and the inside of the mouth. This Morphus channels and generates energy that causes the character to faintly glow and crackle with ripples of energy, be it fire, electricity, or other type of energy. The color of the energy can be almost anything. Any super-hero style costume may reflect the character's energy power or not. **Bonuses:** +2 to P.P., +1D6x10+20 S.D.C., resistant to energy (takes half damage) and is able to fire an energy blast (fire, electricity, laser beam, energy beam). <u>Energy Blast (special)</u>: 3D6 damage +1 point per level of

experience; double damage to the Nightlords, their demonic minions, all creatures from the Nightlands, and all demons. Range: 200 feet (61 m) +20 feet (6.1 m) per level of experience. Each blast counts as one melee attack. **Penalties:** -4D6+6 from the 'Bane's permanent P.P.E. base, -2 from M.A. and M.E., -50% to Prowl, Disguise, Seduction, and Undercover Ops in Morphus, and tends to be aggressive and violent in Morphus form and enjoys combat and violence.

71-80% Technonaut or Cyborg: The Morphus is that of a half-man, half-machine monster with bionic or Biomechanical or bio-engineered (could be chitinous or bone) body parts and living armor that is part of the head, face, neck, shoulders, arms, hands, thighs and lower legs. Whatever the material – metal, ceramic, resin, bone, chitinous shell, etc. – it is a living part of the Nightbane's body. This may have grown out of the fact that the character loves technology and/or science fiction, or the idea of human-alien hybrids or cyborg-like characters such as Mr. Spock, Mr. Data, the Borg, Cylons, Darth Vader, Terminator, etc. **Bonuses:** +1D6 to P.S. and +2D6 to Spd, +1D6x10+80 to S.D.C., Natural A.R. 14, +1 to Horror, Factor and has one of the items listed under *81-90% Gadgeteer*, below, with double the range (where applicable). The mechanical or non-flesh and blood components of the Morphus self-repair and completely regenerate at twice the rate that the Nightbane heals. **Penalties:** -2 to M.A., M.E. and P.B. attributes, -2D6 from permanent P.P.E. base, -30% to skills like Disguise, Impersonation, Prowl, Seduction and Undercover Ops in Morphus form, and -3D6 P.P.E. points from the permanent P.P.E. base.

81-90% Gadgeteer: This individual probably thinks of himself as a super-spy or ninja and the Morphus reflects that. The typical Morphus is a super-spy type jumpsuit with mask and may include a high-tech pair of gauntlets or gloves that go up to the elbow, and maybe an eyepiece or goggles (whether it actually does something or is strictly for show), as well as gadgets that are either built into or strapped onto his body, or carried in a backpack (may be a hard-shell backpack), web vest, and/or utility belt that is part of the Morphus. The gadgets, even if seemingly loose objects like a gun, tools, boots, backpack, etc., are literally a part of the character and cannot be used by anyone else (they do not work for anyone but that specific Nightbane).

Bonuses: +1D4 to I.Q. and M.A. attributes, +1D4x10+10 to S.D.C., +5% to Prowl and any Espionage or Rogue skills, and gets 1D4+3 of the gadgets listed below. The mechanical or non-flesh and blood components of the Morphus self-repair at the same rate that the Nightbane heals. If destroyed or lost, it takes 24 hours for a gadget to re-materialize. Each gadget has only 20 S.D.C. unless otherwise noted. **Penalties:** -1D4 to P.S., -2D6+16 from permanent P.P.E. base, -20% to skills like Disguise, Impersonation, Seduction and Undercover Ops while wearing all of his gear and gadgets in Morphus form. When most of his gadgets are destroyed, out of ammo or lost and only one or two remain, the Nightbane loses his confidence and is -30% to the performance

of all skills, -1 melee attack, and all combat bonuses are reduced by half.

The Gadgets: Choose 1D4+2 of the following.

1. **Lock Pick Tool**: A small tool (or cybernetic finger) that looks like a lock pick or serrated spike that fits into a lock. It has a 92% ability to Pick Locks the same as the skill when used to pick civilian grade locks of all kinds, within 1D4 melee actions; -20% to pick high-tech locks, military grade locks or alien locks. This device can also be used to start any car and most vehicles (G.M. discretion). It also imparts upon the Nightbane the Locksmith and Safecracking skills at a base level of 50% (does not improve with experience), but they are only available in Morphus form.

2. **Eggshell Grenades**: 1D6+2 small spheres that emit a thick cloud of smoke when shattered. The smoke obscures vision in a cloud that covers a 10 foot (3 m) radius, imposing a -8 penalty to combat rolls for all inside the area of effect (including the Nightbane). Eggshell grenades are intended for distraction and evasion purposes.

3. **Glide Pack**: This is a small backpack or folded membrane mounted on the Nightbane's back that opens up and extends into glider wings. While this set of wings does not provide powered flight, it does enable the character to leap from a rooftop, skyscraper, high place or aircraft and make a controlled descent from any height. Piloting the glider is done with a 74% proficiency +1% per level of experience, and the Nightbane is +1 to dodge while gliding. The wings have 50 S.D.C. each.

4. **Grapple Gun**: The item may appear to be an oversized flare gun or something built into or attached to the forearm (point and shoot). Regardless of the form it takes, this tool actually fires a mechanical or magnetic grapple attached to a 100 foot (30.5 m) spool of high-test cable that is itself anchored to a miniaturized winch on the "gun" or in his back or backpack. Hits on a successful strike roll of 8 or better (-2 if shooting at a moving target or he is moving, -2 if the target is smaller than a microwave oven; penalties are cumulative). The cable has 20 S.D.C. per foot (0.3 m) and can hold up to 1,000 pounds (450 kg).

5. **Laser Torch**: This miniature cutting laser is either a hand-held device or Biomechanical unit built into one of the fingers or forearm (there may be a Biomechanical cable that leads to the fuel canister on his hip, back or backpack). The laser can slice through most materials in seconds! Wood, plaster, plastic, ceramic, aluminum, rubber, and other soft materials can be cut at a rate of 15 feet (4.6 m) per melee round, while concrete, stone, ballistic ceramics, iron, steel, safes or molecular bonded super-materials/alloys are cut at a speed of one foot (0.3 m) per melee round (15 seconds). It can be used as a weapon but has the same range as a punch, is -2 to strike and inflicts 2D6 damage. Each laser strike counts as one melee attack. The payload for the torch is effectively unlimited and it has a range of six inches (0.15 m).

6. **Mini-Map**: This is a device that uses a variety of sensors to display a rough map of the surrounding 50 feet (15.2 m) and up to one story above and below the character's current location. The display includes an icon for the character as well as a compass bearing and GPS coordinates and is projected onto a visor, eyepiece, or wrist-mounted digital screen. This tool adds +30% to all Navigation skill rolls and ensures that the Nightbane always knows the lay of the land even on unfamiliar turf. Must have GPS access outdoors and computer access to floor plans or tap into the existing security camera systems. If neither is available (like inside most homes, old warehouses, factories and buildings, caves, and sewer systems, etc.), there is no map or floor plan/ layout available.

7. **Multi-Optical System**: High-tech or unusual looking goggles are part of this character's suit and headgear, or Biomechanically built right into his face! It provides: Laser rangefinder and telescopic zoom (2 mile/3.2 km range), low-light compensation (passive nightvision; range: 1,000 feet/305 m), infrared and ultraviolet view modes (range: 1,000 feet/305 m), macro-lens (20x magnification), and an auto-tint feature that protects against sudden flashes of light.

8. **Rebreather Mask**: This is a small mouthpiece or half-mask that fits over the nose and mouth and may be part of the character's mask, helmet or head gear. It enables the Nightbane to breathe underwater for up to 1D4 hours. Needs the same amount of time to recharge with a new oxygen supply.

9. **Rocket Jump Boots**: Slightly oversized boots or Biomechanical lower legs provide the Nightbane with the ability to perform thruster assisted leaps. 50 feet (15.2 m) high or 12 feet (3.7 m) high and 100 feet (30.5 m) across. Engaging the rocket boots when dropping or falling from a height of up to 200 feet (61 m) high enables the Nightbane to land on his feet with a soft thud and no damage. It slows the descent from higher falls, but the Nightbane still takes half damage. Rocket powered leap kicks or body block, count as two melee attacks but do an additional 10 points of damage and have a 01-50% chance of knocking a human-sized opponent off his feet (victim of knockdown loses initiative and one melee attack).

10. **Stun Bola**: The bola consists of two or three lengths of high-tensile cord with weighted ends. These can be fired from a gun or from a Biomechanical weapon built in the forearm, or twirled and thrown to wrap around a humanoid target in an attempt to lash together the legs or to knock a weapon or device out of an opponent's hands (-2 to disarm and requires a Called Shot, the intended victim can only try to dodge). It takes 1D4+2 melee actions to untangle the legs, or a Supernatural P.S. of 30 or greater to snap the cords in one melee attack, or 30 S.D.C. to cut yourself free. PLUS the bola releases a burst of electricity meant to stun or incapacitate its victim. A roll of 13 or higher is needed to save. A successful save means one point of damage but no penalties. Failure to save means the victim is stunned, -2 attacks for that melee round and -3 on all combat rolls for 1D4 melee round (15-60 seconds). If the roll to save was 5 or lower, the victim is dazed and unable to attack and is barely aware of what's happen-

ing around him for 1D4 melee rounds. **Note:** Has three sets of bolas. Stun bolas can be recovered and reused, unless damaged or destroyed, in which case it takes 24 hours for them to reappear.

91-95% Mutant or Alien: The superbeing has muscles and chiseled features, wears a super-hero costume and/or cape, but has an unearthly skin color (blue, green, red, orange, white like snow, black like pitch, etc.) and inhuman features – think Star Trek aliens or the X-Men. **Bonuses:** +1 attack per melee, +1 to I.Q., +1D6 to P.P. or P.S. (pick one), +2 to M.A. attribute, +1D6x10+12 to S.D.C., +1 to Horror Factor, and +10% to Public Speaking and Seduction (though no true hero would do the latter). **Penalties:** -2 to the M.E. attribute, -3D6 to the permanent P.P.E. base, -10% on the performance of all skills, and may underestimate his opponent and overestimate his own abilities.

96-00% Theme Music: Dramatic or heroic music follows the Nightbane wherever he or she goes. These melodies seem to emanate from the air around the character or may play through speakers on Biomechanical Nightbane. The music automatically matches the mood of the Nightbane (up-tempo when fighting, slow and plaintive when contemplative, perplexed or depressed, light when happy, bold when triumphant, etc.). When the character wishes to make a grand entrance or attempts some daring feat, one particular song will play, giving him or her a personal theme song. This music may be silenced at will, but the Nightbane must concentrate to do so. **Bonuses:** +1 to all saving throws and +2 to Awe/Horror Factor at all times. The character gets an additional +1 melee attack, +4 to damage, and +1 to strike, parry, dodge or disarm, but only when his music is playing! **Penalties:** Other than possibly annoying others, Prowl is impossible while the music is playing, and when the theme music is NOT playing, the Nightbane is -1 melee attack, -2 on all combat maneuvers, -2 to save on all saving throws, -2 to save vs Horror Factor, and -15% on skill performance.

New Common Talents

The number in brackets indicates which level of experience some powerful Talents become available.

All-Nighter
[3] Ashes to Ashes
Blast Wave
[4] Bomb-Maker
Bookworm
[3] Brain Freeze
Bypass
[2] Chain Lightning
Channel Speed
Channel Strength
[4] Chronosphere
[5] Darkblast
[2] Dark Edge
[2] Darkmetal Infusion
Death-Grip
Down the Drain
[7] Dust in the Wind
[3] Earthworks
Eavesdrop
Encryption
[2] Fear No Evil
[4] Flurry
[7] Form-Lock
[2] Frightener
Ghost Tag
Gunslinger

Hotwire
[4] Hound Leash
[2] Hyper-Awareness
[3] Ignorance is Bliss
Inferno Fist
Iron Will
Jam Senses
[6] Killing Spree
Launch
Leap
[2] Leave No Trace
Livewire
[2] Mage Siphon
[7] Mass Transit
[2/4] Mimic Spell
[2] Mimic Talent
Mirror Sense
[4] Mirror Shield
[4] Nega
[2] Open Channel
Phantom Limb
Pipe Bomb
Pocket Change
Raven Wings
[4] Reality Mooring
[3] Skill Stealer

Sky Writer
[3] Solar Flare
Switchboard Operator
Trap Shadow
Ultra-Vision
Wall Runner
[2] Wall Whisperer
Witch-Hunter's Sight

All-Nighter

Since Nightbane still need a relatively normal amount of sleep, this simple Talent can be incredibly useful. Using All-Nighter staves off the effects of sleep deprivation for an entire day at a time and enables the user to remain fully awake and be completely alert without sleep. This can be particularly useful when on guard or lookout duty, on the run from the authorities, or when trying to maintain a dual-identity as an average citizen and resistance fighter. Using All-Nighter also gives the Nightbane a slight Perception bonus of +1 and a +3 to save against sedatives or sleep-inducing powers.

Limitations: Using this Talent only delays the need for sleep, so eventually the character will have to catch up on rest to the tune of at least four hours for each day of sleep that was skipped. All-Nighter can only be activated once per day, and may not be used on an unwilling subject.

Note that while it is technically possible to stay awake indefinitely with this Talent, it is not natural and feels uncomfortable to go more than 3-5 days without sleeping. After 7 consecutive days of being awake, roll once each day on the Random Insanity Table on page 44 of the **Nightbane® RPG**. These insanities are temporary and disappear after the required amount of rest.

<u>Range</u>: Self or one other by touch.

<u>Duration</u>: 24 hours.

Cost: One P.P.E. to acquire permanently. Twelve P.P.E. per use.

Ashes to Ashes

To activate this Talent, the Nightbane must be holding or touching a combustible object/item to sacrifice so that he may transfer the fiery damage to his intended target. The item held or touched is reduced to ashes in a flash of flames destroying it utterly. In the same instant, that fire is directed at the true target of the character's choosing; line of sight required. The damage unleashed depends on the weight of the sacrificed object.

1-2 pounds (0.45 to 0.90 kg) = 1D6 damage: Heavy books, a medium-sized carved statue, axe handle, hockey stick, shovel handle, broom, mop, cane, fallen branch, a pair of blue jeans or slacks, a dress, a heavy jacket, a typical bed pillow, and similar items.

3-5 pounds (1.3 to 2.25 kg) = 2D6 damage: Large, heavy books, baseball bat, staff, a large picture frame, and similar.

6-20 pounds (2.7 to 9 kg) = 4D6 damage: Very large, heavy books, small shelving, small or light table, most simple wooden chairs, wooden folding chairs, very large picture frame, small split log, and similar.

25-35 pounds (11 to 16 kg) = 1D4x10 damage: Hollow-core interior door, small coffee table, desk chair/office chair, folding wooden table, wooden chest, and similar.

40-80 pounds (18 to 36 kg) = 2D4x10 damage: wood pallet, bookshelf, wooden kitchen table, large coffee table, solid-core door (usually an exterior door), light to medium desk, medium dining room table, armchair/easy chair, large log for fireplace and similar.

85-120 pounds (38 to 54 kg) = 2D6x10 damage: Heavy wood table, picnic bench, large heavy desk, large dead tree branch, log, and similar.

The target has no chance to dodge out of the way because he is just suddenly consumed in flames. HOWEVER, living targets (as opposed to an inanimate object, fence, wall, streetlight, vehicle), get to save vs magic. A roll of 15 or higher is needed to save. Failure means full damage. A successful save vs magic means the intended victim takes only 20% damage (round down). Note that the target of the attack can be something like an object or structure and does not have to be flammable to be damaged.

Limitations: This Talent can only be performed when in Morphus and it is not available until third level of experience. Only a single, *combustible* object (generally nothing larger than a love seat) can be sacrificed and its energy channeled to another target, and not anything like an entire house or the front porch, or part of a fence or wall. The item must be combustible, items made of ceramic, metal, plastic, stone, or concrete cannot be used. Limited to wood, paper, rubber and fabric. Magic items cannot be sacrificed nor can a living tree/plant, person or animal. Portions of objects cannot be sacrificed either, it's all or nothing. Damage is always done to a target's armor or magical shields first, and beings impervious to fire take no damage, though clothing and personal belongings on the target's person may be burned to a crisp. Those resistant to fire take half damage.

<u>Range</u>: Touch for the sacrificed object that is turned into ash, and 100 feet (30.5 m) for the attack delivered upon the real target.

<u>Duration</u>: Instant.

Cost: Thirteen P.P.E. to acquire permanently. Two P.P.E. for every weight category.

Blast Wave

This Talent enables a Nightbane to generate a powerful concussive shock wave that originates from his person. This wave of force expands rapidly outward in all directions or just in front of him, sending anyone and anything not sufficiently heavy or secured, flying several yards/meters away, and shattering fragile objects like windows. While this is primarily a defensive Talent meant to force back enemies within melee range, under the right circumstances it can be used to deadly effect; such as on the roof of a skyscraper. Victims caught in the shock wave are thrown 1D6 yards (0.9 to 5.5 m), take 2D6 damage, lose initiative, lose two melee attacks and are shaken up; -5% on the performance of all skills for one melee round. Reduce damage, but not penalties by half with a successful roll with impact of 16 or better.

Limitations: The user can only expend 6 P.P.E. per level of experience on this Talent's activation. Also note that the Nightbane cannot selectively affect those within the radius or forward arc of the blast. Everyone takes damage and is thrown. The only exceptions are those inside a vehicle or one to two people in physical contact with the Nightbane who are willed to be protected from the wave.

Range: 20 foot (6.1 m) radius around the Nightbane, or a wide, forty foot (12.2 m) swath in front of him. Can control range/area of effect in increments of three feet (one yard/meter).

Duration: Instant.

Cost: Six P.P.E. to acquire permanently. Double this activation cost if used in Facade form.

Bomb-Maker

Most common among Nightbane belonging to the Resistance or Warlords factions, this Talent enables the user to transform inert substances into a variety of lethal explosives. For instance, a glass bottle of olive oil can be changed into a gasohol-filled Molotov cocktail, a barrel of sawdust into one of gunpowder, or a handful of clay or putty into C-4. While these explosives mimic the properties of their real-world equivalents (nitroglycerin is unstable, gunpowder won't ignite when wet, etc.), the blast radius and damage they unleash depends on the P.P.E. used to transform the substance as well as the amount.

Damage: 4D6 S.D.C. from "low-grade" explosives like TNT or gunpowder per 10 P.P.E. points spent, makes a one liter or one pound (0.45 kg) amount of low-grade explosive with a blast radius of 4 feet (1.2 m).

15 P.P.E. creates a half pound (0.225 kg) of high-explosives like plastique that does 1D4x10 S.D.C. damage with a blast radius of 3 feet (0.9 m).

Any explosives created with this Talent are indistinguishable from the genuine explosives, which also means they can be detected and neutralized in the same manner. These substances are NOT magical in nature and will not do extra damage to beings vulnerable to magic. It is interesting to note that this Talent is similar to abilities over matter and energy exhibited by the Nightlords, which if brought to the attention of Spook Squad would only serve to reinforce their suspicions and fears about the Nightbane.

Limitations: Nightbane can only use this Talent in Morphus form. Not available until 4th level. Only the explosive substance is created, not the containers for or means to detonate it. This means that for something like C-4, an electronic detonator will be required for it to be of any use. Likewise, to create things like grenades or land mines, the Nightbane or allies will have to acquire the proper casings in which to install the explosive (or substance to be converted).

Range: Touch to transmute into an explosive material.

Duration: The explosive material remains viable for 6 hours per level of experience. After that the explosive becomes inert and reverts back to its original material.

Cost: Seventeen P.P.E. to acquire permanently.

Bookworm

With this Talent active, a Nightbane is able to quickly obtain any knowledge written on paper or similar material. To do so, the book, magazine, scroll, or whatever written source is devoured whole. While this may seem odd, it actually has a couple of advantages. The first is that once the pages are swallowed, every word is instantly known by the Nightbane. Another advantage is that the language the text is written in does not prevent the Talent user from understanding the content, even if it is as obscure as an ancient and/or forgotten language.

The bonuses/effects vary depending on what information is consumed. Eating a book or magazine, the character knows and remembers everything in it as if he had just read it. A diary or a handwritten journal could reveal a critical clue relevant to an investigation. Technical or instructional material temporarily gives the Talent user the information in the book AND 1-4 skills at 90% (or boosts existing skills to the 90%+1D6% level) required to use that knowledge (i.e. repair an engine, computer programming or operation, piloting an aircraft, etc.). On the rare occasion the pages of a spell book or scroll is devoured, it temporarily enables the Bookworm to cast that spell (or spells) contained in it, but only if the Talent user can already cast spells. If there is no understanding of magic, the Nightbane cannot cast spells.

Devoured text is not subject to any real biological processes and simply ceases to exist after being eaten – its knowledge or abilities available one melee round (15 seconds) after being eaten. It should be noted that Nightbane in the Seekers might be in the best position of any of their brethren to use this Talent, though a very few do so as destroying knowledge is tantamount to heresy for this covetous Faction. Many Nocturne Nightbane, however, have been known to make use of

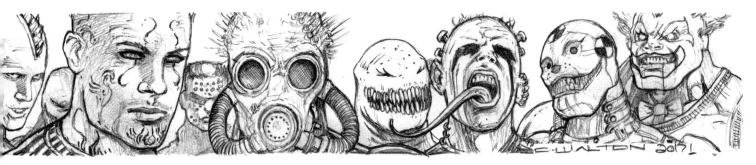

Bookworm for a quick knowledge boost in times of need. This fact has caused no small amount of friction between these two groups.

Limitations: Usable in Morphus form only. Any source devoured is utterly destroyed. Only biological material can be devoured, meaning that items like stone inscriptions, overhead transparencies (printed on clear plastic), photos on photographic paper, slides, and similar are unable to be absorbed. Devouring enchanted or cursed tomes may have unforeseen consequences, so G.M.s should use their best discretion. Any knowledge gained is *not* permanent, and disappears whenever the duration of the Talent lapses.

<u>Range</u>: Self.

<u>Duration</u>: One hour per level of experience.

Cost: Seven P.P.E. to acquire permanently. One P.P.E. per 25 pages of most mundane texts, but 2 P.P.E. *per each page* of a spell book or page equivalent for a scroll.

Brain Freeze

When a person consumes a cold substance too quickly, it can cause acute pain often referred to as "brain freeze." This Talent allows the Nightbane to induce a similar experience in others, but magnified to a much greater and debilitating degree. If the target fails to make a saving throw vs magic of 15 or higher (include any P.E. bonus), then he is stricken by a severe, temporary pain that seems to spread from between his eyes straight to the back of the skull. When in the grips of Brain Freeze, the victim is -5 on Perception Rolls, -2 on all combat rolls, automatically has initiative last, skill performance is done at -30%, and spell casting or the use of psionics or Talents is impossible until the duration of Brain Freeze expires. And unless it is obvious, the victim cannot remember what he or she was about to say or do. If in the middle of a skill, he cannot remember the next step until the freeze is over.

Limitations: Can only be used in Morphus form. Not available until 3rd level. Has no chance to affect immortal beings or supernatural creatures with physiologies radically different than humans (such as Nightland Hounds, Hunters, Hollow Men, Tarantuloids, etc.), though it *will* affect Night Princes (but not Nightlords), vampires, and Nightbane in Facade form or very human-looking Morphus forms.

<u>Range</u>: 200 feet (61 m), +20 feet (6 m) per level of experience; line of sight required.

<u>Duration</u>: 1D4 melees (15-60 seconds), though this can be extended (see cost below).

Cost: Ten P.P.E. to acquire the Talent permanently. Six P.P.E. for the initial attack and 1D4 melee round duration. If the target fails to save, the Talent user can choose to spend an additional 6 P.P.E. at the beginning of each subsequent melee round to extend the duration for another melee (15 seconds) up to eight times in a row.

Bypass

As the name suggests, this Talent allows users to disable both conventional and high-tech locks and electrical surveillance systems and cameras. This includes padlocks, magnetic seals, deadbolts, camera systems and alarms. Even complex electronic locks and alarms such as those used in high-security corporate and government facilities can be sprung given enough time.

Simple locks like those on store-bought diaries, cheap jewelry boxes, file cabinets, bedroom doors, or bathroom stalls are the easiest and quickest to bypass. Instant, counts as one melee attack/action.

Standard locks are those found on most houses and common businesses, and include the majority of padlocks, handcuffs, security doors, car doors, car trunks, car ignitions, and similar. Takes 1D4 melee rounds (15-60 seconds).

Complex locks are more robust than standard locks, such as those on prison-cell doors, locked hospital wards, commercial security doors, common safe/combination locks, keyless automobile ignitions, simple/basic commercial alarm and video systems, and similar. Shuts off the alarm and its sensor systems and any video cameras without triggering the alarm. However, the video feed goes dark and anyone watching the monitor screens will notice that the feed went dark, but no alarms were tripped (just a glitch or investigate?). Takes 1D4 minutes.

Advanced locks, high-tech safes and security systems as found in the highest security areas, including bank vaults, high-risk research and medical facilities, top-secret data centers, government and military facilities, and similar. These locks are almost impossible to crack under normal circumstances and require significant time and P.P.E. expenditure to get through even with this Talent. 4D4 minutes!

Limitations: Only usable in Morphus form and only affects a single lock per activation of this Talent. Use of Bypass disables locking mechanisms and any alarms, video cameras and other security systems that are tied into the lock/door. Does not work on magic locks or magical protections.

<u>Range</u>: Touch.

<u>Duration</u>: Varies as noted above.

<u>Saving Throws</u>: Locks also get a saving throw or difficulty quotient: 15 for advanced (and alien locks), 8 for complex, 5 for standard, 2 for simple. The Talent user needs to roll higher than the saving throw number on a D20 to successfully open the lock. A failed roll means it is still locked, try again.

Cost: Six P.P.E. to acquire permanently. One P.P.E. per use for simple locks, 2 P.P.E. for standard, 6 P.P.E. for complex mechanical or simple electronic locks, and 14 P.P.E. for the most advanced electronic locks or vault doors.

Chain Lightning

This Talent enables the Nightbane to unleash a devastating electrical attack capable of striking multiple enemies in close proximity to one another within a 30 foot (9.1 m) radius. The chain lightning jumping a second apart from one target to the next. The bolt of lightning generated strikes the first target for the full amount of damage, then moves on to another target to inflict one die less damage, and the next reduced by another die, until striking the last target for 1D6 damage. For example, if a character spent 9 P.P.E. to send out a bolt then the first target would take 3D6 damage, the second would take 2D6 damage, and the third target would sustain 1D6 damage. Chain lightning only travels from one living creature to the next and starts with the initial target and then leaps to the next closest, and the next closest after that in descending order. The Nightbane can dictate which targets will be hit beyond the first and the order of preferred targets, but this costs him two melee attacks. Otherwise, targets beyond the first are determined via proximity to one another.

The Chain Lightning Talent is useful against groups of enemies or adversaries, but can be especially effective on Hounds, Hound Masters, Great Hounds, Hunters, and anyone using *Darksteel* weaponry or armor. These enemies must make a saving throw of 12 or higher including any P.E. bonus or they become dazed! Dazed targets lose initiative and two attacks for that melee; these penalties *are* cumulative with successive attacks. Furthermore, Hunters and other flying creatures take additional damage from this Talent (use eight-sided rather than 6-sided dice for damage).

Limitations: Usable only by the Morphus. Not available until 2nd level. The maximum P.P.E. used to activate this Talent is limited to 9 per level of experience. Only damages living beings, not inanimate objects. Each individual in the area of effect can only be struck once per attack, so any damage capability remaining after all available targets are struck dissipates.

Range: 100 feet (30.5 m) +20 feet (6.1 m) per level of experience to a 30 foot radius (9.1 m; double distance and radius of effect in the Nightlands). Ideal against a cluster of enemies and users of Darksteel.

Duration: Instant.

Cost: Ten P.P.E. to acquire permanently. Nine P.P.E. for a 3D6 damage lightning blast to the initial target (2D6 to the next victim, 1D6 to the third). The amount of damage can be increased in increments of 1D6 at the cost of 3 P.P.E. per each 1D6 points of damage up to a maximum of 7 times, making the blast to the first target as much as 10D6 (or 1D6x10) damage! Then 9D6 damage to the next target, then 8D6, then 7D6, then 6D6, then 5D6, then 4D6, then 3D6, then 2D6 and finally 1D6, affecting as many as 10 targets within the area of effect. Most attacks, however, are less than this, usually starting out at 6D6 damage.

Channel Speed

One of a handful of Talents meant for use only in the *Facade form*, Channel Speed taps into the power of the supernatural Morphus form to temporarily add 6 points to the P.P. attribute and 10 points to the Spd attribute for a brief period. The character also gains +1 to initiative and +2 to strike, parry, and dodge (in addition to any possible bonuses from improved P.P.). While this Talent is active, the user's eyes dim and wisps of shadow rise like thin smoke from the hands and feet. Even though the Nightbane is in Facade form, he registers as a supernatural being for the duration of this Talent to any beings able to sense such things.

Limitations: Can only be used in Facade form. Only the bonuses listed above are added, do NOT add bonuses from Morphus features.

Range: Self only.

Duration: See cost below.

Cost: Eight P.P.E. to acquire permanently. Eight P.P.E. per two melee rounds (30 seconds).

Channel Strength

One of a handful of Talents meant for use only in the Facade form, Channel Strength temporarily adds 10 points to P.S. and 6 to P.E. in addition to providing 60 S.D.C. to the user. Any damage dealt to the character is subtracted from this additional temporary S.D.C. first. The character also gains +2 to save vs poison and disease, and +2 to save vs psionics, in addition to any possible bonuses from improved attributes. The Facade's strength is converted to Supernatural for the duration of this ability. While this Talent is active, the user's eyes dim and wisps of shadow rise like steam from the body, arms, and legs. Even though the Nightbane is in Facade form, he registers as a supernatural being for the duration of this Talent to any beings able to sense such things.

Limitations: Can only be used in Facade form. Only the bonuses listed above are added, do NOT add bonuses from Morphus features.

Range: Self.

Duration: See cost below.

Cost: Nine P.P.E. to acquire permanently. Nine P.P.E. per two melee rounds (30 seconds).

Chronosphere

Activating this Talent alters the temporal flow in the Nightbane's immediate vicinity. Anyone of the user's choosing within the affected radius must make a saving throw of 16 or higher including any P.E. bonus or find themselves temporarily moving at half their normal speed. Those affected have half the number of melee attacks (rounded up), as well as a -2 penalty to all combat rolls against anyone unaffected by the Chronosphere Talent. Anyone entering the area of effect after the initial activation must make the save as well or suffer the slowing effects. Likewise,

projectiles or other non-magical attacks leveled against those within the Chronosphere are -4 to strike and do half damage as they slow upon entering the affected area.

Note that Chronosphere is one of a handful of very rare Talents that can be used even in Facade form without any visual manifestation other than the slowed movement of those affected. The Talent user is not affected, but everyone else is. Those who can sense magic or anomalies in space and time will detect the Chronosphere.

Limitations: Not available until level four.

Range: Five foot (1.5 m) spherical radius per level of experience; double the radius for those with a Morphus feature from the Athlete Table.

Duration: See cost.

Cost: Sixteen P.P.E. to acquire permanently. Fourteen P.P.E. per melee round of effect (21 P.P.E. in Facade form). This Talent cannot be extended, but may be reactivated after the duration expires or it is canceled, provided the user has sufficient P.P.E.

Darkblast

The Darkblast Talent can be thought of as an improved *Shadow Blast*. Unlike the latter Talent which is almost instantaneous, this Darkblast causes shadows to gather around two arms as the attack "charges." Once fully charged, the two limbs are brought together to fire a large stream of dark energy that packs even more punch than a Shadow Blast. In the alternative, the blast may be fired from the eyes or mouth (or approximate area thereof). Users are +2 to strike with this attack.

Prerequisites: This Talent cannot be selected until fifth level, and even then the Nightbane must have the *Shadow Blast Talent* before acquiring Darkblast.

Limitations: Usable in Morphus Form only. The Nightbane can spend only 3 P.P.E. on this Talent per level of his experience and must already know Shadow Blast.

Range: 1,500 feet (457.2 m).

Duration: It takes a few seconds to charge, meaning each Darkblast counts as two melee attacks.

Cost: Eleven P.P.E. to acquire permanently. Two P.P.E. per 2D4 damage dealt, up to a maximum of 16 P.P.E. for a 1D6x10 damage blast.

Dark Edge

Many Nightbane have seen the destructive power of *Darkblades* first-hand. While some liberate those weapons to use against the Nightlords and their minions, many refuse to use weapons that are tainted by evil and may falsely mark them as a Ba'al sympathizer. Instead many Nightbane develop the Dark Edge Talent to even the odds.

Using Dark Edge on any mundane blade temporarily imbues it with the same abilities as a Darkblade, and even turns the blade's edge to an ebony hue. While the Talent is in effect, the blade can be used to parry Darkblades without fear of damage, ignores an opponents' A.R., and inflicts double the normal damage dealt out by the weapon (e.g. a combat knife that normally does 1D6 damage would instead inflict 2D6 damage). An imbued blade may also be handed off to a friend or ally to use in combat.

Limitations: The character must be at least level two before selecting the Dark Edge Talent, and it can only be used in Morphus form. This Talent can only be used on non-magical blade weapons. It has no effect on magical blades or Darkblades. Weapons that are part of a Morphus are also ineligible for use with Dark Edge.

Range: Touch.

Duration: Four minutes per level of the Talent user.

Cost: Eight P.P.E. to acquire permanently. Ten P.P.E. per use.

Darkmetal Infusion

Activating this Talent reinforces a single stationary object (or portion thereof) with some of the strength of *Nightlands Darkmetal*, the substance used to create the infamous Darkblades. This ability might be used to prevent a door from being breached, a ceiling from collapsing under someone's weight, or just to beef up the protection of a concrete barricade in the middle of a firefight. The effect of this Talent will likely be obvious, though, as the object targeted blackens and takes on a dull sheen like that of Darkmetal ore.

In addition to strengthening the object against attack, this Talent also prevents anything from piercing the barrier and damaging anything behind it. Even high-power firearms and Darkblades cannot punch through the object's A.R. Only by depleting the total S.D.C. of the reinforced object can it be breached.

Limitations: Only usable in Morphus form. Not available until level two. Only 8 P.P.E. per level of experience may be spent to activate Darkmetal Infusion. The object being reinforced cannot be moved in any way or this Talent's effects are immediately negated.

Range: A 3 foot by 3 foot (1 x 1 m) area per level of experience up to 3 feet (1 m) away.

Duration: One minute per level of experience.

Cost: Eight P.P.E. to acquire permanently. Five P.P.E. per 100 S.D.C. added to the reinforced object, with a maximum of 500 S.D.C.

Death-Grip

With a name like "Death-Grip" it may confuse some people that this Talent inflicts no damage whatsoever. What this Talent does is allow the user to hold tight to objects or opponents with an unbreakable grip stronger than any vise. This ability has a number of uses. First, when subduing an opponent it requires a total Supernatural Strength twice that of the Talent user to even

attempt to break free. Even then, the target and any would-be rescuers still have to beat the Nightbane's P.S. x2. Second, the Nightbane cannot be disarmed of any handheld weapons, nor can an object be pulled or pried from his grip. Finally, Death-Grip can be exceedingly useful when hanging on to a moving vehicle, aircraft, flying monster, or object in order to prevent oneself from falling off or being knocked down. It also adds +20% to the Climbing skill and a +3 bonus to entangle for the duration of the Talent.

Limitations: Death-Grip can only be used in the character's Morphus form. Even if used on a fragile object or a victim's throat, this grip delivers NO damage, but the grip is strong.

Range: Touch/grasp.

Duration: See cost below.

Cost: Four P.P.E. to acquire permanently. Six P.P.E. per melee round of use.

Down the Drain

Primarily meant as a means of escape in urban settings, this Talent enables the user to liquefy himself and his belongings in order to travel through plumbing or other pipe or sewer systems. The Nightbane can control his movement as liquid (along with one or two passengers) through the pipes, including being able to move against water pressure, tide, waves, gravity, etc. If the duration ends before the user has reached a place that can accommodate his returning to humanoid form and normal size and shape, the liquefied traveler must automatically reactivate the Talent at the usual cost.

No matter whether the liquid looks like motor oil, sludge, sap, or blood, the movement speed is a constant 1,000 feet (305 m) per minute unless the current is faster. In liquid form the Nightbane and any passengers are immune to toxins/poisons and all physical attacks, but cannot attack either, not even with psionics. Even being forced through sewage filtration systems will not have any detrimental effect, though users will most likely find the experience to be disorienting and rather unpleasant.

Limitations: Available in Morphus form only. Other than escaping down a drain, moving through plumbing, or extending or deactivating this Talent, a Nightbane in liquid form can take no other actions. Also, all liquefied travelers are -4 on Perception Rolls as the surroundings and sensations are distorted and disorienting. Only the user and as many as two others, and their personal clothing/gear, can be transformed and travel via this Talent. Any large, heavy objects such as a large suitcase, duffel bag or piece of equipment are left behind. Unwilling travelers get to roll a saving throw vs magic to resist being transformed and transported in liquid form; they need a 12 or better.

Range: Self and up to two others by touch. Must be within 3 feet (0.9 m) of a drain or other open plumbing.

Duration: Varies (see cost below).

Cost: Ten P.P.E. to acquire permanently. Six P.P.E. per five minutes in liquefied form.

Dust in the Wind

For a certain number of Nightbane, especially among those who could be considered *ancient* (more than 100 years old), the preservation of their own life is of paramount importance to them. This mindset has led to a handful of older Nightbane acquiring the ability to be blasted or hacked to bits and still survive. If this Talent is activated *before* the character reaches zero Hit Points, then instead of falling into a coma or perishing, he appears to disintegrate into millions of black dust particles that are whisked away on a magical breeze.

Once this cloud has reached a predetermined safe point (up to 2,000 feet/610 m away), the dust particles reconstitute into the physical Nightbane. This leaves the character in a coma, trapped in whatever form he was in when reduced to zero Hit Points until he regenerates back to *full* Hit Points and at least half his S.D.C. If for some reason more than 20% of the dust is prevented from traveling toward this safe point, the Nightbane will remain in dust form for 1 hour per point of M.E. attribute. After that time, reconstitution and regeneration into physical form begins wherever the character is currently located, but reforms without an arm or leg and -10 Hit Points for every 10% of him that was missing. The lost limb and Hit Points are permanent losses that diminish the character.

Limitations: Usable in Morphus form only and not available until 7th level. Before this Talent can be used, a return point or safe haven has to be designated. This is the place he will return to and reconstitute. While in dust form, the Nightbane is effectively unconscious and unaware of his surroundings. He or she is only able to mindlessly home in on this safe haven (at a speed of 40 mph/64 kph). This could be the trunk or backseat of a car, the back of a box truck, under the stairs of a warehouse or building, an abandoned building, behind a dumpster, inside a supply closet, a dark corner in a parking structure, a rooftop, a ditch, and so on. The user is immune to physical attacks in this granular state of being, but any spell, psionic ability, or Talent that deals sufficient damage to the dust form to reduce the Nightbane to below zero Hit Points more than his P.E. attribute number, kills him.

Range: Self, but travel distance is 2,000 feet (610 m).

Duration: Changing to dust that is swept away by wind takes but a few seconds equal to two melee attacks (about 5-6 seconds) and then he is gone. As noted above, he remains a pile of dust in his hiding place until all Hit Points and half of his S.D.C. are regenerated (heals as normal for Nightbane).

Cost: Twenty-five P.P.E. to acquire permanently. 25 P.P.E. to activate.

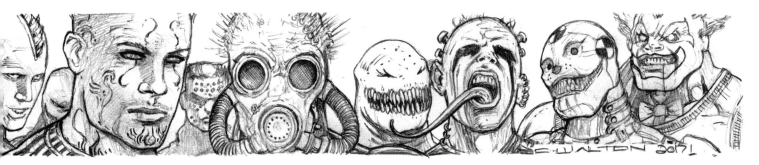

Earthworks

This Talent gives its user the power to shape the ground beneath him at will, whether it is completely natural such as rock or dirt, or manmade materials such as asphalt or concrete. Earthworks is typically used as a defensive power to create walls, barriers, cover to hide behind, trench to hide in, or even escape tunnels.

Any roll to strike that beats the Natural A.R. penetrates the barrier to hit something on the other side, but is the equivalent of shooting wild or shooting blind.

Dirt Barrier: 200 S.D.C. and an A.R. of 11 for a 10x10 foot (3x3 m) section that is 3 feet (0.9 m) thick. Light and medium caliber firearms will not penetrate the dirt wall, with each blast to the dirt barrier doing only one point of damage. Heavy weapons like machine-guns, high-caliber rifles and explosives do 70% of their normal damage to the barrier, but have a good chance of shooting right through the dirt wall.

Clay, Sand or Gravel Barrier: 300 S.D.C. and an A.R. of 14 for a 10x10 foot (3x3 m) section that is 3 feet (0.9 m) thick; small and medium caliber firearms, shotguns and similar inflict only one point of damage to these walls and will not penetrate the A.R. Heavy weapons like machine-guns, high-caliber rifles, explosives and energy blasts do half their normal damage to the barrier, and have a good chance of shooting right through the wall.

Asphalt or Cinder Block Barrier: 400 S.D.C. and an A.R. of 16 for a 10x10 foot (3x3 m) section that is 3 feet (0.9 m) thick; small and medium caliber firearms, shotguns and similar inflict only one point of damage to these walls and will not penetrate the A.R. However, energy blasts and heavy weapons like machine-guns, high-caliber rifles, explosives and energy blasts do one half their normal damage to the barrier, and have a poor chance of shooting right through the wall.

Stone or Concrete Barrier: 500 S.D.C. and an A.R. of 18 for a 10x10 foot (3x3 m) section that is 3 feet (0.9 m) thick; most caliber firearms including high-caliber rifles do no structural damage to these walls and will not penetrate the A.R. Only heavy weapons like heavy machine-guns, armor-piercing rifle rounds, rocket launchers, bazookas, explosives and energy blasts do one third their normal damage to the barrier, and have a fair chance of shooting right through the wall.

Any physical attack that penetrates the A.R. of a stone or concrete barrier only does half or one third damage to the wall and half damage to anyone it may hit on the other side. Shots that penetrate the barrier are the equivalent of shooting wild or partially blindly and are -6 to strike, and an attacker cannot make a Called Shot unless he can see his target, which a barrier may prevent.

Offensive Uses: Rolling Earth. The ground underneath one or more enemies can be made to rise a couple of feet and *roll*, knocking them off their feet and causing them to lose initiative and one melee attack. Those driving in moving vehicles must make a Piloting skill roll with a -20% penalty or drive off the road or crash. This can be done with earth, gravel, sand, clay, mud, asphalt or concrete roads and sidewalks. When the ground stops rolling as if it were a wave of water, the ground or concrete looks perfectly fine and normal.

Crash barrier. If the Talent user can erect the barrier fast enough, he can place the wall in front of a vehicle. Roll initiative. If the Nightbane using the Talent wins initiative, the wall goes up in front of the vehicle and it crashes into it. The vehicle can try to dodge by making a successful Piloting skill roll with a -30% penalty. A successful skill roll means one of three possible outcomes: a) the vehicle is able to stop just in time, b) is able to swerve around the barrier, or c) drives fast enough that the barrier goes up behind him and the vehicle is on the same side of the barrier as the character using the Talent, which could be a problem. A failed roll means it crashes into it. Of course, the range is very short (see Limitations, below), so this is only effective under certain circumstances.

Limitations: Can only be used in Morphus form. Not available until level three. This power will not work on plastic, rubber, or metal.

Range: 5 feet (1.5 m) +5 feet (1.5 m) per level of experience. The total area affected per load is 360 cubic feet (10.2 cubic meters) if shaping the earth. This amount is doubled if only tunneling, meaning the Nightbane can create a tunnel that is 6 feet by 6 feet (1.8 x 1.8 m) and 20 feet (6.1 m) in length. One additional load can be affected per activation at levels 7, 11, and 15.

Duration: The ability to control and shape a load of earth lasts for one melee round (15 seconds). Walls, barriers, trenches and tunnels remain in place for 2D4+2 minutes, unless made permanent. If the changes the Nightbane makes are not made permanent, the load of earth, stone or concrete returns to its original shape and location after 2D4+2 minutes.

Cost: Six P.P.E. to acquire the Talent permanently. Five P.P.E. for each temporary barrier. 32 P.P.E. if the structure is made to be permanent.

Eavesdrop

A very simple yet useful Talent, Eavesdrop allows a Nightbane to listen in on any conversations within range. When activated, the user's hearing becomes equivalent to a parabolic listening device. That means that the Nightbane can focus in on one person or a small group of people and listen to what they are saying from hundreds of feet (meters) away while simultaneously blocking out all but the loudest background noises. Even if the target(s) is behind a thin wall or a window, the conversation can be heard as if standing in the room with them.

Limitations: Does not provide any kind of language translation ability. If the target(s) is speaking on a phone or other device, the conversation intercepted may be one-sided unless audio from the phone could be overheard while standing adjacent the target (this relies mostly on the volume level of the device; rare).

Range: 200 feet (61 m) +50 feet (15.2 m) per level of experience. At least one target or a specific location (street corner, rooftop, window, etc.) must be visible for the Nightbane to Eavesdrop.

Duration: One minute per every 2 P.P.E. expended.

Cost: Four P.P.E. to acquire permanently. Two P.P.E. per minute of use.

Encryption

When active, this Talent automatically encrypts any form of communication the Nightbane uses and allows only intended recipients to hear and understand him clearly. If used when writing a note, a series of symbols is inscribed instead. If shouting a warning or orders, nonsense syllables or just a roar of sound is heard in place of intelligible language by everyone but the person or people the warning is intended for. Even surface thoughts are scrambled, making them nearly impossible for someone using Telepathy to understand. The only means of defeating this Talent is magical translation via the Tongues or Eyes of Thoth skill, or somehow recording the message and attempting to use the Cryptography skill to decipher it at a -40% skill penalty.

Limitations:

Range: Self.

Duration: See cost.

Cost: Three P.P.E. to acquire permanently. One P.P.E. per minute of use.

Fear No Evil

Many seasoned Nightbane become hardened and desensitized to the terrifying reality of fighting for survival against the supernatural horrors that hunt them. Those newly inducted into this war in the shadows are usually not so lucky. Since giving in to the all-too-human emotion of fear can cost precious seconds, some individuals find it prudent to develop a way to negate the fear, at least temporarily. Thus, Fear No Evil can be used before entering a conflict with supernatural foes like the Nightlords, Night Princes and their demonic minions, or any demonic or monstrous enemy, including fellow Nightbane. For the duration of this Talent, the user is rendered immune to the effects of Horror Factor. Even temporarily negates the fear caused by Phobias.

Limitations: Only usable in Morphus form, and not until second level. If the user is still engaged with an opponent when Fear No Evil lapses and Horror Factor either wasn't rolled or was failed, that character must immediately roll to save vs Horror Factor. While using this Talent the Nightbane is also -2 on all Perception Rolls.

Range: Self.

Duration: Two minutes (8 melee rounds).

Cost: Seven P.P.E. to acquire permanently. Eight P.P.E. to activate. By expending an additional 4 P.P.E. the Nightbane can keep Fear no Evil in place for one additional minute.

Flurry

This Talent is named for the amount of blows it allows the Nightbane to rain down upon opponents. Upon activation, Flurry grants the Nightbane preternatural combat speed +2 attacks per melee round, +2 on initiative, +2 to strike, parry, and disarm, +3 to dodge, with an additional +1 melee attack and +1 bonus to each when directly fighting a Nightlord, Night Prince, Night Princess or Greater Demon or dark god of any kind.

Limitations: Can only be used in Morphus form and cannot be selected until level four. Flurry can NOT be used in combination with other Talents that provide bonus attacks such as Firebreather or Dervish Dance.

Range: Self.

Duration: See cost below.

Cost: Seventeen P.P.E. to acquire permanently. Ten P.P.E. per melee round it is in place.

Form-Lock

With a disproportionate number of the supernatural beings involved in the *War of Light and Dark* being able to shape-shift or otherwise transform, some Nightbane have understandably developed Talents specifically intended to neutralize this ability.

When a shape-changing being is targeted by this Talent, and it fails to make a save vs magic at 15 or higher, the creature is unable to alter its physical form or have it altered by any other means for two minutes (or longer depending on how much P.P.E. is spent). It does not matter if the shape-changing ability is natural, magical, or via some other means. An affected vampire, for example, can't change into mist or an animal form, Nightlords cannot alter their size or appearance (though their ability to alter other matter is unaffected), and Nightbane are trapped in their current form, Facade or Morphus, until the effects of this ability lapse. This makes Nightbane with Form-Lock a potentially grave threat to their brethren as many are practically defenseless if trapped in their Facade. Thus, if a character is known to possess this Talent it will likely result in a certain amount of suspicion and fear from other Nightbane.

Limitations: Available in Morphus form only and not until 7th level.

Range: Line of sight up to 500 feet (152 m) away.

Duration: Two minutes plus, depending on the amount of P.P.E. expended.

Cost: Twenty P.P.E. to acquire permanently. 20 P.P.E. to Form-Lock one target for two minutes (successful or not, the P.P.E. is spent) and 20 P.P.E. per additional one minute to extend the Form-Lock.

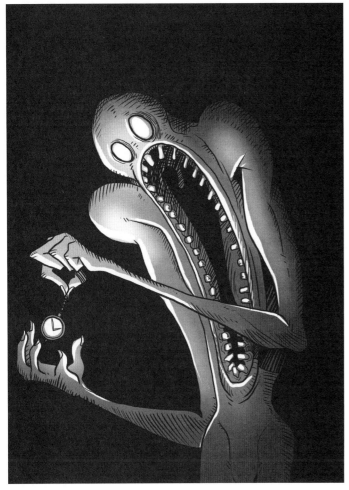

Frightener

Not every Nightbane is a terrifying monster to behold. For those who recognize the utility of being able to scare the living daylights out of opponents, the Frightener Talent provides that chance. Even Nightbane who usually have an Awe Factor (like many Barbies and Kens) will see that become a Horror Factor for the duration of the Frightener Talent.

While the exact manifestation of this Talent is as individual as each user, the commonality is that the character is made to seem scarier and more intimidating. The eyes might glow eerily or radiate a black aura, or bleed, or shadows around the Nightbane may deepen, and the character may even appear to grow in stature or become more corpse/zombie-like in appearance. In reality, any changes are really just magical illusions created by the Frightener Talent.

Limitations: Only able to be used in Morphus form and not available until level 2. The user is unable to select who is and isn't affected by this Talent, though allies who know about the Nightbane and know about this Talent are immune to the Horror Factor unless having to fight or restrain the character. The maximum Horror Factor possible while using this Talent is 15.

Range: Self, but the added fear level affects others who see the character up to 90 feet (27.4 m) away, +10 feet (3 m) per level of experience.

Duration: One melee round (15 seconds).

Cost: Eight P.P.E. to acquire permanently. Two P.P.E. per each +1 bonus to Horror Factor desired, up to a maximum Horror Factor of 15.

Ghost Tag

An interesting form of communication, this Talent allows Nightbane to leave messages by means of words or images that only certain others can see. These messages can be left on any surface such as a wall, sidewalk, table, etc., and are almost as common in some urban areas as common graffiti. The sides of buildings, doors, walls, fences, curbs, objects, vehicles, clothing, and even people can be "tagged" with a message, though they have to remain still while the message is placed on them.

Nightbane, Guardians, Astral Travelers, and *individuals who can See the Invisible* (even if by spell or psionics), can see these spectral messages. Psychics with at least one power from the Sensitive category may be able to see Ghost Tags, but only when looking for them or if the psychic knows they are present; requires a Perception Roll of 12 or better to find and read each message for these characters. If the psychic without See the Invisible does not know the Ghost Tag is present or is not actively looking for one, he needs to make a Perception Roll of 16 or better.

Though very few people realize it, Nightlords, their avatars, and Night Princes are also able to see Ghost Tags, though the latter have to roll for Perception the same as a psychic without the See the Invisible power would. Strangely, Hounds and Hunters are completely unable to see Ghost Tags, which causes some to speculate that Ghost Tags are a kind of illusion. Other minions can NOT see Ghost Tags unless a See the Invisible incantation is cast or they are a psychic sensitive with the ability.

Limitations: G.M.s should use their discretion regarding the size of the message, but 30 words in a minute is a good rule of thumb using 4-6 inch (10-15 cm) lettering.

Range: A Ghost Tag can be written by the Nightbane using his finger to write in the air and cast it upon a surface up to 6 feet (1.8 m) away.

Duration: The message can last for up to one week per level of the Nightbane, unless it is removed by its creator (at no P.P.E. cost) or tagged over by another character with this Talent.

Cost: Three P.P.E. to acquire permanently. Two P.P.E. to write a message of 30 words or less or draw a recognizable image. To write more, the Nightbane must extend the talent at a cost of 2 P.P.E. per each additional minute and another 30 words. Most Ghost Tags are kept short, such as, "The NSB is watching this place." "Safe Zone (and probably a date the message was left)." "Not safe (and probably a date)." "Staying at Jake's." "Meet us at Doug's." "Todd knows the way." "Nightbane are welcomed

here. Ask for Death Blade." "Nightbane stay out." "Mike Silva is an Ancient Nightbane – he can help you." "Be warned, Senator James Brown is a Night Prince." "Victor holds the answer." "Guardians are watching." "NMI was here." "This place is under the protection of the Shadow Slayer gang." "Don't trust anyone here." "Portal to the Nightlands." "Traitor." "Servant of the Nightlords." "Police here all Hollow Men and Doppelgangers." "Spook squad hunting ground. Be careful." "Steve is the spy." "Nightbane Underground Railroad." "Nightbane unite." "Join the Lightbringers." "Warlords rule." "Nocturne territory." "Scott is a Guardian you can trust." And so on.

Gunslinger

While most Nightbane come to rely primarily on their natural strength and abilities, there is a small minority who still place their faith in human technology, and more who see the benefits of having superior firepower. This Talent may be most common among Nightbane with a military, paramilitary, or police background, as well as anyone who finds themselves on the front lines of heavy conflict against the Nightlords and their minions. And then there are those Nightbane who just wish to emulate the "gun-fu" they see in movies and video game aficionados.

When activated, the Gunslinger Talent turns its user into a savant with modern firearms from revolvers and pistols to rifles, assault weapons, rocket launchers and any gun that fires a projectile. Whatever firearm is held in the hands of the Nightbane becomes like an extension of the Morphus form, allowing for its competent use whether the Talent user was trained to use it or not. From a .22 caliber derringer to a laser-guided Stinger missile, when wielded in conjunction with this Talent, the Nightbane uses it with expert precision and skill.

While the Gunslinger Talent is active, the user is +1 attack per melee round with any type of firearm, +3 to initiative when drawing or firing the weapon, +2 to strike and disarm with an Aimed Shot or a Called Shot even when on the move, +1 to strike with a burst, +2 to strike and parry when using the gun as a melee weapon like a club or bayonet, and does NOT suffer any penalty for shooting while on the move/running (can leap and shoot with the same accuracy and bonuses) or from a speeding vehicle or from an unconventional position like hanging upside down or swinging from a rope. This is in addition to the bonuses from any corresponding W.P. skill (Weapon Proficiency) the character may already possess. Furthermore, the Talent user can actually "see" through the weapon's sights or barrel in addition to their own eyes, allowing for accurate shots while blindfolded or temporarily blinded, shooting behind the back (weapon must be pointed in that direction), and in similar situations.

Note: Nightbane using this Talent on a firearm that is part of their Morphus/body get an additional +1 to strike on all ranged attacks when using it.

Limitations: Can only be used in Morphus form. Only a single type of firearm can be used with this Talent at one time. Though more than one weapon of that type may be used at once, but this does not multiply the bonuses gained. Other weapons can also be used at the same time the Gunslinger Talent is in place, but they do not get the bonuses given to firearms.

Range: Self.

Duration: One full melee round (15 seconds) per 10 P.P.E. spent.

Cost: Eleven P.P.E. to acquire permanently. Ten P.P.E. per melee round of use.

Hotwire

Similar to the elite *Deus ex Machina Talent*, Hotwire allows Nightbane to temporarily take control of any motorized vehicle when he sits behind the wheel. The Hotwire Talent enables him to unlock the door or trunk of any vehicle, start (and stop) any vehicle at will without requiring the key, deactivate car alarms, operate minor automated systems such as electronic door locks or windshield wipers, and pilot the vehicle even if he has never driven one before; base skill is 66% +2% per level of experience (starting at level one).

Stunt driving and trick maneuvers are performed at half the penalties. If the Nightbane can already pilot the type of vehicle affected then add a +15% bonus to their piloting skill as long as Hotwire is active.

This Talent is wildly popular among members of the Warlords Faction as it makes stealing cars a breeze. Members of the Resistance and even the Nocturnes find it useful for hijacking aircraft, boats and military vehicles without the need for the intense training normally required to learn to pilot them.

Limitations: This Talent only affects vehicles that travel under their own power. The vehicle's controls must still be physically operated by the Nightbane, though minor electronic systems may be manipulated through sheer force of will. While piloting the vehicle, the Talent user is unable to do anything other than speak. If contact with the vehicle is broken or the Nightbane is forced to do something like engage in hand to hand combat, then control is automatically lost, though it only takes a single melee action's worth of concentration to re-establish the link as long as the Talent remains active. Control can also be usurped by another using Hotwire, though the usurper has to defeat the first user's control. This is done by rolling a D20 and adding each character's M.E. bonus (if any), high roll wins, defender wins ties. **Note:** The *Deus ex Machina Talent* will ALWAYS succeed in usurping control over Hotwire.

This Talent is meant to be used for vehicles that require only a single pilot. For larger vehicles that require a crew, the Nightbane can only manipulate those controls that would normally be the responsibility of the pilot/helmsman, not operate other positions and equipment such as that of a co-pilot, gunner, navigator, sen-

sor operator, communications officer, engineer, etc. He is just the driver.

Range: Touch.

Duration: 15 minutes per level of experience.

Cost: Fourteen P.P.E. to acquire permanently. 15 P.P.E. per use.

Hound Leash

It is arguable that the primary military might of the Ba'al comes in the form of the dreaded *Hounds*. It is these Nightlands demons that are often tasked with hunting down and slaying troublesome Nightbane and other powerful enemies of the Nightlords. In the years since Dark Day, however, some Nightbane have begun to develop Talents specifically intended to fight back against these monstrous foot soldiers.

One such Talent is Hound Leash, which gives Nightbane the chance to temporarily take control of Hounds, Hunters, and Great Hounds (but not Hound Masters). These supernatural thralls can then be verbally commanded like trained guard dogs and made to protect the Nightbane using the Hound Leash, even against other minions. While this Talent starts out able to affect only a single Hound or Hunter, an additional Hound may be controlled at levels 6, 9, 12, and 15. Note that if not all of the targets succumb to this Talent, it can be used again on a number of targets up to the maximum amount able to be controlled without having to relinquish control of those that were affected.

Limitations: Usable in Morphus form only and not until 4th level. The Nightbane must have previously encountered a Hound, Hunter, etc., before selecting this Talent. The Hound or Hunter the Nightbane hopes to "leash" gets a chance to save against magic, but needs to roll a 15 or higher to succeed. Hound Masters are impervious to this Talent and get really angry when their control over their lesser minions is momentarily stolen from them. The Leashed Hound or Hunter can be made to attack and even destroy another one of its own kind, but cannot be made to destroy themselves nor to attack and slay a Hound Master. Commanding them to do so instantly breaks the influence of the Hound Leash Talent and is likely to have them turn on the mortal who was just controlling them! Each Hound controlled reduces the Nightbane user's own number of attacks per melee round by one, and if the Nightbane is knocked unconscious or forced beyond the range of this Talent, the Leash is broken, control is lost, and the monster is free to follow its own instincts and commands of its usual superiors.

Range: 10 feet (3 m), +2 feet (0.6 m) per level of experience.

Duration: One minute. May be extended for additional P.P.E. cost.

Cost: Thirteen P.P.E. to acquire permanently. Ten P.P.E. per each Hound or Hunter that is Leashed. (Or attempted to be leashed. P.P.E. is spent whether the creature becomes temporarily enslaved or saves and remains outside the Nightbane's con-

trol.) The duration can be extended on those who fail to save for one more minute (no saving throw) at a cost of 5 P.P.E. per EACH Hound or Hunter that is leashed.

Hyper-Awareness

This Talent greatly increases the awareness and observational capacity of the user. Upon activation, the character's eyes glow faintly and ears enlarge slightly. This provides a +3 bonus to all Perception Rolls, +1 to dodge, and a +10% bonus to skills that require awareness such as Detect Ambush, Detect Concealment, Seduction, Surveillance Systems/Tailing, Tracking, and similar.

Limitations: The character must be level 2 or higher to acquire this Talent and in Morphus form to use it.

Range: Self.

Duration: One minute per 5 P.P.E. spent.

Cost: Seven P.P.E. to acquire permanently. Five P.P.E. to activate and 5 P.P.E. for each additional minute, as desired.

Ignorance is Bliss

For those Nightbane who had loved ones witness their transformations or innocent bystanders see a bloody battle between monsters, the value of keeping the average citizen unaware of supernatural events occurring in front of them is all too well known. To enable such a veneer of normalcy and/or concealment, a Talent for tricking mortal beings into seeing and remembering what they want to see, rather than deal with the truth/reality, has been developed.

For example, when the Ignorance is Bliss Talent is used, witnesses do NOT remember seeing a child being rushed to safety in the arms of a hulking, slobbering ursinoid Nightbane, instead they remember seeing the child running to safety on her own, holding an oversized teddy bear as big or bigger than she was. Meanwhile, the child may remember being carried to safety by a giant, cuddly teddy bear who cradled her in its strong fluffy arms and told her not to be afraid as she was carried to safety – not the 10 foot (3 m) tall, blood spattered, man-eating grizzly bear-looking Nightbane who really rescued her. Or witnesses might remember seeing a big, husky bear-of-a-man who rescued the girl and then must have run off.

Similarly, a nosy Preserver Activist (aka, Preevert) street patrol could be made to see a scuffle between a group of teenagers or gang-bangers rather than a brawl between a group of Nocturnes fighting off some Hounds or Hunters. Or witnesses cannot remember any faces or details, because "it all happened so fast," or "I don't know, I must have been in shock," or "I ran inside and hid, I didn't see anything," or, "I remember shouting and screaming, and gunfire, and then that explosion. There was smoke and people running everywhere. It was terrible. Then the police showed up. I'm sorry I can't be more helpful."

Being complicit in the Nightlords' policy of keeping the public in the dark has several upsides for Nightbane. First, innocent bystanders are not unduly traumatized. Second, their existence remains unknown, which reduces the number of monster hunters stalking the streets. Third, ignorance prevents panic. Using this Talent can help on all those fronts and keep Nightbane safe by preventing reports from being made to the authorities about "weird activity," "costumed hooligans," "weird things like magic," or "monsters running amok in the streets." Any of which could bring unwanted attention from the NSB, Hounds or Hunters, and other authorities or enemies of the Nightbane. Civilian involvement in battles between Nightbane and the minions of the Nightlords can be deadly for Nightbane because most people do not take the time to sort out the "good guys" from the "bad guys" before opening fire with their trusty weapon, especially when what they see is *monsters* fighting other monsters (or the NSB and other agents of the Nightlords). So in the end, the use of this Talent can save a lot of headaches and lives for Nightbane and civilians alike. If poor Mr. Wilson down the street thinks the neighbor kids trashed his rose bushes rather than the death throes of the Ashmedai your group just took down, it is probably for the best.

Limitations: This Talent can only be used in Morphus form and not until level three. Can only be used to disguise the supernatural from *those who do not believe* – or do not *want* to believe – such nightmares exists. Which is a surprisingly large percentage of people. Even this helps to diffuse and conceal the presence of the Nightbane and the supernatural, because eyewitness reports contradict each other. "I'm telling you, this ... this bear-monster rescued the little girl." "The little girl was rescued by a large man." "I think a policeman pulled the little girl from harm's way." "No, it was heavy-set woman." "You're all crazy, she ran off by herself and hid under the stairs. Smart kid."

This Talent conceals nothing from other supernatural beings, psychics, magic users, or anyone with a solid belief and/or first-hand experience with the paranormal, Nightbane or the minions of the Nightlord; only people who don't want to believe any of that is real. Believe it or not, most Preeverts, local police and firemen not under the thrall of the Nightlords, and the public at large *DO NOT* believe in the supernatural (though this is slowly changing). Anyone with reason to try to see beyond the Ignorance is Bliss enchantment, or who suspects that something is not right and wants to know the truth, has to roll a save vs magic of 15 or greater see through Ignorance is Bliss. A failed roll means they remember the false illusion of what transpired with normal if implausible or inconsistent events explaining what occurred. "Monsters? What? I was there. It was a gas explosion like they said on the news. Killed two people and injured four others. Terrible accident. Don't believe that 'ever since Dark Day' nonsense on the Internet. Nothing supernatural happened here."

Range: All people in a 50 foot (15.2 m) radius per level of the Nightbane's experience can be influenced by Ignorance is Bliss.

The enchantment can be cast up to 60 feet (18.3 m) away per level of experience.

Saving Throw: 15 or greater to save. Those who do not want to believe their eyes and don't want to believe in monsters, magic or scary things, do not roll to save, they automatically succumb to Ignorance is Bliss and remember events that are explainable and have nothing to do with monsters or the paranormal.

Duration: This Talent was designed to be used either when something has just happened that the Nightbane would like to cover up, or when something is expected to happen in the next few minutes. Therefore, when first activated, Ignorance is Bliss instantly affects everyone within range who is susceptible to it (see above). This is great for when a fight has just happened in front of witnesses, because Ignorance is Bliss will let those witnesses convince themselves that what they just saw was really something else, something ordinary. When used in this way, events that happened as much as 2 minutes per level of experience *before* the Talent was activated can be concealed and covered up, as long as the witnesses are still within the area of effect.

Ignorance is Bliss can also be used preemptively, when trouble is expected and witnesses are likely to be drawn by the noise. In this case, the Talent stays active for 2 minutes per level of experience, and anyone who comes within range during that time is affected, and anything they see while in range can be misremembered as described above.

In either case, the effects of Ignorance is Bliss are permanent for those who don't want to believe what they saw. Their false memory is real to them.

Cost: Ten P.P.E. to acquire permanently. Ten P.P.E. to let everyone in the radius of effect believe and remember what they want to believe.

Inferno Fist

Upon activating the Inferno Fist, one of the Nightbane's appendages becomes wreathed in a nimbus of flame. The fire adds 2D6 damage to his punches. It also allows the 'Bane to parry magic weapons and energy weapons with his flame covered hands. While Inferno Fist is active, he is +1 to parry all conventional melee weapons, sword, club, etc., with his bare, fiery hand. Alternatively, the power may be used to parry an incoming energy blast, but with a -3 penalty. Whatever the case, upon a successful strike or parry, the Inferno Fist is used up and the Talent must be reactivated for further use.

Limitations: Usable only in Morphus form. Will not work in conjunction with a weapon of any sort, though any object held by the flaming appendage is not damaged. Only 2 P.P.E. may be spent on the activation of this Talent per level of the Nightbane's experience.

Range: Self. Melee combat/arm's length, for attacks.

Duration: The fiery fist lasts for one melee round (15 seconds). If it isn't used by that time or the Nightbane is knocked unconscious, the fire is extinguished.

Cost: Five P.P.E. to acquire permanently. Five P.P.E. for one melee round.

Iron Will

Not having psychic abilities can put Nightbane at a disadvantage, especially when facing an opponent capable of manipulating minds and fooling the senses. Iron Will enables its user to level the playing field by strengthening his mind's natural defenses. Upon activation, this Talent boosts the character's resistance to mental attacks, making him +3 to save vs mind control, psionic attacks, illusions, and pain, +4 to save vs possession for the duration of the Talent's influence, and negates skill performance penalties for being under duress or under fire. In addition, the Nightbane will know when psionic powers are being used against him and that someone or something is trying to breach his mental defenses.

Limitations:
Range: Self.
Duration: One melee round (15 seconds) per level of the user's experience.
Cost: Six P.P.E. to acquire permanently. Six P.P.E. to activate this defense.

Jam Senses

Any Nightbane that has tussled with a Hound or one of its ilk knows how dangerous their ability to track supernatural beings can be. The Jam Senses Talent was developed to counter these dogged hunters by fouling their supernatural senses, and has allowed Nightbane and their allies to make good an escape on numerous occasions. Any targeted Hound that fails a save vs magic of 16 or higher is temporarily robbed of their ability to sense and track the supernatural as well as their immunity to illusions and concealment powers. The golem-like monstrosities also find themselves slightly disoriented, suffering a penalty of -1 to initiative, strike, parry, and dodge.

Limitations: The Nightbane must have previously encountered a Hound, Hunter, etc., before selecting this Talent. A single target may be affected per each of the user's levels of experience, though the activation cost must be paid for each target. This power only affects the supernatural senses of these creatures of the Nightlands, and they can continue to hunt and track by sight, scent and skill.

Range: 20 feet (6.1 m) per level of experience.
Duration: One minute per level of the Nightbane's experience.
Cost: Five P.P.E. to acquire permanently. Three P.P.E. per each enemy targeted. P.P.E. is spent whether the creature fails to save or succeeds.

Killing Spree

Thought to be a relatively new Talent, this power is rumored to have first been developed by a younger Nightbane who was an avid player of "first-person shooter" computer games. What is certain is that Killing Spree can be an incredibly powerful ability in the right hands, wherever it came from. While Killing Spree is active, half of the remaining P.P.E. of any being killed by the Talent user is stolen and temporarily added to his or her own for the duration of this Talent. The stolen P.P.E. is immediately available to fuel Talents, spells, etc.

There is one major downside to this ability, however. Absorbing the P.P.E. from a kill provides a kind of rush similar to using a chemical stimulant or a berserker rage. Between this effect and the boost in power, a Nightbane can descend into a murderous frenzy. For every 50 P.P.E. absorbed within a one hour period, there is a *cumulative 10% chance* that the user will need to make a mental endurance save of 15 or better. On a failed roll, the Nightbane loses control and becomes little better than a semi-intelligent predator seeking its next kill. Those with good alignments will not harm non-combatants and selfish individuals aren't likely to do so either, but any enemies present – no matter how powerful – or anyone who attacks him first, is assaulted until they flee or are killed. No mercy. No prisoners. Nightbane with an evil alignment who succumb to the Killing Spree attack may slaughter every living being they encounter while in the killing frenzy, regardless of who or what they are. Only henchmen, allies and friends may be spared, but only if they get out the killer's way and take no actions to stop him or defend anyone he may have targeted.

While locked in this killing frenzy, the Talent user has little regard for his own well-being. This makes the Nightbane immune to pain and provides the following bonuses and penalties: +2 on initiative, +2 to strike, +1 to entangle, and +2 to save vs Horror Factor, but is -4 on Perception Rolls, -3 to parry, dodge, disarm, and roll with punch, fall, or impact, will not pull punches and is -35% on the performance of all skills EXCEPT those that apply to hunting (like tracking) and killing, such as W.P.s. Hands, feet, claws, fangs, and the occasional simple melee weapon are the weapons of choice, and the berserker may even stop to drink some blood or tear out a hunk of flesh of his latest victim before moving on to kill some more. Any other Talents used will are limited to offensive ones only, like Shadow Blast, or enable the Nightbane to reach a target, such as using Lightning Rider to get at someone hiding in a locked room, but only if there is not another target available to him.

Such a loss of control lasts until all viable targets are gone (an unlikely scenario in a city environment as there are plenty of people to kill and he will go looking for them), the Nightbane is killed, incapacitated or subdued, or the Nightbane has expended all available P.P.E. and the Killing Spree's duration ends.

Limitations: Not available until 6th level and can only be used while in Morphus form. To absorb a victim's P.P.E., the user must actually strike the killing blow and not just be party to the death.

While Killing Spree is active and the Nightbane is locked into a killing frenzy, he is unable to willingly share P.P.E. with anyone else and always attempts to save (with a +1 bonus) against any attempt to siphon it off. Likewise, drawing on sources other than kills, such as ley lines or nexuses, is not possible during this state of mind. A Nightbane lost to a killing spree is irrational and lost in the primordial killing spree, cannot cast spells, and no strike bonuses apply for ranged weapons.

<u>Range:</u> Self for the ability. Touch, i.e., the killing blow in order to absorb the P.P.E. of the victims he slaughters. The P.P.E. of anyone killed by other characters or away from the madman cannot be absorbed by him.

<u>Duration:</u> Special. Normally the Talent lasts for one melee round, but when the Nightbane succumbs to Killing Spree and goes on a rampage, his P.P.E. keeps burning to keep the Killing Spree Talent running. And he keeps killing to steal more P.P.E. from the people he slays to keep on killing.

As noted above, the Killing Spree continues until the P.P.E. stolen from those the Nightbane has slain is used up, 20 minutes passes while he is actively hunting for more victims to slaughter during which he cannot find any, or he is subdued and kept from killing for 20 minutes, or he, himself, is slain.

<u>Cost:</u> Twenty-two P.P.E. to acquire permanently. Ten P.P.E. is spent per melee round (15 seconds) the Killing Spree Talent is active. Normally, it lasts for one melee round, but when the Nightbane succumbs to Killing Spree, his P.P.E. keeps burning to keep the Killing Spree Talent running. Another cost may be the character's sanity. Characters of good, selfish and even Aberrant evil alignments have to live with what they did and all the people they hurt or killed while lost in a killing frenzy. Many of whom may have been innocent, friends, allies or other heroes.

Launch

A simple yet effective Talent, Launch allows its user to hurl inanimate objects in a manner similar to Telekinesis; +2 to strike and no other bonuses apply.

Damage from such objects is as follows:

1D4 S.D.C. for up to a two pound object (0.9 kg).
1D6 S.D.C. for up to five pounds (2.25 kg).
2D4 S.D.C. up to 10 pounds (4.5 kg).
3D4 S.D.C. up to 20 pounds (9 kg).
3D6 S.D.C. up to 30 pounds (13.5 kg).
4D6 S.D.C. up to 40 pounds (18 kg).
5D6 S.D.C. up to 50 pounds (22.5 kg).
6D6 S.D.C. up to 60 pounds (27 kg), the maximum that can be tossed in this fashion.

Weights greater than 30 pounds have a 33% chance of knocking down any human or human-sized opponent, causing them to fall down, losing initiative and one melee attack.

Weapons are flung point or blade first and inflict their usual damage +1D6 for the additional force behind it.

Limitations: Usable in Morphus form only. Only ONE object can be hurled at a time. Any object flung must be visible to the Talent user. The target must be visible. Living beings cannot be thrown or pushed with this ability. Fine manipulation (like pulling the pin on a grenade), holding an object suspended in mid-air, or using a launched object to parry, are not possible using this Talent. In order to "throw" an object, the character must make a gesture in the proper direction with a wave of the arm or even a simple nod and glance in the right direction. Hurled objects under 20 lbs (9 kg) can be parried with a -2 penalty, but anything larger must be dodged with a penalty of -1 to dodge.

<u>Range:</u> 50 feet (15.2 m), +20 feet (6.1 m) per level of experience.

<u>Duration:</u> One melee round with each Launch counting as one of the Talent user's melee attacks.

Cost: Eight P.P.E. to acquire permanently. Four P.P.E. per melee round.

Leap

Upon activating this Talent, the user is propelled beyond the scope of his or her normal jumping ability. For every one P.P.E. spent, 5 feet (1.5 m) is added to the character's usual vertical jump limit. When used to make a horizontal jump, this distance is 10 feet (3 m) per P.P.E. point spent. If Leap is used in combination with an attack like a flying tackle or leap kick, add 1D6 S.D.C. damage to it. This power can also be used in an attempt to dodge by leaping out of the way; usual dodge bonuses apply.

While this Talent enables the user to jump great distances, judging those distances is another thing entirely. After a few practice sessions, the average Nightbane is able to determine the approximate distance to a target with just a glance. This effectively gives the character a *Judge Distance* skill of 60% +3% per additional level of experience that should be rolled for difficult jumps such as trying to hit a moving target or a distance greater than 50 feet (15.2 m). On a failed roll, the target is either undershot or overshot with the amount and consequences determined by the G.M.

Limitations: Can only be used in Morphus form. When using Leap to attack, the character is -1 to strike for each 20 feet (6.1 m) of distance covered and spends an additional attack to do so. In any case, the distance and cost are selected upon activating the Talent and may not be altered mid-leap. No more than 4 P.P.E. per level can be spent to activate this Talent.

<u>Range:</u> +5 feet (1.5 m) or +10 feet (3 m) lengthwise per level of experience.

<u>Duration:</u> Instant.

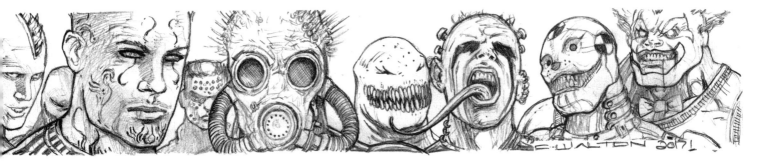

Cost: Six P.P.E. to acquire permanently. Two P.P.E. per each Talent assisted leap.

Leave No Trace

Despite the fact that the Ba'al are not very tech-savvy, modern investigative techniques such as DNA analysis are used by the NSB and local law enforcement. In an effort to remain hidden, some Nightbane have developed supernatural means of thwarting this kind of technological detection. At the basic level, Leave No Trace prevents the beneficiary from leaving behind any trace evidence such as hairs, fingerprints, or blood droplets. It also lets the affected character move about without creating tracks or footprints. This Talent can be boosted to achieve even more astounding effects, though.

If the boosted activation cost is paid the user becomes greatly obscured to all electronic cameras, sensors, and listening devices. This means that security cameras will only capture blurry images with indistinguishable features, wire taps record only garbled static, and devices like laser trip wires, motion detectors and microwave fences will only be tripped 01-30% of the time. Several times since Dark Day, this Talent has caused those who claimed to have evidence of monsters living among the public to lose face when photos or video footage turned out way too blurry to prove anything.

Limitations: Cannot be selected until level 2. Using the boosted version or bestowing the basic benefits on another person can only be done in Morphus form. However, the Nightbane, himself, can use this Talent in both basic or boosted mode in Facade form as well as in Moprhus, but only on himself. The boosted Leave No Trace Talent cannot be used on another individual.

Range: Self or other by touch.

Duration: Five minutes per level of the user's experience.

Cost: Nine P.P.E. to acquire permanently. Six P.P.E. per use for the basic effects or 10 P.P.E. for boosted effects. Leave No Trace has double duration in the Nightlands.

Livewire

Like some otherworldly snake charmer, this Talent enables the Nightbane to command a length of cable or wire to behave like a snake and make it attack or entangle others. The affected wiring or cable rips free from available devices, thin walls, and telephone poles and moves like a serpent writhing through the air at a speed of 36 (23 mph/37 kph). It has two attacks per melee of its own and is +3 to strike, +3 to entangle and dodge. If at any point the cable is severed or destroyed, the enchantment ends. In the alternative, the Talent user can control the cable with his mind and gestures, but each attack counts as one of his own.

In most cases, the cable or wiring available is relatively thin, residential varieties. Such wire has roughly six S.D.C. per foot. Whip attacks do 1D6 damage, and if it is still carrying an electri-

cal current it can shock a target one time for 1D6+2 damage per strike (does not stun). An entangled opponent needs a Supernatural Strength of at least 18 to break free and uses up two melees attacks to do so.

Higher-gauge wire/cable is used for power lines, tow cables, fiber optic cables, cable TV wires, etc. These wires have roughly 20 S.D.C. per foot (0.3 m). Whip attacks inflict 2D6 damage, and if carrying an electrical current, it can shock a target and does 2D6+4 damage, and has a 01-33% chance of stunning its opponent. Victims of a shock must roll a 13 or higher to save vs stun. A successful save means half damage and no stun. A failed roll means full damage and stunned (-2 attacks for that melee round and -3 on all combat rolls for 1D4 melee rounds). Entangled opponents need a Supernatural strength of at least 30 to break free and uses up two melee attacks. Trying to simply untangle oneself while the Livewire is animated is impossible, as the animated wire keeps countering every action. Breaking free or cutting oneself loose is the only solution.

Heavy-duty wire/cable is used for high-test transmission lines, ships' mooring cables, towing cable, construction cable, etc. This wire has roughly 50 S.D.C. per foot. Whip attacks do 3D6 damage, and if carrying an electrical charge it functions same as above, but does an extra 1D6 damage and there is a 01-66% chance of stunning its opponent for 2D4 melee rounds. An entangled opponent needs a Supernatural strength of at least 40 to break free and uses up three melee attacks doing so.

Limitations: Livewire can only be used in Morphus form. The user must either be able to clearly see both the wire and his intended target or otherwise know the location of each with certainty. Reduce the chance for stun/knockout as well as the duration of stun attacks by half against supernatural opponents. A successful save vs electricity of 13 or higher (P.E. bonus applies) by the victim reduces damage by half and prevents stun penalties. Damage from Livewire is not increased for those vulnerable to Nightbane Talents.

Range: Animates a 20 feet (6.1 m) length of wire/cable up to 100 feet (30.5 m) away.

Duration: 30 seconds (2 melees) per level of experience.

Cost: Ten P.P.E. to acquire permanently. Five P.P.E. per use for light cable, 8 P.P.E. for high-gauge, and 12 P.P.E. for heavy-duty cable.

Mage Siphon

One of the vulnerabilities any Nightbane faces is running out of Potential Psychic Energy (P.P.E.) to fuel Talents or magic spells. One answer to that is the Mage Siphon Talent, first developed by ancient Nightbane Sorcerers to supplement their personal P.P.E. reserves. Mage Siphon enables its user to attempt to steal P.P.E. from others. 1D6 P.P.E. is stolen for every one point of P.P.E. channeled into Mage Siphon's activation. A successful

roll to save vs magic of 14 or better prevents the energy from being siphoned away.

Limitations: Usable only in Morphus form and not available until 2nd level. The target must be visible to the Talent user and within 10 feet (3 m) per level of the Nightbane's experience.

Only two P.P.E. points per level of experience may be spent on each use of the Mage Siphon Talent (one point steals 1D6 P.P.E., two points 2D6 P.P.E., three points 3D6 P.P.E., and so on).

Saving Throw: 14

Any magic or psionic barriers (e.g. the Magic Armor spell or Shadow Shield Talent) blocks the Mage Siphon from stealing P.P.E., causing it to instead do damage to the Armor/Shield/barrier in the amount that P.P.E. would have been siphoned, i.e. 1D6, 2D6, and so on, and the saving throw does not apply.

Likewise, any armor that would interfere with spell casting such as metal plate mail reduces the amount of P.P.E. able to be stolen by half.

Range: 10 feet (3 m) per level of experience; line of sight

Duration: Instant results, meaning the Talent user knows if he has been successful stealing P.P.E., but he can only hold on to the extra P.P.E. for five minutes per level of experience so he should use it soon.

Cost: Nine P.P.E. to acquire permanently. One P.P.E. per 1D6 P.P.E. to be stolen.

Mass Transit

One of the few Talents thought to date back to the original campaign against the Ba'al on Earth, Mass Transit enables the user to teleport from Earth to the Nightlands and vice versa, and take several people and/or supplies along with him. Nightbane possessing this Talent are highly sought-after and likely to have two or more Factions routinely competing to recruit them. The Resistance currently has the most members with this Talent and uses them for mass troop and supply movements between their Nightlands outposts and Earth. For this reason, Nightbane with Mass Transit tend to get slightly preferential treatment, are typically heavily guarded on missions, and are often seen as a pampered and as an over-glorified taxi service by the regular fighters.

Limitations: Can only be used in Morphus form, and is not available until 7th level. Only the corresponding point in the Nightlands or a place in the Nightlands the user has visited before, can be reached via Mass Transit. Unwilling passengers/targets can attempt a save vs magic but need to roll a 12 or better to avoid being taken against their will. P.P.E. is still expended in the effort even if the person(s) is able to resist and stays behind.

The Nightbane using the Mass Transit power must go to the other dimension with everyone or everything else, for the Talent to work, and he must know the exact location he is going to.

Range: Can affect anything within a 20 foot (6.1 m) radius at 7th level, +10 feet (3 m) for each level beyond 7th.

Duration: The Nightbane must concentrate for one melee round (15 seconds) per each 10 P.P.E. expended before the dimensional jump to the Nightlands (or vice versa) can be made. He has enough control that he can grab and transport specific people and objects within his radius of influence.

Cost: Twenty-four P.P.E. to acquire permanently. 20 P.P.E. to transport self, +10 P.P.E. for each additional individual or equivalent object like a satchel, trunk, crate or container of weapons or supplies weighing up to 400 pounds (180 kg) each.

Mimic Spell

The casting of a spell almost always leaves a kind of short-lived echo or trace of it on the metaphysical fabric of reality. A Nightbane with this Talent is able to expend P.P.E. to reactivate this trace as long as he observed its casting or any tell-tale effects. This Talent essentially captures and copies a previously cast spell at the same level it was cast, only this time the Nightbane is able to cast it again as if it were coming from him, meaning he can direct it at a target of his choosing, regulate the level of damage, etc. Mimic Spell is a favorite Talent among Nightbane Sorcerers and Nightbane Mystics, as it can be used to quickly recast a favorite spell that may otherwise take several moments to cast, or use a spell which is unknown to them!

Limitations: Available in Morphus form only.

Magic-using Nightbane can select this Talent at 2nd level, but all others must wait until 4th level.

This Talent is unable to mimic rituals or any spell that requires additional physical or spiritual components (such as a circle of blood or link with the elements, etc.) unless the Talent user possesses them as well. In situations where multiple spells have been cast in roughly the same area, the user of Mimic Spell can only mimic the last spell cast in that area.

Time Limit: The Mimic Spell Talent can only recreate a spell that has been cast within the last six minutes. Any trace of a spell that was cast longer than that is too weak and deteriorated to mimic, and all trace of it is gone within 1D4x10 minutes.

Range: Mimic Spell can recreate a spell that was cast within 200 feet (61 m) of a Nightbane who desires to recast it himself. The range, duration, damage and effects of the reactivated spell are the same as the original that was cast just moments earlier, though the Mimic can adjust it within the usual parameters of the spell as he desires.

Duration: The captured, mimicked spell must be cast within one melee round (15 seconds) or it is gone. As noted above, traces of the spell that has been cast lingers for six minutes before it is no longer available for mimicking and recasting. The duration of the mimicked spell is the same as the original unless it is deliberately altered by the user of the Mimic Spell Talent.

Cost: Twenty-five P.P.E. to permanently acquire this Talent. Ten P.P.E. to activate the Talent PLUS the usual P.P.E. cost required to cast the spell being mimicked. If a spell costs 4 P.P.E.

the Nightbane must spend 10 P.P.E. +4 (14 total). If the spell costs 25 P.P.E., the Talent user must spend 10 P.P.E. +25 (35 total) to cast a duplicate of the spell.

Mimic Talent

In much the same way as the Mimic Spell ability above, this Talent enables the user to duplicate the effects of almost any other Nightbane Talent he witnesses within 100 feet (30.5 m) of him. This temporarily available Talent is only good for a single activation, but is fully under the control of the user of Mimic Talent. For instance, if the user witnesses a Nightbane use the Doorway Talent to escape but the observer does not possess that Talent himself, Mimic Talent can be used to *duplicate it one time*. However, since the Talent is now controlled by the user of Mimic Talent, the doorway will NOT open to the same location as the original unless the mimic knows the original's exit point and chooses to follow. He can, however, use the mimicked Talent to go somewhere else.

Limitations: Can only be used in Morphus form, but cannot be selected until level 2. The user must meet all the requirements of the Talent he is intending to copy, including any level or Morphus restrictions, loss of Hit Points, loss of P.E. attribute points, and so on. This Talent can only duplicate the last Talent the user witnessed with his own eyes.

Time Limit: The Mimic Talent ability can only mimic a Talent that the Nightbane sees performed with his own eyes and must be mimicked within 60 seconds (four melee rounds) after witnessing it in use.

Range: Within 100 feet (30.5 m) of the original Talent user; line of sight required. The range of the mimicked Talent is roughly the same as what he saw.

Duration: The Talent being mimicked is instantly available to the Nightbane who is mimicking it, but the duration of the mimicked Talent itself is half. Otherwise, it has the same level of power and capabilities as the person it is copied/mimicked from, NOT the Nightbane's own level of experience. The mimicked Talent is used once and cannot be duplicated again unless the Nightbane sees a fellow Nightbane use it in front of him again and he chooses to mimic it.

Cost: Thirty P.P.E. to acquire permanently. Ten P.P.E. to activate Mimic Talent PLUS the usual P.P.E. costs required to use the Talent being mimicked.

Mirror Sense

Activating this Talent lets the Nightbane sense the presence of any mirrors in the vicinity that have a connection to the Nightlands. Any such mirror within range can be felt with pinpoint precision, so the user of Mirror Sense knows exactly how many there are, what direction they lie in, and how far each is from him. By spending a few seconds concentrating on a single mir-

ror the Nightbane can tell if it is linked to the dreaded realm of the Nightlords, and if so, a blurry, shadowy image of the Nightlands appears to him. It does not reveal anything or anyone in the surrounding area there, except a shadowy reflection of the same room in which the Nightbane is standing. It is worth noting that ANY Nightbane can tell by simply looking at a mirror whether or not it connects to the Nightlands. This Talent enables him to sense those mirrors in a large area before looking into their mirrored surfaces.

Limitations: Only detects mirrors with a counterpart in the Nightlands, not any other kind of dimensional portals, breaches, or other anomalies. Thus the Talent user will know that X number of mirrors in a neighborhood are connected to the Nightlands, and which houses they are in. Getting into the home, apartment, office building, of facility may be another story. And just because a place has a mirror connected to the Nightlands does not mean everyone inside the building is evil or a Doppelganger, though there are likely to be a few (or more).

Range: 500 foot (152.4 m) radius +100 feet (30.5 m) per level of experience.

Duration: Five minutes per level of the Nightbane.

Cost: Three P.P.E. to acquire permanently. One P.P.E. to activate.

Mirror Shield
(Parry Bullets and Energy)

Drawing on the reflective nature of mirrors, the Mirror Shield Talent summons a protective shield capable of deflecting attacks leveled at the user. This shield may take the form of anything from a buckler (a small, round shield worn on the forearm) or a larger, medium-sized shield of any shape, covered in a mirrored surface, but strong as steel. Whatever the physical appearance, the protection it offers is the same: The shield itself has 75 S.D.C. but is only damaged if targeted, and provides a bonus of +3 to parry (no other parry bonuses apply except those from a high P.P. attribute number).

The advantage of the Mirror Shield is that it can be used to parry energy attacks and projectile attacks from bullets to magical fireballs and energy blasts — the normal penalty to parry projectiles is negated with this Talent. Any parried attack may, however, hit nearby people or objects for half damage, so this power must be used carefully if collateral damage is to be avoided.

Limitations: Usable only in Morphus form. Unable to be selected until 4th level. The shield remains on the user's arm or in his hand for the duration and cannot be dropped or passed on to another, but may be canceled at any time.

Range: Self.

Duration: 10 minutes per level of experience or until the shield is destroyed.

Cost: Eight P.P.E. to acquire permanently. Six P.P.E. per use.

Nega

This Talent provides the ability to temporarily counter and terminate any spell, psionic power, Talent, or other supernatural ability that is specifically directed at the Nightbane with this Talent. He can also use it to negate the effects of an area effect spell or Talent, but only he is spared its enchantment and any corresponding damage, penalties, etc. Once the Nega Talent is activated, any power affecting him is nullified. P.P.E. cost requires the Nightbane to spend the same amount of P.P.E. as the spell or Talent directed at him. Not applicable to true psionic attacks (I.S.P.). Nega can be applied to as many as two others at a time by touch.

The Seekers and Nocturnes are known for having members with this Talent and assigning at least one to any team tasked with hunting down any mages or powerful supernatural beings in order to counter magic and Talents.

<u>Limitations:</u> Can only be used in Morphus Form and cannot be selected until 4th level. Can only negate abilities that are fueled by psychic or magic energy (i.e. P.P.E., I.S.P., etc.). The Talent-user does not get to pick what is countered and what isn't; this includes the character's own powers. If the user doesn't have enough P.P.E. to match the cost of an incoming power then that power works as normal.

<u>Range:</u> The area of effect can be restricted to the user or expanded out to a maximum of 2 feet (0.6 m) from the user at level 4 and an additional 2 feet (0.6 m) at levels 6, 8, 10, 12, and 14.

<u>Duration:</u> Determined by the activation cost paid (see below), but this Talent automatically lapses when the user reaches 0 P.P.E.

<u>Cost:</u> Fourteen P.P.E. to acquire permanently. P.P.E. cost requires the Nightbane to spend the same amount of P.P.E. as the spell or Talent directed at him. Nega can be applied to as many as two other people at a time by touching each and using Nega on them at the same time, or himself and one other person by touch. This negates the spell on two for the P.P.E. cost of one. **Note:** Not applicable to true psionic attacks (I.S.P.).

Open Channel

Opening oneself to the supernatural is a skill that many mystics and psychics have used across the ages to detect the presence of unearthly beings. This Talent simulates that ability, but with a narrower scope. Upon activation, the user chooses a single species. Once chosen, the Nightbane can sense the presence of all members of that species in the area. In the converse, however, every one of those individuals can also sense the presence of the Talent user! Examples would include being able to detect all nearby Guardians, Wampyrs, Ashmedai, Hounds, Hunters and so on.

This ability takes the form of a kind of gut-feeling that the creature(s) is nearby. An average person unused to the supernatural might pass it off as just a weird feeling, but this is a dead giveaway to beings like Hounds and Hunters that a Nightbane is nearby. The Open Channel indicates whether there is: one or two, a few (3-6), several (7-16), many (17+), or a great many (50+) of a specific type of supernatural being. Thinking "minions of the Nightlords" or "creatures of the Nightlands" is too broad and undefined, but trying to sense a Nightlord or Night or Prince, or Hounds, or Hunters, or Namtars, etc., or whatever the one chosen species is, works just fine. **Note:** It does NOT indicate an exact number nor where they may be located, though the Talent user does get an idea of whether they are near or far. Practitioners of magic and psychics are NOT sensed by this ability. However, *Nightbane in Morphus* (not Facade) can also be sensed via this Talent. **Reminder:** Whatever creature the Talent user is trying to detect also senses him, and each one of that supernatural species in range now knows that a Nightbane is in the area and lurking around someplace not terribly far away. This may or may not put such creatures on the alert, or even on the hunt for this Nightbane.

<u>Limitations:</u> Usable in Morphus form only. Unavailable until 2nd level. The sense provided by Open Channel does not indicate exact location, distance or numbers, only the presence or absence of supernatural beings and only of the one, specific supernatural species focused upon. To sense a different species, new P.P.E. is spent and the Open Channel Talent must be reused.

The Nightbane using the Talent can restrict this sensing ability to a 100 foot (30.5 m) radius or in 100 foot (30.5 m) increments to the full range available to him.

<u>Range:</u> 100 feet (30.5 m) per level of experience.

<u>Duration:</u> One minute per level of experience.

Cost: Four P.P.E. to acquire permanently. Three P.P.E. per use.

Phantom Limb

For any Nightbane who has ever wished for another set of hands, the Phantom Limb Talent is a convenient solution. Useful for more than just physical combat, this Talent can come in handy (no pun intended) when moving loads of equipment, performing repairs, or scaling a cliff. For many who develop Phantom Limb, the use of this Talent becomes second nature, as they seem to activate the ability almost absent-mindedly when needed.

Activating this power summons one or more ghostly appendages that function as additional limbs. These limbs can look like almost anything from an extra pair of human arms and hands to lobster claws or tentacles. What is the same for all of these limbs is that they are translucent with a faint glow, and appear to be made of something like ectoplasm.

From one to several arms may be summoned at the same time depending on the amount of P.P.E. spent. One extra limb adds a bonus of +1 to parry and entangle. Each *pair* of arms also adds a bonus of +1 additional attack/action per melee round, and +5%

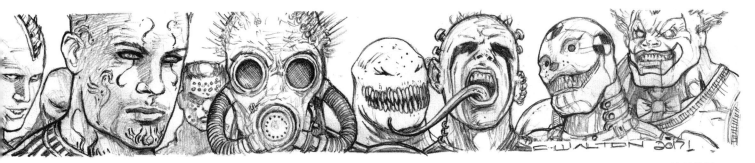

to the Climbing skill. Each limb has a Supernatural P.S. of 16, which means that normal hand to hand strikes deal 1D6 damage.

Limitations: This Talent is usable only in Morphus form.

Number of Limbs: One limb can be summoned for every 3 levels of the user's experience, so one extra phantom limb at level three, two at level six, three at level nine, four limbs at level 12, and five at level 15. If the arms are meant to be used for activities such as operating a computer or shooting a gun they must have fingers or similar digits and an opposable thumb.

Range: Self, only.

Duration: One minute (4 melee rounds) per level of experience.

Cost: Ten P.P.E. to acquire permanently. Six P.P.E. per each Phantom Limb activated.

Pipe Bomb

Dark energy coalesces around the Nightbane, forming a physical shell that looks like the *Shadow Shield Talent*. Only other Nightbane are able to tell the difference between a Pipe Bomb and Shadow Shield. People used to fighting Nightbane will think it is the Shadow Shield, and will not know otherwise until it explodes at some point!

Like the Shadow Shield, Pipe Bomb creates a form-fitting protective shield around the Nightbane, but provides only 10 S.D.C. protection per every two 2 P.P.E. spent upon activation of this Talent. The big difference is when this barrier is depleted or upon the command of the Nightbane wearing it, the Pipe Bomb shell explodes outward in a sphere of explosive power. Only the Nightbane it was covering is unscathed. Everything else within its explosive radius takes damage equal to 1D6+1 S.D.C. per every 2 P.P.E. spent when the Pipe Bomb Talent was activated and the Pipe Bomb shield was created (every 2 P.P.E. = 10 S.D.C.).

Limitations: Can only be used by the Morphus form.

The Talent user is NOT able to select targets; everyone and everything within the blast radius takes damage regardless of whether they are friend, foe or innocent bystander. Also note that activating this Talent and then intentionally detonating the field counts as two separate melee attacks.

P.P.E. expenditure is capped at 4 P.P.E. and 20 S.D.C. (2D6 damage) per level of experience.

Range: Self.

Blast Radius: 15 foot (4.6 m) blast radius.

Duration: 10 minutes per level or until S.D.C. of the Pipe Bomb shell is depleted or willfully detonated. If the Pipe Bomb is not detonated and the duration comes to an end, the shell crumbles away and vanishes without exploding or inflicting damage. It can also be cancelled at any time by the Talent user.

Cost: Ten P.P.E. to acquire permanently. Two P.P.E. per 10 S.D.C. of the shell which equals 1D6+1 explosive damage. Spend four P.P.E. equals 20 S.D.C. and 2D6+2 explosive damage, eight P.P.E. equals a 40 S.D.C. shell and 4D6+4 damage, 12 P.P.E. equals 60 S.D.C. and 6D6+6 damage, and so on.

Pocket Change

Throughout history there have been millions upon millions of individuals who have wished for more money. For a Nightbane with this Talent, he can turn such a wish into reality, even if only for a limited amount of time. To accomplish this feat, the Nightbane simply closes his eyes, pictures the amount of money he requires, and activates this Talent. Upon expending the P.P.E., a physical dollar appears in his hand for every P.P.E. point spent. This currency is, for all intents and purposes, the real thing and will pass any inspection or test to verify it is not a forgery. Also, the money appears in the form that the Nightbane chooses, allowing for the creation of coins or paper notes up to the maximum P.P.E. spent.

Limitations: Since the Nightbane must picture the currency they wish to create, familiarity with that specific type of money is required, and it is best if he has an example of it to focus on when using this Talent. For instance, a Nightbane in Germany or elsewhere in the European Union (EU), would need to know the denominations of Euros – both their value and appearance – to be able to produce them. Another potentially dangerous limitation is that money created by this Talent only remains in existence for a very limited amount of time.

Range: Self.

Duration: 10 minutes per level of experience, then vanishes completely.

Cost: Six P.P.E. to acquire permanently. One P.P.E. per dollar (or local equivalent).

Raven Wings

The dream of free flight has been common among mankind for centuries. It should be no surprise then that many Nightbane wishing for new Talents may develop a means to take wing and soar through the clouds like a great bird. This Talent tends to manifest as large, black wings composed of solid shadow (can look like anything from a raven's to an eagle's wings), but may also appear as a flying apparatus as long as it has wings. The means of flight has no actual physical substance, does not impair movement, and cannot be damaged.

Limitations: Only usable by the Morphus.

Since this is magically powered flight there is no strain on the Nightbane other than exposure to the elements, and no altitude limit to speak of. However, the air does get too thin to breathe around 20,000 feet (6,096 m). Flight speed is limited to 20 mph (32 kph) per level of experience. Also, although no piloting skill is needed to maneuver/fly using this Talent, it also imparts no special combat bonuses other than a +2 to dodge while in flight.

Duration: 10 minutes per every 4 P.P.E. after activation cost and the first 10 minutes.

Cost: Twelve P.P.E. to acquire permanently. Six P.P.E. to activate for 10 minutes of flight and four P.P.E. for each additional 10 minutes sustained.

Reality Mooring

While some might discount the danger of incorporeal beings, eventually Nightbane that live long enough are likely to encounter so-called spirits, ghosts, Entities, Astral Beings, and other ethereal creatures employed as spies by the Ba'al or other enemies. The Reality Mooring Talent is a specific effort to combat Astral creatures and the like that can normally float through solid objects like walls and are immune to most sources of damage. When this Talent is activated, every incorporeal being within its area of effect needs a roll of 16 or better to save vs magic to prevent being forced to manifest on the physical plane or vanish to the Astral Plane or wherever they came from.

Those incorporeal beings who save are not effected. Those who fail can immediately return to the Astral Plane or whatever unearthly plane of existence they come from (cannot return for 1D6 days) or become corporeal. As a physical being their movement is limited, they cannot pass through walls, they take physical damage and can be captured, interrogated, tortured and killed. *Astral Travelers* who have simply left a physical body via Astral Projection are instantly snapped back to their own Physical body and cannot Astral Project again for 24 hours. Other Astral Beings are forced back to the Astral Plane and cannot leave it for 1D6 days.

Likewise, it is impossible for characters within the area of effect to leave their bodies and Astral Project or to become intangible/ethereal for the duration of this Talent. Beings such as ghosts and Entities which are incapable of manifesting physically are forced outside the Talent's area of effect and are unable to return for 1D6 days. If Reality Mooring is used on the Astral Plane, only Astral Travelers are forced back into their bodies outside the Plane. **Note:** For ethereal creatures (including Astral Beings), being forced to manifest physically can be frightening and has a Horror Factor of 15 when it is discovered that they are no longer invisible and intangible. Regardless of the type of intangible creature, being turned physical in the physical plane is disorienting and they suffer the following penalties: -2 on all Perception Rolls, -2 on initiative, -1 attack per melee round, -2 to all combat rolls and -20% on skill performance for 1D4 melee rounds. Those beings who do not immediately flee are likely to lash out at those nearby out of fear and/or confusion, so this Talent should be used with caution.

Limitations: Can only be used while in Morphus form, but cannot be selected before level four.

Range: 15 feet (4.6 m) radius per level of experience.

Duration: One melee round (15 seconds).

Cost: Sixteen P.P.E. to acquire permanently. 15 P.P.E. per melee of use.

Skill Stealer

As the name suggests, this Talent enables Nightbane to temporarily rob another sentient being of a single skill. The intended victim gets to roll a save vs magic (needs a 14 or better to save). A failed save means a single skill of the Talent user's choosing is completely forgotten for the duration of this ability! That skill is temporarily transferred to the Nightbane using the Skill Stealer Talent. The stolen skill has the same percentage of success and expertise as possessed by the character whom it was stolen it from. Skill Stealer can also be used to steal a skill already known by the Nightbane just to prevent the enemy from using it or to increase his own ability with it. In this instance, if the stolen skill is known at a higher percentage of success by the person it was taken from, the Nightbane gets to use it at that level of expertise. If the stolen skill is lower than the Nightbane's own skill, he ignores it and uses the skill with his own superior ability.

Limitations: Usable in Morphus form only and not until third level.

Only a single skill can be stolen per use of this Talent. If a skill is stolen before the duration of a previously stolen skill, the newly stolen skill replaces the last one.

This Talent can be used on physical skills and Weapon Proficiencies, EXCEPT it only grants the thief the knowledge of the skill itself, but NONE of the *combat bonuses* to strike, parry, dodge, extra melee attacks, etc. However, the Nightbane's P.P. and other bonuses may provide some bonuses with a weapon.

Of course, only sentient beings (living or undead) who possess skills are affected by this Talent, not animals or monsters with instincts and innate abilities.

Range: By touch or up 40 feet (12.2 m) away, provided the intended victim can be seen.

Duration: 10 minutes per level of experience, though he can give it back (or let it go, depending on how you look at it) at any time.

Cost: Sixteen P.P.E. to acquire permanently. 12 P.P.E. per use.

Sky Writer

This Talent is like a more limited version of the *Storm Bringer Talent*, affording the user the ability to manipulate clouds in a few useful ways. First, as the name might suggest, the Nightbane can utilize clouds to write messages in the sky that are clearly visible to everyone in a 5 mile (8 km) radius. If the day is completely clear, thin clouds can even be conjured out of thin air to work with. Second, clouds can be slowly moved around the sky to temporarily block out sun or moonlight, used to obscure the view of airborne foes, or even just to create animated "cloud art."

Finally, Sky Writer can be used to tint or darken clouds to make it appear as if it will storm, for dramatic effect (but it doesn't).

Limitations: Can only be used while in Morphus form.

Range: Can affect any cloud within a 5 mile (8 km) radius.

Duration: Two minutes (8 melee rounds) per level of experience.

Cost: Two P.P.E. to acquire permanently. One P.P.E. per 6 letters or six symbols formed to "write" in the sky. 5 P.P.E. to shift a cloud's position, and 10 P.P.E. to darken or tint clouds within the radius of effect. Double all P.P.E. costs if the clouds have to be conjured rather than working with existing ones.

Solar Flare

No doubt a development that came from interactions with the enigmatic beings known as Guardians, this Talent summons up a small orb of sunlight. This small "flare" can be held in the Talent user's hand to light up a 5 foot (1.5 m) radius as a lantern. It is bright enough to read by, and it also keeps vampires and other creatures vulnerable to sunlight from entering the illuminated area, but does not otherwise hinder or harm such beings.

Unlike the spell incantation *Globe of Daylight*, this Talent also has distinctly offensive uses as well. The Solar Flare can be launched at one enemy to inflict 5D6 damage (+3 to strike). Damage is inflicted by this laser-like bolt of light whether the target is vulnerable to sunlight or not; double damage to vampires and Shadow creatures. Or it can be launched up into the air for a more dramatic effect against those vulnerable to sunlight.

If launched into the air, the flare explodes with a flash that lights up a 1,000 foot (305 m) diameter as bright as daytime for 1D4 seconds (counts as one melee attack). This effect damages beings vulnerable to sunlight within 100 feet (30.5 m) of the flare's user. The flash does not blind, but when used at nighttime it does have a Horror Factor of 12 to vampires and other creatures vulnerable to sunlight, and may blind creatures that are sensitive to light. The flare is likely visible for 2D4 miles (3.2-12.8 km) at night, making it a great signal or distraction (+2 to the initiative roll of the user and any allies for the first melee round, while everyone else is surprised).

Limitations: Not available for selection until level 3. Usable by the Morphus only. Only 4 P.P.E. per level of the user can be spent to activate this Talent.

Range: 1,000 feet (305 m).

Duration: The flare can be held and used as a lantern for up to one melee round (15 seconds) per level of experience. Near-instant once it is released.

Cost: Eight P.P.E. to acquire permanently. 5D6 damage when fired as a laser bolt at any one target (double damage to creatures vulnerable to sunlight). Gone the instant it is fired. Or fired into the air to create a Sunlight flare blast that does 2D6 damage for every 4 P.P.E. spent to all vampires, shadow beings and other creatures vulnerable to sunlight and caught in the radius of sunlight created by the flare. No damage if shielded in darkness or indoors and away from windows.

Switchboard Operator

Like old telephone switchboard operators of the past, this Talent enables Nightbane to communicate with multiple people at once, like a conference call or Skype call (without video or the need of a computer). When the Operator Talent is active, the Nightbane acts as a supernatural switchboard or communication hub to provide a sort of short-range, telepathic communication network that cannot be detected, hacked, or jammed by technological means. No device is need, it all happens in the participants' own heads. However, they do need to actually speak aloud, even if it is a whisper, to be heard. Only a psionic Mind Block and the Anti-Magic Cloud spell will prevent someone from being connected via this Talent, and the psionic ability of Telepathy can be used to eavesdrop on the conversation, but only if the psychic knows the communications is happening and he or she has access to one of the participants.

Limitations: A Nightbane using this Talent has to be in Morphus form, and he can use no other Talents while using Switchboard Operator. The Switchboard Operator Talent makes the Talent user "the" switchboard operator, the hub through which ALL participants are linked and able to communicate.

This is an open line to ALL participants, so anything spoken by them is heard by them all.

The Nightbane using the Talent, and as many as two additional people per level of the Talent user's experience, can be "hooked in" to this magical communications network, but any more than six people (plus himself), causes the following penalties for the Nightbane who is the Switchboard Operator: Perception Roll bonuses are reduced to zero, -4 on initiative, -4 on ALL combat roll (strike, parry, dodge, etc.), -2 melee attacks and -40% on skill performance because he is too distracted by the chatter going on in his head.

Likewise, when there are eight or more participants, EVERYONE else suffers similar penalties, as follows: Perception Roll bonuses are reduced to zero, -2 on initiative, -2 on ALL combat roll (strike, parry, dodge, etc.), -1 melee attacks and -20% on skill performance.

All participants must speak aloud, even if it is a whisper, in order to be heard by the others. However, only the voices of the participants are heard loud and clear and without any background noise; no sounds of traffic, shooting, screaming, etc. If one of the participants linked to Switchboard Operator begins to speak to any third party, only his voice, not the other person or people, is heard via this link; just like hearing one side of a telephone conversation. However, the voices of the other participants speaking to him are only heard by him, so they can speak and offer advice without anyone around hearing them – unless a telepath is present and tries to read his thoughts. This connection lets him hear

everyone and he can eavesdrop on everything said by everyone connected.

Nightbane using this Talent can only connect with *willing participants*, and even willing targets have to be within range. So if a participant needs to break the connection he can do so at any time, but only the Nightbane serving as the communications hub realizes it immediately. However, as long as they stay within range, those linked can move freely without fear of losing contact.

Range: 1,000 foot (305 m) radius per level of experience.

Duration: 10 minutes per four P.P.E. invested.

Cost: Eight P.P.E. to acquire permanently. Four P.P.E. for the first 10 minutes, +2 P.P.E. for each additional 10 minutes thereafter.

Trap Shadow

Nightbane involved in the struggle against the Nightlords and their minions rely mainly on guerilla warfare tactics. This means making quick, surgical strikes in small numbers and disappearing into the night before the Ba'al can bring their might to bear on attackers. Booby-traps can be an invaluable part of these strikes. Such traps serve to delay and disable the enemy and pursuers. This Talent converts an ordinary patch of shadow into such a trap, lashing out whenever an enemy comes within range.

The trap itself can appear as any variety of things, from impaling spikes of solid darkness to black tendrils that grab and hold or even painfully constrict and crush its victim. Trap Shadows are mentally "programmed" to activate automatically whenever any number of criteria are met. For instance, it may be set to only be triggered by a particular type of Nightlands monster, or NSB, or only when two or more enemy targets are in range, or anyone who comes within range, and so on. Trap Shadows can also be activated at will by the Nightbane who set it, though this requires the character to maintain line of sight.

Victims who fail to make a saving throw of 15 or higher (include any P.E. bonuses to save) are dealt 3D6 damage and are immobilized in the shadow for one melee round per level of the Nightbane. Those who successfully save take half damage and are only trapped for one melee round (15 seconds). Also note that the damage from these traps is not "physical" in the traditional sense, so while a victim may appear to be impaled by a half dozen black spikes, this does not cause wounds the way real metal spikes would. Once the duration of the immobilization expires, there is little physical evidence that the victim was attacked (for humans, only minor welts remain), even though the damage is quite real. Those killed by a Trap Shadow will appear to have died from cardiac arrest.

Limitations: Usable in Morphus form only.

Trap Shadows affect only a one target per each level of the Nightbane's experience.

There must be a shadow or patch of darkness at least five square feet (0.46 square meters) for the Trap Shadow to be set; often a much larger shadow.

Consumed by the Trap Shadow. Those dragged into the Trap Shadow seem to be so heavily cloaked in darkness that they are barely visible and their cries of fear and distress barely audible. (Must come within four feet/1.2 m of the shadow which could make you a victim!) This means those trapped are temporarily removed from play, but cannot be attacked while trapped inside the Trap Shadow.

Range: Entering the shadow itself triggers it, but also coming near it can cause it to trigger, reach out and grab enemies to pull into the trap. This reach is a one foot (0.3 m) radius per level of its creator. The creator can trigger the trap from up to 100 feet (30.5 m) away per level of experience.

Duration: The Trap Shadow can be set and left behind where it lasts until someone triggers it or for 10 minutes per level of the Nightbane, whichever comes first. When triggered, whether by one or several victims, each victim takes initial damage and is trapped for one melee round per level of the Nightbane. After that the trap releases them and tosses them out of the shadow. If they step back into the shadow they are attacked and held again, and the same happens to new enemies who may arrive.

Note: A strong, bright light (more than a flashlight) will destroy the Shadow Trap after being exposed to it for more than 1D6+1 minutes.

Cost: Eleven P.P.E. to acquire permanently. Seven P.P.E. per Trap Shadow created.

Ultra-Vision

Originally developed by a few Nightbane working with the Lightbringer faction, Ultra-Vision grants the user the ability to see in several spectrums of light as well as telescopic (4-8x30 magnification) and microscopic (2-20x magnified) vision. Seeing into spectrums beyond visible light can be useful for things like spotting laser trip wires or targeting lasers, examining physical traces like hand prints on a wall, and even being able to read various "invisible" inks sometimes used in espionage. Even limited X-ray vision is possible, enabling the character to see through low-density, non-metallic materials like cloth, tents and flesh.

Limitations: Electromagnetic frequencies in the microwave range and lower are not visible, nor are high-powered X-rays or above.

Range: 2 feet (0.6 m) for microscopic and X-ray vision, standard visual range for non-telescopic sight such as infrared and ultraviolet, and up to 2 miles (3.2 km) for telescopic vision.

Duration: See cost below.

Cost: Three P.P.E. to acquire permanently. Two P.P.E. for the first two minutes and one P.P.E. for each subsequent 2 minutes of use.

Wall Runner

Primarily of use in urban environments, the Wall Runner Talent allows a Nightbane to defy the laws of gravity and move up or across vertical surfaces as if they were the ground. Speed as well as carrying capacity and combat ability are unaffected, and any opponent fighting the Wall Runner at a 90 degree angle is going to be at a disadvantage (-3 to strike, parry, and dodge) due to the novelty of the situation and the Nightbane's unique angles of attack and movement.

Limitations: Usable only by the Morphus form. Most windows and glass sides of skyscrapers will support the weight of someone running over them, however those of smaller buildings and homes usually won't (G.M. discretion). If the Nightbane loses contact with the vertical surface he is traveling on, his defiance of gravity ends and he will fall back to Earth. Falls from great heights (four stories or more) are likely to be deadly!

Range: Self.

Duration: Two minutes plus.

Cost: Five P.P.E. to acquire permanently. Four P.P.E. for the first two minutes and two P.P.E. per one minute after that.

Wall Whisperer

It is a commonly accepted fact among Nightbane that this Talent has its origins in the old saying, "If only these walls could talk." At least to users of this Talent, walls really can talk and reveal things that happened within them as early as the day construction was finished. This is similar to the psychic power of Object Read but expanded to an entire section of a wall or building.

To establish such a communion, the Talent user simply touches the chosen wall and activates the Talent. Once that is done there are a few different ways to view what the wall has "witnessed." The first is to call up the events that took place at a specific time, usually something recently, but can be a specific date and time. The second is to start at a specific day and time and scroll forward or backward to scan for a specific person, event, or maybe until something catches the eye, but even fast-forwarding through images takes time. The final method is to simply open oneself up to whatever highly emotional occurrences have taken place with 20 feet (6.1 m) of the wall. Emotionally charged events always leave the strongest impression, so they are what appear when opening up to random, strong events. Examples of this could include happy events such as a marriage proposal or birth or good news, or darker occasions such as a robbery, accident, murder, arson attempt, bad news, and so on that has taken place within range of a wall in a particular room or facing the backyard, front yard, porch, sidewalk, street, entranceway, tunnel, bridge, etc.

The perspective that events are viewed from can be from anywhere on the chosen wall and can reveal things happening on either side of the wall, including things that might be glimpsed through a window from a distance. Sound and images can be viewed this way, though not smell nor the sensation of touch. It is the psychic imprint left in the area that is being read, the wall is just he focal point and angle of view and details may be sketchy due to the emotion of the situation and lighting when it took place. Similarly, an entire conversation may not be available, just key snippets, especially if it took place more than four feet (1.2 m) from the wall, and if spoken in a foreign language, that is what the Nightbane hears.

Limitations: May only be used in Morphus form and is not available until level two.

Particularly momentous and traumatic events leave such strong impressions on a space that a Nightbane using this power will have to make a save vs psionic attack of 17 or better to have any option but to relive these powerful happenings. Certain measures can hinder or prevent use of this power as well, such as the spell Sanctum.

Range: Touch for activation. 20 feet (6.1 m) on both sides of the wall for a 20 foot length. The latter increases by an additional 10 feet (3 m) per level of the Talent user.

Duration: Minutes to hours. Each activation has a maximum of one hour to review and experience memories left at the wall.

Reviewing and reliving psychic imprints left on a particular area may take 1D6 minutes if the Talent user knows an exact time and date or a specific event like the attack on the Carmichael family, October 22, 2011. Otherwise, it could take hours sampling random times and events or fast forwarding through hours or days or months of impressions. While doing this, the Talent user falls into a trance and may completely lose track of time. Viewing events carefully takes the same amount of time as those events did.

Cost: Nine P.P.E. to acquire permanently. Eight P.P.E. per activation of the Talent.

Witch-Hunter's Sight

Using this Talent allows P.P.E. to be seen as a bluish glow emanating from beings or objects that have a significant amount (more than 30 points). Smoke, mist, and thin material like cloth or cardboard will not hide this glow, but it does not shine through walls, doors, heavy crates, and similar objects. Ley lines and nexus points are also clearly visible to the Talent user even in daytime. The potential uses for this power are many and various, including picking out potentially disguised supernatural creatures, magic users, Nightbane, creatures of magic, spotting magical objects, seeing through illusions (+4 to the user's save versus illusion), etc. With a little practice, this Talent can even be used to estimate the general amount of P.P.E. a person or object has in reserve plus or minus 1D4x10%.

Limitations: When this Talent is active, non-magical objects and living beings with very low P.P.E. (less than 12) do not register.

When the Talent is activated, it imposes a -3 penalty to all Perception Rolls because the user is focused on finding beings or objects with high P.P.E., like trying to spot a Hollow Man sneaking toward him. Since the magic energy is viewed as a bluish glow, being on a ley line or at a nexus is akin to trying to see through a dense fog (-6 to Perception Rolls involving vision). Likewise, looking directly at any being or object with 500 or more P.P.E. is uncomfortable and gives the user a penalty of -4 to all combat rolls against that being while this ability remains active. Looking directly at anything with over 1,000 P.P.E. is positively blinding, causing the user to be -8 on all combat rolls. Luckily, these penalties vanish as soon as the Talent's duration expires or it is canceled.

<u>Range</u>: Equal to the Nightbane's natural nightvision range.

<u>Duration</u>: One minute per level of experience.

Cost: Four P.P.E. to acquire permanently. Two P.P.E. to activate.

New Elite Talents

The numbers in brackets indicate which level of experience some powerful Talents become available.

Listed in parenthesis are the level the Talent becomes available and the type of Morphus that would be most appropriate and likely to select a particular Elite Talents. A bit of help to provide a development path for you character. This is just a suggestion.

[6] Beguiling Beauty (Angelic, Superbeing, or Unnatural Beauty)

[4] Beyond the Call (Occupation, Soldier, or Superbeing)

[3] Choke (Artisan, Athlete, Hobbyist, Occupation, or Infernal)

[6] Contortionist (Disproportional, Unnatural Limbs, or Victim)

[4] Corrupting Influence (Infernal, Substance Abuse, or Unearthly Beauty)

[2] Dark Dreams (Mythical Creature, Nightmare, Substance Abuse, or Victim)

[3] Dark Fathom (Aquatic Animal or Aquatic Biomech)

[7] Diamond-Hide (Artificial Appearance, Mineral, or Mythical Creature)

[7] Divine Wrath (Ancient Warrior, Angelic, or Fantasy)

[5] Epic Proportions (Dinosaur, Mythical Creature, Nightmare or Sci-Fi)

[5] Fan Club (Artisan, Athlete, or Superbeing)

[6] Ghost Ship (Ancient Warrior, Fantasy, or Undead)

[5] Hatred's Mirror (Alien Shape, Disproportional, or Unusual Facial Feature)

[4] Hysterical (Artificial Appearance, Artisan, or Clown)

[5] Legionnaire (Ancient Warrior or Artificial Appearance)

Living Nightmare (Alien Shape, Nightmare, or Stigmata)

Master Stroke (Artisan or Hobbyist)

[5] Mystic Amplifier (Angelic, Fantasy, or Mythic Creature)

[7] Nature's Fury (Plant Life, Mineral or Superbeing)

[5] Necrosis (Nightmare, Pestilence, Stigmata, or Undead)

[3] No Rest (Ancient Warrior, Occupation, Soldier or Superbeing)

[4] Overdrive (Aquatic Biomech, Biomechanical, Sci-Fi or Superbeing)

Pariah's Mantle (Clown, Disproportional, or Unusual Facial Feature)

[7] Passing the Torch (Athlete, Stigmata, or Superbeing)

[3] Payday (Athlete, Hobbyist, or Occupation)

Rallying Cry (Ancient Warrior, Athlete, or Soldier)

[2] Revolting Spit (Dinosaur, Snake, Extra-Terrestrial, or Mythical Creature)

[4] Rigor Mortis (Pestilence, Undead, or Unnatural Limbs)

[6] Seedling (Alien Shape, Angelic, Mythical, Plant Life, and Unnatural)

Shadows of Despair (Nightmare, Pestilence, Substance Abuse, or Victim)

[3] Shadow Swarm (Animal, Pestilence, or Undead)

[5] Share the Needle (Substance Abuse or Victim)

[2] Sideshow (Athlete, Clown, or Disproportional)

[6] Summoner (Infernal, Fantasy, or Nightmare)

[6] The Ties that Bind (Infernal, Nightmare, or Stigmata)

[5] Too Much Stereo (Artisan, Biomechanical, and Hobbyist)

[6] Urban Golem (Artificial Appearance, Gear-Head, Fantasy, or Mineral)

[4] War Cry (Ancient Warrior, Dinosaur, or Fantasy)

Beguiling Beauty

Upon activating this Talent, the unnatural good looks of the user become, quite literally, stunning. Anyone who looks directly at the Beguiling Beauty must make a save vs magic roll of 12 or higher. Any person who saves is unaffected, but those who fail are awestruck at the mere sight of the Nightbane and blissfully unaware of anything other than the character's beauty and what she or he is doing. Victims stand slack-jawed staring at the Beauty while a bank vault is emptied, prisoners escape, etc. After the individuals snap out of being beguiled, the only part of the experience they remember is the image of the Beguiling Beauty who so transfixed them. Opponents not beguiled are still a bit distracted by the Beguiling Beauty

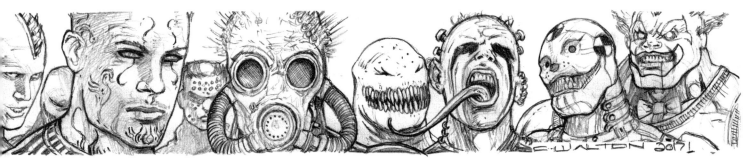

and are -1 on all combat rolls and -5% on the performance of skills.

Prerequisites: The character must have at least one feature from the Unnatural Beauty, Angelic, or Superbeing table as well as an experience level of 6 or greater before Beguiling Beauty may be selected.

Limitations: Only usable in Morphus form. Beguiling Beauty will not keep the victims from reacting to attacks directed at them by anyone other than the Beguiling Beauty, but they only fight to defend themselves or to quickly take down their attacker so they can return to admiring the beauty. Any hostile or aggressive action on the part of the Nightbane who is the Beguiling Beauty immediately cancels this Talent's effects and those who were enthralled snap out of the enchantment as if waking from a dream.

This Talent does not work on those impervious to illusion or mind control.

Range: 8 foot (2.4 m) radius per level of the Nightbane's experience.

Duration: See cost below. Trance lasts for 1 minute (4 melee rounds) after the Talent lapses or the affected person is no longer within range.

Costs: Twelve P.P.E. to acquire permanently. Nine P.P.E. per melee round.

Beyond the Call

History is full of stories of relatively unremarkable individuals performing extraordinary feats of courage, endurance, strength, etc. With this Talent, a Nightbane can channel magical energy to accomplish similarly astonishing results. When activating Beyond the Call, the player selects ONE of the following traits to temporarily boost to a superhuman level: I.Q., Mental Endurance, Physical Strength, Physical Prowess, Physical Endurance, Speed, and/or S.D.C.

Prerequisites: The Nightbane must be at least level 4 and have one or more features from the Soldier (any), Superbeing, or Occupation table.

Limitations: Only usable in Morphus form.

Temporary Augmentation: +200 S.D.C. points, +30 to Spd, +12 to P.S., +12 to I.Q., +10 to P.E., +8 to M.E., or +8 to P.P.; make sure all appropriate bonuses are applied for the duration.

Range: Self only.

Duration: Two melee rounds (30 seconds).

Costs: Fourteen P.P.E. to acquire permanently. Eight P.P.E. to select any ONE of the temporary boosts described above to enable the Nightbane to perform above and beyond the call of duty.

Choke

This Talent enables the Nightbane to cause opponents to suddenly *fail the next action he takes.* Whether it is a combat roll to strike, parry, dodge, etc., a Perception Roll, a saving throw, skill roll, etc., the opponent who fails to save vs magic automatically fails his next action and suffers the consequences for it (if any). To save, the victim needs a 15 or better to save vs magic. Targets who do save are not impacted by this magic.

Prerequisites: At least one feature from the Athlete, Artisan, Hobbyist, Occupation or Infernal table, and the Nightbane must be at least level 3 to acquire the Choke Talent.

Limitations: The Nightbane must be in Morphus form to use this Talent.

The user of Choke typically has no way of knowing for certain what a target's next action will be, meaning guesswork, timing and a bit of luck are often involved when using this Talent.

Range: 100 feet (30.5 m) per level of experience and the target must be visible; line of sight.

Duration: Affects only the next action of a one specific character, but his failure could have lasting consequences, like failing to save vs poison or mind control, or he may lose control and crash his vehicle for flubbing a roll, or get captured becaue he missed a Perception Roll, etc.

Costs: Sixteen P.P.E. to acquire permanently. Eight P.P.E. per use of this Talent.

Contortionist

A brutal yet effective means of attacking and debilitating opponents, this Talent enables the user to violently manipulate the limbs of his victims. Upon activating Contortionist, the Nightbane dislocates one of his or her own limbs or digits (1D4 damage to the user). The target of the Talent then must attempt to save vs magic of 12 or better. If the save is unsuccessful, an arm, leg, tentacle, etc., is twisted and contorted out of socket. This attack does 2D6 damage and inhibits the use of that limb until medical attention is provided, or the damage is healed.

Having one's limb dislocated in this way is incredibly painful, causing most ordinary human victims to pass out for 1D4 melee rounds (15-60 seconds). A roll to save vs pain of 14 or better (using any M.E. bonuses) allows the victim to stay conscious. Even if the target remains conscious, however, the pain is distracting and causes the loss of two melee attacks, -3 penalty on initiative and all Perception Rolls, and Skills are performed at -15%. Losing the use of one arm imposes a -3 penalty to strike, parry, disarm, and entangle, as well as preventing the use of weapons or tools with that limb. Losing the use of half of all legs drops Spd by 70% and imposes a penalty of -6 to dodge. Losing use of a wing, fin, or other appendage prevents winged flight, reduces swimming Spd by 70%, inhibits the use of any special attack, and so on, as is appropriate (G.M.s, use your discretion).

The Contortionist Talent can be used multiple times consecutively on the same limb to overcome a victim's supernatural healing rate (penalties last until all damage done to the limb by this Talent is regenerated). For lesser targets like normal humans,

healing is likely to take 1D4 weeks unless psionic or magical healing is used.

Prerequisites: The Nightbane must be at least level six before acquiring this Talent and must have at least one Morphus feature from the Unnatural Limbs, Victim, or Disproportional Tables.

Limitations: Only usable in Morphus form. The user must have some kind of appendage or digit that can be dislocated as well.

Range: Touch or four feet (1.2 m) away; line of sight.

Duration: Instant. Penalties last until a successful First Aid or higher medical skill is used to reset the limb in the socket or damage is regenerated/healed.

Costs: Sixteen P.P.E. to acquire permanently. Ten P.P.E. per use.

Corrupting Influence

Temporarily turning the Talent user into the archetypical "silver-tongued devil," the Corrupting Influence Talent makes victims more susceptible to suggestions relating to their darker nature. Such suggestions might play to a target's greed, jealousy, anger, lust for revenge, etc. For instance, a bullied teenager might be talked into attacking the bully, an ambitious gang-banger into skimming profits from his crew's drug sales, or a jealous wife into trying to kill her husband's coworker.

Whatever the task the Talent user wants to accomplish, there must be a justifiable motive for the person affected to do it, which is likely to require some intelligence-gathering on the player's part. The assigned task can even be something the target normally wouldn't do as long as it isn't more than one alignment below their current alignment. So a person who is Scrupulous could not be made to torture another person for fun, but they could be made to threaten torture and maybe slap their prisoner around, or lie to another good person since that is allowed under an Unprincipled alignment. Submitting to a Corrupting Influence does NOT make that character become an evil alignment, it means he was pushed to do something he normally would not. His alignment does not drop though he may feel guilt and regret. FYI: A Selfish or evil aligned character can just as likely be convinced to perform a good deed.

Potential victims can attempt to save vs magic to prevent the effects of Corrupting Influence. Those of *good alignment* need a 12 or better to save, *selfish characters* need a 14 or better, and *evil characters* require a 16 or better to do something that is morally questionable or reprehensible. A Nightbane using this Talent can tell whether or not it is successful before they make the suggestion.

Prerequisites: The Nightbane must be at least level 4 and have one or more features from the Infernal, Substance Abuse, or Unearthly Beauty table, and the Nightbane's own alignment must be Anarchist or evil to take a Talent that manipulates and corrupts people.

Limitations: See description, above.

Those affected by this Talent can NOT be made to seriously injure themselves or a loved one. If the Talent user or a recognized ally attacks a person under the sway of Corrupting Influence, its effects are immediately negated the moment after the deed is done.

Range: Touch or 10 feet (3 m) and must be able to hear the Talent user speak.

Duration: The Talent is only good for a single suggestion per use.

Costs: Sixteen P.P.E. to acquire permanently. Four P.P.E. per suggestion for targets with an *evil* alignment, 8 P.P.E. per suggestion to those of a *selfish* alignment, and 12 P.P.E. per suggestion for those of a *good* alignment.

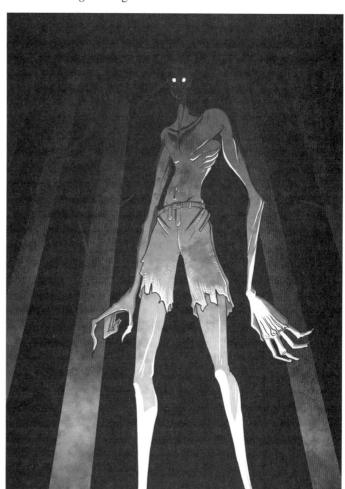

Dark Dreams

This Talent has a handful of different uses involving nightmares and the manipulation of dreams. First, it can be used on a sleeping target to attempt to impose a nightmare. If the victim fails the saving throw, a nightmare with the chosen level of Horror Factor invades his dreams. The victim must then attempt to

save vs the nightmare's Horror Factor or awaken within 1D4 melee rounds feeling robbed of any sleep previously attained – no restored Hit Points, S.D.C. or P.P.E. or I.S.P. While this may not seem powerful at first glance, if used over a long period of time and even combined with other tactics, it can debilitate or even drive people insane.

If the Talent user is capable of entering Dream Pools (page 83 of **Nightbane® World Book One: Between the Shadows**), Dark Dreams can be used to orchestrate a nightmare from within and even engage in dream combat. In this case, activating the Talent lets the user try to "darken" or reshape the surroundings in a way that makes the Dream Pool scarier and more menacing. If the dreamer fails to resist, the environment takes on a Horror Factor of 5 plus the Talent user's experience level (e.g. a result of 9 if the Nightbane is 4th level, 15 if the Nightbane was 10th level, etc.). From there, the Nightbane can even turn dream constructs native to that Dream Pool against the dreamer or level Dream Manipulation attacks as per Dream Combat rules (see pages 89-91 of **Between the Shadows**) with a +3 bonus.

Prerequisites: At least one feature from the Nightmare, Victim, Substance Abuse, or Mythical Creature table. The character must be level 2 or higher to select this Talent.

Limitations: Can only be used in Morphus form.

This power can only cause or worsen nightmares, it cannot be used to end a nightmare, decrease its intensity or to give it a happy ending. Dark Dreams also cannot be used in the Dream Pool of the Talent's user. Only the dreamer and any dream constructs native to the Dream Pool can be affected with the exception of dream attacks.

The maximum possible Horror Factor for an imposed nightmare is 15, while the limit when darkening a Dream Pool is 17.

Range: Up to 3 feet (0.9 m) from the target when imposing nightmares. Affects a single target's Dream Pool.

Duration: 1D4 minutes for imposed nightmares, otherwise see cost below.

Saving Throws: Resisting an imposed nightmare requires a save vs magic of 14 or better. The same is required for a dream construct to resist the Nightbane's control. Resisting the manipulation of one's own Dream Pool requires dream combat rolls, and can be rolled at the beginning of each melee round the dreamer's Dream Pool is under the Talent-user's influence. If the dreamer wrests control back from the Nightbane, all capability to manipulate constructs and bonuses to dream attacks end.

Costs: Thirteen P.P.E. to acquire permanently. Five P.P.E. to impose a nightmare (+1 P.P.E. per additional point of Horror Factor), 12 P.P.E. per minute to darken a Dream Pool, 8 P.P.E. per minute to manipulate a dream construct, and 2 P.P.E. per dream attack.

Dark Fathom

Aquatic Nightbane can use this Talent to temporarily change the water nearby to that of the darkest ocean depths. Inside the affected area, no light penetrates from the outside, meaning that even passive nightvision does not work, though flashlights, sonar, and other means of navigating underwater still function. Magical or Supernatural nightvision works, but at half the usual range. For some reason natural buoyancy is also reduced, preventing victims from simply floating back to the surface.

Despite the fact that people and creatures caught in a Dark Fathom might have means of seeing, the experience is still frightening. Veteran divers must save vs a Horror Factor of 10, but sea creatures and inexperienced divers are more likely to panic and need to save vs a Horror Factor of 15. Those who fail to save, panic and become disoriented. Roll again every melee round (15 seconds) to see if the victim can get a grip and act rationally. Until such time as a person saves, they swim in confused circles trying to remember how to get back to the surface. In this panicked state, the victim is also more vulnerable to attack: -4 to all combat rolls and Perception Rolls, double if blind, and unable to perform skills other than *Swimming*. Sea creatures almost always flee the dark waters as quickly as possible.

Without an oxygen supply, a panicked character only lasts 10 seconds per each P.E. attribute point before drowning! Those with an oxygen supply use it up twice as fast from being panicked. Meanwhile, the temperature of the darkened water drops to a chilly 39 degrees Fahrenheit (4 degrees Celsius), which can cause unprotected swimmers to suffer the effects of hypothermia within 1D4 minutes (-20% to skills, -1 attack, and -2 on all combat rolls). Even with oxygen, a normal person will slip into unconsciousness within 5D6 minutes (+1 minute per point of P.E.) of exposure to the frigid Dark Fathom and likely drown. Supernatural beings like Nightbane and Guardians who do not have special protection from the cold will take 4D4 minutes to suffer from hypothermia and 2D4x10+P.E. attribute in minutes before falling unconscious.

Prerequisites: At least one feature from an Aquatic Animal table or the Aquatic Biomech table. The Nightbane must be at least level three to acquire this Talent.

Limitations: The Nightbane must be in Morphus form to utilize Dark Fathom.

Range: Up to 100 feet (30.5 m) away +10 feet (3 m) per level of experience. Affects a 20 foot (6.1 m) radius per level of experience.

Duration: See cost below. Hypothermia penalties last for 3D6x10 minutes after drying off (1D4x10 for supernatural creatures).

Costs: Ten P.P.E. to acquire permanently. Six P.P.E. to activate and 4 P.P.E. for every additional minute sustained.

Diamond-Hide

This Talent is used to greatly increase the Talent user's resistance to damage for a time, turning them into a supernatural juggernaut capable of shrugging off a hail of attacks. This is especially useful for Nightbane who already have a Natural A.R. as it costs less to boost the existing Natural A.R. than generating one from scratch. While Diamond-Hide is active, the skin of the user takes on a sheen like a rough-cut gemstone or volcanic glass. All of the normal features of the Natural A.R. function as usual, only the numerical value is enhanced.

Prerequisites: Not available until level 7 and the Talent user must have at least one feature from the Mineral, Mythical Creature, or Artificial Appearance Table.

Limitations: Can only be used in Morphus form.

The maximum boost allowed is limited to 2 A.R. points per level of the Nightbane up to a cap of A.R. 18. This only affects the Nightbane and not any equipment or armor in the possession of the user.

Magical and psionic attacks ignore any boost provided by Diamond-Hide, meaning attacks from spells like Call Lightning, Talents like Shadow Blast, and psionics like Pyrokinesis use the original A.R. (if any) to determine if damage is inflicted upon the Nightbane.

Range: Self only.

Duration: One minute.

Costs: Nine P.P.E. to acquire permanently. Five P.P.E. per each point of Natural A.R. added.

Divine Wrath

In an impressive display of supernatural power, the user of Divine Wrath appears to call down devastating retribution on anyone unfortunate enough to be in the area of effect. Once this Talent is activated, the Nightbane becomes wreathed in a halo of light or fire, and appears to float weightlessly into the air. Maximum speed is unchanged and floating height is only 5 feet/1.5 m per level of experience. By pointing or gesturing at a nearby area, a rain of destruction is called down from on high to strike any being caught within.

Whether this attack takes the form of bolts of lightning, a rain of fire, shafts of searing light, or something similar, the damage and effects are always the same. Any target struck by this attack – or physically striking or grappling with the Nightbane while wrapped in the halo of light or fire – takes damage based on his or her alignment: Good beings take only 2D6 damage, selfish take 4D6 damage, and evil beings take 1D6x10 damage! *Double the damage* to supernatural beings and magical creatures, and *triple* damage against demons, Nightlords, their avatars and all evil creatures from the Nightlands! The Talent user of Divine Wrath is +5 to strike with this onslaught, but only rolls once per melee attack. Targets within the area of effect may try to dodge, there is no saving throw. The area affected can be changed each time the Nightbane attacks.

Prerequisites: At least one feature from the Angelic, Fantasy, or Ancient Warrior table. The character must be at least level 7 before acquiring Divine Wrath.

Limitations: Only usable in Morphus form, typically in dire circumstances.

Can only be used once every four melee rounds (60 seconds). While using the Talent the Nightbane can use no other Talents, spells, or abilities and can only attempt to dodge incoming attacks (use normal bonuses).

Range: 10 foot (3 m) diameter of effect per level of experience up to 500 feet (152.4 m) away +50 feet (15.2 m) per level of experience.

Duration: One melee round (15 seconds), four energy blasts from Divine Wrath in that one melee round. Uses up ALL the Nightbane's attacks.

Costs: Twenty-five P.P.E. to acquire permanently and 30 P.P.E. per use.

Epic Proportions

As the name suggests, this Talent enables the Nightbane to temporarily grow to a massive size, up to 30 feet (9.1 m). **Bonuses:** Temporarily double the Talent-user's weight and add 100 S.D.C. per every 10 feet (3 m) of height to the character's current amount (Hit Points are unchanged). Add +10 points to the P.S. (and adjust the damage inflicted by punches, kicks and stomps), and +10 to Spd attribute. **Penalties:** -1D6 points from the P.P. attribute, all combat bonuses of the Nightbane are halved if the P.P. attribute falls below 8 and negated entirely at a P.P. attribute of 2. Horror Factor is increased by one point per each 10 feet of height up to a maximum of 18. Keep in mind, though, that the bigger and scarier the character becomes, the more likely it is that enemies (and mistaken allies) will attack the giant

Prerequisites: At least one feature from the Mythical Creature, Dinosaur, Nightmare or Sci-Fi table. This Talent cannot be selected until level 5.

Limitations: Can only be used while in Morphus form. No other Talent may be used by the character while Epic Proportions is in effect.

Range: Self.

Duration: One minute (4 melee rounds) per level of experience.

Costs: Eighteen P.P.E. to acquire permanently. Fifteen P.P.E. per 10 feet (3 m) of additional height.

Fan Club

In much the same way that god-like beings can call upon the support of worshipers to increase reserves of magical energy, a Nightbane with this Talent can draw strength from his or her own

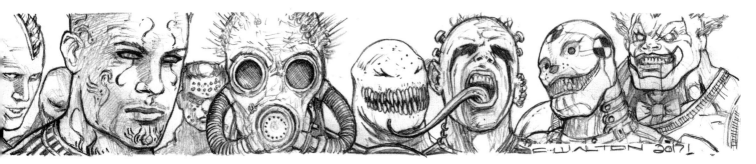

ethereal fan club; i.e. members of his team or Faction (player characters and NPCs), and any people rooting for him or for the downfall of his opponent, such as a Nightlord or his minions. The Fan Club Talent does not actually take a perceptible amount of P.P.E. from the teammates or bystanders but rather generates P.P.E. from their focus and emotions.

When the Fan Club Talent is activated, a low chanting or cheering can be heard near the Talent user and the Nightbane suddenly feels inspired and cheered on just like when a crowd of fans support a sports hero or team against the opposition. This gives the Nightbane a mystical energy bump and he suddenly finds himself with an extra 2D6+15 P.P.E. available to use for the activation of other Talents or the casting of spells. For the duration of this ability, every melee round the Talent user needs to expend P.P.E., the cheering grows a bit louder and the 2D6+15 P.P.E. is available to him. The Fan Club also gives him a temporary bonus of +1 on all saving throws and +20 to save vs coma/death.

Prerequisites: A feature from the Athlete, Artisan, or Superbeing table. Not available until 5th level.

Limitations: Can only be used in Morphus form.

A maximum of 27 P.P.E. may become available every melee round while this talent is activated to supplement his own.

Range: Self, or other by touch.

Duration: 1D4 melee rounds +1 melee round per level of experience.

Costs: Twenty-seven P.P.E. to acquire permanently. Twenty P.P.E. to activate.

Ghost Ship

This Talent gives the user the ability to summon a supernatural conveyance in the form of a large, ghostly sailing vessel. This ship is roughly the size of a Corsair/large cutter approximately 80 feet (24.4 m) long and 20 feet (6.1 m) wide. With the amount of space available, 30-50 passengers plus 40 tons of cargo can be carried onboard the Ghost Ship. Despite the ship's size, the only crew needed is the Nightbane Talent user. He controls every aspect of it.

While the aesthetics of the ship may vary widely from user to user, the basic abilities are the same: 50 S.D.C. per level of the Talent user, sails seeming to blow in the wind and like the legend of the Flying Dutchman, it floats silently through the air, so it functions on dry land as well as over water and has a *Prowl of 50%*. The maximum altitude is 1,000 feet (305 m), but it manages a respectable 60 mph (96 kph) at "full sail" without actually needing any winds. This top speed is increased to 90 mph (144 kph) if traveling along a ley line or within a ley line triangle like the Bermuda Triangle. The Ghost Ship seems to bring a fog with it that makes the ship appear to be floating on a small cloud. When moving at 20 mph (32 kph) or slower, the fog envelops the entire ship and it is not recognized as anything but a fog bank (+30% to Prowl).

Used for transporting people and cargo. No weapon capabilities.

Prerequisites: Unavailable before level 6. The Nightbane must have at least one feature from the Ancient Warrior, Fantasy, or Undead table before Ghost Ship can be selected.

Limitations: Can only be used in Morphus form.

Range: Self. The user must remain onboard the ship at all times. If he leaves the ship the Talent is cancelled and the vessel vanishes.

Duration: 20 minutes per 30 P.P.E. expended, but the Talent may be sustained for three times as long when on a ley line. Fog is maintained indefinitely as long as the Talent remains in effect.

Costs: Twenty-three P.P.E. to acquire permanently. Thirty P.P.E. to activate and for every additional 20 minutes of travel. No additional P.P.E. is needed to sustain the ship if it stays within one mile (1.6 km) of a ley line.

Hatred's Mirror

Typically developed by Nightbane who know what it is to be ostracized and abused, this is a powerful Talent capable of turning aside any attack born of anger, hatred, or other ill intent. Furthermore, for the duration of this ability, any opponent with foul motives who attacks the Talent user will discover the true price of hatred as the damage that would normally be dealt to his victim is instead inflicted upon the aggressor! This reflects the fact that hatred can destroy one's own soul just as surely as it can destroy one's enemies.

The type of attack leveled at the Nightbane under the protection of Hatred's Mirror does not matter. Whether it is a punch, psychic attack, spell, or Talent, if the user is targeted then Hatred's Mirror will redirect the effects back to the point of origin. If the attack has an area of effect it centers on the person who launched it. In the case of spells, psionics, and Talents, some, like a Domination spell, simply fail to work, and the attacker whose own magic is being turned on him still gets to attempt to roll a saving throw but with a -2 to save penalty.

It is important to note that some redirected attacks go completely unnoticed by the attacker. This is especially likely if opponents are in a blind rage or blood frenzy. For the first attack redirected by Hatred's Mirror, roll a Perception check for the attacker to see if he realizes what just happened. If the result is lower than a 12 (may be higher for enraged, insane, or slow-witted opponents), the self-inflicted damage goes unnoticed. Continue to roll for each attack until he realizes what is going on, at which point the aggressor understands his attacks are only hurting himself, and not the Talent user.

Prerequisites: The Nightbane must have at least one feature from the Unusual Facial Feature, Alien Shape, or Disproportional table as well as reach 5th level before this Talent can be obtained.

Limitations: Can only be used in Morphus form.

Only malicious attacks are redirected by Hatred's Mirror. If the aggressor is simply trying to restrain the Nightbane, protect others, or otherwise has good intentions behind any offense, it is not redirected back at him.

The Talent user cannot make any kind of attack against anyone while this Talent is active or it is immediately canceled.

Range: Self.

Duration: One melee round.

Costs: Twenty-four P.P.E. to acquire permanently. Sixteen P.P.E. per melee round.

Hysterical

Humor has long been a part of human interaction, and those who can make others laugh possess a special kind of power. The Hysterical Talent takes this humor and laughter into the realm of the supernatural. Use of the Talent enables a Nightbane to imbue an object or himself with the ability to cause uncontrolled bouts of hysterical laughter in others.

If used on oneself, the character has to do something funny to afflict other people with laughter. This may be a silly face, funny little jig, telling a joke or saying or doing something that most people will find funny. Objects enchanted by this Talent must look funny or be used in a comical way, even if it is just a hand drawn alteration to a photograph, like drawing a silly mustache on a portrait.

Any person who sees the cartoon, photo, video, etc., or hears the joke, goofy song, pratfall, slapstick or pantomime, etc., must save vs magic of 15 or higher or succumb to a laughing fit.

At first glance, this may not seem very horrifying or debilitating, but anyone who has ever been unable to stop laughing for a prolonged period can relay how uncomfortable and even frightening such a loss of control can be. This laughing fit is even worse, causing loss of motor control, pain in the chest and throat, the face turns red, and each victim has difficulty breathing. Anyone caught in the grips of such a laughing spell automatically has last initiative, his attacks per melee round are reduced by half, -5 to all combat rolls, -50% to skill performance. If attacked by the Talent user, the hysterical person is unable to defend against his first attack because he is laughing too hard.

Prerequisites: Hysterical is not available until level 4, and even then only to Nightbane with at least one feature from the Clown, Artisan, or Artificial Appearance table.

Limitations: Can only be used in Morphus form, and victims can only be affected by this Talent one time per 12 hour period. Hysterical only works on intelligent beings with a relatively human sense of humor. Animals, wholly alien beings, and most supernatural monsters, and the like, are unaffected. However, Nightlords, Night Princes and Princesses, Doppelgangers, Guardians, and similar supernatural beings are susceptible, as are any who have human sensibilities about humor. In short, anyone who smiles, chuckles or laughs at the Talent user's antics is af-

fected, and that includes multiple people. Anyone watching who finds it funny will become hysterical. If a victim is attacked in any way while under the influence of Hysterical, the influence and penalties end in 1D6 seconds.

Range: Self or an object/prop up to 10 feet (3 m) away. The power then affects anyone that sees or hears the humor.

Duration: The power can be activated and remain latent for up to one day per level of the Talent user. Once the power becomes active, it can affect people for 5D6 minutes. Those who fail to save against this Talent suffer penalties for 1D6 minutes, +1 minute per level of the Talent user.

Costs: Sixteen P.P.E. to acquire permanently. Fourteen P.P.E. per use.

Legionnaire

Nightbane who choose this Talent gain the ability to create shadowy copies of themselves to help even the odds when outnumbered. These copies of the Morphus form have half the Talent user's combat bonuses reduced by half, half the number of attacks per melee round, skills are performed at half his ability, and each copy has only 30% of their creator's S.D.C. and no Hit Points. The P.S. of these copies is also reduced by half (minimum P.S. of 10), but is still Supernatural. Even if the

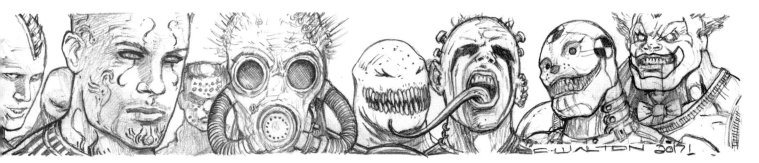

Nightbane's Morphus has a Natural A.R., it does NOT apply to copies created via Legionnaire. The shadow copies of the user act on their own to defend the person they are a copy of, as well as any of his nearby associates, but can also be ordered by their creator to perform specific tasks. Each simple command takes a single action.

If a Legionnaire is destroyed by reducing its S.D.C. to zero, it disappears into fading bits of shadow, leaving no trace it ever existed. Copies can also be dispelled by things such as an Anti-Magic Cloud incantation or the aura from an Anti-Arcane Talent, and take double damage from light-based attacks such as a Guardian's light blast. They may be fooled by illusions, but any spell, psionic, or other ability that targets the mind such as Hypnotic Suggestion or Telepathy fail. Shadow copies Prowl at 70% in shadows and dark environments, they do not emit heat, and will not set off pressure-plates, though tripwires, surveillance cameras, and motion detectors will catch them.

Prerequisites: Nightbane selecting this Talent must have at least one Morphus feature from the Ancient Warrior or Artificial Appearance table and be at least 5th level in experience.

Limitations: Can only be used in Morphus form. Copies of the user created by this Talent are unable to speak, cast spells, or activate Talents. For every pair of copies created, subtract one melee attack/action from the user. If reduced to no attacks/actions the Nightbane is unable to do anything but direct the created copies and no more can be created until one or more is dismissed or destroyed.

Range: The copies must stay within 10 feet (3 m) per level of experience of the user.

Duration: One minute at level 5, but add an additional minute for each subsequent level after 5.

Costs: Seventeen P.P.E. to acquire permanently. Fifteen P.P.E. per each individual copy created.

Living Nightmare

Upon activating this Talent, the Nightbane becomes the epitome of fear. Each person within the area of effect must roll a save vs magic or save vs illusion of 14 or higher. For all who fail to save, the Talent user appears to change into whatever it is each individual fears most. This gives the 'Bane an effective Horror Factor of 14+1D4 to each affected person. Victims must then roll a save against this new Horror Factor without the aid of *any* bonuses. Failing vs this Horror Factor means the victim is willing to do almost anything to get away from the horrifying Talent user, even trampling others that are in his path of escape. Unlike normal Horror Factor, though, the first attack directed at the terrified victim does NOT automatically succeed. In fact, those affected are +3 to dodge the Nightbane and want nothing more than to get away.

Prerequisites: One or more features from the Nightmare, Stigmata, or Alien Shape table.

Limitations: Can only be used in Morphus form. Powerful supernatural creatures such as Nightlords, Night Princes, Reshapers, and Ancient Nightbane are immune to this Talent, as are animated dead, Golems, and any other beings who do not experience fear. Anyone affected by this Talent can attempt to re-roll the save vs Horror Factor at the beginning of each new melee round.

Range: Self, but targets are affected up to 20 feet (6.1 m) away per level of experience; line of sight required.

Duration: The Nightmare lasts 30 seconds (2 melee rounds) per level of experience, but victims are affected until they flee from sight or roll a successful save vs Horror Factor.

Costs: Fifteen P.P.E. to acquire permanently. Eight P.P.E. per use.

Master Stroke (In the Zone)

Many artists claim to fall into a certain state of mind when at peak performance. This state is referred to by many different names: being "hot," "in the zone," and "creating up a storm" to name a few. The Master Stroke Talent taps this phenomenon and enables the Talent user to boost the performance of any one skill to phenomenal quality if so desired. Any recipient of this boon feels focused, refreshed, and ready to tackle the task at hand. Once underway, inspiration comes fast and furiously, with work completed at a breakneck speed (half the normal rate) without any reduction of quality. If the skill roll is successful, the quality of the work is impeccable.

Some downsides to the use of the Master Stroke Talent do exist. First, anyone engaged in using the skill boosted by Master Stroke is totally focused on the task at hand. The worker does not stop to eat, sleep, and may not even take a bathroom break. They are -10 to Perception Rolls to notice anything going on around them, and if roused from the task, have half the normal attacks per melee and no combat bonuses whatsoever! Second, this heightened state is exhausting, feeling like twice the amount of effort expended. It isn't uncommon for a person to fall into a deep sleep for 10 or more hours after the Talent lapses and need a giant meal once awakened.

There is the dark truth that people can become addicted to the effects of Master Stroke. There is a certain rush when engaged in an activity one is good at, as well as a sense of fulfillment with a job well-done. Given that most would rather be naturally gifted than work long and hard to become masterfully skilled, the shortcut to greatness offered by this Talent can be a powerful temptation. Unscrupulous Nightbane over the centuries have used Master Stroke to empower and enthrall renowned artists, inventors, and even politicians. These 'Bane then became the muse, consultant, or advisor to these powerful figures and reaped the rewards.

Each time an individual is affected by this Talent, a Mental Endurance saving throw should be rolled (12 or better is needed). A failed roll causes a -10% penalty to the skill that lasts for 2D4

days due to lack of self-confidence. Upon failing three consecutive rolls, the unfortunate soul is addicted to Master Stroke and suffers a -20% penalty to all the skills that have been previously augmented by this Talent, and -5% to all others. This makes him want, even need, to be under the influence of Master Stroke. Kicking this addiction should be role-played, and may include a group intervention, counseling, or even a major confidence restoring success with the skills while not aided by this Talent. G.M.s may reserve level related skill growth to any skill used in conjunction with this Talent.

Prerequisites: The Nightbane must have a feature from the Artisan or Hobbyist table.

Limitations: Can only be used in Morphus form. The maximum possible bonus is +5% per level of the Talent user's experience. Master Stroke does not work on combat skills such as hand to hand combat or W.P.s, or special abilities like track by scent. Only skills may be affected. Anyone other than the user can only be affected once per day by this Talent. Unwilling targets get a chance to save vs magic (12+ saves).

Range: Self, or other by touch.

Duration: Varies by task; 24 hours maximum.

Costs: Eleven P.P.E. to acquire permanently. One P.P.E. per percentage point of the skill bonus imposed by this Talent.

Mystic Amplifier

This powerful Talent increases the P.P.E reserve of the Nightbane for a limited duration. Upon activation, the user's remaining P.P.E. is doubled. Any P.P.E. expended by the user is subtracted from the added points first before the personal reserve is used. However, this additional P.P.E. is made freely available to any person within range who can draw upon it, including enemy magic-users. Another pitfall of Mystic Amplifier is that any being sensitive to magic energy can track a Nightbane using this Talent from an additional 500 feet (152 m) away.

While the Nightbane's P.P.E. base is amplified, he becomes a transitional place of power that increases the range and duration of incantations 50% by any spell caster within 20 feet (6.1 m) of him, as well as any spells or other Talents he may cast himself.

Prerequisites: Mystic Amplifier is unavailable until level 5. The Nightbane must have at least one Mythical Creature, Fantasy, or Angelic Morphus trait.

Limitations: Can only be used in Morphus form. The maximum P.P.E. amplification possible is 150%. The bonuses to magic range, duration, and damage do not stack with other Talents, abilities, or even phenomena like ley lines or celestial alignments. Simply use the more powerful of the two effects in such situations.

Range: Self, but the added P.P.E. can be drawn on at twice the normal distance. The magic amplification affects a 50 foot (15.s m) radius per 50% P.P.E. bonus.

Duration: 1D4 melees, +1 melee round per level of experience.

Costs: Twenty-two P.P.E. to acquire permanently. Ten P.P.E. per 50% P.P.E. bonus.

Nature's Fury

One of the most destructive Talents known to exist, this ability calls on the awesome power of nature to carve a swath of devastation. While similar in some ways to the Storm Maker Talent, Nature's Fury is narrower in scope and purpose. It is used solely to damage or destroy large areas by creating localized natural disasters. Though the area of effect is smaller than Storm Maker, Nature's Fury puts a much wider variety of damaging forces at the disposal of the Talent user.

While the Nightbane is immune to the destruction (buildings collapse around but not on the user, can walk through burning buildings without singeing a hair, etc.), use of this Talent will make the user a *priority target* to his enemies, as well as any Nightlords, Avatars, Night Princes or Princesses, Hound Masters and NSB agents. Good and even selfish characters are highly unlikely to unleash such destruction when innocent people are in harm's way, and anyone who acts to the contrary of their alignment will see it drop to the next level (Scrupulous to Unprincipled, Unprincipled to Anarchist, and so on). Moreover, any character who uses Nature's Fury in a populated area is likely to incur the wrath of local factions and heroes who do not condone such callous behavior or drawing such attention to themselves.

The following are guidelines for the most common natural disasters created. Or use the descriptions and stats presented in the Dead Reign Sourcebook: Hell Followed.

Blizzard/Ice Storm: The temperature of the entire affected area plunges to -6D6 degrees Fahrenheit (21 to 37 degrees Celsius) below freezing within 1D4x10 minutes of the Talent's activation. Once it does, 3 inches (7.6 cm) of snow or one inch (2.5 cm) of icy precipitation will fall per hour of duration (half for the secondary radius). This precipitation falls so quickly it reduces visibility to a mere 5D6 feet (1.5 to 9.1 m), halting almost all traffic (-80% to speed, -60% to piloting skill rolls, and -80% to navigation or tracking rolls). Old or shoddy structures may start to see some structural damage such as roof collapses at 12 inches (30 cm) of snow or 4 inches (10 cm) of ice (and building codes aren't what they used to be on Nightbane Earth). Anyone exposed to this weather can survive just 6D6 minutes +1 minute per point of P.E. without protection so shelter should be sought immediately. Every five minutes of exposure imposes a cumulative -5% penalty to skills, -1 attack per melee, -2 to all combat rolls, and -15% to speed. Supernatural creatures can survive for four times the norm and take four times as long to suffer penalties.

Earthquake/Landslide: The entirety of the primary radius is rocked by a powerful earthquake and then 1D4 aftershocks per hour. Trying to stand or walk is next to impossible with the ground bucking and roiling, leaving victims the only option of crawling at 1/4 normal speed. 1D4x10+40% of all non-hardened buildings

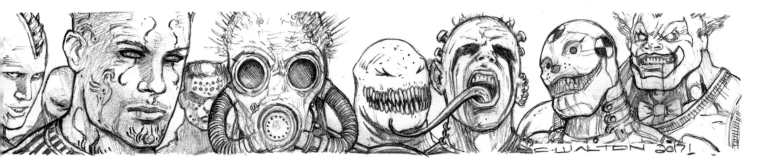

in the radius are reduced to rubble in 2D4 melees with anyone inside or hit by a landslide being dealt 1D4x10 damage. There is a 50% likelihood of being trapped/buried in such a collapse (half that for beings with Supernatural Strength). The secondary radius is rattled, with 5D6% of buildings partially or completely collapsing (3D6 damage from debris and a 30% chance of being trapped) and half that suffering structural damage such as cracked foundations. As this is an unnatural occuranc, aftershocks do not follow.

Flash Flood/Tsunami: A sudden torrential downpour or tectonic activity affecting a nearby body of water sends a large wave racing through the area. This wave is an average of 4D4+6 feet (3.1-6.7 m) tall, and demolishes any one-story building and damages average two-story houses, as well as knocks out power and other utilities, and completely floods basements and underground structures. The churning, debris laden water does 2D6 damage to victims caught on first impact and every minute trapped in the rushing water from being hit by debris and/or smashed into obstacles. Swimming is done at -50%, but three successful skill rolls (roll one per melee round) carries a character to relative safety on high ground or behind the wave. Vehicles are swept away by the tide and submerged, likely trapping any occupants inside. Anyone trapped underwater for more than 15 seconds per point of P.E. will drown. After the initial wave, residual flooding stands at 2D4 feet (0.6 to 2.4 m). The secondary radius will see minor flooding of 1D4+1 feet (0.6 to 1.5 m) and sporadic utility outages.

Thunderstorm: Heavy rain causes minor flooding to the primary radius and low-lying areas nearby like creeks and storm water canals. High winds make flying and road travel difficult: Reduce visibility to 200 feet (61 m) and -30% to piloting and navigation skills. Characters who can fly see their speed reduced by 20%, they get drenched and there is a 50% chance of getting struck by lightning every minute they are airborne (6D6 damage and there is a 20% chance of being knocked unconscious for 1D6 melee rounds). Anyone on foot gets drenched and battered by the wind, sees their speed reduced by 20%, and are -1 attack and -1 to all combat rolls (double these penalties for those in the air).

Each hour, there is a 40% chance of large hail that will deal 2D4 damage per melee round to any unprotected person and vehicles in the primary radius for 1D6 melee rounds.

Volcanic Eruption: Only applicable where there is a volcano within 50 miles (80 km). It either causes a volcano to erupt or a magma vein near the surface cracks open and creates small lava vents in the primary radius of effect. Either of these effects causes the ground to fissure and vent superheated gases. Anyone caught within 10 feet (3.1 m) of such a fissure unprotected suffers 2D6 damage per minute from the incredible heat. Unless impervious to heat, fire and/or smoke, the heat and gases makes it difficult to breathe and function: Reduce Spd, the number of melee attacks, all combat bonuses and skill performance by half. Falling into a lava flow means almost certain death, suffering 2D6x10 damage per melee round!

When a volcano erupts, chunks of molten rock and hot ash rain down on the whole area, reducing visibility by half and inflicting 2D6 damage per melee round to anyone who is outside unprotected and Wildfires (see below), could start.

Wildfire: Engulfs the primary radius within 6D6 minutes. Anyone inside who is unshielded from the fire takes 5D6 damage per melee round from the flames and 3D6 damage per melee from smoke inhalation (the more common killer in fires). The pervasive smoke will also reduce visibility by 80%. Anyone who sees the fire start and is willing to flee immediately, is likely be able to escape even on foot (80% chance). Hesitation for any reason lowers this chance by 10% per melee round. In urban settings, there is an average 30% chance of survival by sheltering in place, which drops to 10% elsewhere. 6D6% of all buildings will be gutted or reduced to ruins per hour of the fire if unchecked. Halve this percentage if there is a swift emergency response. Most property such as vehicles will be destroyed if reached by the fire. Secondary effects include minor fire and smoke damage; reduce nearby buildings' S.D.C. by 5D6% and anyone caught in a smaller fire suffers a total of 4D6 damage per melee round.

Prerequisites: 7th level is the earliest Nature's Fury can be acquired, and then only if the Nightbane has a Morphus feature from a Mineral, Plant Life, or Superbeing Table.

Limitations: Can only be activated in Morphus form. The type of disaster created must make sense for the area affected (e.g. no blizzards in the middle of a Death Valley summer). This Talent has no effect on places such as the Astral Plane or the Dreamstream. While the origin of the disaster is magic, any damage dealt is not. Note that activating this Talent requires a 1D4 minute trance wherein the Nightbane communes with nature. If this process is interrupted the P.P.E. is lost and the Talent fails to activate.

Range: The most powerful effects will be localized to the primary 1/2 mile (0.8 km) radius, but secondary effects (half damage and penalties) are felt for an additional 1D4 miles (1.6 to 6.4 km) radius.

Duration: 15 minutes per level of the Talent user's experience or until he is slain or cancels the magic.

Costs: Thirty-five P.P.E. to acquire permanently. 120 P.P.E. per use.

Necrosis

This malicious Talent is capable of inflicting grievous damage on living flesh by accelerating the natural processes of decay. For this power to be effective, the target must have unhealed wounds of some sort, or a stigmata. The injuries can be recent or something still healing from days or weeks before, but do not include long-term wounds that have healed as much as possible such as old scars or a missing limb. A target with such unhealed injuries must save vs magic of 15 or greater or suffer damage from this Talent as the wounds necrotize and the surrounding tissue decays.

A failed roll inflicts 1D6 damage first to S.D.C. then to Hit Points per one point of P.P.E. expended in the use of the Talent. In addition, the victim of Necrosis feels weak and feverish: -2 to attacks per melee, and reduce combat bonuses, Spd, and skill performance by half for 1D6 melee rounds, and are -3 to save vs disease for 1D4 hours. **Note:** Biomechanical, Plant and Alien morphuses suffer half damage and penalties. Mineral Morphuses are immune.

Worse, Nightbane and other beings with regenerative powers, see their healing abilities temporarily shut off! And do not regenerate for five minutes per level of the Talent user! After that, they heal/regenerate as normal. Of course, psionics and magical healing can be used to restore Hit Points and S.D.C. as per the ability or spell.

Characters who successfully save against this Talent suffer no damage, do not lose any melee attacks, heal/regenerate just fine, but feel a bit shaky and are -1 on all combat rolls and -5% on skill performance for 1D6 melee rounds.

Prerequisites: Not available until 5th level, and then the character must have at least one feature from the Undead, Nightmare, Pestilence or Stigmata table.

Limitations: Can be used only in Morphus form. This Talent only affects living creatures; machines, mineral, Greater Demons, undead and other non-living targets are unaffected. Wampyrs and Nightbane with features from the Artificial Appearance, Biomechanical, and Substance Abuser tables are +2 to save against this Talent. The maximum damage that may be inflicted by Necrosis is 1D6x10 (or 10D6). A wound may only be affected once by this Talent, but a different cut or wound on the same person can be attacked and worsened in another use of this Talent. **Remember,** a wound, cut, deep scratch, bullet wound, bite, etc., must have existed before this Talent can be used to make it fester and get worse.

Range: Touch or up to 10 feet (3.1 m) per level of experience; line of sight is required.

Duration: Instant effect and damage with lingering penalties.

Costs: Sixteen P.P.E. to acquire permanently. Every two P.P.E. points spent on Necrosis inflicts 1D6 damage (and penalties) up to a maximum of 1D6x10 damage! **Note:** The amount of P.P.E. expended on this Talent should always be selected by the user BEFORE the intended victim rolls to save. The full P.P.E. amount is spent whether the victim saves or not.

No Rest

Like All-Nighter, this Talent enables the user to go for long stretches with no sleep without needing the assistance of chemical stimulants. Using No Rest totally eliminates the effects of sleep deprivation for an entire day per level of experience and allows the user to remain fully awake and alert. This Talent also gives the Nightbane a Perception bonus of +1 and a +5 to save against sedatives and sleep inducing powers.

Using No Rest as an attack: Unlike the All-Nighter Talent, No Rest may be used on unwilling targets. Those who attempt to resist must roll a Save vs Magic of 14 or better. Failure to save sees the target fatigue as normal, but is completely unable to sleep. The physical and mental toll this takes on the victim is quite debilitating, and may even be considered a form of torture: For every 24 hours without sleep, the victim is -1 melee attack, -1 on Perception Rolls, initiative and all combat rolls (strike, parry, etc.), including rolls to save, and -10% on the performance of all skills. Penalties are cumulative. After 72 hours, all regeneration, whether it is of S.D.C./Hit Points, P.P.E., I.S.P., or the like, is reduced by half. After 120 hours (5 days) of no sleep, regeneration stops, and the victim prays for sleep but it may not come. After a full week (168 hours), roll to save vs insanity (16 or higher to save) each day. On a failed save, roll for a Phobia or an Obsession each subsequent day, and the character is probably too weak and disoriented to do much of anything but sit or lay in bed wishing for sleep. If sleep deprivation goes 13 days, roll on the Random Insanity Table (see the **Nightbane® RPG**). All penalties are reduced by half and insanities disappear after the victim finally gets 10 or more hours of sleep. He is fully restored after two consecu-

tive nights or days of at least 8 hours of sleep, but there is a 50% chance that a single insanity may remain if it went 10 days or longer.

Note that the effects of this Talent can be canceled at any time by the Talent user regardless of distance between him and his victim. Also, magic and psionic abilities that induce sleep may be used to counteract No Rest, but the person under its effects automatically attempts the appropriate saving throw (wanted or not). This Talent may also be used in a Dream Pool to immediately awaken the dreamer, without need of a saving throw, and expel any intruders.

Prerequisites: No Rest is not available until reaching 3rd level or higher. Even then at least one trait from the Occupation, Soldier, Ancient Warrior or Superbeing table is required.

Limitations: Can only be used in Morphus form, though the effects will continue even when the Nightbane shifts back into the Facade. The physical need for rest is removed by using No Rest. Characters can stay awake using this Talent for a number of days equal to their M.E. attribute. Beyond that, each day requires a save vs insanity to prevent acquiring a random insanity. Any insanity gained is luckily temporary and goes away after at least 8 hours of sleep. Going without sleep for long periods takes a psychological toll on almost anyone, especially when used on someone other than the Talent user.

Range: Self and one other by touch with good intentions. Touch or 30 feet (9.1 m) when used on one victim as an attack.

Duration: 24 hours per level of experience.

Costs: Seven P.P.E. to acquire permanently. Ten P.P.E. per use. +3 extra P.P.E. to raise the saving throw by one point (with a maximum of 15).

Overdrive

Activating this Talent drastically increases the maximum speed of the user or whatever means of conveyance is transporting the Nightbane. That speed limit is boosted to 500 mph (800 kph)! There is always a corresponding physical change while Overdrive is in effect. Concealed thruster ports might open and fire or the Morphus might reconfigure to a more aerodynamic shape and thrusters may appear. Different sounds may also accompany the high speed travel such as the roar of a rocket booster or whine of a supercharger.

In addition to enhanced speed, the perception and reflexes of the 'Bane (or whoever is at the helm) are heightened to be able to maneuver at such a perilous pace. As long as the Talent is active, add +2 to Perception Rolls when looking ahead for trouble and +2 to dodge while in motion.

If used on a vehicle or riding animal, the pilot enjoys a +30% to the appropriate *Piloting* skill and reduce penalties for high-speed maneuvers by half. Luckily, hitting objects under 10 pounds (4.5 kg) harmlessly knocks them out of the Talent user's path. Collisions with anything over that inflicts 1D4x10

damage to the Nightbane or the Overdrive vehicle or animal and whatever they have collided with and the Talent is immediately canceled.

The energies channeled by Overdrive are such that anyone or anything under its effects do not suffer physical strain from traveling at high speeds and do not damage surfaces traveled over unless there is a sudden stop or crash. Any flat surface, even bodies of water, can be traversed as if they were dry pavement. Of course, this Talent can be utilized to boost flight, swimming on or underwater, and running or driving across the ground. Once the power's duration lapses or is canceled, anything under its effects slows to normal maximum speed within a half mile (0.8 km), which takes 2-3 seconds.

Prerequisites: The Nightbane must be 4th level or above and have at least one Morphus feature from the Biomechanical, Aquatic Biomech, Superbeing or Sci-Fi Table.

Limitations: Overdrive can only be used in Morphus form. While using this Talent, combat is largely impossible outside of dodging incoming attacks, firing at something ahead, or ramming an opponent (see collision damage, above). Other than the changes mentioned in the description, above, the user and/or vehicle remain the same. Any altitude or depth restrictions, S.D.C. values, and so forth, are unchanged. This means that Mom's minivan still won't fly like a fighter jet, a helicopter still can't travel underwater, and whatever it is must still have a working engine and drivetrain. Bear in mind that using this Talent is an all or nothing proposal as the user does not get to slow down his traveling speed without canceling Overdrive. He has to go 500 mph (800 kph) or his normal speed. Nothing in between.

Range: Self, riding animal or vehicle by touch.

Duration: Special, see cost below.

Costs: Eighteen P.P.E. to acquire permanently. Sixteen P.P.E. per 100 miles (160 km) traveled, +8 P.P.E. per additional 100 miles. Double the P.P.E. cost for vehicles with up to 4 passengers or 800 lbs (360 kg) of cargo; triple P.P.E. cost for vehicles able to transport 20 passengers or 10 tons of cargo.

Pariah's Mantle

In olden days, pariah, or outcasts, were ridiculed and even attacked by mobs for such simple things as a physical deformity. This practice may be on the rise once again thanks to the Nightlords' corruption and disintegration of society, but those with the Pariah's Mantle Talent have found a use for drawing the ire of others to them. This power may be used to create a distraction, ensure weaker allies are not attacked, etc. Whatever the utility, all those within range of this talent and selected by the Nightbane to be affected, must roll a saving throw of 15 or better using any bonuses from a high M.E. attribute or be overcome with revulsion and violent hatred toward the user of Pariah's Mantle. They respond toward the character by threatening and hurling insults at him, and engage in physical assaults within 1D4 melee rounds,

even if unprovoked. Anyone affected who already disliked or wanted to attack the character does so immediately.

During this time, everyone affected and probably most, if not all bystanders and observers, have their eyes on the pariah and the people assaulting him and are unlikely to notice anyone one else slipping away, entering a secure building, stealing a car, on the Prowl or doing anything that involves stealth or secrecy. Any Perception Rolls that might apply are -6.

Prerequisites: At least one Morphus feature from the Disproportional, Unusual Facial Feature, or Clown Table.

Limitations: Usable in Morphus form only. Anyone affected by this Talent that is harmed in any way will immediately be released from its effects and is immune to this power for 24 hours. Range: 20 feet (6.1 m), +5 feet (1.5 m) per level of experience. Any intended target with a *good alignment* gets a +2 to save, while total pacifists are +5. Duration: See cost below.

Costs: Five P.P.E. to acquire permanently. One P.P.E. per minute of use.

Passing the Torch

This is the extraordinary ability to turn ordinary individuals into Nightbane, even if it's only for a short time. The recipient of this enchantment immediately undergoes the Becoming and for the duration of this Talent, is in an exact copy of the Talent user's Morphus form. Alternatively, the G.M. can elect for the recipient to manifest a brand new Morphus if time is available to create it. For all intents and purposes, the person under the effects of this power is a Nightbane and is affected by spells and such that specifically affect Nightbane. The character has all the usual abilities of the R.C.C. such as Mirror Walk and the ability to sense fellow 'Bane. Available Talents can be a copy of the original Nightbane's or Talents may be selected as a level one Nightbane (again, depending on time-constraints and the desires of the player and G.M.). As usual, this Talent may be canceled at any time by the Talent user, but also automatically ends if the person under its effects is slain.

The shock of Becoming is much less if the recipient knows what is coming and what he'll look like, since he has, presumably, been a friend, teammate or associate of the Nightbane who uses this Talent on him. Still, it is more exhilarating and disorienting than most people expect so the following penalties apply to the temporary Nightbane: -1 melee attack, -1 on all combat rolls and -10% on skill performance.

Truly Passing the Torch: It is also possible to use Passing the Torch to turn the recipient permanently into a Nightbane, but only if that person is certain he wants this, the Talent user is prepared to die, and the Game Master approves of it. In this case, the Nightbane Talent user must have at least 20 P.P.E. available to him and is willing to make the ultimate sacrifice. This transformation is often a deathbed sacrifice and is permanent and irrevocable. It kills the Nightbane Talent user in the process, so he

is quite literally passing the torch, which makes such an event *exceedingly* rare to say the least. The new Nightbane retains his own Facade attributes, skills and knowledge at whatever level he is at the time of the transformation. Otherwise, he possesses all the abilities and P.P.E. (minus 12 P.P.E. permanently expended in passing the torch) of the Nightbane who passed his or her Nightbane Morphus on to the recipient. This new Nightbane is likely to need some time to adjust, but he is now a Nightbane who resembles the 'Bane who passed his appearance/Morphus and powers on to someone else. Presumably to carry his legacy or to avenge his death.

Prerequisites: Nightbane selecting this Talent must be at least level 7 and have one or more features from the Superbeing, Athlete, or Stigmata tables.

Limitations: Can only be used in Morphus form. While the more common temporary Passing the Torch is in effect, the Talent user is limited to his Facade form. As soon as this Talent is activated in Morphus form, the Nightbane Talent user immediately reverts to the Facade. This Talent only works on willing targets. Anyone unwilling to become a Nightbane or those who are incapacitated, automatically save. Only mortal races without psychic abilities can receive Passing the Torch – cannot affect psychics, supernatural beings, or creatures of magic.

Range: Touch or 10 feet (3 m).

Duration: See cost below.

Costs: Ten P.P.E. to acquire permanently. Twelve P.P.E. per hour for someone else to operate in his Morphus. If that person is slain, the Morphus returns to the Talent user and he'll know the recipient has died. The Talent user can also cancel this Talent at anytime, returning the recipient to his normal state of being and returning the Morphus back to its true Nightbane.

Payday

Similar to the *Pocket Change* Talent, Payday allows the Nightbane to conjure money out of thin air. Upon expending the P.P.E. to activate this Talent, ten physical dollars appears in hand for every one P.P.E. spent. This currency is the real thing and will pass any inspection to verify it is not a forgery. This money works at cash registers and vending machines, etc. The money appears in the form that the Nightbane chooses which allows for the creation of coins or notes up to the maximum P.P.E. spent in the currency of whatever country the Nightbane finds himself. Created currency stays in existence for a longer time than with Pocket Change, but will still disappear from pockets, tills or bank vaults when the duration of Payday expires.

Prerequisites: Must possess at least one feature from the Occupation, Athlete, or Hobbyist Table and is cannot be selected until level 3 or greater before Payday.

Limitations: Since the Nightbane must picture the currency they wish to create, familiarity with that specific type of money is required. For instance, a Nightbane in Europe would need to

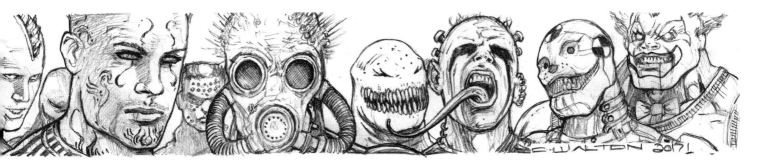

know about the Euro and/or have an example of the currency in hand in order to produce them.

Range: Self.

Duration: One hour per level of experience.

Costs: Seven P.P.E. to acquire permanently. One P.P.E. per 10 dollars (or local equivalent) created. The Nightbane with this Talent can also conjure up 100 dollars per point of his P.E. attribute. Same duration of the money's existence and it takes 24 hours to recover each P.E. attribute point expended in this manner. Adjust bonuses and saving throws accordingly.

Rallying Cry

Harkening back to the ancient battlefield, rallying cries were meant to lift the spirits of embattled warriors and refocus their efforts. In more modern times, such cries are more commonplace in sports arenas as a team tries to come from behind to win a game. The Rallying Cry Talent bestows a supernatural version of this time-honored tradition to the Talent user. The actual cry may be a favored sports team, a command to regroup, or have historical significance such as Easy Company's "Currahee!" "Never give up, never surrender," or "Avengers Assemble" or "It's clobberin' time" from characters in Marvel comic books. Whatever is chosen, the effects on others are the same.

When this Talent is activated, and the rallying cry is shouted out, allies and supporters in the area of effect experience a brief surge of energy and a renewed confidence or commitment. This translates to a +2 bonus on initiative, +1 to strike, parry and dodge, a +1 bonus to all saving throws, and +5% bonus on all skills. Any affected ally that's under the effects of a demoralizing or manipulating power (failed Horror Factor, psionic mind control, etc.) *immediately* gets to roll another save with the new bonus added.

In addition to the standard effects, the Nightbane may also choose to expend double the usual amount of P.P.E. on any number of specific allies to try to remove any penalties imposed by enemy powers, injuries, side effects of poisons, etc. Such targeted allies roll another saving throw against any negative effects currently suffered, and if successful, ignore the penalties for the duration of this Talent. For any penalty not resulting from something that has a saving throw, a 14 or better including applicable bonuses, temporarily saves against it. For instance, injury penalties from the Optional Damage Chart would use the 14 number to save and any P.E. bonuses would be applied to it.

Prerequisites: For a character to select Rallying Cry, he or she must have at least one feature from the Ancient Warrior, Athlete, or Soldier Table.

Limitations: Can only be used in Morphus form. A user must have at least a general idea of the presence and location of each target to be affected. The bonuses granted by this Talent will NOT accumulate with multiple uses.

Range: Every ally or supporter within a 10 foot (3.1 m) radius of the Nightbane Talent user per level of experience, or specific people within range and line of sight.

Duration: The cry is instantaneous, but its positive effects and corresponding bonuses last for one melee round per level of the Talent user's experience.

Costs: Eight P.P.E. to acquire permanently. Six P.P.E. per Rallying Cry unleashed.

Revolting Spit

Inspired by the theory that certain dinosaurs had caustic venom that could be spit into the eyes or face of its prey or enemies, this Talent lets the Nightbane secrete a mild organic acid in his mouth. This acid can then be held in the mouth and delivered via a *bite attack or spit* at an enemy. Each use of this Talent counts as two attacks. The first to conjure the acid and the second to bite or spit. A bite with Revolting Spit deals normal damage for that particular Morphus plus the acid spit. The acid itself does damage each melee round for 1D4 rounds (15-60 seconds), and causes temporary blindness if the target is hit in the face. To hit an opponent in the face requires a *Called Shot* and a roll of 14 or better, and normal strike bonuses do NOT apply, only a Natural, unmodified roll. The intended victim can attempt to parry the spit with a shield of any size or using an equivalent shield-like object, or he can try to parry with his hand or forearm.

If the Revolting Spit hits an opponent in the face, but the victim makes a successful save vs nonlethal poison of 13 or higher, the penalties are comparatively minimal. But the eyes water and the fumes make it difficult to breathe: -1 melee attack, -1 to all combat rolls, -2 on Perception Rolls, and -10% to the performance of all skills.

If the victim fails to save, he suffers 1D4 damage and is temporarily blinded and overwhelmed by the strong nauseating fumes. Penalties last for 1D4 melee rounds.

Prerequisites: The Nightbane must be at least 2nd level and have one or more features from the Dinosaur, Snake, Extra-Terrestrial, or Mythical Creature tables.

Limitations: Can only be used in Morphus form. Inorganic material like glass, ceramics, crystal, stone, plastic and metal take no damage, including Nightbane in full environmental suit or armor, and those with a mineral-based Morphus form as well as Elementals, Flint People, Hounds and Hunters. Face protection such as a gasmask will prevent the penalties from this Talent, but only if eyes, nose, and mouth are covered. Goggles, visors, and eye-wear will prevent blindness as soon as they are removed, but the penalties from the noxious fumes still apply and the eyes are now vulnerable to another attack. Eye-wear can be used again after washing the spit off of them with soap and water. Clothing and most natural fabrics (cotton, wool, etc.) take damage from the acid, as do plants and wood. **Note:** Water completely neutralizes the acid, immediately stopping both damage and penalties.

Range: Bite or 10 feet (3.1 m) per level of experience.

Damage: The acid spit does 1D4 damage from the initial attack and +1 point of additional damage per each of the next 1D4 melee rounds, and penalties last until the duration ends or until the spit is washed away, whichever comes first. Simple water will do the trick. Washing the acid away and flushing the eyes with water takes 1D4 melee rounds. Also see Penalties, below. **Note:** The acid is especially vicious if it comes into contact with exposed cuts that inflicted three or more points of damage and other vulnerable tissue such as the inside of a throat. In such instances, the acid does double damage, and half of that damage is *direct to Hit Points.* Acid spit does double damage to Nightlords and the Denizens of the Nightlands. Depending on what part of the body is damaged in this way, G.M.s may elect to use the *Optional Side-Effects Table* on page 39 of the **Nightbane® RPG,** but give player characters the benefit of the doubt with least damage and successful recovery.

Penalties: Being blind has the following penalties: -10 to all combat rolls (strike, parry, dodge, etc.), and skills requiring sight are -80% if they can be accomplished via touch. Zero if sight is a must to perform the skill, like walking a tightrope or performing surgery. Talent is also useful for covering the lenses of surveillance cameras. In fact, they remain "blind" until the sticky spit is washed away.

The noxious fumes from the acid spit also impairs the individual who does not successfully save vs this attack: -2 melee attacks, -2 to all combat rolls, -2 on Perception Rolls, and -20% to the performance of all skills.

A Called Shot is required to strike a target in the face.

Duration: The attack is instant, but damage and penalties last for 1D4 melee rounds. Once secreted, the acid may be held in the mouth until used to attack, but it prevents the character from speaking and drool may dribble from his lips.

Costs: Nine P.P.E. to acquire permanently. Six P.P.E. per spit projection; counts as two melee attacks.

Rigor Mortis

This Talent mimics the effects of rigor mortis, the stiffening of muscle tissue after death. This talent can be used in Facade or Morphus form. Using it on oneself makes the Nightbane appear to be a dead, stiff corpse. Heartbeat fades to almost nothing, core temperature cools to that of the surroundings, and breathing stops completely. Even if the character is hooked up to modern medical equipment such as an EKG, no sign of life can be detected, not even brain activity. Only a successful skill roll using *First Aid* at -90%, *Paramedic* at -70%, or *Medical Doctor* at -50% reveals what is essentially a state of suspended animation. While in this state, the person uses just 5% of the normal oxygen required, does not require food and water, and will cease to metabolize any drugs or poison in the body. Despite this catatonic state, the individual is still able to see, hear, smell, etc.

When used on unwilling subjects, a failed save vs magic (needs a 12 or higher to save) instantly causes the muscles to stiffen and makes movement a difficult, forced effort. Victims see their P.S., P.P., and Spd attributes as well as attacks per melee round, combat bonuses and skill performance reduced by 20-80%, depending on how much P.P.E. was spent on the attack by the Talent user (see Cost below).

Prerequisites: At least a single feature from the Undead, Pestilence, or Unnatural Limbs Table. This Talent is unavailable until level 4.

Limitations: Can be used on oneself in Facade or Morphus form. When used as an attack upon another person, The Talent can only be used in Morphus form. **Note:** When a character is a willing participant feigning his own death, the effects of Rigor Mortis can be cancelled should his "corpse" fall under attacked. It is his choice as to when to cancel the Talent, so even being stabbed does not automatically cancel the Talent unless he wants it to. It all really depends on how far he wants to carry the pretense that he is dead. If his life is in jeopardy, he will know it, and he can immediately negated Rigor Mortis to fight back or attempt to escape. The newly revived individual functions without penalties and is likely to catch his attackers completely off-guard when he seems to come back to life with a vengeance.

Range: Touch or up to 20 feet (6.1 m), +5 feet (1.5 m) per level of experience.

Duration: One minute per level of experience against opponents; one hour per level of experience when used on oneself or a willing target to feign death.

Costs: Seventeen P.P.E. to acquire permanently. Three P.P.E. on oneself or a willing participant who wants to appear to be dead. Five P.P.E. per -20% penalty imposed upon an unwilling victim; 80% maximum. At 80%, most victims of Rigor Mortis can barely move and have no or few bonuses and only one or two attacks per melee round.

Seedling

By all accounts, this is one of the odder Talents known. Seedlings allows the user to plant a seed imbued with a fragment of life essence. After 2D4 weeks, this seed grows into a small (1D4+4 feet/1.5-2.4 m tall) tree, but it also resembles the Morphus form of the Nightbane who planted it in some way. For instance, a Nightbane with the *Crystalline* feature will create a tree with a blocky, geometric shape, and there will be some quartz stones or crystals at the base of the tree; whereas the seedling of a character with *Nightmare* features might resemble a gnarled or dead tree; a Snake Morphus will create a tree that resembles a coiled rattlesnake or cobra, or may have obvious roots that spread out in a snaking pattern; an animal morphus results in a tree that my have a shape of that animal, and so on. (FYI: We have seen real trees with branches that resemble the head of a rabbit, and a tree that resembles a bird with tail feathers and wings out like it is

flying. People in the neighborhood uses it as a landmark and call it the "bird tree.") The supernatural nature and appearance of the plant can be masked, but only for a short time (see costs below). Appearance aside, once the seedling has sprouted, the Nightbane who created it can see, hear, and feel everything within a 20 foot (6.1 m) radius around the tree as if he is standing right next to the sapling. This can be done by spending a minute concentrating on the tree, no matter the distance between the two, as long as the Nightbane is on Earth.

After 1D4+2 months, the Seedling doubles in size. At this stage and beyond, whenever in the presence of the seedling, the Nightbane who planted it can meld with it to hide within the tree. While inside the tree the character cannot be sensed or located by conventional or paranormal means. Also, while inside the tree, the Nightbane heals at double the normal rate, does not need to consume food or water (draws nourishment from the tree), and feels calm and content to the point that time spent inside the tree counts as meditating for the purpose of rest and P.P.E. recovery. The Nightbane inside remains aware of everything going on around the tree for an extended 200 foot (61 m) radius; line of sight, in the same manner as mentioned before. Furthermore, the tree serves as a living P.P.E. battery with 5D6+6 P.P.E. the Nightbane can draw upon up to one mile (1.6 km) away.

After an additional 1D6+6 months, the seedling doubles in size a final time. Once at this state, the tree continues to grow at a normal rate and lives for as long as the Nightbane who created it lives. In fact, being linked to the living tree provides the following benefits: the Nightbane is +30% to save vs coma death no matter the circumstance or level of treatment, he or she can breathe without air for two minutes per P.E. attribute point, is immune to carbon dioxide, and has a battery of secret Hit Points that even he may not realize he has until the day he needs them. When the Nightbane's own Hit Points drop below zero, he falls into a coma. Under normal circumstances, he might die without medical treatment and even then will require a successful save vs coma and death to survive. However, in the case of a Nightbane who has his own Seedling, he drops into the coma state and appears to be dead or dying. However, he actually has an additional 1D6+1 Hit Points per level of his experience via his life connection to the Seedling. As a result, even in a coma state, he is not at death's door (unless damage is more than the extra Hit Points provided by the tree, then it is a save vs coma death situation), and his body continues to regenerate as usual! This temporary healing coma state lasts until the character has regenerated to 1D6+10 Hit Points above zero. At that point he awakens from the coma and is back in action, though he should probably rest or switch to Facade until more Hit Points are regenerated. The Tree also extends the Nightbane's lifespan by decades. For all these reasons it is sometimes referred to as the *Life Tree*.

Prerequisites: Must be at least level 6 and have one or more features from the Angelic, Alien Shape, Mythical Creature, Plant Life, and Unnatural Limbs tables.

Limitations: Must be in Morphus form when planting the Seedling, after that it can be used in Facade and Morphus forms. Only ONE seedling can be planted at level 6 for the lifetime of the Nightbane.

<u>Range</u>: Touch to plant a seedling.

<u>Duration</u>: The Seedling will live for decades or until destroyed. Having a Seedling guarantees the Nightbane's lifespan is extended 1D6x10+60 years, provided the Seedling also remains alive and healthy. If the tree is cut down or destroyed, all of the bonuses and abilities it provides are gone, though the Nightbane will continue to live out his extended life. When the Nightbane dies, the tree lives only another 1D6x10 years.

Costs: Sixteen P.P.E. to acquire permanently. Five P.P.E., one Hit Point and one P.E. attribute point are permanently lost, placed into the Seedling when it is planted. To outsiders, the Seedling is just an ordinary tree, perhaps with an odd shape, but the Nightbane can always recognize and find it. Communing with or hiding within a Seedling has no cost.

Shadows of Despair

This Talent manipulates the emotions of its victims, plunging them into the depths of despair. Individuals targeted must roll a 13 or higher to save vs magic to resist. On a failed, save the world seems too dim for the victim as colors wash out into gray or sepia-tones. Feelings of hopelessness, helplessness, and worthlessness assail the person's self-confidence. Life seems to lose meaning and even menial tasks appear daunting. Those afflicted are likely to withdraw from others, give up on any current goals, and may stop taking proper care of themselves. This character is likely to crack under interrogation (the interrogator is +20%) and in combat the victim is -6 on Perception Rolls, -6 on initiative, -6 to save vs Horror Factor, -3 on saving throws and all other combat bonuses, -25% on skill rolls (-50% when skill performance is a matter of life and death!) and reduce all remaining combat bonuses by half. Victims also fatigue twice as fast as normal and heal/bio-regenerate at half the usual rate. And are likely (60%) to flee or surrender when their Hit Points have been reduced to half unless a Mental Endurance saving throw of 16 or higher is made. **Note:** While Shadows of Despair can make a target depressed, it can NOT make someone suicidal. Any effects on an already suicidal person are left up to individual G.M.s to determine.

Prerequisites: A Morphus feature from the Nightmare, Pestilence, Substance Abuse, or Victim table is needed to be able to select this Talent.

Limitations: Can only be used in Morphus form and can only affect living beings capable of human-like emotion. Even if they can be affected, magical, supernatural, and alien beings get a +5 to save vs this Talent. If a target successfully saves against this Talent he is not affected and is immune to further Shadows of Despair attacks for 24 hours.

Range: Two by touch or one target up to 100 feet (30.5 m); line of sight.

Duration: 1D4+1 melee rounds per 12 P.P.E. spent on this Talent.

Costs: Fourteen P.P.E. to acquire permanently. Twelve P.P.E. per 1D4+1 melee rounds of depression. By spending 120 P.P.E. the effects of Shadows of Despair last for 1D4+2 days.

Shadow Swarm

Upon activation, Shadow Swarm creates a horrific illusion of what appears to be a swarm of vermin moving about in the shadows. A swarm that seems to single out one specific target or small group clustered close together. The swarm can be any of the following: mice, rats, frogs, snakes, spiders, beetles, cockroaches, a swarm of flies, and similar creepy crawlers all moving at a speed just less than their victim. The effect being that they are nipping at his heels.

The swarm illusion has a Horror Factor of 15 for the average person, H.F. 12 for the typical Nightbane, H.F. 17 for those with a phobia about such creatures, darkness or shadows. The usual penalties for failure to save vs Horror Factor, apply. What is worse, even if the potential victim(s) escapes the first swarm, the vermin swarm seems to be lurking in every shadow or dark corner. This alone may be enough to send people screaming and running away or locking themselves inside a vehicle or a well lit room. And even those who save vs Horror Factor might run away with the rest of his friends or a large group of panicked people.

The Shadow Swarm will not enter a brightly lit area, not even under a lamppost, but will swarm and circle all around just beyond the edge of the light, effectively corralling victims into one location. Which is often the intention of this spell. Shadow Swarm is often done to corral an opponent or group, chase away innocent bystanders, discourage opponents from getting within melee range, to create a distraction (a mob of screaming people running across a parking lot or down the street can make a wonderful distraction), or make good an escape by momentarily holding off one's enemies.

Being caught by the Shadow Swarm or stepping in the Shadow Swarm seems to engulf its victim(s) and pulls him or them into the shadows or darkness where their screams stop and they seem to *vanish*. It is a terrifying sight that is likely to have those who witness the event scream, weep and even faint. And it certainly keeps them clinging to the light and away from the darkness. Those who vanish are gone for one melee round, +10 seconds per level of the Talent users. For them, everything suddenly gets calm, and quiet, even peaceful. Regardless of how long they were actually gone, for them it only feels like 10 seconds have passed. They are unhurt in any way, and reappear, safe and sound at the location from which they vanished.

Prerequisites: The Nightbane must have at least one Morphus feature from the Animal, Pestilence, or Undead Table and must be level three or greater before selecting Shadow Swarm.

Limitations: Can only be used in Morphus form. Shadow Swarms cannot enter light and are held at bay by it.

The swarm is an illusion that effects everyone in a 30 foot radius (6.1 m) who does not save against the illusion's Horror Factor (15 or higher to save). Shooting in to the swarm seems to kill them but there are so many, it does not seem to make a difference!

Damage: None. See vanishing and fear in the description above.

Range: The illusion of the Shadow Swarm effects everyone in a 30 foot (9.1 m) radius, +5% per level of experience, but it can be cast up to 200 feet (6.1 m) away. Of course the Talent user is not effected and he can control the spell enough to have it not affect teammates or only affect certain people within the radius of effect. Those who save vs the Horror Factor of this illusion and those spared the illusion do not see the swarming vermin, only those who fail to save.

Duration: One melee round (15 seconds), +8 seconds per level of the Nightbane. Typically used to make good an escape, hold people at bay or chase them away without inflicting harm to those plagued by the Shadow Swarm. Even after the illusion stops, many people will refuse to go back where the vermin are swarming, and the rest need 1D6+4 melee rounds to screw up the courage to go back. Half for heroes.

Costs: Twelve P.P.E. to acquire permanently. Eight P.P.E. to activate.

Share the Needle

This Talent gives the user the ability to recreate some of the worst effects of drug addiction and withdrawl. This can be done to debilitate an enemy, teach a lesson to a youth on the wrong path, or just out of spite or cruelty. Whatever the case, the user must select one of the following symptoms and expend the P.P.E. while in physical contact with the intended victim. If the victim fails to save vs magic (15 or higher), he suffers the symptoms of one of the following. Only one can be inflicted at a time, no multiple afflictions. A successful save means the character is completely unaffected; no symptoms.

Anxiety/Restlessness/Wired: The victim is keyed up and on edge, finding it difficult to relax or even concentrate on tasks. -20% to all skills, -1 to Perception Rolls, and -3 to save vs Horror Factor.

Cold Sweats: This condition does not impose penalties beyond making the victim highly uncomfortable and -5% on all skills. Clothes are soaked within minutes. Any attempt to track the victim by scent is at +15%.

Dizziness: Equilibrium and balance are thrown off as the victim feels like the world is spinning. Feels relief when laying down, even if it is on the ground, but moving faster than a Spd of four or trying to engage in combat, the victim is -2 attacks per melee, -4 to strike, parry, dodge and all other combat rolls, -40%

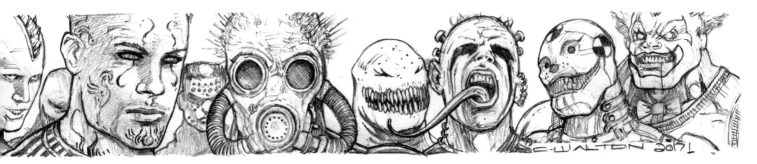

on all skills, and any attempts to maintain balance, such as walking a tightrope, Climbing and Swimming, are impossible; falls down onto the ground.

Fatigue: The victim feels exhausted no matter how much rest or sleep is gotten. Reduce Spd, number of melee attacks and all combat bonuses by half; -10% to all skills and the victim fatigues twice as fast.

Headache: This causes a throbbing headache which approaches the magnitude of a migraine. -1 to initiative and Perception Rolls, -20% to all skills, and -1 to all saving throws.

Muscle Cramps: The target is wracked with moderate to severe muscle cramps all over the body. Reduce P.S., P.P. and Spd attributes by half, as well as all combat bonuses by half.

Nausea/Vomiting: The victim is always nauseous, but moving faster than half his Spd, being jostled or bounced about, or engaging in strenuous activity like combat, has a 0-75% chance per melee round of causing vomiting. Having to stop and vomit uses up all but one melee attack for that round, and the character has no initiative.

Tremors: Motor control is compromised as the target is afflicted with constant trembling and shaking of the body. Reduce P.P. and Spd attributes by half, skill performance by half and -6 to strike with ranged weapons like bow and arrow, guns and even thrown weapons.

Sober Up: One final use of Share the Needle Talent enables the Nightbane user to completely alleviate the temporary effects and high of recreational drugs or alcohol, making them sober within 1D4 melee rounds and reducing any subsequent hangover/withdrawal symptoms by half. The target may resist and remain under the influence by rolling a standard save vs spell magic of 12 or higher. More than one Nightbane with this Talent works with the Lightbringers Faction ministering to people struggling with substance abuse and dependence all over the world.

Prerequisites: Unavailable until level 5. The Nightbane must have at least one trait from either the Substance Abuse or Victim table.

Limitations: Only available in the Morphus form. Penalties and effects are at half when applied to supernatural or magical creatures.

Range: Touch.

Duration: See cost below.

Costs: Sixteen P.P.E. to acquire permanently. Five P.P.E. per 1D6 minutes or 20 P.P.E. for 1D4x10 minutes.

Sideshow

A Nightbane who uses Sideshow gains the remarkable ability to move like a trained acrobat or gymnast while in and out of combat. The equivalents of the following skills are all gained for the duration of the Talent at an 86% proficiency: Back Flip, Climb Rope, Sense of Balance, Walk Tightrope/High-Wire, and Work Parallel Bars & Rings. Users also get a +2 bonus to parry and dodge, and a +3 bonus to roll with punch/fall/impact. In combat, the Nightbane moves with preternatural grace, flipping and tumbling around opponents like a character in a kung-fu movie or circus performer – no strike penalties are applied for attacking on the move, +2 to strike with kick attacks, +2 to disarm and +3 to roll with punch/fall/impact.

Prerequisites: Sideshow cannot be selected until 2nd level, and can only be selected by a Nightbane with a Morphus feature from the Clown, Athlete, and/or Disproportional tables.

Limitations: Can only be used in Morphus form.

Range: Self.

Duration: One minute per level of experience.

Costs: Twelve P.P.E. to acquire permanently. Ten P.P.E. to activate this Talent and 6 P.P.E. to sustain it.

Summoner

The Summoner Talent lets the user summon demonic minions to serve his or her will. It is unknown whether these beings are true demons from some hellish dimension or creations of pure magical energy given substance by the summoner. What is known is that the summoned minions are completely loyal to the Talent user to the point of self-sacrifice if it is required of them. For the duration of the Talent the demons carry out any orders to the best of their ability and then disappear as suddenly as they appeared.

Upon activating the Summoner Talent, one or more portals appear near the Nightbane. Within 1D4 seconds, the summoned demon(s) appear from these portals and are ready for action. The appearance of the portal and demons may vary with each individual Nightbane, from hellish insectoids emerging from pitch-black sphere to classic flaming demons crawling from cracks in the earth. Regardless of appearance, the quick-stats and enhancements below may be used to generate these minions. Alternatively, with the G.M.'s approval, the Red Flame Demons (**Nightbane® World Book 2: Nightlands**) or demons from other Palladium books and settings may be used.

Sub-Demon: 100 S.D.C., 20 Hit Point, and Natural A.R. 11, P.S. 20, P.P. 16, P.E. 14, Spd 24, and Horror Factor 10. All other stats are average. Claw attack adds 1D6 to supernatural punch damage. Three attacks per melee round, +1 to all combat rolls, +2 to damage, and +1 on all saving throws.

Lesser Demon: 150 S.D.C., 30 Hit Points, and Natural A.R. 12, M.E. 16, P.S. 25, P.P. 18, P.E. 18, Spd 20, and Horror Factor. 12. All other stats are average. Claw attack adds 1D6+3 to Supernatural Punch damage. Four attacks per melee round, +2 to all combat rolls, +6 to damage, and +2 on all saving throws.

Greater Demon: 250 S.D.C., 50 Hit Point, and Natural A.R. 13, I.Q. and M.E. 18, M.A. 20, P.S. 30, P.P. 20, P.E. 22, Spd 16, and Horror Factor 14. All other stats average. Claw attack adds 2D6 to Supernatural P.S. punch damage. Six attacks per melee

round, +4 to all combat rolls, +10 to damage, and +3 on all saving throws.

The following enhancements may be added when the minions are first summoned (see cost below):

1) Strength: Adds +5 to Supernatural P.S. (boosts punch damage by 1D6) and +50 to S.D.C.

2) Flight: With or without wings, the demon is able to fly at a Spd of 1D4x10+20 and is +2 to dodge in flight.

3) Stealth: The minion gets the Prowl skill at 65% and Shadow Meld as per the spell at will.

4) Biting Jaws: Provides a bite attack that deals half of Supernatural P.S. punch damage and provides one additional attack per melee round.

5) Armament: Adds a single melee weapon that inflicts 3D6 damage in addition to Supernatural P.S. punch damage. The minion is +2 to strike and parry with this weapon.

6) Firepower: Can cast a Fire Ball as per the spell at no cost (5D6 damage) or breathe fire for 5D6 damage at a range of 50 feet (15.2 m) with a +3 to strike bonus. Each fire attack counts as one of the demon's melee attacks.

Prerequisites: Level 6 must be reached before selecting this Talent. The Nightbane must have at least one Infernal, Fantasy, or Nightmare Morphus trait.

Limitations: Can only be used in Morphus form. As many as three Sub-Demons may be summoned. Two Lesser Demons may be summoned or one Greater Demon may be summoned via this Talent.

<u>Range:</u> Portals can be opened up to 30 feet (9.1 m) from the user and the summoned demons can travel up to 1,000 feet (305 m) away from their Summoner per level of the Nightbane's experience.

<u>Duration:</u> Sub-Demons: 40 minutes. Lesser Demons: 20 minutes. Greater Demon: 10 minutes.

Costs: Twenty-three P.P.E. to acquire permanently. Twenty P.P.E. per Sub-Demon, 40 P.P.E. per Lesser Demon, and 80 P.P.E. per Greater Demon summoned. Each enhancement adds 5 P.P.E. per each demon to this cost and is limited to a total of three enhancements.

The Ties that Bind

This power creates one or more ensnaring chains, razor wire, tendrils, etc., that materialize out of thin air to shoot out and hold an opponent in place. These tendrils are often gruesome, with things like rusty razor-wire, barbed wire, chains, barbed tentacles, and hooks and chains being fairly common. Each is capable of inflicting damage and inflicting breathtaking pain. Each tendril has a supernatural P.S. of 16 and is +3 to strike and entangle (the Nightbane's usual bonuses to strike, entangle, etc. do not apply). A strike with one of these tendrils does 4D6 damage whether the target is mortal, Nightbane, demon, Shadow Beast or other supernatural creature. Damage is 6D6 when used against the Night-

lords, their demonic minions and all Denizens of the Nightlands. If the tendril entangles a target, the unfortunate victim is held in place and is vulnerable to subsequent attacks from other tendrils, constriction, or agony pulses.

Being entangled by a single tendril imposes a -2 penalty to all subsequent combat rolls. This same penalty doubles to -4 when held by two tendrils. Being held by three or more tendrils prevents any defensive action other than parrying with a free limb at -6. Tendrils can also be used to lift a target into the air, robbing the victim of mobility and leverage.

Constriction attacks only do half damage (2D6), but cannot be defended against. A roll to strike is still necessary in the case of a target with a Natural Armor Rating, but in the case of body armor, half the damage from the attack is dealt to the armor and the remaining half to the target's S.D.C./Hit Points. If the tendril entangles the target's throat (requires a Called Shot of 16 or better with NO bonuses added), a constriction attack cuts off the victim's airway and strangles. This results in unconsciousness in a matter of 1D6+4 melee rounds for normal mortals, coma after 1D4+2 minutes, and death after an additional 2D4 minutes.

Agony pulses are a special, magically induced pain that travels down the tendril and into the pain centers of the victim. This causes intense pain experienced as a burning or stabbing sensation wherever the tendril makes contact. A save vs pain of 12 or better (adding any P.E. bonuses) is necessary for the victim to prevent losing two attacks and being unable to use any spells, psionics, Talents, skills or do anything but scream for the duration of that melee round (15 seconds). A successful save still robs the victim of a single melee attack and leaves the person -1 to save against the next agony pulse. If multiple tendrils ensnare a target, an agony pulse can be sent down each one simultaneously. Doing so imposes a -2 penalty to the saving throw for each tendril beyond the first.

Prerequisites: One or more features from the Infernal, Nightmare, or Stigmata table and is not available until 6th level.

Limitations: Can only be used in Morphus form. Targets must be visible and within range to be attacked with this Talent. Victims MAY attempt to break free if they have a Supernatural P.S. equal to or greater than the combined strength of the entangling tendrils. Such an attempt takes two melee actions and inflicts 2D6 damage per each tendril to the victim whether the victim is freed or not. Tendrils may be severed by doing 26 S.D.C. damage in a single attack, but are only vulnerable to spells, psionics, Talents, magical weapons and Supernatural beings, like Nightbane and demons, and their Supernatural P.S., claws and bites.

<u>Range:</u> 20 feet (6.1 m) +5 feet (1.5 m) per level of experience.

<u>Duration:</u> One minute (4 melee rounds) per level of experience.

Costs: Twenty P.P.E. to acquire permanently. Fifteen P.P.E. per tendril created, +1 P.P.E. per additional point of P.S. of the tendril (maximum of 24). Each agony pulse costs 2 P.P.E. per each tendril used.

Too Much Stereo

Using this Talent turns the Nightbane into the equivalent of a stadium quality sound system. The character can choose to project their own voice or favorite music at up to 150 decibels. Whichever is projected, it can clearly be heard up to 2 miles (3.2 km) away if outdoors. The sound is so loud that nearby objects will rattle and vibrate and anyone within 500 feet (152.4 m) without some kind of hearing protection, finds it difficult to verbally communicate with others – must shout – and is -3 on Perception Rolls (-6 if Perception requires hearing), -2 on initiative, -2 to parry and disarm, -4 to dodge and -15% on skill performance for as long as the music is blasting. Communications range is limited to 5 feet (1.5 m) shouting.

In addition to this sound amplification, the Nightbane can channel more energy to create a powerful sonic blast once per melee round that is capable of destroying fragile objects and knocking people to the ground. This can be done as a directed attack that affects a column 6 feet (1.8 m) in diameter originating with the Talent user, or with a cone-shaped area of effect in a 45-90 degree arc. Targets hit by such a blast suffer 2D6 damage, are knocked off their feet and lose initiative and two melee attacks.

Note: This Talent may be used to create confusion, interfere with ground communications, and create a distraction. It should be noted that it is most certainly going to attract the attention of the authorities, NSB agents, and probably supernatural minions of the Nightlords.

Prerequisites: The Nightbane must be at least 5th level and have one or more Morphus features from the Artisan, Hobbyist and/or Biomechanical tables.

Limitations: Can only be used in Morphus form. Targets may not be selected individually for this Talent, everyone within the area of effect is affected.

<u>Range:</u> Column shaped blasts reach up to 600 feet (183 m) while cone-shaped blasts have half that range.

<u>Duration:</u> Sound amplification lasts up to one minute per level of the Nightbane's experience while a sonic blast can only be fired once per melee round and counts as one of the Nightbane's melee attacks.

Costs: Fourteen P.P.E. to acquire permanently. Two P.P.E. if only amplifying the Nightbane's voice like a megaphone, 10 P.P.E. to blare music. Each directed sonic blast requires an additional five P.P.E. and can only be fired once per melee round.

Urban Golem

(Inspired by an idea by Reed Dees)

The Nightbane with this Talent is capable of quickly cobbling together a Golem-like automaton from man-made materials like brick, steel, and glass. Such an Urban Golem is too dull-witted to carry out complex orders, but is great backup in combat as conjured muscle. The construct will even continue to function if its creator is not nearby.

The ultimate appearance and abilities of an Urban Golem depends on the will of its Talent user and what materials are on hand to work with, but always has the following basic stats:

- I.Q. 5, M.E. 6, M.A. 6, P.S. 22, P.P. 10, P.E. 10, P.B. 4, Spd 14. Strength and Endurance are Supernatural.
- Four attacks/actions per melee and is +2 to strike, parry, and dodge, and +3 to roll with punch/fall/impact.
- Punch as per Supernatural P.S.: 3D6 damage, 6D6 for Power Punch but it counts as two melee attacks. Bites do 2D6 damage.
- Claw Strikes (if applicable): 4D6.
- 7-10 feet (2.1 to 3 m) tall and weighs up to 3 tons (sinks like a rock in deep water).
- Horror Factor of 1D4+9.
- Does not require food, water, air, or rest. Immune to poisons, illusions/mind control, and Horror Factor.
- S.D.C. and Natural A.R. depends on the materials that comprise the automaton, so it will have a range of durability as follows:

  <u>Cardboard, Plastic, and/or Other Trash:</u> 2D4x10+20 S.D.C. and a Natural A.R. of 8. Fire-based attacks ignore A.R. and do 50% more damage.

  <u>Wood, Plaster, and/or Glass:</u> 2D6x10+40 S.D.C. and a Natural A.R. of 10.

  <u>Brick, Asphalt, and/or Concrete:</u> 1D4x100+60 S.D.C., a Natural A.R. of 13.

  <u>Lightweight Structural Metal or Metal Scrap:</u> 1D6x100+80 S.D.C., Natural A.R. 15.

  <u>Structural Steel and/or Reinforced Concrete:</u> 2D4x100+120 S.D.C., Natural A.R. 16.

Prerequisites: One or more features from the Artificial Appearance, Fantasy, Gear-Head or Mineral tables, and must be 6th level or greater before selecting Urban Golem.

Limitations: Usable in Morphus form only. Urban Golem only works on man-made or processed materials like cut lumber, broken furniture, bricks, cinder block, engine blocks, scrap metal, etc., like those listed above under S.D.C. Only a single Golem-like automaton can be created and controlled by the Nightbane Talent user.

<u>Range:</u> The Urban Golem can be created up to 50 feet (15.2 m) away and commanded for up to a distance of 600 feet (183 m) away from the Talent User. It never goes farther and requires the Nightbane who created it to command its actions. Without him doing so, it just stands there, swatting at whoever comes within range. The Nightbane loses all but two of his own attacks per melee round while he is controlling his automaton.

<u>Duration:</u> 10 minutes per level of experience.

Costs: Thirty P.P.E. to acquire permanently. Varies based on the materials used to create it.

<u>Cardboard, Plastic, and/or Other Trash:</u> 20 P.P.E.

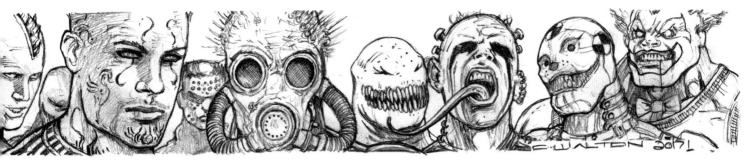

Wood, Plaster, and/or Glass: 30 P.P.E.
Brick, Asphalt, and/or Concrete: 60 P.P.E.
Lightweight Structural Metal or Metal Scrap: 90 P.P.E.
Structural Steel and/or Reinforced Concrete: 150 P.P.E.

War Cry

From the bellowing roar of an angry beast to the shouted invocations of patron spirits, war cries have been part of martial combat since before the time of man. This Talent enables the user to unleash a howl powerful enough to demoralize and cow enemies. Failure to save vs Horror Factor affects every enemy who hears it. 1D4x10% of all enemies who hear the War Cry and fail to save vs the amplified H.F. run away. The rest fight at -1 melee attack and all combat bonuses are reduced by half for 1D4 melee rounds. Not effective against Nightlords, their avatars, Night Princes and Princesses, and Greater Demons, or the Nightbane's allies and supporters.

In game terms, this war cry raises the Nightbane's Awe/Horror Factor in accordance with the P.P.E. spent to activate the Talent (see cost below). While the maximum saving throw able to be imposed is 18, boosting Horror Factor beyond this number serves to counteract victims' bonuses to save on a 1:1 basis. For instance, augmenting to a Horror Factor of 20 will counteract two points of any bonus to save vs Horror Factor a victim may have, though the number needed to save will remain 18 or better.

Prerequisites: One or more features from the Ancient Warrior, Dinosaur, or Fantasy tables and at least 4 levels of experience.

Limitations: Can only be used in Morphus form. Each use of this Talent uses half of the Nightbane's attacks for that melee round.

Range: Affects anyone not considered an ally up to 1 mile (1.6 km) away as long as the victim is able to hear the cry. This area of effect can be reduced down to as little as 150 feet (45.7 m) at the user's will.

Duration: Instant results that last for 1D4 melee rounds.

Costs: Twelve P.P.E. to acquire permanently. Five P.P.E. per each +1 bonus to the Talent user's Horror Factor and the volume and ferocity and menace of his War Cry.

Talent Creation & Conversion

A Game Designer's Advice

While this book doubles the number of unique Talents, one must remember that Nightbane can wish to be capable of *anything* and likely end up with an ability that is at least somewhat similar to what is desired. Therefore, no number of sourcebooks large or small could possibly hope to cover all the possibilities G.M.s and players *might want* to include in their games. To help fill your every desire, the following section should help gamers convert many of the various spells, psionic abilities, super-powers, and even racial or character class special abilities to Nightbane Talents, and even design brand new Talents from scratch.

Before even considering the two routes, however, it is useful to think about whether the Talent will add anything not already available as a Talent. Is it just going to be *Shadow Blast* with a different name? If yes, why not just select *Shadow Blast* and get to the fun of gaming? If no, then read on. Just remember that the G.M. is the final arbiter of what is allowed in a game or campaign. If the G.M. denies any or all "non-canon" Talents, try to remember that the point of gaming is to have fun, not argue over rules. Don't create a fuss or create hard feelings, go along with him. The Game Master needs to feel comfortable and enjoy the game too.

To Convert or Create?

That is the question. When a player or G.M. wants to add a Talent, it would behoove them to compare the concept to the hundreds of abilities already conveniently available in other Palladium source material, especially in **Beyond the Supernatural, Heroes Unlimited, Palladium Fantasy®,** and **Rifts®.** If the idea is similar enough to another power, the process might be as simple as tweaking it to fit the Nightbane setting and calling it finished. Even if there is only some level of similarity, the abilities already written can serve as a touchstone or jumping-off point in designing this new power. If your proposed Talent is totally unique, that might mean more thought and work will be involved. But don't worry, if we writers can do it, so can you.

Think like a Nightbane

This is a role-playing game and you are a role-player, so think like a Nightbane. Whether converting or creating new Talents, it is useful to keep in mind exactly who is creating and using them. That, for anyone still lost on the subject, would be the *Nightbane*. Put yourself in a Nightbane's shoes.

What problems do the Nightbane have to deal with? What would a 'Bane find useful to be able to do? When asking such questions, also keep in mind that most Nightbane are teenagers and young adults, which means thinking like a teen or twenty-

something. That means some Talents may not necessarily be the most practical or take into consideration all the ramifications, but they will likely be "cool" and helpful. It also means that Talents may be inspired by popular culture.

Since Talents can be individual creations they are likely to reflect personal biases, fears, stereotypes, misconceptions, and personal experience (or lack thereof). Anything from a slang term or popular phrase to a song lyric, comic book hero, personal experience, etc., can inspire a Talent's manifestation. The *Bookworm Talent* is a great example of the former, where the slang term for a heavy reader was twisted with some Nightbane flavor to create an ability that allows the user to eat books to temporarily gain the knowledge contained in them. On the other hand, the *Bypass* Talent could have been born from experience where a character repeatedly failed to succeed at the Pick Locks skill, and created the *Bypass* skill to make his life as a thief or spy easier.

Not only should you think like a Nightbane, you should also try to think like the character developing the Talent. What are the things he or she likes? What hobbies do he have? What skills or experience might affect how he or she views the world? These questions are important because Talents should fit into the persona of the character, not just give the best bonuses and powers. For example, what are the chances that a reclusive Seeker sorceress is going to develop a bunch of combat based Talents unless she has an experience that leaves her wanting to better defend herself? The answer is: Not that great. Such a character would be much more likely to develop a Talent to, say, speed up her magical research or keep herself hidden. The need to study and research could be fulfilled by the psionic power of Speed Reading, but since Nightbane cannot possess psionics, it opens an opportunity to convert or create a new Talent.

This process all might sound a bit odd, but it is exactly how we write the games and books you enjoy. We put ourselves in the shoes of the character, and our readers, and ask ourselves all these questions and more. And like magic, the ideas start coming and we have new Talents and spells to share with you in books like these. The same process will work for you to develop you own ideas.

Converting to Talents

As mentioned previously, almost any power or ability can be converted into a Talent. This is much easier with spells, psionics, and some abilities because of one key factor: cost. Establishing a fair cost is essential for Talents, so when one already exists, the conversion process is greatly simplified. Of course, if the parameters of the ability are altered in any way, the existing cost should be altered as well. But let's take this process one step at a time.

There is no hard and fast formula for establishing the cost of a Talent. That's okay, this is magic and the supernatural we are dealing with, not linear equations. Even without a clear formula, one fundamental rule is that Talents should almost always cost at least a little bit more than the original ability or spell being converted. Why? Because upping the cost of the Talent preserves the usefulness of the original power or spell. Think about it. If every psionic ability in the book was available as a Talent and at the same cost or lesser to Nightbane, why would players ever want to play a psychic character?

The P.P.E. cost for a psionic power converted into a Talent will be P.P.E. that is the equivalent to the I.S.P. x2 or x3. So if a psionic power cost 4 I.S.P., is costs 8 or 12 P.P.E. as a Talent. Likewise a spell converted into a Talent costs two or three times more P.P.E. than it costs to cast the spell.

If a spell is from a specialized school of magic like Necromancy or Elemental magic, tripling or even quadrupling the cost for an identical Talent should be considered. Psionic abilities unique to a specific class of psychic should cost triple or quadruple as a Nightbane Talent. And do NOT make every spell or psionic power available as a Talent.

Of course, altering the cost of a converted power is not the only way to preserve the integrity or specialty of the original. Other restrictions may be made to the Talent version of the power or spell, like reducing the effects, duration, damage or range, or requiring a higher level for access, or adding some negative consequence not present in the original power. For details on such restrictions and how they might affect a Talent's cost, read on about *Talent Creation/Alteration*.

As for super abilities and other such abilities lacking any point based cost to begin with, there are two good ways of dealing with their conversion to Talents. The first is to simply find a point-based power that is relatively close to the one you wish to convert and use it as a gauge in conjunction with the guidelines above. Just do not forget to compare the relative power of the super ability to the point-based equivalent and increase or decrease the base cost (or the ability) accordingly. The second method is to use the Talent Creation/Alteration guidelines, below, to reach your own conclusions regarding the cost of the ability.

Creating & Altering Talents

So you've decided that creating a brand new Talent or modifying an existing one is warranted. Now what?

First off, it's important to realize that writing up powers like Talents is an art, not a science. What has been created up to this point was not done using a codified set of rules. Not every Talent is created equal and trying to apply the following logic to previous material may leave you completely vexed. That's because what you are about to read are *guidelines* to help shepherd you through the creative process while maintaining some reasonable limitations on the Talents you might create. They are NOT hard and fast rules that are guaranteed to statistically balance your creations with what has already been written.

Siembieda's Design Thoughts

That said, you should always try to keep power levels in check and consider game balance when you are creating a new Talent, spell or power, character, weapon or whatever it is. One way to do this is to think about how such an ability would impact your own character if it was used on him. For example, the target of a Talent or any power should always have a genuine and fair chance to survive. No automatic kill shots. No situations where one failed roll means death. No absolute control over another character or permanent debilitation. Why? Role-play this scenario in your head.

"Okay, Brandon. Your Nightbane is enveloped in a swirl of energy. Roll to save vs magic. And roll high, because you need an 18 to save. Oh man, a 15. Sorry, dude, your character is dead. Next."

How much fun was that?

NONE. The fate of your character hinged on one single roll whether your character was playing smart or not. Fail it, and you die. Roll high and you live. That sucks. A character you may have spent an hour creating and weeks, months, or even years playing is gone, in a heartbeat. It feels unfair. And where is the drama, fun and "role-playing" in that?

Sure, you might argue that it is realistic, but this ain't reality. This is a game of heroes. It is supposed to be challenging and fun. Why is it the main hero in any (okay, most) movies, TV shows, books, comics, etc., is never killed by a sniper's bullet or miraculously survives an explosion that collapses an entire building and kills everyone else?

Because he or she is the hero.

We want the hero to survive and live and see justice served. Sure, we want drama and suspense. Yes, the hero can get hurt and almost killed, but in the end we want the hero to win. And your player characters are the heroes in your stories. They should ALWAYS have a fair chance at surviving. When they die, it should be because they knowingly, bravely sacrificed their lives so that others would win or to make sure the Big Bad perished with them. Or because the character did something stupid or foolish despite hints and clues from the G.M. that it was a dangerous or foolish thing to do. This advice comes from a Game Master who has played thousands of games and seen his share of characters die for both reasons. It works. It is fair. And it feels right for everyone.

So while it may sound cool to give your hero a Kill Shot Talent or an incredible power, Talent, or magic weapon that crushes

the enemy, it is not so cool or fun when that power is turned back on you or your fellow player characters. Remember that. Too deadly and too powerful is bad. Large areas effected abilities are often bad, too. The duration of a paralysis, stun or other severe incapacitation is also bad, because while the Talent or spell did not kill the character per se, it played a big part in it, because you made it impossible for him to have a chance to defend himself or escape, and any bad guy can just walk up and put a bullet in his head or slice his throat. Again, not fun or cool.

This is a phantasmagorical setting with heroes that are more than human. The player characters are the X-Men or the Avengers, or John Wick, or Ripley or Han Solo and company. Yes, death should always be a real possibility, but it should not come easy for our heroes, and whenever possible, they should have some input in how they choose to die. I often refer to **Nightbane®** as a "super-hero horror game." A setting populated with heroes who possess superhuman powers and abilities and who take a stand against impossible odds. Heroes who must turn into monsters themselves to use their powers and fight fire with fire. It raises the question, are they monsters or heroes? And what is it that makes a hero? An attractive appearance or what's in their hearts and souls? The Nightbane are tortured, yet noble heroes unlike those in any other role-playing game. Heroes who become something inhuman in order to protect the innocent and to battle the cunning and insidious forces of evil. That core premise is considered and reflected in every part of this game, from the characters and their Morphuses to their Talents, spells and everything else. That and fun. Never forget this is a game and it is supposed to be fun.

– Kevin Siembieda

Step #1:
Select One or More Base Effect(s)

Base Effects:

This is a list of general Talent types. Some Talents may not fit one of these categories or might fit into more than one category simultaneously. Note the base cost for a Talent of that type involves adding together or averaging costs as appropriate for Talents with more than one effect.

Note: Remember, this is just ONE part of the total cost. See ALL of the steps to determine the final cost.

Boost Stats/Skills: Two P.P.E. per attribute point or 1 P.P.E. per 5% skill boost.

Communication: 1-4 P.P.E.

Control: 10-15 P.P.E. for natural phenomena like weather, 12 P.P.E. per target for sentient beings, 3 P.P.E. for animals, or 2 P.P.E. per inanimate object.

Damage: Costs one (sometimes two) P.P.E. per 1D4 or 1D6 points of damage delivered by the Talent. One cost element is the damage at one or two P.P.E. per 1D4 or 1D6 dice. So if a Talent inflicts 2D6 damage the cost consideration amount is probably 2 P.P.E., 3D6 costs 3 P.P.E., 4D6 costs 4 P.P.E., and so on, usually with a high end of 6D6 or 1D4x10, and sometimes as much as 1D6x10 damage.

This damage may be spread over time (typically X damage per melee round). A good rule of thumb is to limit damage to 6-12 points per each 2-4 P.P.E. points of cost when the damage is dealt out as so much per melee round.

Debilitation: Two P.P.E. points per -1 or -5% skill penalty.

Detection/Discovery: Two P.P.E. per mile (disregard range-based cost modifiers) when locating something specific, and 2-3 P.P.E. for sensing or revealing entire categories of things (supernatural creatures, magic items, secret passages, etc.).

Creation: The same as Summoning, below, for minions, 1-5 P.P.E. for most small to medium objects (man-portable), 5-10 P.P.E. for large objects (up to 10 feet or 3m), and 10-20 for very large objects (larger than 10 feet/3 m).

Healing: One P.P.E. per each Hit Point/S.D.C. restored. This amount may be doubled if spread over time such as 10 Hit Points/ S.D.C. (or 2D6 Hit Points) per melee round or per minute.

Movement/Travel: Three P.P.E. to change movement type (flying, swimming, etc.), 5 P.P.E. to increase speed, and 8-24 P.P.E. to breach dimensional boundaries.

Protection: One P.P.E. per 10 S.D.C. or +1 to a saving throw, and 2-20 P.P.E. for immunity to a specific threat.

Stealth: 5 P.P.E. to hide from natural senses; 10 P.P.E. to hide from supernatural senses.

Manipulation/Illusion: Five P.P.E. for sentient minds and 8-10 P.P.E. to manipulate physical forms.

Summoning: One P.P.E. per 10 S.D.C. or Hit Points above 15, and 1-5 P.P.E. per additional perk.

Transformation: 5-10 P.P.E. depending on how drastic the transformation.

NOTE: While the base costs and any of the aspects of a Talent may be fixed numbers, it is likely that one or more may be scaled on a "per level" basis, such as a Talent lasting for "X minutes per level." In such a case, use that per level value x1 as the indicator when determining cost. For example, a protection Talent that provides 10 S.D.C. per level would have a base cost of one while 50 S.D.C. per level would have a base cost of 5.

Step #2: Modify the Base Cost depending on Key Elements of the Talent

When creating a new Talent, simply add up the modifiers for each applicable aspect (number of targets, range, and/or duration) and apply the total modifier to the base cost. **Example:** A healing Talent that restores 10 H.P./S.D.C. (or 2D6 points) would have a base cost of 10, but add the modifiers for two targets, 100 foot (30.5 m) range, and instant duration, and the activation cost

would rise to 25 since the total modifier is +150% to the base cost. Keeping it simple keeps the cost down.

Modifying existing Talents works a bit differently. Instead of using the modifiers listed, increase or decrease the cost by 50-100% per level altered. **Example:** Changing the *Shadow Blast Talent* into an area effect attack that hits everything in a 5 foot (1.5 m) radius up to 2,000 feet (610 m) away would add 100-200% to the cost (double or triple the norm) because the number of targets and range are both improved by one level.

Duration

This is how long the Talent's effects last. The longer the duration, the higher the activation cost. Note that for game balance purposes, combat-focused Talents tend to have relatively brief durations (seconds to a few minutes).

Instant: The effects occur upon the Talent's activation and last only 1D4 seconds with instant results. This also means EACH use/activation costs whatever the P.P.E. amount is. Instant is the base duration for damage, healing, and detection/discovery Talents. P.P.E. cost is zero.

Melee Round: The effects/Talent lasts for one melee round or 15 seconds. (Increase the cost of the Talent +25%).

Quick: Up to 1 minute. (+50%)

Brief: 1-45 minutes. (+100%)

Moderate: 1-24 hours. (+200%)

Lengthy: 1-7 days. (+400%)

Extensive: 1-4 weeks. (+900%)

Protracted: 1-3 months. (+1,400%)

Epoch: From 3 months to many years. (+1,900%)

Permanence: This is a special case and almost always included as a secondary and optional duration when five to ten times (5-10x) the normal activation cost is paid. Making the effects of a Talent permanent is also likely to require some additional cost such as sacrificing a small number of P.P.E. or Hit Points, or requires a lengthy period of meditation, etc.

Sustaining Cost Note: If there is a separate cost to sustain or continue a Talent it is *typically* 25-50% lower than the final activation cost.

Number of Targets

This is the number of things, individuals, or the size of the area affected by the Talent, and how each affects the activation cost.

One Person/Object: The base number of targets for all Talents. P.P.E. cost is zero.

Two People/Objects or a Small Area: The Talent affects up to two targets simultaneously or a radius of up to 5 feet (1.5 m). (+50%)

Three+ Targets or an Intermediate Area: The effects cover three people/objects or a radius of up to 10 feet/3 m. (+100%)

Medium Area: The Talent covers a radius of up to 20 feet (6.1 m). (+200%)

Large Area: A radial effect up to 50 feet (15.2 m) in size. (+400%)

Massive Area: A radial effect up to 100 feet (30.5 m) in size. (+900%)

Colossal Area: A radial effect up to 500 feet (152.4 m) in size (+1,900%).

Beyond Colossal: While area effects of more than 500 feet/152.4 m in radius are possible, these are generally seen when dealing with forces like weather that do not follow the same scale since they naturally affect large areas. G.M.s should use discretion and common sense as always if a Talent is to have such a large area of effect.

Range

The following is a list of potential ranges and associated cost modifiers.

Self Only: This is the starting range for all beneficial Talents and has zero P.P.E. cost.

Touch: Physical contact with the target is required. This is the base range for detrimental Talents. (+25%, but only if the Talent can be used on oneself and one other.)

Melee Range: Up to 10 feet (3 m) away. (+50%)

Short-Range: 10-100 feet (3-30.5 m). (+100%)

Medium-Range: 100-995 feet (30.5-304 m). (+200%)

Long-Range: 1,000 feet to one mile (304.8 m to 1.6 km). (+400%).

Extreme-Range: 1.1 miles to 20 miles (1.7 to 32 km), or any range measured in multiple miles (or kilometers); rare. (+900%)

While ranges beyond extreme are possible, they tend to only be needed with travel or discovery Talents. For such Talents, G.M.s may also wish to reduce the above range modifiers by a level or two.

Other Aspects

These are other parameters of a Talent that can influence its cost. While it is technically possible to reduce the final activation cost by over 100% by combining the following modifiers, no Talent will have an activation cost of less than one P.P.E. Rather than combine the following modifiers, in some instances it might make more sense to just use the greatest cost modifier.

Facade Form: If a Talent is able to be used in Facade form as well as Morphus, the final cost should be increased by 100%. NOT available to Talents that have offensive capabilities or cost more than 20 P.P.E. before this feature is added to it.

Morphus Form: This is the default for all Talents, meaning it should be presumed that the Talent only works in Morphus form unless the increased cost to use it in Facade Form is paid; see above. Cost to use a Talent in Morphus form only is zero.

Material Requirements: Requiring some kind of object or material for the Talent to be used reduces the base cost by 25-50%.

<u>P.P.E. Caps:</u> While limiting the amount of P.P.E. that can be spent at any one time to activate a Talent does not affect the base or final cost, they can be an important way to maintain game balance. A typical cap will be 1-4 times the activation cost per level of experience.

<u>Penalties/Disadvantages:</u> If using the Talent also penalizes the Nightbane somehow, subtract 10-40% from the final cost depending on how severe the disadvantage.

<u>Prerequisites:</u> These are criteria that must be met to even be able to acquire the Talent. -5% to final cost per level necessary requirement beyond the first, up to -30% for an Elite Talent, and up to -10% for other prerequisites like a certain alignment or possessing a different Talent. Keep in mind that particularly powerful Talents should be *level restricted* as a matter of principle; typically not available until levels 3,4, 5, 6 of 7, sometimes as soon as level two.

<u>Restricted Target:</u> Limiting the effects of a Talent to only a certain class or type of opponent, or giving it some kind of Achilles' heel (such as a relatively common object that protects against its effects), can drastically impact cost, reducing final cost anywhere from 10-90%! This reduction depends entirely on how restricted it makes the Talent. **Example:** Limiting the Talent to a broad category like supernatural creatures only might reduce the cost by 10-20% while only being able to target vampires might reduce the cost by 30-50%. Of course, if the targets are particularly powerful or common in your campaign, a cost reduction may not be necessary at all.

<u>Saving Throws:</u> The base saving throw is 12. Raising the number required increases the P.P.E. cost. Lowering the number required to save reduces the P.P.E. cost. For each one point increased (to a maximum of 15) the cost is +10-20% higher. For each point less (i.e. Saving Throw is 11, or lower), reduce the cost by -10-20%. If a successful saving throw only limits effects, cost should usually be increased by an additional 50-100%.

<u>Speed of Use:</u> For a large number of Talents it only takes 1D4 seconds to activate and use it; the equivalent of a single melee attack. Zero cost modifier.

Reduce P.P.E. cost of the Talent 30% if each use of the Talent counts as two melee actions.

Reduce cost 50% if a Talent can only be used once per melee round.

Reduce cost 70% if a Talent can only be used once every minute or longer.

Purchase Cost

Now that the scope and activation cost of the Talent have been established, how much will it cost for characters to "purchase" or acquire permanently?

A simple way to determine purchase cost is to set it at 1.5x to 2x the activation cost, though this method will almost always under-value Talents that work on an "X P.P.E. per something" basis.

The best way to determine purchase cost is to use existing Talents as a template and compare your new power to similar Talents, setting a higher cost if superior and a lower cost if inferior. If done right, the experience level at which the Talent becomes available can also provide some guidance.

The following list presents the average P.P.E. purchase cost (the first number) and the typical range (the second number) by level (applicable to spells and psionic powers that are converted). Note that Elite Talents usually have higher purchase costs than most Common Talents available at the same level.

<u>Level 1</u>: 7 P.P.E. on average with a typical P.P.E. range of 4-12.

<u>Level 2</u>: 9 P.P.E. on average with a typical P.P.E. range of 7-12.

<u>Level 3</u>: 12 P.P.E. on average with a typical P.P.E. range of 8-15.

<u>Level 4</u>: 14 P.P.E. on average with a typical P.P.E. range of 13-19.

<u>Level 5</u>: 16 P.P.E. on average with a typical P.P.E. range of 15-20.

<u>Level 6</u>: 18 P.P.E. on average with a typical P.P.E. range of 16-22.

<u>Level 7</u>: 22 P.P.E. on average with a typical P.P.E. range of 20-25.

Step #3: Wrapping Up
Make certain the Talent "fits"

So, you've worked through the previous steps and come up with a new Talent with all the proper parameters in place. Congratulations. But there may be a few more things you can consider to really set your creation apart.

First, double-check the statistics you've come up with and see how they compare with similar Talents. While it does not have to be perfectly balanced with what is already established, you certainly don't want any glaring flaws that dissuade players from using it. On the same token, an extreme advantage over similar Talents that isn't compensated for by cost could make those Talents obsolete. This has the potential to not only wreck game balance, but also diminishes the diversity of the characters as everyone scrambles for the "latest and greatest" new Talent. Keep in mind that if the players can access this power, opponents can too (and vice-versa).

Next, consider the setting. Nightbane is a dark, horror-themed "urban fantasy" world with a bit of a superhero flavor thrown in. Is there anything you can do with the Talent you've created to emphasize the *supernatural/horror* aspects? Take the Infectious Control Talent as an example. While it could have been just another domination/control ability, C.J. played up the horror by

SIEMBIEDA 2017

highlighting the grotesque nature of how the Talent user seizes control of another being. Is there anything about your Talent that could be made more gruesome or gritty?

Along those same lines, adding unique "quirks" can make powers much more interesting. Take the new Talent *Ashes to Ashes* as an example. This power could have been yet another ranged damage-dealing ability. Rather than rehash the fireball, a material cost was added so that some object would have to be sacrificed when using the Talent. This serves to not only limit a powerful attack, it also plays on a passage from traditional burial rites. Additionally, this limitation fundamentally alters the playing experience for players that have a character with Ashes to Ashes. They have to think about how to carry around or scrounge up items in the environment for "fuel" to use against opponents and may even be able to exploit this "limitation" in certain situations by thinking outside the box. What interesting twists can be added to your Talent?

Finally, everyone involved with such creations, from player to Game Masters, should think of it as a *work in progress*. As has been said above, creating Talents is an art rather than a science. If you or your players use the above guidelines and the end result doesn't quite seem right, do not be afraid to tweak it to make it work for your game. If the Talent is too powerful, tone it down some or raise the P.P.E. cost. If it's too weak, then amp it up until it feels balanced with other powers or reduce the P.P.E. cost to make it an inexpensive alternative. Even if there is some unique mechanic or element that is not accounted for from the previous sections, don't be afraid to experiment and see what you come up with. However, it can't be stressed enough that the G.M. is the final arbiter of what is allowed in the game. So even if a newly created Talent is approved that doesn't mean it cannot be adjusted or disallowed at a later date. If some loophole is discovered or the power gets out of hand, it needs to be modified or removed. After all, this kind of game is about everyone getting to have fun, so don't spoil it by abusing a created Talent or arguing over rules.

Ancient Nightbane

Survival of the Fittest

Some of the most enigmatic and powerful beings on the face of Nightbane Earth are the Ancient Nightbane. Some of these individuals are known to have lived for hundreds of years while the truly ancient, rare even among the Ancient Nightbane, are said to have lived for a millennium or more. Ancient Nightbane are much rarer than the current generation due to a number of different factors. First, there were only a tiny number of Nightbane prior to Dark Day. Second, some Nightbane who existed before Dark Day, perished combating supernatural monsters, powerful mages, and rival Nightbane. Third, some left Earth for other dimensions seeking a safer or more interesting place where a supernatural being such as themselves might fit in or be able to rise to a place of power and prominence. Fourth, during and after Dark Day, some of the Ancient Nightbane who stuck their necks out to help innocent humans or to protect new Nightbane were slain by the minions of the Nightlords. Since then, Ancients have been relentlessly hunted by the Nightlords and their henchmen to prevent the Ancient 'Bane from becoming mentors and generals to the growing army of new Nightbane appearing across the globe. Fifth, of those who did not die or leave, some withdrew from an unforgiving world seeking tranquility or just not wanting to watch family and friends perish time and again.

The moment Dark Day happened, all Ancient Nightbane knew they were on the Nightlords' "hit list" and would be relentlessly hunted down by their demonic minions and human henchmen.

Thus, Ancient Nightbane have gone into hiding and are keeping a low profile. They help newborn Nightbane and people in danger from the shadows or via the anonymous Internet. No one knows how many Ancient were able to either escape notice or evade assassination and live to fight another day. Then again, nobody knows how many Ancient Nightbane existed prior to Dark Day to begin with. Most believe there were only a few thousand spread across the entire globe hidden among the 7+ billion people on the planet. However, there could have been two or five times that number, or many fewer, perhaps only a few hundred Ancients, nobody knows.

Today, Ancient Nightbane are an important element in the secret war against the Nightlords. Most of the major factions have one or more Ancient Nightbane as founding members, executive leadership, or both. Many have poured the accumulated wealth and resources of several lifetimes into helping bankroll one or more factions or independent *Night Crews*. Many Ancients who are not affiliated with any existing faction or group are known for being amenable to lending a hand to help other 'Bane survive these dark times. Some do so out of a sense of responsibility or as an act of charity, others in exchange for something tangible, or for a bit of information or to be owed a favor he can cash in at a later date. Other Ancients have no desire to be tied down with bureaucratic red-tape, politics, or the ethics of some committee or group. They prefer to fight the Ba'al on their own terms either as lone hunters and saboteurs or by forming their own, handpicked team.

SIEMBIEDA 2017

Just because many Ancient Nightbane fight against the Night-lords it does not mean they all do. There are those who choose to sit things out (at least for now), or find ways to profit from the secret war. Others are away from the planet and have not yet heard mention of the invasion. A very small minority have thrown in with the Ba'al, reasoning that it is the best chance of survival or a shortcut to greater power. But even when dealing with those struggling against the Nightlords, it is important to remember that the surviving Ancients are almost assuredly the canniest of the original lot and are known for being secretive and harboring dark secrets. They are survivors for a reason. And that may mean not just being smart and cagey, or ferocious in combat. It may mean knowing when to cut their losses and betraying their comrades. Not all Nightbane, whether aged or Became recently, are good or heroic. Some are self-serving. Some are ruthless. And some are capable of great scheming and treachery. Think *Game of Thrones* or the movie *Braveheart*.

Becoming an Ancient

Unlike most R.C.C.s, the Ancient Nightbane is essentially added to the standard Nightbane R.C.C. (or that of the Nightbane Mystic or Sorcerer). This allows any Nightbane to transition from being a normal 'Bane to an Ancient. If the Game Master (G.M.) deems it appropriate in the context of the campaign, a player character may even be allowed to become an Ancient Nightbane.

So what makes an Ancient?

First, the character must be at least 120 years of age. It isn't known why this is the case, but some theorize the transition to greater power can only take place when the last vestiges of a normal mortal life are stripped away by living beyond a standard lifetime. Second, the character must be at least 9th level, needing a vast amount of experience and perspective to make them capable of transcending the usual Nightbane form.

Once both of the above requirements are met, the Nightbane is capable of ascending to the status of "ancient." Of course, how this process takes place is as individual as each Nightbane. Some achieve this new level of power and ability by isolating and meditating on the metaphysical nature of the Nightbane. Others have a kind of "baptism by fire" and come out of a trying crisis with newfound strength and perspective. And still others simply wake up one morning and realize that they are ancient. Regardless of how it happens, there are certain benefits to being an Ancient Nightbane.

Creating an Ancient Nightbane

While it is possible for Ancient Nightbane to be player characters, it is much more likely for them to be used as NPCs (Non-Player Characters). The following rules and tables are applicable to both player characters and NPCs. Player characters would, of course, be the newly ascended and a comparatively young, 120-190 years old, Ancient Nightbane who is much more limited. Still, a young Ancient is quite powerful and probably not appropriate for most campaigns.

These powerful beings make great villains, benefactors, mentors, helpers, secret supporters and quest-givers. They may also be used as leaders of factions or advisors to them or the player group, and on rare occasions, to go rescue an outmatched player group or provide critical guidance to progress a stalled adventure. But beware, Ancient Nightbane seldom do anything without an ulterior motive, whether it be magnanimous like training heroes to battle the darkness, self-serving like getting rich or even robbing the Nightlords, a business or Nightbane faction, to revenge against a specific Nightlord or one of his minions (or a good guy or group of heroes, if he is selfish or evil).

Whatever the case may be, G.M.s should be careful not to overuse any Ancient Nightbane NPCs and to keep from regularly overshadowing or rescuing the player group. With that in mind, Ancient Nightbane can be created using the rules that follow.

Automatic Bonuses for Ancient Nightbane

The following are applied to the character upon reaching Ancient Status: +1 to I.Q., +2D6 to Hit Points, and +2D6 to S.D.C., applicable to the *Facade*.

AND the following bonuses apply only when the Ancient Nightbane takes his Morphus form: +2D6+6 to Hit Points, 4D6+6 to S.D.C. and +3D6+10 to P.P.E. in *Morphus* only.

Ancient Random Age Table

First, roll or select one of the options for age. Usually the older the Ancient, the more powerful he or she will be. Note that while Ancient Nightbane *may* exist that are older than what is found on this table, they are exceedingly rare, and none are currently known to exist on Nightbane Earth.

01-40% Recently Ascended: 120-190 years old. Roll one area of focus.

41-65% Industrial Age Ancient: 200-290 years old. Roll one area of focus.

66-85% Exploration Age Ancient Nightbane: 1D4x100+200 years old. Roll two areas of focus.

86-95% Medieval Ancient: 2D6x100+300 years old. Roll three areas of focus.

96-00% A.D. Ancient: 1D10x100+1,000 years old! Roll four areas of focus.

Areas of Focus and Corresponding Special Abilities & Bonuses

The benefits gained by each Nightbane for reaching the status of Ancient and surviving each subsequent century are largely determined by the individual's focus and activities during his lifetime.

Select one of the *Areas of Focus*, below, for every 300 years of life, up to 4x maximum. This demonstrates how the Nightbane has spent most of the previous centuries.

01-15% Material Focused: The Nightbane has spent time pursuing material wealth, possibly with aspirations of building a personal empire. **Wealth:** This focus yields additional resources and contacts to the tune of 1D10 million dollars per every 200 years of life. Much of his wealth is likely to be "hard assets" such as land, gold, silver, jewelry, works of art and antiques.

This Ancient also has 1D4+3 high-level contacts in the world of collectors and dealers in such items. This may include some high-level collectors, dealers, smugglers and thieves who traffic in stolen and illegal items. Each high-level contact can be traded off for two mid-level or four low-level contacts or a combination of one mid-level and two low-level. At the G.M.'s discretion, a portion of the material wealth may include things like modified vehicles, mundane or magic weapons, or spell tomes. See *Current Equipment and Assets* under Stats, below, for additional ideas.

If selected again, double the number of dice rolled for money (2D10 million dollars, *instead* of the initial roll) and add double the number of contacts.

16-30% Morphus Focused: The character has spent much more than the average amount of time in Morphus form and/or contemplating or studying the true nature of the form and its relationship to the Facade. This leads to much greater control over the Morphus form and some unique abilities.

- +1D6 to Hit Points.
- +2 to the amount of Hit Points and S.D.C. regenerated per melee round!
- The character no longer needs to roll an M.E. save when undergoing the Becoming, as he is now able to choose how fast or slow to transform.
- One NEW Morphus feature can be rolled or selected from any of the Morphus tables.

If this focus is selected a second time, the long-lived Ancient Nightbane gets all the bonuses, above, but the maximum number of Morphus features that can be displayed at once is 10. From this point on, the character may decide how many features are present at the time of each Becoming (minimum of one feature). Features not selected to be present do not manifest, meaning any bonuses or penalties associated with them are not in effect. Cannot be selected a third time.

31-40% Power Focused: The Ancient Nightbane craves power and influence. This means he has accumulated a small fortune (2D6 million for every 200 years of age), but more importantly, has learned the art of deal making, diplomacy and politics. Preferring to operate from the shadows, this Nightbane is not likely to put himself in the limelight, but rather pulls the strings of the puppets whom he has helped to put into power. He or she is the power behind the crown. This means the Ancient Nightbane is a skilled manipulator, liar, and schemer and is not beneath using threats, lies, blackmail, intimidation tactics and perhaps even more extreme measures to get the power he covets. **Bonuses:** +1D4 to M.A., and over time, has acquired the following skills, all currently at 96%: Barter, Escape Artist, Forgery <u>or</u> Interrogation (pick one), Networks, Palming <u>or</u> Undercover Ops, Seduction, Streetwise, and Surveillance Systems.

This Ancient also has 1D4+4 high-level contacts in the world of politics and government. Each high-level contact can be traded off for two mid-level or four low-level contacts or a combination of one mid-level and two low-level.

41-50% Skill Focused: Whether trying to keep a low profile, deny the supernatural nature of Nightbane, loves knowledge, or some other reason, the character has spent a great deal of time in academia learning a wide range of things. He may be an expert in multiple fields or know many diverse things. Select the following skills:

History <u>or</u> Philosophy at 98%.

Basic and Advanced Mathematics <u>or</u> Art and Mythology at 96% each.

Four Language (spoken) <u>or</u> Literacy (written) skills, all at 90% each.

Four Lore skills, all at 92% each.

Four skills of choice from any Skill Category. These are new interests, and each starts at level one proficiency but get a +30% bonus.

Money is not what's important to this character, but the Ancient has squirreled away 1D6x100,000 dollars per every 200 years of life.

This Ancient also has 1D4+3 high-level contacts in the world of academia, such as college professors, historians, heads of private and institutional libraries of which he can gain access to, scientists, advisors to government or business, and perhaps, Guardians, sorcerers and other Nightbane. Each high-level contact can be traded off for two mid-level or four low-level contacts or a combination of one mid-level and two low-level.

If selected a second time, the Nightbane gets a +5% bonus on all existing skills (where appropriate), four new skills of choice from any Skill Category with each starting at level one proficien-

cy but get a +30% bonus, and another 1D4+3 high-level contacts. Cannot be rolled or selected for a third time.

51-60% Talent or Magic Focused: The Nightbane .has spent a great deal of time and effort manipulating magic energy through the use of spells. As a result, six extra common Talents or six spell invocations from levels 1-7 may be selected at no cost. These may be traded on a two-to-one basis for Elite Talents or higher level spells, or ALL six Talents or spells can be traded for one Spell of Legend. Also, +1 to Spell Strength, and increase the range and duration of the all Talents or Spells (whichever is the focus) by 25%.

This Ancient also has 1D4+1 high-level contacts in the world of the Nightbane and/or magic, including practitioners of magic, Guardians and fellow Ancient Nightbane. Each high-level contact can be traded off for two mid-level or four low-level contacts or a combination of one mid-level and two low-level.

The same bonuses and number of contacts are added if this Focus is rolled or selected a second time. Cannot be selected a third time.

61-70% Fame Focused: This Nightbane is focused on being famous probably as a Nightbane, within the world of the Nightbane and/or the Nightlords. The Ancient may be infamous among the Nightlords and their minions if he opposes them or is a great warrior or leader of the Nightbane and/or other resistance factions, or infamous among the Nightbane if he is a wild card lone wolf or famous for something specific (a legendary feat or accomplishment, battle, leadership, etc.) or infamous because he serves the Nightlords or is known to hunt, kill or betray fellow Nightbane.) Or he may be famous for his skill or occupation as a gunslinger/assassin/warrior or mage or scholar, or arbiter, etc. Whatever it is that the Ancient Nightbane is famous for, his fame and preserving or improving his reputation is the most important thing to this character. **Bonuses:** +1 to I.Q., +3 to M.A. attribute, +5D6 P.P.E. and +1 attack per melee round or +2 Common Talents or +1 Elite Talent.

This Ancient has 1D4+6 high-level contacts in the world regarding whatever area of fame or infamy that is appropriate. If a famous leader he is likely to have contacts among other Nightbane Factions and/or other groups such as Guardians, practitioners of magic, secret societies, maybe vampires and others. If a renowned assassin, his contacts are likely to be with the Mafia and other criminal organizations, gangs and possible corrupt governments, and so on. Each high-level contact can be traded off for two mid-level or four low-level contacts or a combination of one mid-level and two low-level. This Focus can only be selected once.

71-80% Combat Focused: This Ancient Nightbane has focused on perfecting martial combat with physical training and weapon skills. This also means learning to control his anger and fear, and fighting with a cool head, awareness, and tactical superiority.

- +1 melee attack for every 200 years of life up to a maximum of five.
- +1 on Perception Rolls related to field combat, like sizing up an opponent, recognizing a likely ambush, trap, concealment, etc., for every 200 years of life up to a maximum of five.
- Demon slayer strike. This Ancient's punches, kicks and attacks with melee weapons (sword, spear, club, etc.) inflicts double damage to all demons and Shadow creatures. Double damage +20 to the Nightlords, Night Princes and Princesses, Demon Lords and dark gods. This damage bonus does not apply to bows and arrows, guns or any weapon that fires projectiles or a set energy blast.
- +4D6 to Hit Points.
- +2 to the amount of Hit Points and S.D.C. regenerated per melee round!
- +2 Elite Talents of choice.
- Recognize Weapon Quality skill at 98%.
- Combat Driving or Prowl or Land Navigation at 86% (pick one).
- Four skills of choice from Espionage or the Military Skill Category (pick a Category), and each skill has a 92% proficiency.
- Four Ancient W.P.s of choice, each at 9th level proficiency and two Modern W.P.s at 7th level proficiency regardless of the Ancient's actual experience level.
- Money is not what's important to this character, but the Ancient has squirreled away 1D4x100,000 dollars per 200 years of life and has a large collection of weapons, with at least four varieties for each W.P. as well as other weapons, and 1D6 types of body armor (G.M.'s discretion).

Note: This Focus can only be selected once.

81-90% Well-Rounded: The Nightbane has striven for balance rather than choosing a specific focus, and enjoys the following: 2D6x100,000 dollars hidden away, 1D4 high-level contacts (may be exchanged as usual, see those above), +1 to the Becoming saving throw, +1D6 to Hit Points, +3D6 to S.D.C., +1 new Common Talent (or one new spell from levels 1-5), +1 Elite Talent, and +3 new skills of choice from any Categories, each at 90%. This Focus can only be selected once.

91-00% Seeks Justice and Harmony: This Ancient wants to bring a sense of peace, purpose and place to his fellow Nightbane in the world of humans. However, he is well aware of the Nightlords and the consequences of Dark Day, and knows there can be no peace for humans or Nightbane as long as they are in the world. Thus, he fights the Nightlords and their minions and henchmen, but will be satisfied with sending them back to the Nightlands rather than utterly destroying them. This Ancient is on an eternal quest for personal enlightenment and enjoys sharing what he has learned, and what he believes is an honorable, moral and just way to live. In combat he is fierce and relentless in his crusade to drive the Nightlords and their minions from Earth, but can also be compassionate and merciful when appropriate.

Bonuses: +1D4 to I.Q. and M.A. attributes, +1 Elite Talent and +2 spells selected from levels 1-7, +1 to disarm and dodge, +2 to pull punch, and, over time, has acquired the following skills, all currently at 96%: Barter, Firefighting, Law, Paramedic, and Philosophy. This Focus can only be selected once.

This Ancient also has 1D4+3 high-level contacts with leaders among the Nightbane and other nonhuman Factions like the Guardians and vampires, and he may be an advisor to a group, Faction, or government, or may lead his own Faction or movement (especially if an NPC). Each high-level contact can be traded off for two mid-level or four low-level contacts or a combination of one mid-level and two low-level.

Ancient Nightbane R.C.C. Stats

Also Known As: Ancients, Elder 'Bane, and Methuselahs.

Alignment: Any, though many Ancient Nightbane may become somewhat jaded by multiple lifetimes hiding in plain sight and/or working against the Ba'al and other evil supernatural beings and rivals. Thus, Principled Ancient 'Bane are rare, with Scrupulous, Unprincipled and Anarchist representing the majority.

Attribute Requirements: An I.Q. and M.E. of 9 or greater. Those Nightbane not meeting these requirements never seem to achieve the level of self-awareness required to survive for generations, grow old and attain Ancient status.

Ancient Nightbane R.C.C. Skills: All skills progress normally as per the original R.C.C., though G.M.s should award the *Lore: Nightbane* and *Lore: Nightlands* skills based on the character's experiences (if these skills aren't already known). Hand to Hand bonuses while in Morphus form are as follows:

Level 16: +1 to strike and pull punch.

Level 17: +1 to roll with punch/fall/impact and +5% to invoke trust or intimidation.

Level 18: +1 additional attack per melee round and +2 to physical damage.

Level 19: +2D6 to Hit Points and 3D6 to P.P.E.

Level 20: +1 to entangle and Critical Strike on Natural 17-20.

Level 21: +1 to disarm and +5% to invoke trust or intimidation.

Level 22: +1 Common Talent <u>or</u> two magic spells from levels 1-5.

Level 23: +1 to save vs possession and +6D6 to P.P.E.

Level 24: +1 Elite Talent <u>or</u> two magic spells from levels 6-10.

Level 25: +1 Common Talent and +1 Elite Talent <u>or</u> five new spells total, with selections made from levels 1-10.

Level 26: Bio-Regenerates from damage at *double* the usual rate!

Current Equipment and Assets: Any player character just becoming an Ancient Nightbane retains their current posses-

sions and gets the usual a bonus of +6 to Hit Points and +10 to P.P.E. and +2D6x10,000 extra cash in savings or perhaps a sudden and unexpected boon.

For long-lived NPCs, those who still value material possessions (some find owning things less meaningful and a hindrance, while others covet wealth and possessions more than ever), will likely have what they consider the best of everything. Whether this is a hedonist who lives in a large mansion or a military-style survivalist with a firearms collection that rivals that of most small countries, it is easy to accumulate "things" over the course of multiple centuries. Others may have money, but it is liquid, and have gotten rid of possessions because they find it ties them down and limits them. These Ancients prefer to be mobile and invisible with no landholdings or possessions that could be used to find them or slow them down.

Game Masters can elect to either choose exactly what the Ancient Nightbane has or roll on the following table for a random determination, and then modify it to best suit the character.

<u>01-15% Saver:</u> The character has been a miser and hoarded the money he has accumulated over the decades, saving it for a rainy day or has hit it big in the stock market. In any case, the character has 2D6x10 million dollars. Roughly 90% of the character's wealth is "liquid" in the form of currency, gems, and precious metals. The money is likely to be kept in several banks with 1D4x10% stashed away in one or more secret locations while the Nightbane lives like ordinary working-class people in mundane to downright austere conditions.

<u>16-30% Antiquities Collector:</u> Much (50-90%) of the Nightbane's wealth has been spent on anything from valuable works of art to military hardware and other antiquities (old books, coins, furniture, etc.). This collection is worth 2D6x10 million dollars.

<u>31-45% Modern Collectibles:</u> Much (50-90%) of the Nightbane's wealth has been spent on modern collectibles such as toys, stamps, baseball cards, books of the last 150 years, comic books, modern art, animation cells, dinosaur fossils, and pop-culture memorabilia (Hollywood movie and rock-n-roll collectibles, etc.). This collection is unlikely to fetch what was spent on it over the years (2D4x10 million dollars), since demand for goods fluctuate and some have dropped to an all-time low, but in a pinch it can be auctioned for 1D4x10+20% of its original value. Also has 1D4 million in available cash.

<u>46-60% Land Baron:</u> The character has invested in real-estate. Whether it is numerous commercial properties on one or several continents to private land for development, to wilderness reserves; 30-70% of his or her wealth has purchased deeds to land and/or buildings. Estimated value is 2D6x100 million dollars plus 2D6 million in liquid funds.

<u>61-75% Major Shareholder:</u> Whether private or public, the Nightbane invested 60-80% of his accumulated wealth into

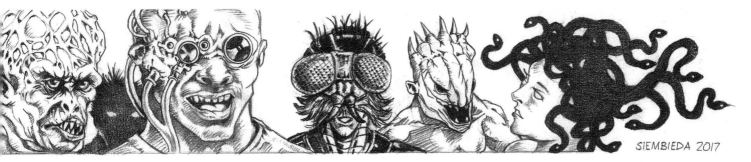

SIEMBIEDA 2017

one or many business interests. While this can be risky, it is also one of the few uses for wealth that pays dividends. Estimated value is 2D6x100 million dollars plus he has 3D6 million dollars in liquid funds. At any point in time, the stocks can be sold off for 2D6x10% of the purchase price. The character is also likely to have a controlling interest in one or more businesses, even if it's just a small, local business that he probably uses as a front for his current operations.

76-85% Hard Times: Both money and possessions have been destroyed, stolen, or otherwise lost. The Nightbane is left with 1D6x100,000 dollars in cash plus some basics like a 1D4 year old vehicle, a basic wardrobe, cell phone, laptop, basic electronics and common assets and equipment of the working middle class. Time to reinvent himself and rebuild.

86-93% Major Losses: The Ancient may have been a victim of theft, mismanagement or the NSB froze bank accounts and seized property, etc. The latter has happened to more than one Ancient Nightbane since Dark Day as the Ba'al try to wipe them all out. Bank accounts are being frozen by law enforcement, property seized or destroyed, and many Ancients are lucky to get away with their lives. Since Dark Day, the global economy is in turmoil as the Nightlords dismantle humanity bit by bit, so many investments have gone bust and not enough money circulates to support a healthy market for commodities. Now the Nightbane is forced to rebuild and perhaps seek revenge.

Whatever the case, he has lost everything! He has the clothes on his back, a 1D6 year old vehicle, and 2D6x1,000 in cash. For some Ancient Nightbane this is time for revenge against the Nightlords, for others it may be better to lay low, operate from the shadows against the Nightlords or cut his losses, move on and quietly rebuild.

94-00% Criminal on the Run: Similar to Major losses, the Nightbane has been branded a criminal, his criminal operation(s) shut down, assets seized by the authorities, and he is a wanted criminal on the run. The charges may be trumped up, but odds are this Nightbane has been making his fortune with one or more criminal enterprises for half his life (drug dealer, illegal gambling operation, sex trade, money laundering, racketeering and extortion, hit man, etc.) In any case, the Ancient Nightbane has changed his identity and gone underground. Good or evil, the Ancient harbors a grudge against the Nightlords and whatever government agencies they have in their pocket that shut his criminal business down. As a result, this crooked Nightbane is likely to make them the targets of his new criminal enterprises, everything from robbery and extortion to murder and creating public scandal for them.

However, this Ancient always has an eye out for making himself a pile of money in the process, even when extracting revenge. For example, he might attack and hijack/rob a military convoy or base, or armory, killing whoever gets in the way – hopefully that includes Nightlord minions, their hench-men and maybe even a Night Prince or Nightlord Avatar – and selling the weapons for a tidy profit to Nightbane factions and freedom fighters who will do more damage to the Nightlords and their plans.

Current assets of the criminal Ancient Nightbane are a paltry 1D6 million dollars, though the criminal or vengeful Ancient is likely to have a small, loyal crew of his own (3D4 henchmen), 1D4 contacts and connections in the criminal underworld he can still rely upon, and 1D4+1 favors he can call in among his criminal underworld associates or corrupt business people.

Ancient Nightbane Personality and Insanity Table

To live several hundred years to a thousand or more is a long time for a being to live, much less a being that begins life with a mortal perspective and human value system. Add to that the shock of finding out one's supernatural nature, both of which necessitates losing friends and loved ones, and gaining knowledge about magic and otherworldly forces that defy science and logic, and you are going to have someone who has experienced his share of mental and physical trauma. Top that off with Dark Day, the Nightlords' conspiracy to infiltrate and takeover the Earth and an overwhelming evil force hellbent on hunting you down, and you have a recipe for a host of interesting ... um ... quirks.

The following is a random table of just some of the possible effects of life as an Ancient Nightbane. Roll for every two centuries of life.

01-20% No Insanities: No major psychological problems yet, though the character probably seem at least a little eccentric or antiquated.

21-40% Phobia: Any are possible. See the **Nightbane® RPG** for some ideas.

41-44% Ascetic: Has no want for material possessions beyond what is necessary to survive. This Ancient gives away or spends any worldly assets on others in need, living a very simple and austere life. He values and enjoys life and is willing to fight injustice and wickedness, he just wants to live a simple life without being tied down by possessions and desires.

45-48% Cryptic: Has a tendency to communicate in riddles or lapse into vague metaphysical ramblings that make little to no sense to most others; -15% to all Communications and Language skills. This is most common among Ancient Nightbane Sorcerers.

49-52% Doomsday Speaker: This Ancient has given up hope and is either apathetic, believes Dark Day is the beginning of the end, or seems to fight with a death wish for a chosen cause. Either way, none of it matters since the Nightlords will win eventually. -2 on Perception Rolls, -5% to all skills and -2 to dodge.

53-56% Eternal Warrior: The Nightlords must be defeated, costs be damned. The character is willing to sacrifice fellow

Nightbane, innocent civilians, and even themselves if it means striking a blow against the Ba'al, though for most, this isn't done wantonly. +1 attack per melee and +1 to strike when fighting Nightlords or their minions. This extreme stance can alienate even long-time friends and allies.

57-60% Extreme Paranoia: There is the healthy level of paranoia that keeps all Ancients alive, and then there is this. The Nightbane trusts no one but themselves. He is constantly questioning the motives and actions of others. The slightest hint of suspicious activity often prompts swift action to neutralize a potential threat whether that means defensive, evasive, or even aggressive action toward a former ally or associate, or even a passing stranger who says the wrong thing. Such Ancient Nightbane tend to eventually withdraw from society and end up as a solitary hermit living in a secluded area or even a nomad that's constantly on the move. On the plus side, such characters are always on edge and expecting a fight, so add a +2 bonus to both initiative and Perception Rolls regarding danger and potential attack.

61-64% Hates Nightbane: Yes, this Ancient Nightbane hates his own kind. This may be due to his own self-loathing, or resentment or trauma from being betrayed by fellow Nightbane in the past. This character views himself and other Nightbane as dangerous monsters who need to either be destroyed or exiled to the Nightlands. As a result, he tries to avoid contact with Nightbane; or may manipulate and use fellow Nightbane for assorted "dirty work" or to help humanity with little or no regard for them (the Nightbane); or deliberately kill (or cause to be killed) Nightbane who try to enlist his aid or will not leave him alone; and some who fell this way may become serial killers who stalk only Nightbane, probably young Nightbane who are confused and easily misled and destroyed. **Note:** As much as this character hates Nightbane, he hates the Nightlords more, and never willingly serves them. Working with other enemies of the Nightbane may be another story.

65-68% Hedonist: This character feels that you might as well have the best time you can in the time left, because it is only a matter of time before something brings you low or kills you. He may still be willing to help others, especially if the 'Bane stands to benefit somehow, even if it is accolades or favor, but will always look out for numero uno above all others. -10% to all non-leisure skills and -1 to all combat rolls. Good alignments are not possible for hedonists given their pervasive self-interest. Anarchist at best.

69-72% Hermit: The Ancient Nightbane has retreated from the world for any one of a variety of reasons. He or she wants nothing to do with the Nightlords, the war, fellow Nightbane, and maybe even former associates. The character may be terrified about being discovered by the Ba'al or anyone, even humans, and is cantankerous and aggressive toward anyone who disturbs the quiet new life of solitude he is trying to hold onto. It will take some really smooth talking or something big/important to bring this Ancient back to the real world or to stand up to the Night-

lords. Even then, the character is not confident or focused and may have other insanities and quirks, including -10% penalty to all skills and still tends to be quiet, keep to himself and distrustful of others.

73-76% Kingpin Obsession: The Ancient has become obsessed with building and ruling a personal empire and will likely resort to any means necessary to achieve power and influence. This character wants to be a major player in Machiavellian political, military or business scheme, but is so driven he makes bad choices based on impulse without full research or vetting, especially when he thinks there is a big payoff for him. This can get him involved with the wrong people, and he tends to backstab his partners and associates before they do it to him. The Ancient never truly trusts anyone for long, because he knows he can never be trusted himself.

77-80% Megalomaniac: Power-mad, this Ancient Nightbane will stop at nothing to become the most powerful being the world has ever seen. This may lead to alliances with powerful, otherworldly forces such as the Ba'al, demons, or vampires. Also likely to seek out lost artifacts and forbidden magic/knowledge. Good aligned characters may be misguided and believe their ascent to power is what's best for the country or the world. Evil aligned characters want what they want and don't care who gets hurt in the process. Tends to be ruthless and brutal in all his dealings. Distrusts others, especially if they are powerful or seek power like him. This Ancient Nightbane sees anyone who is not subservient and fiercely loyal to him or his cause as a potential rival or enemy.

81-84% Nightbane Supremacist: The Ancient Nightbane sees "his people" as the future, period. Everyone else can either serve them in the coming new world order, leave Earth/the Nightlands, or be destroyed. This Ancient Nightbane sees anyone who is not subservient to him or his cause as a potential enemy. All non-Nightbane are to be manipulated and used to facilitate the rise of the Nightbane to their rightful place as leaders in human societies. May still work with non-Nightbane, but only if the means justify the end, or lies and uses them as expendable pawns.

85-88% Pacifist: Refuses to take part in the war against the Nightlords, rivals, Factions or anyone else for that matter. Believes that to do so simply perpetuates the negative cycle of violence and retribution. The character may still try to protect innocent people from harm, help in rescue operations, and intercede in fights to prevent serious injury or death, but otherwise sticks to the sidelines or uses nonlethal means to stop the fighting.

89-92% Wanderlust: This Ancient has a driving need to see what is beyond the horizon, exploring the far-flung corners of Earth and even other dimensions. He may stick around for up to 2D6 months at a time if needed, sometimes much longer if things are interesting or challenging, but will eventually become uncomfortable and leave on another expedition.

93-96% Random Insanities: Roll 1D4 times on the Random Insanity Chart on page 45 of the **Nightbane Main Book** or the

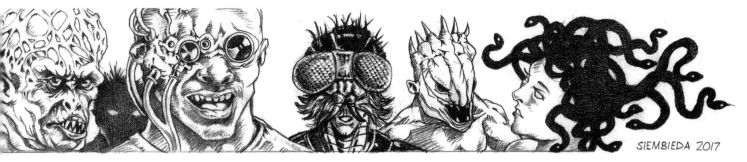

SIEMBIEDA 2017

Nightbane-Specific Insanity Table on pages 66-67 of the **Nightbane Survival Guide**.

97-00% Roll Twice: Roll two results on the chart above and keep both. If this result is rolled again, ignore it and re-roll.

Ancient Nightbane Experience Table

Use the same table as the starting R.C.C.; the following table is for levels beyond 15.

16: 600,001-800,000
17: 800,001-1,000,000
18: 1,000,001-1,250,000
19: 1,250,001-1,500,000
20: 1,500,001-1,800,000
21: 1,800,001-2,100,000
22: 2,100,001-2,500,000
23: 2,500,001-2,900,000
24: 2,900,001-3,400,000
25: 3,400,001-3,900,000
26: 3,900,001-4,500,000

Ancient Nightbane Sorceror / Mystic Experience

Use the same table as the starting R.C.C.; the following is for levels beyond 15.

16: 800,001-1,000,000
17: 1,000,001-1,250,000
18: 1,250,001-1,500,000
19: 1,500,001-1,800,000
20: 1,800,001-2,100,000
21: 2,100,001-2,500,000
22: 2,500,001-2,900,000
23: 2,900,001-3,400,000
24: 3,400,001-3,900,000
25: 3,900,001-4,500,000
26: 4,500,001-5,100,000

Plot Hooks for Ancient Nightbane

Help Wanted: One or more players are offered a job working for what turns out to be an Ancient Nightbane. Might this be a benefactor that can support the party's efforts and adventures? Does the Ancient have a different, and perhaps nefarious, agenda? The players will likely only find out if they take the offer.

Quest for the Holy Grail: The Ancient 'Bane has found "it" but needs the players' help. This may be a powerful artifact, a secret weapon to use on the Nightlords, the truth of the Nightbane's origin, or some other suitably tantalizing goal. Whatever the case, the Ancient can't recover it alone and decides to call on the player group. Whether "it" really is what the old Nightbane thinks it is, was moved or stolen long ago, or the Ancient double-crosses the group and steals it away, G.M.s should certainly think twice before giving the players a real shot at something potentially game-breaking.

A Call to Arms: An Ancient known for his success in fighting the Nightlords has put out a call to any fellow Nightbane who will join a new offensive. He claims to know how to hit the bastards where it will hurt the most and strike a major blow in this secret war. Is this a fool's errand or is he right? Even if the strike is successful, what will be the consequences? Might this just spark open war on Earth and hasten its demise? Perhaps the characters will be the deciding factor.

Guardian Angel: One or more times the group has received important guidance or been delivered from harm's way by a mysterious stranger. Now that stranger is revealed to be an ancient Nightbane who shows up to collect on the debt the players owe.

I Bequeath Thee: An Ancient Nightbane has died or disappeared, leaving something of value to one or more players. This inheritance may have unforeseen consequences like stipulations in the will or covetous enemies that want what the players now have. Perhaps it is a clue to finding the Ancient's killer or a long-lost treasure. Whatever the case, it should prove interesting.

The Sleep of Ages: The group learns of the resting place of a fabled Nightbane warrior who led the battle against an ancient scourge (a previous Nightlord invasion, vampire colonization, or demon raid?). In the end, this warrior fell in battle, was imprisoned by the enemy, or was incapacitated by powerful magic. The catch is that the hero was said to be immortal and it was prophesied that they would be found and freed when needed most. To complicate matters, the foes defeated by this ancient warrior have discovered the hidden location as well and seek to destroy the Ancient Nightbane once and for all. Can the players free the endangered legend in time?

Of Ancients and Plowshares: Somehow the group becomes aware of an Ancient Nightbane that disappeared and was thought dead long ago. As it turns out, the Ancient simply lost faith in the fight against the Ba'al and now just wants to be left alone. Perhaps the characters can convince the Ancient to come out of self-imposed retirement, but how? To complicate matters, perhaps this Ancient possesses some key information or some source of power the characters need to defeat a powerful foe, free a trapped friend, etc.

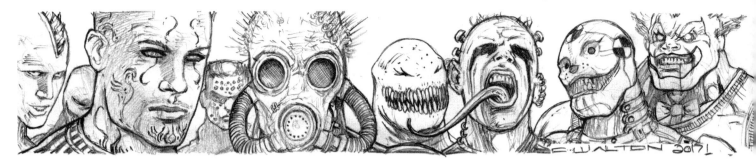

Questions & Answers

How do you deal with damage to Nightbane as they are changing forms?

Answer: Subtract any damage done to a Nightbane in transition from the Morphus form regardless of which form the Nightbane is transitioning from. The same logic applies for any saving throws such as those against psionics or magic spells, use the Morphus form's bonuses when in transition and ignore those of the Facade. And finally, if a Nightbane is killed while transforming then only a dissipating pool of darkness is left behind.

Can Nightbane or Guardians draw P.P.E. from outside sources such as ley lines, amulets, or blood sacrifice?

Answer: For the most part, no. Normal Nightbane and Guardians are unable to draw P.P.E. from anywhere but their own personal reserve (though this does not prohibit them from allowing others to draw on said reserve). However, Nightbane Mystics and Nightbane Sorcerers are capable of doing so due to their training in the magical arts. G.M.s may also allow Nightbane or Guardians who obtain the *Principles of Magic* skill to draw on outside P.P.E. sources.

Do new Talents start at level one proficiency?

Answer: No. Much like magic spells, the power level of Talents is based on the general level of experience of the Nightbane rather than how many levels they have been known.

Does activating and using a Talent take separate attacks?

Answer: Not normally. For instance, Shadow Blasts only take a single action to use (as the Nightbane expends the P.P.E. a split-second before firing the blast) and Shadow Shields are erected in the same attack the Talent is activated.

If Talents can be used in the same action in which they are activated, how does the free attack from the Fire Breather Talent in the Nightbane Survival Guide work?

Answer: Fire Breather is one of the few exceptions to the above rule. Activating this Talent takes a melee action in which the attack can't be used. However, it gives the Nightbane a free attack to be used at any point in the melee after the Talent is activated. Since sustaining a Talent doesn't take an action, if Fire Breather is extended past the initial melee of use, the Nightbane gains +1 attack (the fire breath) per melee as long as the Talent is in use. Do note that both the Talent and breath attack are *both* limited to one use per melee.

What is the range of the Borrow Morphus Talent in the Main Book?

Answer: The Talent-user must be within 100 feet (30.5 m) of the Morphus form intended to be copied.

How far away can a portal created by the Doorway Talent be generated, how big can they be, and how long do they last?

Answer: A "doorway" can be generated up to 10 feet (3 m) away from the Nightbane per level of experience. The doorways themselves can be up to 5x10 feet (1.5x3 m) and last for one minute.

What is the range of the Infectious Control Talent in the Main Book?

Answer: The range of the initial attack is 10 feet (3 m), but an infected target can be controlled at up to 300 feet (91.4 m) away.

What is the duration of the Nightbringer Talent in the Main Book?

Answer: The effects of Nightbringer last for a single melee round (15 seconds), but may be sustained for the same cost. Altering the magnitude of the darkness would require a new activation.

In the Reshape Facade Talent's description it mentions an increased cost for more drastic changes, but how does this work?

Answer: The activation cost is paid for each feature changed. For example, simply changing the hair color of the Facade costs 6 P.P.E., but to change the hair color and shape of the nose would take 12 P.P.E., and further adding a change in height would make the cost 18 P.P.E. To simplify complete appearance changes, G.M.s may allow such total transformations to cost 30 P.P.E. for activation and 20 P.P.E. per additional hour.

What is the range of the blood attack from the Bloodbath Talent in the Main Book?

Answer: The range of the Bloodbath Talent is 10 feet (3 m) per level of experience.

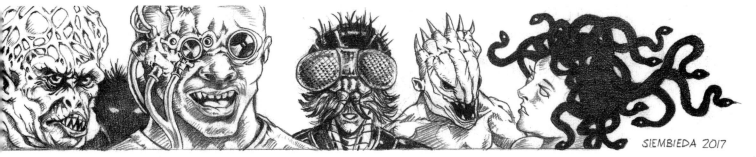

SIEMBIEDA 2017

What is the duration of the See Truth Talent in the Main Book?

Answer: The user can see the true nature of the targeted object or individual for one minute per level of experience.

What is the range of the Darkbonds Talent in World Book 2: Nightlands?

Answer: Darkbonds can be created up to 300 feet (91.4 m) away, but the Talent-user must have line of sight.

Can a Nightbane be possessed by a spirit or alien being?

Answer: It depends on what is doing the possessing. Remember that Nightbane are immune to any physical transformation other than the Becoming, certain Talents and mind control. This means that any being like an Elemental (see **Rifts® Dark Conversions**) or Chinese animal spirit (**Rifts® China 2**) that usually alters the host would be unlikely to even try to inhabit a Nightbane. Likewise, a slain demon attempting to be reborn through a mortal mother (see **Dimension Book 10: Hades**) can't use a Nightbane for such a purpose.

Beings that do not physically alter the Nightbane host may try to possess the body but not the mind. This means that the possessing force has to assert itself as the body's conscious mind rather than take control of said consciousness. Therefore, there is no access to the Nightbane's personality, skills, memories, etc. The entity is also unable to trigger the Becoming and is stuck in whichever form it possessed. As an alternative, a possessing being can hide within a Nightbane without trying to take control. They may even be able to use psionic or magic abilities to try and communicate with and/or influence the host, but the Nightbane's consciousness is secure against direct manipulation.

Could a character such as a super-being from Heroes Unlimited™ or a Juicer from Rifts® be a Nightbane?

Answer: Theoretically, in most cases, yes. As long as the character is a mortal being with a human-like brain and no psionic ability, it has the potential to be a Nightbane. In the case of someone with superpowers or similar innate abilities, those powers/psi-abilities would only be available in Facade form.

A Juicer would be handled a bit differently since a Facade's increased healing would interfere with the action of drugs from the harness. The only way Nightbane could morph into a Juicer would be under the Substance Abuse Table for a Morphus, and he only becomes a Juicer, with collar and armor, in Morphus form. The Facade is likely to be a scrawny, sickly or crippled person, or even a child or teenager. Otherwise, any Nightbane who tried to become a Juicer (or Crazy for that matter), would undergo a kind of forced detox and healing, and lose all Juicer powers and abilities. Nightbane cannot become Crazies.

With all that said, as a G.M. I probably wouldn't allow characters with super-powerful Facades in the interest of maintaining at least some control on the power level of the game. Not to mention the dichotomy between the relatively fragile Facade and super-powered Morphus is part of what defines Nightbane characters.

Can a Nightbane have a hand to hand skill other than martial arts?

Answer: The facade form can be skilled in any hand to hand style of combat, but for almost all Nightbane, the Morphus form uses Hand to Hand: Martial Arts. This is not to say that all Nightbane are inherently masters of Kung-Fu, just that the instinctive fighting style common to Nightbane is best expressed by the bonus structure of Hand to Hand: Martial Arts.

Even if the Facade has a hand to hand skill which offers better bonuses than Martial Arts, this style does *not* carry over to the Morphus, because the two forms are physiologically distinct. Any practiced martial artist can tell you that it is not just skill acquisition that defines a hand to hand style. There are physiological elements to Martial Arts training such as body hardening, muscle memory, and kinesthetic awareness that would not function the same way if you suddenly found yourself in a different body.

So, other than the modifications found under the Ancient Nightbane in this book, future supplements might have additional options for Nightbane hand to hand skills. Until that time, unless your G.M. says otherwise, the Morphus form sticks to the equivalent of Martial Arts.

Natural Armor Rating in Nightbane®

Some fans noted after the **Nightbane Survival Guide** was released that Morphus features gave Armor Ratings for the first time. Some felt this was slightly unbalancing given the absence of A.R. in previous books. To address this, the following errata for previous Morphus features have been derived:

Nightbane® RPG:

Metal Exoskeleton (Biomechanical) provides a Natural A.R. of 14.

Bony Exoskeleton (Alien Shape) provides a Natural A.R. of 13.

Armorgraft (Biomechanical) provides a Natural A.R. of 12.

Crystalline (Alien Shape) provides a Natural A.R. of 11.

Full Arachnid (Arachnid), and Giant Insect Nightbane (Insectoid) provide a Natural A.R. of 10.

Spider/Scorpion (Arachnid), Insectoid Centauroids (Insectoid), and Bark-Like Skin (Alien Shape) provide a Natural A.R. of 9.

Were-Arachnid (Arachnid), Were-Insect (Insectoid), Giant Reptile (Reptile), and Wheels or Treads (Biomechanical) provide a Natural A.R. of 8.

Humanoid Arachnid (Arachnid), Humanoid Insectoid (Insectoid), Were-Reptile (Reptile), Reptile Centauroid (Reptile), and Full Snake (Snake) provide a Natural A.R. of 7.

Limbed Snake (Snake) and Humanoid Snake (Snake) provide a Natural A.R. of 6.

Nightbane® World Book 2: Nightlands™

Rough Metal Body (Mineral) and Metal Statue (Mineral) provide a Natural A.R. of 14.

Rough Stone Body (Mineral) and Living Statue (Mineral) provide a Natural A.R. of 13.

Crystalline Body (Mineral) provides a Natural A.R. of 12.

Part Inorganic (Mineral) and Part Inorganic with Weapons (Mineral) provide a Natural A.R. of 11.

Humanoid Tree (Plant Life) provides a Natural A.R. of 10.

Thorn Skin (Plant Life) and Bark Skin (Plant Life) provide a Natural A.R. of 9.

Note: All Armor Ratings given for Nightbane or other supernatural and magical creatures are considered "Natural," meaning that any strike rolls under the number will usually fail to do *any damage* even if the strike connects. This is the result of supernaturally tough hides being able to turn aside many blows. An exception is made when Supernatural Strength or certain magic weapons (most notably, Darkblades) are involved. In the case of a punch or kick from a Nightlord, Nightbane or other being with Supernatural P.S., or the slash of a Darkblade, failure by the attacker to exceed a target's Natural Armor Rating means the damage from the attack is half instead of ignored. When a Darkblade is used in conjunction with Supernatural Strength, Natural A.R. is effectively ignored.

Hounds/Hunters are another special case: The A.R. of Hounds is considered Natural A.R., but is ignored by magical and supernatural attacks such as magic spells and weapons, psionic powers, and Nightbane Talents. It is NOT ignored by strikes from Supernatural Strength, though any successful physical attack using Supernatural Strength will still deal at least half damage as per the explanation of Natural A.R. above.

Appendix Morphus Tables

For your convenience, we have reprinted the Morphus Tables from the **Nightbane® RPG** and select sourcebooks.

Morphus Tables from the Nightbane® RPG

Creating the Nightbane

One of the unique characteristics of the Nightbane is that they have no set shape or qualities. There are literally thousands of variations, and it is said that no two Nightbane are exactly alike. In general, the Nightbane's Morphus (true form) will reflect some part of the character's personality. For example, a character who was fascinated with (or afraid of) snakes might turn into a were-snake creature or have scaly skin or a serpent's tongue. A shy and/or unattractive character might actually transform into an awesomely beautiful, albeit inhuman, form, or see himself as a monster and turn into a hulking beast.

To simulate the variety of forms, a number of **Appearance and Shape Tables** have been set up in the following section. Making *random rolls* to select the appearance, abilities and limitations of the Nightbane is in many ways the easiest and always fun. This method is quick, but may leave the player unsatisfied with the results for his character. On the other hand, play tests determined that it was fun to decide why the character's Morphus looked like the randomly-rolled result. It turned out to be similar to interpreting a horoscope or Tarot Reading, and it actually gave players some ideas and insights on how to role-play their character.

Game Masters may alternatively allow the players to pick some selections and randomly roll on others. For example, the aforementioned character who is fascinated by snakes would get to *select* the Snake Form Table, and roll randomly to see what snake characteristics would occur. The combination works best if

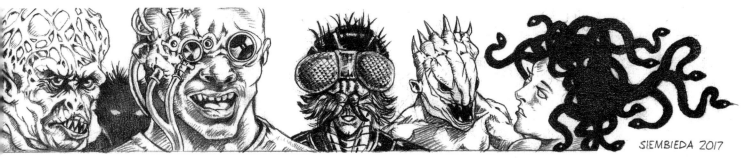

SIEMBIEDA 2017

the player has an idea of what kind of Nightbane he'd like to play, but wants some randomness to add spice.

The last way is to simply hand-pick the selections the player wants for his or her character. This option can lead to abusive players trying to design super-powerful Nightbane "killing machines" without regard for balance or role-playing, so the Game Master is cautioned not to use it unless his players are not likely to abuse their freedom, or he is not particularly concerned with game balance – and let's face it, fun may come ahead of both game balance and realism; although the **Nightbane RPG** can be used for moody, "dark" and introspective games, it can also be a "supernatural superhero" game (and lots of things in between); it's up to you.

Creating New Tables/Forms: Even all the tables below can't hope to compete with the imaginations of players and Game Masters. As usual, these tables are provided as a guideline, thus a player may randomly roll for appearance and shape, make deliberate selections, or come up with his own (subject to G.M. approval). Game Masters and players are encouraged to add their own forms and concepts to the mix.

Game Masters and Players' Note: Flexibility and imagination are the key. If a combination of rolls produces a ridiculous result, the description could be altered to fit the player's conception or re-rolled. Players should get a Nightbane character they enjoy playing, but they shouldn't try to optimize their characters and turn them into ultra-powerful beings. Game Masters might decide to put a "cap" on the number of attribute and S.D.C. bonuses if they feel their players are just trying to stack bonuses for the sake of power. Also, if the game is meant to have a serious bent, "silly" or humorous forms shouldn't be allowed (on the other hand, a touch of humor might be appropriate for some campaigns). Don't let die rolls rule the game. Be imaginative and have fun.

Nightbane® RPG Appearance Table

Roll for random determination or select one.

01-20% Almost Human: The Nightbane's Morphus is almost totally human, except for one inhuman trait that might be disguised or concealed – although sometimes the one trait is inhuman enough to give away the character's true supernatural nature. Roll once on the *Nightbane Characteristics Table* to determine unusual characteristics. If the result asks for more than one characteristic, ignore it and reroll.

21-30% Inhuman but Beautiful: The Nightbane combined a beautiful appearance with rolls on the *Unearthly Beauty Table* and the *Nightbane Characteristics Tables*.

31-45% Marred Beauty: The character has a beautiful True Shape, but it is marred by a gruesome stigmata. Make rolls on the *Unearthly Beauty Table*, the *Stigmata Table*, and the *Nightbane Characteristics Table*.

46-60% Lycanthrope: The Nightbane's Morphus is a mixture of animal and humanoid traits. Roll once on the *Animal Form Table*.

61-75% Monstrous Lycanthrope: Not only is the Morphus form animal-like, it has hideous deformities that give it a terrifying appearance. Roll on the *Animal Form*, *Stigmata* and *Nightbane Characteristics Tables*.

76-90% Inhuman Shape: The Nightbane's True Shape is a gruesome mockery of humanity. Roll on the *Stigmata* and *Nightbane Characteristics Table*.

91-00% Bizarre: Roll on the *Unearthly Beauty*, *Nightbane Characteristics*, *Animal Form*, and *Stigmata tables*. Then exercise your imagination to combine the alien result.

Nightbane Characteristics Table

01-20% Unusual Facial Features: Roll on the *Unusual Facial Features Table*.

21-40% Biomechanical: Roll on the *Biomechanical Table*.

41-60% Alien Creature: Roll on the *Alien Shape Table*.

61-80% Unnatural Limbs: Roll on the *Unnatural Limbs Table*.

81-90% Two Characteristics: Roll or select two categories. Ignore any result of 61% or higher (alternatively, roll 1D6x10% to get a result between 10-60%). If you get the same characteristic twice, roll twice on the appropriate table.

91-95% Three Characteristics: Roll or select three categories. Ignore any result of 61% or higher (alternatively, roll 1D6x10% to get a result between 10-60%). If you get the same characteristic twice, roll twice on the appropriate table.

96-00% Four Characteristics: As above, but roll four times.

Morphus Tables

Unearthly Beauty Table

Not all Morphus are horrible to behold. Some have a terrible beauty that produces fascination and awe instead of fear or loathing. Nightbane students are divided as to whether these shapes are the result of inner beauty brought to the fore, or an incarnation of some darker facet of the Nightbane's personality. Although there aren't any statistical figures to confirm this, it is widely believed that more female Nightbane have beautiful qualities than their male counterparts. The argument is that females are more concerned about their appearance, and this comes through when their Morphus manifests. Modern-minded Nightbane consider this to be so much male chauvinism and ignore it.

Beautiful Nightbane are often met with anger and contempt by others of their kind. The current nickname for attractive and not terribly deformed Nightbane is "Barbie" or "Ken" (some of the older Nightbane use "Venus" or "Adonis" instead). The "Barbies" inspire a great deal of jealousy among some Nightbane, who feel they got the short end of the stick. Also, a few "Barbies" claim that their beauty is the result of their purer or superior spirits or souls ,which does not endear them to the rest.

01-10% Doll-Like Appearance: The Nightbane's body is tiny and toy-like. His or her skin becomes unnaturally smooth and featureless (no fingerprints), size is reduced by 2D6+10 inches (0.3 to 0.55 m), and body temperature is inhumanly cold. The character's P.B. is raised by 6 points and from a distance, the character will be mistaken for a small child. If standing perfectly still, he or she might pass as a storefront mannequin. In a good light, the inhuman features of the Nightbane have a frightening aspect, providing a Horror Factor of 10.

11-30% Animal Magnetism: The Nightbane's P.B. and M.A. are increased by 8 (minimum P.B. and M.A. is 20!). Not only is his/her Morphus incredibly beautiful, it radiates charisma. This is a mixed blessing, however, for the attraction the character exerts cannot be turned off. This can lead to a number of distractions, annoyances and even hazards, as total strangers make advances towards the character, or try to force their affections on him/her.

31-50% Elfin Features: The character has slender and delicate features, oversized eyes and vaguely pointed ears, reminiscent of the legends of elves and faeries. Increase P.B. by 7 points (minimum 17) and size by 1D6 inches (1.5 to 15.2 cm). Their unusual appearance has a Horror Factor 6.

51-70% Physical Perfection: The Nightbane's True Shape is at the peak of physical condition, with perfectly delineated muscles and a shape somewhere between a gymnast and a bodybuilder. Increase P.B., P.E. and P.S. by 1D4 each and S.D.C. by 4D6. The character projects an aura of danger that intimidates those around him, giving the Nightbane a base Horror Factor of 6.

71-90% Fallen Angel: A Nightbane with inhuman beauty; increase P.B. by 6 and S.D.C. by 3D6. Fallen angels also have feathered wings on their backs which provide slow flying (Speed of 4D6 in the air).

91-95%: Combination of Two: Roll two times (ignore and reroll any result of 91% or higher) and combine the two results.

96-00% Other: The Game Master and player can develop a different form of unearthly beauty. The physical attractiveness could be balanced by an inhuman or intimidating feature. Alternatively, roll three times and combine the results, as per 91-95%.

Animal Form Table

About one-third of Nightbane have animal shapes or characteristics in their Morphus. In earlier times, the animal characteristic was even more common, so these transformed Nightbane were believed to be the living embodiments of their animal totems or were-beasts. Animal shapes seem to reflect parts of the Nightbane's personalities. For example, a strong-willed person (or, often, somebody who wants to be strong but was not in his normal life) could turn into a bear or a wolf-like creature. Free-spirited wanderers often take on the form of birds and other fliers. Curious, coy or feminine people may have feline qualities, sneaky or weasely fellows may have the characteristics of a weasel or rodent, and so on. Other forms just seem to be the result of interests and hobbies: many an insect-collector has turned into a giant equivalent of a prized specimen! Warrior types often transform into wolf, lion or tiger form, while city-rats might actually become so in literal truth!

Even while rolling randomly, deciding what aspect of the character has been reflected in the Morphus might provide ideas on the specifics. The actual animal species is left to the player's discretion. If the player rolls a Canine Form, is his character a wolf (warrior, team player), a dog (loyal companion, guardian), or a fox (wily trickster)?

All animal forms are capable of full human speech; the words may be twisted by the Nightbane's inhuman shape, or they could be perfectly human-like (player's choice). Hearing words coming from an animal adds +1 to the Horror Factor of the creature the first few times until the person gets accustomed to it. In most cases, Disguise and Undercover Ops are impossible.

SIEMBIEDA 2017

01-07% Bear: All large ursinoids. Roll on the *Bear Table*.

08-14% Amphibian: Mostly frogs and toads. Roll on the *Amphibian Table*.

15-20% Insectoid: All types of insects, from beautiful butterflies to disgusting dung-beetles. Roll on the *Insectoid Table*.

21-27% Rodent: Rats, squirrels, beavers and similar creatures. City-bred Nightbane tend to favor rats, while those who grew up in the country often transform into wilderness varieties. Roll on the *Rodent Table*.

28-35% Arachnid: Spiders and scorpions. Roll on the *Arachnid Table*.

36-44% Bat: All varieties of pointy-eared flying mammals, including vampire bats, fox-bats, and others. Roll on the *Bat Table*.

45-53% Feline: All cats, from the great predators to small house cats. Roll on the *Feline Table*.

54-62% Snake: All crawling non-legged scaly creatures, from the huge anaconda to the tiniest garden snake. Roll on the *Snake Table*.

63-71% Avian: Any bird species can be selected (most of them are predatorial or scavenging birds, however). Roll on the *Avian Table*.

72-79% Canine: Dogs, wolves and foxes. Roll on the *Canine Table*.

80-88% Reptilian: Lizards (snakes have their own table) of all kinds. Roll on the *Reptilian Table*.

89-95 % Equine/Bovine/Deer: Includes not only horses and cows, but all kind of hoofed plant-eaters such as goats, deer, antelope, zebras, etc. Roll on the *Equine/Bovine/Deer Table*.

96-98% Combination of Two: Roll twice on this table (ignore and reroll any result of 96% or higher), and combine the elements from the two animals. To decide which bonuses apply, roll 1D6; 1-3 means the first animal selection is used, 4-6 means the second one is. **Example:** A Nightbane has snake and equine characteristics. The player decides the character is a centaur with a were-snake upper body. When selecting P.S. bonuses, the player rolls 1D6, and on a roll of 1-3 he gets the snake P.S. bonuses; on a roll of 4-6 he gets the Centaur/horse P.S. bonuses.

99-00% Combination of Three: Roll three times (ignore and reroll any result of 96% or higher) and combine elements from the three animals. To decide which bonuses apply to each attribute, roll 1D6: 1-2 means the first animal selection is used, 3-4 means the second one applies, and 5-6 grants the bonuses of the third selection.

Arachnid Table

Spiders and scorpions are alien-looking creatures that frighten and disgust humans. They symbolize danger and give many people the creeps. Nightbane whose Morphus have arachnid elements often felt like outsiders even before their Becoming. Spider Nightbane are often good schemers who like to spin complex webs of intrigue, for good or ill. Scorpion beings tend to be vicious predators, stubborn and unwilling to compromise. Due to the natural human revulsion towards these creatures, they are among the most fearsome Nightbane forms. All arachnid characters instinctively have the base skills of Climbing at 55% and Prowl at 25% whenever they change into their Morphus shape. In most cases, Disguise and Undercover Ops are impossible.

01-20% Full Arachnid: The Nightbane's Morphus is a giant spider or scorpion. In either case, the creature gets the following. **Bonuses:** +4 to P.S., +2 to P.P., +2 to P.E., +1D4x10 to Speed (can leap 20 feet/6 m), +3D6x10 S.D.C., +1 on Perception Rolls, +2 on initiative, +6 to the Horror Factor.

If a spider, the Nightbane can spin and shoot webbing (range: 60 feet/18.3 m, with 4D6 S.D.C. per length/application), bites inflict 2D4 plus injects a poison inflicting 4D6 (2D6 if a save versus lethal poison is made).

If a scorpion, pincers add one attack per melee round, do 3D6 to hand to hand damage, and the stinger inflicts 3D6 S.D.C. plus it injects poison (same stats as spider's poison, above).

21-45% Were-Arachnid: A vaguely humanoid creature, with two legs and six arms if a spider, or two legs, two arms, two additional arms with pincers, and a tail/stinger if a scorpion. The head is an inhuman horror with four to six eyes, pincer-mouth and chitin or spider-fur instead of skin. The creature could never be confused for a normal human. **Bonuses:** +2 to P.S., +2 to P.P., +2D6 to Speed (can leap 10 feet/3 m), +2D4x10 to S.D.C., +1 on initiative and +1 on Perception Rolls; add one additional attack per melee from the extra limbs. Add 1D4+2 to the Horror Factor.

If it is a spider shape, the Nightbane can spin and shoot webbing (range: 60 feet/18.3 m, has 3D6 S.D.C. per application), and its bite inflicts 1D6 plus injects a poison inflicting 4D6 (2D6 if a save versus lethal poison is made).

If a scorpion, pincers add 2D6 to hand to hand damage, and the stinger inflicts 3D6 S.D.C. plus it injects poison (same stats as spider's poison, above).

46-70% Humanoid-Arachnid: A "man-spider" or "man-scorpion," with a mostly humanoid shape, but with chitin or hair-covered skin, clawed hands, and either two additional spider-arms, or a scorpion's stinger. **Bonuses:** +2 to P.S., +1 to P.P., +1D6 to Speed (can leap 6 feet/1.8 m) and +1D6x10 S.D.C. Add 1D4 to Horror Factor.

If a spider, add one additional attack per melee round from the extra arms; the clawed limbs inflict 3D6 in addition to hand to hand damage.

If a scorpion, add one additional attack per melee round from the extra stinger which inflicts 2D6 plus poison that does 4D6 (2D6 if a save versus lethal poison is made).

71-90% Scorpion Pincers/Spider Limbs: The character has a normal human shape – except for the hands, which are tipped by either pincers or bony, hair covered fingers tipped with claws. The character's face also has a strangeness to it; the look of a predator always sizing-up its prey. **Bonuses:** +2 to P.S., +1 to

P.E., +3D6 to S.D.C. and +1 to Horror Factor. The pincers inflict 3D6 in addition to normal hand to hand damage, spider-clawed hands do 2D6 damage. **Penalties:** On the downside, the Nightbane's hands cannot grasp tools and weapons properly: -5 to use them and -30% to the performance of skills that require dexterity and sensitive touch.

91-00% Spider/Scorpion Centauroid: The Nightbane is a huge creature with the lower body of a spider or a scorpion, and the upper body of a humanoid-arachnid. The result is much taller and heavier than a normal human, making it difficult to fit into vehicles and enclosed spaces. **Bonuses:** +2 to P.S. +2 to P.P., +1 to P.E. and +3D6 to Spd (can leap 12 feet/3.7 m), +3D6x10 to S.D.C. and +1D6 to Horror Factor.

If a spider, the Nightbane can spin and shoot webbing and its bite inflicts 2D4 plus injects a poison the same as the giant spider.

If a scorpion, pincers add 3D6 to hand to hand damage, and the stinger inflicts 3D6 S.D.C. plus it injects poison (same stats as spider's poison, above).

Avian/Bird Table

The player get to select the bird's species. Nightbane tend to become predatory or scavenger birds, such as hawks, eagles and vultures, although all kinds are possible. Avian Nightbane are often wanderers by heart, or those who covet the freedom to fly away from one's problems.

01-15% Full Bird Form: The character has almost no humanoid features, and basically appears as a giant bird of the player's choice. +1 P.S., +3 P.P., +3D6 S.D.C., Speed flying is 2D6x10. Exceptional vision (can see a rabbit or read a sign two miles/3.2 km away): +2 to initiative, +3 to all Perception Rolls using sight, and +1D4 to Horror Factor. Beak slash/peck does 3D6 S.D.C. plus P.S. bonus. Feet claws add 1D6 S.D.C. to kick damage. While in this form, the Nightbane cannot manipulate guns and normal weapons (arms have been replaced by wings); most skills requiring manual dexterity will be at -40%.

16-30% Were-Bird: The Nightbane is a bird-man (or woman), with hands at the end of the wings, a full bird's head, clawed feet, and a feather-covered body. +2 P.S., +2 P.P., +3D6 S.D.C. Speed flying is 2D4x10. Exceptional vision: +2 to initiative, +2 to all Perception Rolls using sight, and +1D6 to Horror Factor. Beak slash/peck does 2D6 S.D.C. plus P.S. bonus. Feet claws add 1D6 S.D.C. to kick damage. **Penalties:** While in this form, guns and hand weapons are at -4 to strike. Skills requiring manual dexterity will be at -25%.

31-45% Man-Bird: The character has separate wings and arms, and fully developed hands ending in claws. The body is still covered by feathers, and the character has a small beak, nearly useless in combat. +2 P.S., +2 P.P., +3D6 S.D.C. Exceptional vision: +1 on initiative, +2 to all Perception Rolls using sight, and +1D6 to Horror Factor. Beak bite does 1D4 S.D.C. (no P.S. bonus). Speed flying is 1D6x10.

46-55% Bird Head: The character looks like a normal human except for his head, which is that of a bird. Beak slash inflicts 3D6 S.D.C. plus Supernatural P.S. punch damage. **Bonuses:** Exceptional vision, +1 on initiative +2 to all Perception Rolls using sight, and +1D6 to Horror Factor.

56-66% Bird Face: The Nightbane looks like a normal humanoid, except for large, round eyes and an oversized beak protruding from where his mouth and nose would be! Beak slash does 3D6 S.D.C. plus P.S. bonus. Add 1D4 to Horror Factor and +1 on initiative.

67-80% Talons: The character's hands and feet turn into oversized bird-like talons. **Bonus:** +1 to P.S. Claws add 2D4 to punch and kick damage. Add 1D4 to Horror Factor. **Penalties:** Normal shoes and gloves are uncomfortable and painful to wear, reduce Spd by 30% and skills requiring a delicate touch are -10%.

81-90% Feather "Hair": Instead of hair, the character's head is covered by feathers. Small feather growths appear throughout the body. **Bonuses:** 2D6 to S.D.C. and +1 to Horror Factor,

91-00% Winged Human: A normal-looking human, except for the wings protruding from the back. The wings can belong to any bird species. **Bonuses:** 2D6 to S.D.C., +1 to P.B., and the character can fly at a speed of 1D4x10.

Bat Table

Bat-like Nightbane have often been confused with vampires and demons. It may not be an accident that many Nightbane with such Morphus were fascinated with creatures of the night before the Becoming. During Dark Day, many an Anne Rice fan found himself or herself turned into something beyond any vampire tales' wildest imaginings. While vampire bats seem to be dominant among these Nightbane, all bat species can be found in one shape or another. All bat characters instinctively have the base skills of Climbing at 45% and Prowl at 20% whenever they change into their Morphus shape. In most cases, Disguise and Undercover Ops are impossible.

01-20% Full Bat: The Nightbane has the shape of a giant bat, typically with a wingspan of over seven feet (2.1 m)! **Bonuses:** +2 to P.S., +2 P.E., +4 to P.P., a flying speed of 1D6x10+20, +2D4x10 to S.D.C., and +1D4 to Horror Factor. Ultra-acute hearing adds +3 to initiative and +4 to any Perception Rolls involving sound. Unlike true bats, the Nightbane's vision is not impaired (same as a human's). The clawed feet inflict 2D6 plus hand to hand damage, and its bite does 2D6 to S.D.C. **Penalties:** Its arms are giant, leathery wings with hands at the middle joint. This limits the character's ability to manipulate tools and use weapons, both of which are impossible when flying, although it can carry small objects in its hands or large items or people in its prehensile clawed feet. -6 to strike, -35% to perform skills.

The bat form is also capable of using its screeching as a form of radar, allowing it to sense invisible figures and obstacles con-

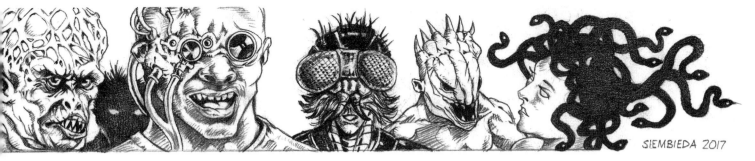

SIEMBIEDA 2017

cealed in total darkness, fog, smoke, etc. Range is 500 feet (152 m).

21-40% Were-Bat: This Morphus is more human-like, although still predominantly bestial. The Nightbane is covered with fur, and its head is animalistic, with a snout and the oversized ears of a bat. Instead of arms it has full bat-wings, but they end in large, clawed hands that can be used to grasp objects and use tools or weapons (-3 to strike, -15% to perform skills; neither can be done while flying). **Bonuses:** +3 to P.S., +3 to P.P., +3 to P.E., the character has a flying speed of 1D6x10, +1D6x10 to S.D.C., +1D6 to Horror Factor. ultra-acute hearing adds +1 to initiative and +3 to all Perception Rolls involving sound. Unlike true bats, the Nightbane's vision is not impaired. The bat form is also capable of using its screeching as a form of radar/sonar, allowing it to sense invisible figures and see with obscured vision at a range of 200 feet (61 m). Claws on hands and feet inflict 2D4 S.D.C. in addition to normal hand to hand damage. Bite does 2D4 S.D.C. Add 1D6 to Horror Factor.

41-60% Humanoid Bat: The Nightbane's skin is sparsely covered by fur, and the face and features are mostly humanoid, with pointy but small ears and sharp fangs marring an otherwise normal face and head. Small bat-wings extend from beneath the arms, making normal clothing very uncomfortable to wear (the wings can be folded, but this restricts movement). **Bonuses:** +2 to P.S., +1 to P.P., and limited flying speed of 1D4x10. +1D4x10 to S.D.C., acute hearing adds +2 to all Perception Rolls involving sound, and +1D4 to Horror Factor. Claws on hands inflict 1D6 S.D.C. in addition to normal hand to hand damage. Bite does 1D6 S.D.C. Add 1D4 to Horror Factor. The Nightbane does NOT have the bat's sonar sense.

61-80% Bat Wings: The Nightbane looks like a perfectly normal human – except for the bat wings protruding from his/her back, which give him a demonic appearance. The wings allow for flight. **Bonuses:** Spd 1D6x10, +1 to dodge when flying, +4D6 to S.D.C., and +2 to Horror Factor.

81-00% Bat Head: A normal human body, topped by a perfect bat's head. **Bonuses:** +2D6 to S.D.C., ultra-acute hearing, +2 to initiative, +4 to any Perception Rolls involving sound, and +2 to Horror Factor. Unlike true bats, the character's vision is not impaired. The bat form is also capable of using its screeching as a form of radar, allowing it to sense invisible figures and see in total darkness, fog or smoke at a range of 500 feet (152 m). A bite inflicts 2D6 S.D.C.

Canine Table

The choice of specific canine species is left to the player to choose. Wolves are the most common canine Nightbane, but dogs of all types, foxes and other canines are possible. Wolf-like Nightbane are often leaders or team players, fiercely loyal to their "pack." Dogs have so many varieties that almost any personality or attitude can be reflected by one or more species, from bestial savagery (a Pit Bull or a Doberman) to dependable companionship (St. Bernard). Fox Nightbane are typically tricksters; they have been fairly common in Japan, perhaps due to the legends of fox spirits. All canine characters instinctively get a base skill of Tracking at 40% and Swimming at 50% whenever they change into their Morphus shape. In most cases, Disguise and Undercover Ops are impossible.

01-20% Full Canine: The Nightbane's Morphus is a large canine, commonly a huge wolf or dog that can pass for a normal member of the species unless other Nightbane characteristics apply. **Bonuses:** +5 to P.S., +1 to P.P., +3 to P.E., +12 to Spd, +2D6x10 to S.D.C., and +2 to Horror Factor. Superior sense of smell and hearing add +1 to initiative and +3 to Perception Rolls, and +15% to the Tracking skills (if the character does not have the Tracking skill, he automatically has it as a base skill at 40% in his Morphus alone). Bite attacks do 5D6 S.D.C. and the wolf form can body-slam enemies (inflicts the equivalent of punch damage), but it cannot punch, kick, or use weapons or tools.

21-45% Were-Canine: A humanoid-canine with full dog/wolf features, covered in fur, with a tail, and bigger than a normal human. **Bonuses:** +4 to P.S., +1 to P.P., +3 to P.E., +6 to Spd, +2D4x10 to S.D.C. and +1D4+1 to Horror Factor, +2 initiative, +2 on all Perception Rolls, and +10% to the tracking skills (if the character does not have a tracking skill, he automatically has it at the base skill of 55% in his Morphus alone). A bite attack does 4D6 S.D.C. and claws add 2D4 to hand to hand damage

46-70% Canine Humanoid: A less extreme version of the above, the character resembles the "wolf-man" of classical movies. The Nightbane has no snout or tail, but is covered in fur and has fangs. Heavy clothing could disguise his appearance to some degree (close up or when clearly visible in a good light, however, it would be obvious that this isn't a normal human being). **Bonuses:** +2 to P.S., +2 to P.E., +3 to Speed (and can leap 12 feet/3.7 m high or lengthwise), +1D4x10 to S.D.C., +1 initiative, +1 to Perception Rolls and +2 to Horror Factor. Bite does 2D6 S.D.C. and claws add 1D6 to hand to hand damage.

71-80% Canine Centauroid: The Nightbane has the upper body of a were-canine (as above) and the lower body of a wolf! This four-legged creature is too big to fit inside most automobiles and may not fit in elevators, cars, and other confined spaces. **Bonuses:** +6 to P.S., +4 to P.E., +4 to Spd, +2D6x10 to S.D.C., +1 to initiative, +2 to Perception Rolls and +1D4 to Horror Factor. Its bite inflicts 4D6 S.D.C., and claws add 2D4 to hand to hand damage.

81-00% Canine Head: A normal looking human with the head of a wolf or a dog! Bite inflicts 4D6 S.D.C., +1 on initiative, +2 on Perception Rolls and +1 to Horror Factor.

Equine/Bovine/Deer Table

This table covers most four-legged herbivores, from domestic cattle to wild deer, bison, antelopes and similar species. Horses and cattle have often been thought of as symbols of power and strength, as well as friends to humankind. The most common Nightbane shapes with these bovine or equine characteristics are the centaur and minotaur. It is very likely that Nightbane gave birth to the legends of the mythical half-man, half-horse (or half-bull). A few Nightbane even transform into normal-looking animals, which may explain stories of magical horses or woodland creatures.

Note: Damage (unless otherwise indicated) is as follows: Kicks and head butts inflict double damage (typically 2D6) and jump and leap kicks do triple damage! If a horned/antlered creature, the Nightbane can head butt and inflicting 4D6 damage. All equine/bovine/deer Nightbane instinctively know Swimming at a base proficiency of 65% and Climbing at 30%. In most cases, Disguise and Undercover Ops are impossible.

01-20% Full Horse/Bovine/Deer Form: The Morphus form is that of a huge creature of the species in the list. The character may pass as a normal, although bigger than average animal and has a mean or tough appearance. **Bonuses:** +12 to P.S., +3 to P.P., +6 to P.E., +1D6x10 to running speed, +1 on initiative, +2 on Perception Rolls, and +1D4 to Horror Factor. The character can also leap 10 feet (3 m) high or 15 feet (4.6 m) lengthwise and gets an automatic dodge (works like a parry and does not use up a melee attack/action). +3D6x10 to S.D.C. **Penalties;** The character cannot use any weapons or tools, and is likely to be too large to fit into most vehicles.

21-45% Half-Man Half-Animal/Were-Animal/Minotaur: The character has the basic bipedal shape of a muscle-bound human, but is covered with fur, has hoofed or cloven feet, a tail, and the head of a horse, bull, deer, or similar animal (the bull is the traditional Minotaur of myth and legend). **Bonuses:** +6 to P.S., +2 to P.P., +4 to P.E., and +4D6 to Spd, +2D6x10 to S.D.C., +2 on initiative, and 1D4+2 to Horror Factor. Kicks and horn attacks inflict an additional 2D6 damage.

46-66% Humanoid Shape: A less extreme version of the above, with a basically human form. Typically, the chest and arms are completely human, but the character has fur covered legs and hoofed/cloven feet. The head is mostly humanoid, but is likely to have horns or antlers and animal features (large eyes, long face, large flat teeth, etc.). These Nightbane may be responsible for myths about satyrs and Pan. **Bonuses:** +4 to P.S., +1 to P.P., +2 to P.E., +2D6 to Spd, +1D6x10 to S.D.C., +1 on initiative, +1 on Perception Rolls and +1D4 to Horror Factor.

67-90% Centaur/Beast-Man: The character has the lower body of a horse, deer, moose, bull, or similar animal and the upper body of a normal man with horns or antlers crowning the man's head. **Bonuses:** +6 to P.S., +2 to P.P., +5 to P.E., and +5D6 to Spd, +3D6x10 to S.D.C., +2 on initiative, +1 on Perception

Rolls, +1D4 to Horror Factor. The Nightbane's body may be too big to fit in vehicles or to maneuver well in most indoor settings.

91-00% Equine/Bovine Head: A normal-looking human body with a full animal head. Bonuses: +1 to P.S., +1D6 to speed, +3D6 to S.D.C., +1 on initiative, +1 on Perception Rolls, and +1D4 to Horror Factor.

Feline Table

The player gets to select the features of a cat. Any feline, from prehistoric sabertooth tigers to household tabbies can be selected. Independent, lazy or sensual Nightbane tend to have some feline elements in their Morphus. Feline Nightbane may have triggered the persecution and killing of cats during the Middle Ages (especially during plague years) when cats were believed to be demonic creatures who had brought plague and disease to the world.

All feline characters automatically get a bonus of +2 to roll with punch, fall or impact, and instinctively get a base skill of Climbing at 45%, Swimming at 40% and Prowl at 20% whenever they change into their Morphus. In most cases, Disguise and Undercover Ops are impossible.

01-10% Full Feline Form: The Nightbane becomes a large (or in the case of household cats, a giant) version of the species in question. **Bonuses:** +6 P.S., +3 P.P., +3 P.E., +3D6x10 S.D.C., Nightvision 1,000 feet (305 m), acute hearing adds +2 to initiative +2 to Perception Rolls involving sound, and +1D4 to Horror Factor. Claws add 2D6 S.D.C. damage to Supernatural Strength. Bites inflict 4D6 S.D.C. Running speed is increased by 1D6x10, and the character can leap 30 feet (9 m) from a standing position and 60 feet (18.3 m) with a running start! **Penalties:** The feline cannot use any weapons, tools or vehicles.

11-26% Were-Cat: A humanoid feline creature, covered in fur and with full feline-shaped head and tail. +4 to P.S., +2 to P.P. and P.E., +1D4x10 to Spd, +2D4x10 S.D.C., +1D6 to Horror Factor, Nightvision is 1,000 feet (305 m), acute hearing adds +2 to initiative and +2 on Perception Rolls involving sound. Claws add 2D4 to Supernatural Strength damage. Bite inflicts 3D6 S.D.C. Can leap 20 feet (6.1 m) from a standing position and 40 feet (12.2 m) with a running start. The paws make it hard to use weapons and tools: -4 to strike with guns and -20% (or -4) to use any weapons, tools or skills that require manual dexterity.

27-42% Fur-Covered Humanoid: The Nightbane could pass for human in bad light, but his/her skin is covered with fur, the ears are feline and near the top of the head, the teeth are sharp feline fangs, has a long furry tail, and the eyes have vertical slits. **Bonuses:** +2 to P.S. and P.P., +3D6 to Speed, +1D6x10 to S.D.C., Nightvision is 800 feet (243.8 m), acute hearing adds +1 to initiative and +2 to Perception Rolls involving sound, and +1D4 to Horror Factor. Claws add 1D6 to Supernatural P.S. damage. Bite inflicts 2D6 damage.

43-58% Cat-like: Appears to be a normal person except for the eyes, which have vertical slits, the teeth (unnaturally long and

SIEMBIEDA 2017

sharp), and the retractable claws in the hands and feet. **Bonuses:** +1 to P.P., +1D6 to Spd and +1D4 to Horror Factor, Nightvision is 800 feet (241 m), and acute hearing +1 to Perception Rolls involving sound. Claws add 1D6 to Supernatural P.S. damage. Bite inflicts 2D6 S.D.C.

59-69% Feline Centauroid: The creature has the lower body of a giant cat, and the upper body of a were-cat! The Nightbane is almost as big as a horse, and cannot fit in most regular vehicles, elevators and even some doorways! **Bonuses:** +2 to P.P., +6 to P.S., +4 to P.E., +1D6x10 to Spd, 3D6x10 to S.D.C., and +1D4 to Horror Factor. Claws add 2D6 S.D.C. damage to supernatural strength and bites inflicts 3D6 S.D.C. The creature can leap 30 feet (9.1 m) from a standing position and 60 feet (18.3 m) with a running start.

70-80% Cat Claws: The Nightbane gains retractable claws. **Bonuses:** +5% to Climbing and inflicts 2D4 S.D.C. in addition to normal Supernatural P.S. damage.

81-90% Cat's Head: The Nightbane has a normal humanoid body but his head is fully feline! Bite inflicts 4D6 S.D.C. **Bonuses:** +1 on initiative, +1D4 to Horror Factor and Nightvision is 600 feet (183 m).

91-00% Feline Features: A lesser form of Cat's Head (see above), in which only some of the person's features have a feline outlook and furry pointed ears near the top of the head. The character gains sharp teeth (bite inflicts 1D8 damage), cat's eyes with vertical slits. **Bonuses:** +1 to Perception Rolls, Nightvision is 500 feet (152 m), and keen hearing.

Insectoid Table

Insect-looking Nightbane became much more common after Dark Day than before. It is believed that the "new generation" of Nightbane feel alienated enough from the world that they subconsciously picked such alien shapes for themselves. Insect shapes range from the beautiful to the grotesque, but most are strange and intimidating. All insect Nightbane instinctively know how to swim at a base proficiency of 50%, and have Acrobatics at 50% and Climbing at 60% (unless stated otherwise), as well as +1 to roll with fall or impact. In most cases, Disguise and Undercover Ops are impossible.

As usual, the players select the insect species for his or character. If desired, Game Masters may modify the bonuses listed below to better represent the insect species picked by the player.

01-15% Giant Insect: The Nightbane becomes a giant insect at least six feet (1.8 m) in length (spiders and scorpions are not insects; ants, bees, wasp, flies, dragonflies, mosquitoes, beetles, praying mantis, butterflies, and moths are some common insect types). Most giant insect forms have at least one or two forms of attack, be it pincers and bite or claws and stingers. Many can fly (with wings that lay on the back of the body like flies or protrude like butterflies) and others can run at great speeds.

Bonuses: +10 to P.S., +3 to P.P., +4 to P.E., and either +1D4x10 to running speed OR a flying speed of 2D4x10. **Bonuses:** +3 on initiative, +3 to all Perception Rolls, +4D6x10 S.D.C. to hard body insects like ants and beetles, or 2D6x10 S.D.C. for soft body insects like flies and butterflies, +1D6 to Horror Factor.

Claws add 1D6 to hand to damage, pincers 2D6, small insect mandibles 2D4 from bite attacks, medium 2D6 and large (like ants and beetles) 4D6 points of damage. Stingers like those of the wasp or bee inflict 2D6 damage from the stabbing attack and an additional 1D6 damage from poison, plus victims of the poison feel woozy and are -2 on initiative and -1 to strike, parry and dodge unless they successfully save vs non-lethal poison. The stinger does not fall off and the creature can sting repeatedly. The Nightbane will be unable to use tools or weapons or perform complex skills (-40% on skill performance that requires human hands and dexterity).

16-35% Were-Insect: A bipedal combination of human and insect, with two pair of clawed, spindly arms, hands and legs, vaguely humanoid shape, and insectoid head complete with antennae, pincer-like mandibles and multi-faceted eyes. **Bonuses:** +6 to P.S., +3 to P.P., +3 to P.E., and either +5D6 to running speed or a flying speed of 2D4x10, +2 on initiative, +3 to all Perception Rolls, +1D6 to Horror Factor, +3D6x10 to S.D.C. to hard body insects like ants and beetles, or 2D4x10 S.D.C. for soft body insects like flies and butterflies. Claws add 1D6 to hand to hand damage, and extra arms add one attack/action per melee round. Mouth mandibles inflicts 3D6 points of damage.

36-55% Humanoid-Insectoid: The Nightbane's Morphus is basically human-like, with an extra pair of arms and a number of insectoid characteristics. The head is human, except for large, round, multi-faceted eyes and antennae. The skin is covered with a chitinous exoskeleton that provides 2D6x10 to S.D.C. to hard body insects or 1D6x10 S.D.C. for soft body insects. The character may have insect wings, but otherwise has no other unusual limbs. **Bonuses:** +4 to P.S., +2 to P.P., +2 to P.E., and either +3D6 to running speed or a flying speed of 1D4x10, +1 on initiative, +2 to all Perception Rolls, and +1D4 to Horror Factor. Claws add 1D6 to hand to hand damage, and the pair of extra arms add one attack/action per melee round.

56-70% Insect Wings: The Nightbane has an otherwise-normal body, except for the insect wings protruding from his back. **Bonuses:** 3D6 to S.D.C. and can fly with a speed 1D4x10+20, and +1 to dodge when flying and +1 to Horror Factor.

71-80% Insect Head: An ordinary-looking human, except for the full insect head. **Bonuses:** 2D6 to S.D.C., +2 on initiative, +3 to all Perception rolls, and +1D4 to Horror Factor. The mandibles bite for 4D6 damage.

81-90% Insect Eyes: The character has multi-faceted eyes. **Bonuses:** Polarized vision (works like sunglasses to reduce glare), can see in the ultraviolet and infrared spectrum of light, is +2 to all Perception Rolls, and +2 to Horror Factor. Unless the eyes are covered with sunglasses or mirror goggles.

91-00% Insectoid Centauroid: The Nightbane has the upper body of an insect-like humanoid with insect mandibles, eyes and antennae, and the lower body of a six-legged, giant insect; the insect body may also have wings. **Bonuses:** +6 to P.S., +2 to P.P., +2 to P.E., +5D6 to running speed, plus 1D6x10 flying speed if it has wings, +1 on initiative, +3 to all Perception Rolls and +1D4 to Horror Factor. Clawed hands add 1D6 to hand to hand damage, and mouth mandibles inflicts 3D6 points of damage.

Reptilian Table

Lizards of all kinds are represented in the shapes of some Nightbane. It is possible that some of the legends of dragons may originate in reptilian-shaped Nightbane. All reptilians instinctively know how to Swimming at a base proficiency of 45% and Climb at 35%. In most cases, Disguise and Undercover Ops are impossible.

01-20% Giant Reptile: The Nightbane has the shape of a giant lizard, typically over seven feet (2.1 m) tall counting the tail (to determine the length of the Morphus, add 1D6 feet (0.3 to 1.8 m) to the character's Facade's height). This giant form may be mistaken by onlookers as Komodo dragons, crocodiles and similar natural large reptilians. The reptile can move in great bursts of speed, but maximum speed cannot be maintained for more than 3D4 minutes. **Bonuses:** +3 to P.S., +4 to P.E. and +3 to P.P., +4D6 to Spd, +3D6x10 to S.D.C., and +3 to Horror Factor. Its bite inflicts 4D6 damage and claws 2D6.

21-40% Were-Reptile: A bipedal mixture of man and reptile, with the reptilian feature predominating. The head is fully animal-like, and the arms and legs are undeveloped but incredibly strong and tipped by sharp claws. **Bonuses:** +5 to P.S., +3 to P.E. and +2 to P.P., +2D6 to Spd +2D6x10 to S.D.C., and +1D4 to Horror Factor. Clawed hands and feet add 2D6 to hand to hand damage and +10% to Climbing skill. The bite inflicts 3D6 damage.

41-60% Humanoid-Reptilian: A human-shaped creature, scale-covered but able to pass for a human if covered up in heavy clothing (e.g., a trench coat or a cape), or seen from a distance or in shadow. **Bonuses:** +3 to P.S., +2 to P.E. and P.P., +1D6 to Spd, 2D4x10 to S.D.C. and +2 to Horror Factor. Clawed hands and feet add 2D4 to hand to hand damage and +5% to Climbing skill. The bite inflicts 2D6 damage.

61-80% Reptile's Head: A human body, except for the fully reptilian head. **Bonuses:** 2D6 to S.D.C. and +1 to Horror Factor. Bite inflicts 4D6 damage.

81-00% Reptilian Centauroid: A huge creature that has the lower body of a reptile with four legs and tail, while the upper body is a scale-covered humanoid torso with a human-like head and features. This huge creature will be hard-pressed to fit into a vehicle or small room. **Bonuses:** +5 to P.S., +3 to P.E. and P.P., +4D6 to Spd, +3D6x10 to S.D.C., and +1D4 to Horror Factor.

Clawed hands and feet add 2D6 to hand to hand damage and the bite inflicts 3D6 damage.

Rodent Table

This category includes all types of rats (the most common), mice, shrews, squirrels, chipmunks, rabbits, moles, and similar animals, whether or not they are actual true rodents, zoologically speaking. Rat-like Nightbane are very common in cities, and their shape often represents a will to survive at all costs, or a desire to hide in the shadows from the dangers of the world. In most cases, Disguise and Undercover Ops are impossible.

01-20% Full Rodent: The Nightbane's Morphus has the shape of a giant rat, roughly the size of a small bear or mountain lion. The creature is so large that nobody (not even New Yorkers) will confuse it for a normal animal. **Bonuses:** +2D6x10 to S.D.C., +4 to P.S and +4 to P.P., +5 to P.E., +4D6 to Speed, are +10 to climb (if no Climbing skill is known the creature can instinctively climb at a base skill of 30%) and can leap 10 feet (3 m) high or lengthwise. The creature's acute senses add +1 to initiative and +3 to all Perception Rolls. Nightvision is 1,000 feet (305 m). The giant rat can use tools or weapons but very poorly (-6 to strike or -30% on skill performance); they cannot punch or kick effectively, but can parry and slash with their claws: 1D6 damage from a claw strike, 3D6 S.D.C. from a bite and a body slam or jump kick does 2D6 damage. Add +1D4 to Horror Factor.

21-45% Were-Rat: A vaguely humanoid rat-creature able to stand on two feet, with a long tail, fairly short arms, clawed hands, and a full rat's head. It is almost impossible to disguise the inhuman nature of the Nightbane, even with heavy clothing. **Bonuses:** +3 to P.S., +3 to P.P., +4 to P.E., +3D6 to Spd and 1D6x10 to S.D.C. Bite inflicts 3D6 S.D.C., and claws add 1D6 to hand to hand damage. The creature's acute senses add +1 on initiative and +2 to all Perception Rolls. Nightvision is 1,000 feet (305 m). Add 1D6 to Horror Factor.

46-70% Humanoid Rodent: A fur-covered humanoid; the head is mostly human-like, but it tends to project forward more than normal, giving the Nightbane "weasel" or "rat" features. The creature has no tail and the fur is sparse enough near the face and hands to allow the character to pass for a normal human in bad light. **Bonuses:** +2 to P.S., +2 to P.P. +2 to P.E., +2D6 to Spd, +4D6 to S.D.C., +1 to all Perception Rolls, Nightvision is 500 feet (152 m), and +2 to Horror Factor. Bite inflicts 2D6 damage, claws add 1D4 damage to Supernatural P.S. punch..

71-90% Rodent Head: The Nightbane's body is a normal human, but the head is that of a giant rat or other rodent! **Bonuses:** +1 to initiative, +2 to all Perception Rolls, Nightvision is 1,000 feet (305 m), and +1D4 to Horror Factor. Bite inflicts 2D6 damage.

91-00% Rodent Centauroid: The Nightbane has the lower body of a giant rat, and the upper body of a humanoid. **Bonuses:** +4 to P.S., +5 to P.E., +2 to P.P., +4D6 to Spd, +3D6x10 to

SIEMBIEDA 2017

S.D.C., +1 to initiative, +3 to all Perception Rolls, Nightvision is 500 feet (152 m), and +1D4 to Horror Factor. Bite inflicts 3D6 S.D.C., and claws add 1D4 to hand to hand damage.

Snake Table

A traditional subject of fear and fascination, the snake is a common motif found among the Nightbane. Snakes are symbols of temptation, hunting, and subtlety. Cobra-based shapes are often found among Nightbane with leadership qualities or ambition. All snake Nightbane instinctively know how to swim at a base proficiency of 55% and climb at 40% (unless stated otherwise). In most cases, Disguise and Undercover Ops are impossible.

01-15% Full Snake Form: The character's Morphus has the shape of a giant snake (at least six feet/1.8 m in length; typically take the height of the Nightbane's Facade and add 1D6 feet/0.3 to 1.8 m to it). Bonuses: +6 to P.S., +3 to P.E., +2 to P.P. and +2D6x10 to S.D.C. The snake form has a base Climbing skill of 60% (or add +20% to the character's current Climbing skill, whichever is greater; applicable in Morphus form only) and +3 to Horror Factor.

If the Morphus is that of a poisonous serpent (asp, cobra, rattlesnake, viper, etc.), its bite inflicts 2D6 S.D.C. plus venom does 6D6 damage (or 3D6 if a successful save versus lethal poison is made). Add another +1 to Horror Factor if poisonous.

A constrictor snake has all the base abilities of the Wrestling skill, plus it can jab with its head or coil from its body to do the equivalent of punch damage. Crushing/constricting attacks do double the character's normal punch damage plus P.S. bonuses. Each act of constriction does damage and counts as one melee attack.

16-30% Limbed Snake: The Nightbane has a pair of scaly, human-like arms, hands and legs stemming from a long, snake-like body. The basic form remains that of a snake, with an over-long "neck" and a snake's head. The snake-man's "torso" can bend and twist with the full flexibility of a serpent and all limbs are double-jointed and ambidextrous. Bonuses: Add one attack per melee round, +4 to P.S., +2 to P.E., +2 to P.P., +2D4x10 to S.D.C., 1D6 to Horror Factor; +15% to the Climbing skill if the character possesses it, otherwise base ability applies.

If the Morphus is that of a poisonous serpent, its bite inflicts 2D6 S.D.C. plus venom does 4D6 damage (or 2D6 if a successful save versus lethal poison is made).

A constrictor snake has all the base abilities of the Wrestling skill, plus it can jab with its head or coil from its body to do the equivalent of punch damage. Crushing/constricting attacks do double the character's normal punch damage plus P.S. bonuses. Each act of constriction does damage and counts as one melee attack.

31-50% Humanoid Snake: The character has the basic build and shape of a human being, but the skin is covered by colorful scales, the head and neck are those of a snake, and it has a long, prehensile tail. In addition to the sharp fangs of a snake, the Nightbane also has sharp claws on his hands and feet that can inflict an additional 1D6 damage from punches/claw strikes and kicks. The bite inflicts 2D6 S.D.C., and if a poisonous variety, will inject a venom doing 3D6 damage (reduced to 1D6 on a successful save versus lethal poison). The tail can be used to hit, hold and carry objects or as an aid in climbing (add +10% to the Climbing skill). Bonuses: Add one attack per melee round from prehensile tail, +3 to P.S., +2 to P.E., +1 to P.P., and +1D6x10 to S.D.C. Add 1D4+1 to Horror Factor.

51-70% Scaly Skin: A normal human body and features except for the scale-covered skin and eyes that are snake-like in appearance. Add 1D6x10 S.D.C. Add 1D4 to Horror Factor.

71-85% Half-Man, Half-Snake: A scale-covered human torso with arms and hands, a human head tops and a long snake-like lower body and tail. This Nightbane has no legs, and must crawl or climb using his/her lower body. The upper torso can bend and twist with the full flexibility of a serpent and all limbs are double jointed and ambidextrous. Bonuses: Add one attack per melee round, +4 to P.S., +2 to P.E., +3 to P.P. and +1D6x10 +10 to S.D.C. Add +20% to the climbing skill if the character possesses it.

If the Morphus is that of a poisonous serpent, its bite inflicts 2D6 S.D.C. plus venom does 4D6 damage (or 2D6 if a successful save versus lethal poison is made). Add 1D6 to Horror Factor.

A constrictor snake has all the base abilities of the *wrestling* skill, plus it can jab with its head or coil from its body to do the equivalent of punch damage. Crushing/constricting attacks do double the character's normal punch damage plus P.S. bonuses. Each act of constriction does damage and counts as one melee attack.

86-00% Snake's Head: The Nightbane has a normal human body, topped by a giant snake's head! Bite inflicts 3D6, plus if poisonous, will do an additional 3D6 damage (1D6 if a successful save versus lethal poison is made). Add 2D6 to S.D.C., and 1D4 to Horror Factor.

Stigmata Table I

Mockingly named after the "sacred wounds" said to appear on saintly people, stigmata are among the most disturbing deformities among the Nightbane. The common characteristic of all stigmata is that the Nightbane appears to be injured. The wound can be an open cut, blister, sore or a foreign object imbedded in the flesh. From time to time the wound will ooze with blood, pus, or other fluid. These wounds never heal, and are often a source of discomfort and pain to the character.

What do these marks represent? Are they an embodiment of the guilt, fears and psychic pain of the Nightbane? In times past, many religious people called Nightbane stigmata a sign of the devil and "the witch's mark." Modern thinkers believe them to be a reflection of psychological trauma. In a few cases, the stigmata

are the result of terrible wounds suffered by the Nightbane just before his transformation: For example: 600 years ago when a young Nightbane first manifested his powers, he was under attack by soldiers. He had been stabbed and slashed repeatedly when the Becoming began, and as a result, his Morphus bore those wounds and they have never healed.

Roll percentile dice to determine a stigmata.

01-05% Bloody Ooze: Covered in a slimy blood-like liquid, making his skin slippery. **Bonuses:** +2 to parry and dodge pins or grappling attacks, and +1D4 to Horror Factor.

06-10% Corpse-Like: The Nightbane's skin is grayish-green, his eyes are sunken, and he looks like a days-old corpse, complete with the odor of death and signs of decay. **Bonuses:** +3D6 to S.D.C. and +1D4 to Horror Factor. Reduce P.B. by 25%.

11-15% Stitches: A crisscrossing of stitches at several points in the skin gives the Nightbane the appearance of a "rebuilt" corpse. Sometimes, the limbs and body may not quite match. For example, the "sewn-on" limbs might belong to an animal, while the torso and head are human-like! This is particularly appropriate for lycanthrope Nightbane who bear stigmata. **Bonuses:** 3D6 to S.D.C. and +1D4 to Horror Factor.

16-23% Nails: Metal nails, pins, spikes or screws protrude from the character's skin. They can be localized to a few small areas on the body (around the eyes, on the forehead, hands, shoulders, torso, etc.), or they can completely cover the character (player's choice). **Bonuses:** 4D6 to S.D.C. and, if covered, a body slam inflicts +2D6 added to normal Supernatural P.S. punch damage.

24-31% Razor Blades: Razor blades are unnaturally attached to the Nightbane. They may have replaced teeth or fingernails, or cover the character like a porcupine's quills. **Bonuses:** +1D4 to Horror Factor, +4D6 to S.D.C., and +1D6 damage added to Supernatural P.S. punch damage. In combat, if the fingernails or teeth have been replaced with razors, +1D6 damage to claw strikes and +2D6 damage to bite attacks. If the blades are on the skin, body slams do +2D6 S.D.C., plus normal punch damage.

32-39% Broken Glass: Jagged pieces of glass are embedded in the character's flesh. They can be located in small specific areas or cover the body. Same damage as #24-31 above. **Bonuses:** +3D6 to S.D.C. and +1D4 to Horror Factor.

40-47% Barbed Wire/Razor Wire: Part of the character's limbs head, neck or torso are wrapped in barbed or razor wire, causing bloody wounds that never heal. Same damage as #24-31 above. **Bonuses:** +4D6 to S.D.C. and +1D4 to Horror Factor.

48-55% Eternal Wounds: The Nightbane bears horrible wounds that never heal. Most often, the wounds are clearly visible and may appear to be deadly, including gaping chest wounds, gashes in the skull, cuts, gouges and other grotesqueries. The wounds cover any clothes the character wears with bloody patches in a matter of minutes, soaking through bandages and dressings after a while. **Bonuses:** +3D6 to S.D.C. and +1D4 to Horror Factor.

56-63% Missing Skin: Patches of skin or even the whole skin (player's choice) are missing, revealing bare muscle and bones. **Bonuses:** +3D6 to S.D.C. and +1D4+1 to Horror Factor.

64-71% Leatherboy/girl: Portions (or all) of the Nightbane's skin seems to have been replaced with shiny, polished leather, belts, bodysuits, and the like. S&M gear like hoods and straps is not uncommon, all grafted to the skin and flesh of the character. Metal studs, chains and other "decorations" finish the grotesque design. **Bonuses:** +5D6 to S.D.C. and +1D4 to Horror Factor.

72-79% Boils or Sores: Areas of the character's body are covered in open sores or festering boils. **Bonuses:** +3D6 to S.D.C. and +2 to Horror Factor.

80-85% Zippers: Zippers close horrible wounds in the character's body. **Bonuses:** +3D6 to S.D.C. and 1 to Horror Factor, but the Horror Factor is increased by 3 if the Nightbane opens the zipper to reveal the pulsing flesh or organs underneath!

86-90% Bones: Some (or even all) of the Nightbane's body has been stripped of flesh and muscle to reveal bare bone. **Bonuses:** +5D6x10 to S.D.C. and 1D4+1 to Horror Factor.

91-96% Biomechanical: Roll on the *Biomechanical Table*, but any modifications will appear to make bloody wounds or sores where the mechanics are attached or placed in the character! For example, if Armorgraft (see below) was rolled, the armor would appear to have been nailed or hammered into the flesh of the Nightbane, and its edges would have a patina of fresh blood! Add 1 point to the normal Horror Factor associated with that Biomechanical characteristic.

97-00% Combination of Two: Roll two times (ignore and re-roll any roll of 97% or higher) and combine the two characteristics and Horror Factor points.

Facial Features Table

Many Nightbane appear completely normal from a distance – until one looks them in the face. In most cases, -40% to the Disguise, Seduction and Undercover Ops skills.

01-07% Oversized Carnivorous Mouth: The Nightbane has supernaturally strong jaw muscles. **Bonuses:** +1 to Horror Factor. Bite attack does 2D6 damage and the character can hold on and continue biting (no strike roll is necessary), but inflicts normal bite damage once at the beginning and once at the end of the melee round until his victim is dislodged or he lets go. **Note:** No other combat actions are possible while using this attack).

08-15% Glowing Eyes: The Nightbane's eyes glow with unnatural light, so bright that they can faintly illuminate a dark area! Normal sunglasses will not be able to hide the glowing eyes, but mirror shades will. **Bonuses:** The Nightbane has enhanced Nightvision able to see in total darkness at a range of 2,000 feet (610 m), and +1 to Horror Factor.

16-22% Cyclops: The character only has one large eye in the middle of his forehead. **Bonuses:** Perfect 20/20 vision and +2 to the Horror Factor.

SIEMBIEDA 2017

23-30% Misshapen Facial Features: Some possibilities: The eyes are in the wrong place, the nose is flat or missing, the mouth is where the eyes should be and vice-versa, the creature has more than one mouth, and other bizarre features. **Bonus:** +1D4 to Horror Factor.

31-38% Extra Eyes: The Nightbane has 1D4 additional eyes (roll or choose from 1-6 total eyes). They are arranged in two or three rows, and they can be human-sized or slightly smaller. **Bonuses:** +2 to Perception Rolls involving sight and +1D4 to Horror Factor.

39-46% Sharp Teeth: The Nightbane has long, fang-like teeth. **Bonuses:** Bite inflicts 3D6 damage, and +2 to Horror Factor whenever the teeth are displayed, in a smile, for example.

47-55% Skull Face: The character's head is a fleshless skull (players may opt to let hair grow on the skull, or leave it bare). The skeletal head is sometimes surrounded by a nimbus of light or flames (1-30%), but is completely without flesh and bare and grotesquely protrudes from a flesh neck (31-60%). This gives the head more of a bony helmet or mask appearance than a real head (61-90%), or has a different, unusual look (91-00%, the player may roll again for unusual facial features that further deform the skull, like small horns, and additional eye sockets), roll or pick one. **Bonuses:** +2D6 to S.D.C. and +1D4 to Horror Factor.

56-62% Small Horns: The Nightbane has small, vestigial horns, typically similar to a goat's or a ram's. The horns can be disguised with a hat or other head covering. **Bonuses:** Head butt does 1D6 S.D.C. damge in addition to Supernatural P.S. damage and +1 to Horror Factor.

63-70% Large Horns: Large horns, often similar to a ram's or deer's. **Bonuses:** +2 to Horror Factor, and a head butt inflicts 3D6 damage addition to normal punch damage. **Note:** The horns are so large that it is impossible to hide them.

71-78% Facial Tentacles: Writhing tentacles protrude from the face of the Nightbane! They can be situated anywhere in the face; some examples include the chin for a "living beard" look, between the nose and mouth for a Lovecraftian appearance, or instead of hair for a Medusa-like look. **Bonuses:** +2D6 to S.D.C. and +1D4 to Horror Factor.

79-85% No Face: The Nightbane has a perfectly smooth face: no eyes, mouth, or nose are visible. The creature can speak, but the voice seems to be coming from inside the smooth surface, and may have an inhuman quality, or simply sound muffled; player's choice. The lack of eyes does not impair the Nightbane's senses; he can see, smell and hear perfectly. To eat, food is seemingly pushed through the skin, like a soft membrane, where the mouth should be. **Bonus:** +1D4 to Horror Factor.

86-90% Biomechanical: Roll on the *Biomechanical Table*, but only apply the results to the face/head of the Nightbane. The rest of the body may be normal or have completely different characteristics.

91-95% Alien Features: The Nightbane looks inhuman and alien. The head may be over-sized with large (or small), black almond-shaped eyes, a tiny nose or nose holes, no facial hair, dark or pale complexion and other inhuman features (fangs, skin patterns, horns, etc.). **Bonus:** +2 to Horror Factor.

96-98% Two: Roll twice and try to combine the result; ignore and re-roll any result of 96% or higher. Some results might not make much sense at first, players are invited to use their imagination. For example: A player rolls for both Cyclops and No Face! In that case, the character has one central eye, and no other facial features. Or maybe he rolls instead Cyclops and Multiple Eyes: simply place one large eye in the middle, surrounded by smaller ones.

99-00% Three: As above, but roll three times.

Alien Shape Table

This category covers a wide variety of unusual shapes and forms that occasionally manifest in some Nightbane. Players are welcome to determine or guess what dark elements of their character's souls or subconscious are embodied in any of the alien forms listed below. In most cases, Disguise, Seduction and Undercover Ops skills are impossible.

01-12% Plasmoid: The Nightbane's body has a semi-liquid consistency; he is made up of jelly-like blood! The basic shape of the character remains that of a bipedal humanoid (it can even have the exact outline of his Facade), but it can be changed at will, stretched, spread or even puddled into any shape the character wills. The character can squeeze through narrow openings (even a couple of inches will do!), slip out of restraints and conceal himself as a glob or goo. **Bonuses:** +4D6 to S.D.C., all physical attacks directed at the character (punches, clubs, bullets, etc.) do half damage, and +1D6 to Horror Factor.

13-24% Bark-like Skin: The character looks like a bizarre combination of tree and human, with bark instead of skin, and often with leaves or vines instead of hair! **Bonuses:** +1D4x10 to S.D.C. and +1D4 to Horror Factor.

25-37% Bony Exoskeleton: The Nightbane is covered with bone-like plates or large scales, often with horn-like protrusions and short spikes. **Bonuses:** +1D6x10 to S.D.C. and +1D6 damage to the usual Supernatural P.S. damage from hand to hand and melee attack, and +1D4 to Horror Factor.

38-45% Thorns: Thorns protrude from the character's body! They may appear to be natural growths, or they might be stigmata-like, appearing to painfully pierce the character's skin! **Bonuses:** +4D6 to S.D.C. and +1D4 to Horror Factor.

46-54% Crystalline: The character looks predominately human, but has crystals that resemble quartz or diamonds growing out of his skin along the fingers, the bones of the hands, along the back of the arms up and down the spine and at the elbow, shoulders and knees. The head can look completely human or the hair can be replaced with a cap of crystals or a crown of tall, jutting crystal. Add 2D4x10 to the S.D.C., heat and fire do half damage, and the character can parry bladed weapons and

fiery torches with his bare hands. The fingernails are replaced by jagged crystals that slash, doing 1D6 plus punch damage and the crystal encrusted hands function similar to brass knuckles adding 1D6 to punch damage. Furthermore, in bright light, the Nightbane glitters like a gem and may (1-60% chance) blind all who look at him from the reflected light. **Bonus:** +2 to Horror Factor.

55-66% Living Tattoos: The Nightbane's skin is covered with tattoos. Unlike normal body decorations, however, these tattoos change and move! The changes may reflect the character's current state of mind (i.e., an angry Nightbane might suddenly display violent or threatening tattoos) or might be controlled directly by the character (50-50 chance or select one). In the first case, the Nightbane has no control over the tattoos, they react to his emotions and may start squirming at any given moment. **Bonus:** +1D6 to Horror Factor whenever someone notices the moving tattoos.

67-77% Unusual Skin Color: The Nightbane's skin has an inhuman hue. The color is too intense and sharp to be normal, body paint or dyes. Colors can include shades of yellows, reds, greens, blues, purple/violets, copper, gold, metallic grey, silver, pitch black, and stark white. Roll or pick one. **Bonus:** +1 to Horror Factor.

78-85% Hulking Monster: The character transforms into a huge, hulking brute with a large barrel chest, hunched back, long gorilla-like arms, and a comparatively tiny (human-sized) head. The face may be human, alien, animal, or monstrous in appearance. The misshapened hulk stands 1D6+6 feet (2.1 to 3.7 m) tall (and that's with a hunched back), and weighs 800 pounds (360 kg) per every foot (0.3 m) of height! **Bonuses:** +1D6x10 to S.D.C., +1D4 to P.S., +2 to roll with fall or impact and add +1D4 to Horror Factor. **Note:** Reduce Spd by 10%.

86-95% Mouth-Covered Body! The Nightbane's body is covered by 2D6x10 tiny mouths! The mouths can make gestures, stick out their tongues, whistle, hoot, growl or even scream in a hellish chorus (adds 3 to Horror Factor when all of them are screaming or screeching at once)! However, they cannot speak. The character can also grapple an enemy and let the tiny mouths bite him (this inflicts 1D4 damage per mouth; typically 1D6 mouths will bite at the same time). **Bonus:** +1D4+2 to Horror Factor.

96-00% Combination of Two: Roll twice more (ignore and re-roll any result of 96 or higher), and then combine the results.

Unnatural Limbs Table

01-10% Prehensile Tail: The Nightbane has a prehensile tail, which can be used to grasp and carry things or help climb. The tail is very strong, able to support the character's full body weight when suspended above the ground. However, it can only carry the equivalent of one third of the character's body weight (typically about 60 lbs\27 kg). **Bonuses:** +20% to Acrobatics (balance) and Climbing when the tail is used, +1 attack per melee and +1 to Horror Factor.

11-20% Spiked Prehensile Tail: Same as above, except that the tail ends in a spike, blade, stinger or club with 2D4 small spikes at the end. Strikes with the tail inflict 2D6 damage.

21-30% Tentacles: The character has two tentacles in addition to his arms! These tentacles are very difficult to conceal (need at least a trench coat, cape or cloak). The limbs can grab and carry objects, but are unable to use firearms or other tools requiring fingers. A pair of tentacle strikes do 1D6 in addition to normal hand to hand damage, and provide one additional attack/action per melee round. **Bonus:** +1D4 to Horror Factor.

31-40% Long, Sensitive Fingers: The fingers on the hands are three times longer than normal. **Bonuses:** Fingers are delicate and sensitive, providing a bonus of +5% to the following skills or skill categories: Medical (all), Demolitions (all), Electronics (all), Climbing, Computers (all), Forgery, Palming, Pick Locks, Pick Pockets, and Safecracking.

41-50% 2D4 Pairs of Tiny Arms and Hands: The character has several tiny arms about one third size of a normal arm, usually located along the length of his forearm(s) or clustered at the shoulder(s). Each has a P.S. of only 1D6 and inflicts only one point of damage in combat (and then only if a foe gets close enough). However, they can grab and carry small and/or light objects or wield razor blades, small knives, or ice picks (1D4 damage each). **Bonus:** +1D4 to Horror Factor.

51-65% Four Arms: The Nightbane has an extra pair of arms and hands. **Bonuses:** +1 attack per melee round, the arms and hands are ambidextrous and double-jointed, and +1D4 to Horror Factor.

66-80% Pseudopods: At will, the Nightbane can extend 1D4+1 tentacle-like limbs from his flesh, much like an amoeba can extend pseudopods. The process of extending these limbs is utterly horrible to a human being, because these fleshy limbs break through the skin as if an unwholesome parasites were climbing out of the character's body! Treat the pseudopods as tentacles (see above). **Bonuses:** +1 attack pe melee for *each pair*, each limb has 22 S.D.C., and +1D4+2 to Horror Factor whenever the pseudopods are extended.

81-90% Articulated Spikes: The character has four spikes or spines that resembles the spine or legs of an insect. Each is about the size of a survival knife, but can extend to twice that length in an instant. They are distributed along the side of each forearm (two on each arm) or on the chest, or sides of the body. These slim, chitinous limbs end in sharp points, and can move independent of each like tiny, stiff arms and even rotate 360 degrees. They are used to parry an enemy's hand to hand attacks (+2 to parry) and to stab or slash opponents who come within arm's length. **Bonuses:** The four spikes provide +1 attack per melee round, inflict 2D6 damage, but they cannot grab or manipulate objects, and +1D4 to Horror Factor.

SIEMBIEDA 2017

91-00% Antennae: A pair of antennae are located on the character's head. Each can move like an arm, independent of each other and can dodge attacks (+3 to dodge; each has 15 S.D.C., and regenerate within 72 hours). They can look like any variety of insect or crustacean antennae and are typically, thin, whip-like limbs that extend 1D4 feet (0.3-1.2 m) in length. **Bonuses:** These sensitive "feelers" enable the Nightbane to move around in total darkness, can measure and detect changes in the air temperature and humidity (automatic), wind movement and direction (automatic), detect and identify common odors (66% proficiency), track by smell (50%), and sense an approaching rainstorm (70%; storm will arrive within 2D6x10 minutes), and +1 to Horror Factor.

Biomechanical Table I

Many occultists point to the existence of Biomechanical Nightbane as proof that the Morphus is some sort of physical manifestation that reflects of the Nightbane's personality. How else could these unnatural and artificial looking components be part of the creature? Even before complex machines appeared, even some of the earliest Biomechanical Morphuses had limbs shaped like swords, metal gauntlets, and other weapons and gizmos. In the time of the Industrial Revolution, some Nightbane were reported to have steam-powered, piston-driven limbs and riveted-metal skins appeared for the first time. In the last years of the 20th Century, "cyborgs" became fairly common. Biomechanicals seem to embody the fascination and love or abhorrence and fear the character has toward machines or science.

Despite their artificial appearance, Biomechanical characteristics are as much a part of the Nightbane's living body as "natural" skin and bones. The Biomechanical components do not have any of the limitations of true cybernetic prosthetics, and heal at the same rate as the Nightbane does. In most cases, Disguise, Seduction and Undercover Ops skills are impossible.

01-10% Armorgraft: Pieces of archaic body armor (helmets, breastplates, gauntlets, chain mail, segmented mail) are fused with the Nightbane's skin. Add 1D6x10 to S.D.C. and +2 to Horror Factor.

11-20% Plastic: Parts or all of the character's skin has been replaced with plastic or rubber (player can pick the colors and texture). **Bonuses:** +5D6 to S.D.C. and +1 to Horror Factor, unless the skin coverings are made up of transparent plastic, revealing internal organs, in which case the Horror Factor is +1D4.

21-25% Rocket Jets: The Nightbane has metallic exhaust tubes and small jet engines growing out of his back! They provide limited flight: 80 mph (128 km), maximum altitude 5,000 feet (1,524 m) and hover capabilities. **Bonuses:** +4D6 to S.D.C. and +1 to Horror Factor. **Penalty:** There is actually a roaring sound of engines when the jets are used so Prowl is impossible even when hovering.

26-30% Metal Teeth and Talons: The Nightbane has metal fangs and talons instead of normal teeth and fingernails (may be retractable). The metal teeth inflict 3D6 points of damage with a bite, and the claws do +1D6 damage in addition to Supernatural P.S. punch damage. **Bonuses:** +2 to Horror Factor.

31-40% Metal Endoskeleton: Metallic bones are mixed with living flesh in grotesque ways. There is always a place where the metal seems to rip out of the skin, usually on the hands, arms, neck, cheeks and legs. **Bonuses:** +2 to P.S., +2 to P.E., +2D4x10 to S.D.C., and +1D4 to Horror Factor.

41-50% Mechanical Limbs: The arms and legs of the Nightbane are obviously mechanical. They may be piston-driven, huge mechanisms of iron and bronze, or microchip covered or chrome-plated creations of "cyberpunk" mythology. These limbs do not bleed when struck, instead a sort of oil or grease may ooze out or wires, metal components and other artificial "guts" be revealed. **Bonuses:** +4 to P.S., +1D4x10 to S.D.C., (if he character has legs, they are also mechanical and get +4D6 to Spd), +1D4 to Horror Factor.

51-60% Weapon Hand: One or both of the Nightbane's hands can metamorphosize, at will, into a hand to hand weapon such as a knife, a sword, battle axe, trident, sickle, etc. The weapon does normal damage for that particular weapon type, in addition to Supernatural P.S. punch damage, and is at no risk of breaking (see Supernatural Strength Damage). **Bonuses:** +1 to strike and parry with his weapon limb and +2 to Horror Factor.

61-70% Metal Exoskeleton: The character is covered in mechanical armor that can look hard and bulky with rivets and seams or smooth and chrome-like – Victorian-era Nightbane often walked the world with riveted iron instead of skin. Modern characters tend to "favor" metallic bands or a combination of metal plates and bands and resemble robots or suits of power armor. **Bonuses:** +3D6x10 to S.D.C., +2 to P.S., +1 to P.E., and +1D4 to Horror Factor.

71-80% Metal Head & Camera Eyes: The character's head looks like a robot or cyborg and instead of eyes, he has two camera lenses protruding from the eye sockets. These artificial eyes raise the character's Nightvision range to 2,000 feet (610 m) and provide him with telescopic sight like a pair of high-powered binoculars, and polarized filters. Even more amazing, the Nightbane can turn his eyes into movie projectors, and show moving pictures of anything he remembers (the depiction will be literally as seen by his eyes and may reflect personal prejudices, bias, and emotions). These two-dimensional projections have no sound, but are otherwise picture-perfect. **Bonus:** +1D4 to Horror Factor.

81-90% Wheels or Treads: Instead of legs, the Nightbane is a two-wheeled man-machine hybrid. The upper body looks human or half human and half cyborg, while the lower body is a machine vehicle. The vehicle part of the body can look like a motorcycle, four-wheeled vehicle or miniature tank with treads. More than one motorcycle enthusiast has found himself grafted to a Harley Davidson, and gun-bunnies or military aficionados to

the chassis of a tank! **Bonuses:** +3 to P.S., +2 to P.E., +2D4x10 to Spd, 3D64x10 to S.D.C. and +1D4 to Horror Factor. **Note:** The Nightbane may find it difficult to operate indoors or in confined spaces, -2 to all combat rolls.

91-00% Gun Limbs: The Nightbane has one or more guns built into his body! The grotesque result is usually a weapon barrel protruding from flesh and muscle. These guns will have normal gun stats; the biggest gun available would be a rifle type doing 6D6 S.D.C. damage. **Note:** This advantage actually requires a permanent P.P.E. sacrifice, equal to 1 P.P.E. per die of damage, and 2 P.P.E. if the gun is an automatic weapon (capable of firing bursts). Additionally, the character has to find bullets for the gun! A maximum of 100 bullets can be "stored" inside the body (to do this, the Nightbane literally has to shove the bullets into his flesh, inflicting 1D6 S.D.C. to himself per 10 bullets). **Bonus:** +1D4 to Horror Factor.

Morphus Tables from Between the Shadows™

Bear Form Table

Bears are respected and feared for their strength and raw power, but they are also seen as relatively benign creatures that rarely kill even for food, let alone sport. Slow to rage, a provoked bear is nonetheless a lethal creature. Many Nightbane who have ursine characteristics are big, gentle people, or strong at heart. The most common bear shapes include the grizzly, polar, black and brown bears. Native American Nightbane seem to subconsciously favor this species. In most cases, Disguise, Seduction and Undercover Ops skills are impossible.

01-20% Full Ursinoid: The Nightbane's Morphus is a large bear, typically close to the largest normal size for the species, and easily confused for the real thing unless other Nightbane characteristics make that impossible. **Bonuses:** +12 to P.S., +1 to P.P., +6 to P.E., +1D6 to Spd, +4D6x10 S.D.C., and +1 to Horror Factor. The bear form cannot use weapons, but its paw attacks do normal punch damage plus 2D6 S.D.C., and its bite inflicts 4D6 S.D.C.

21-45% Were-Bear: A mixture of man and beast, with the beast predominating. Since bears can stand on their hind legs, it is easy to confuse the Nightbane with a normal bear under a bad light, but when clearly seen it is obvious the creature is not natural. This animal form can manipulate objects with its hands/paws, but with some limitations; any task that requires careful manual dexterity (picking locks, typing on a computer, and using most guns) will be at -15%, and using weapons at -2 to strike and parry. Size is usually 30 to 40% larger than the Facade, and sometimes much bigger. **Bonuses:** +8 to P.S., +3 to P.E., +3D4x10

S.D.C. and +2 to Horror Factor. Bite attack does 3D6 damage, and claws add 1D6 to punch damage. Speed is normal.

46-70% Bear Humanoid: A more human-like creature, with a basic human shape, except it is covered with fur and the head and facial features still seem to be bear-like. A cloak, large trench coat and hat or other bulky clothing might hide its appearance at a distance and in the dark, but not for long. The creature will be very tall, at least six feet (1.8 m) or more. **Bonuses:** +4 to P.S., +2 to P.E., and 1D6x10 S.D.C., and +2 to Horror Factor. Bite attack does 2D6 and blunt claws add 1D6 to punch damage.

71-80% Bear Centauroid: The Nightbane has the upper torso of a were-bear and the lower body of a full bear, complete with four legs! This creature is far larger than a normal bear, and will not fit any small, enclosed space, including most vehicles, indoor locations, small elevators, etc. **Bonuses:** +10 to P.S., +1 to P.P., +2 to P.E., +1D6 to Spd, +3D6x10 S.D.C., and +1D4+1 to Horror Factor. Bite attack does 3D6, and blunt claws add 1D6 to punch damage. Speed is normal. **Penalties:** Any task that requires careful manual dexterity, like Picking Locks, Computer Operation (typing on a computer keyboard), and so on are performed at -15%, and -2 to strike and parry with most weapons and guns.

81-00% Bear Head: A normal looking human with the head of a bear! Bite inflicts 3D6 damage. **Bonuses:** +5D6 to S.D.C. and +1 to Horror Factor.

Amphibian Table

This category covers frogs, toads and salamanders. Amphibians have long been part of arcane and occult lore, from quaint "ingredients" in witches' brews to creatures attributed with a number of magical powers. Salamanders have often been associated with the element of fire, and toads and frogs, which nowadays are a subject of amusement, were once regarded with fear. Many stories about people being turned into frogs may have their roots in Nightbane phenomena. In most cases, Disguise, Seduction and Undercover Ops skills are impossible.

01-20% Full Amphibian: The Nightbane is shaped like a giant toad, frog or salamander, typically with the same length as his/her human Facade's height. The creature cannot be confused for a normal member of the species due to its enormous size. **Bonuses:** +4 to P.S., +2 to P.P., +1 to P.E., +2D6x10 S.D.C. and +3 to Horror Factor.

If a toad, the character can jump 30 feet (9 m) from a standing position, and Swimming speed is the same as running speed.

If a frog, can jump 80 feet (24.4 m) from a standing position and swimming speed is double the running speed.

If a salamander, add +1D6 to running speed, and swimming speed is double.

In all cases, bite damage does 2D6, and most creatures have a long, prehensile tongue that can reach targets up to 20 feet (6 m) away. The character can also hold his breath underwater for 3D4 minutes. There is a 10% chance that the Nightbane will have poi-

SIEMBIEDA 2017

sonous glands that cover his skin with a contact poison. Exposure to the poison (touch with bare skin) inflicts a red rash and does 3D6 S.D.C. damage (to human and supernatural characters) unless a save versus lethal poison is successful. A good save means a small rash and only 1D6 damage.

21-45% Were-Amphibian: A barely humanoid frog-man/ amphibian, with overlong fingers and smooth, moist skin (dry and lumpy if a toad). The head is that of a full frog, toad or salamander. **Bonuses:** +3 to P.S., +1 to P.P., +1 to P.E., 2D4x10 S.D.C., the character can jump 30 feet (9.1 m) from a standing position, and up to 40 feet (12.2 m) with a running start, Swimming speed is double the character's running speed, can hold his breath underwater for 2D4 minutes, and +1D4 to Horror Factor. Bite damage does 2D4, and most creatures have a long, prehensile tongue that can reach targets up to 15 feet (4.6 m) away. There is a 10% chance that the Nightbane will have poisonous glands that cover his skin with a contact poison. Exposure to the poison (touch with bare skin) inflicts a red rash and does 2D6 S.D.C. damage (to human and supernatural characters) unless a save versus lethal poison is successful. A good save means a small rash and only 1D4 damage.

46-70% Amphibian Humanoid: The Nightbane has humanoid features, and his basic shape is roughly human, so that the character might hide his deformities under bulky clothing and head covering. The leg shape is still impossibly bow-legged, the fingers and toes are webbed, and the character has a crouched posture most the time, as if getting ready to leap – all of this will inevitably attract attention. Bonuses: +2 to P.S., +1 to P.P. and P.E., 1D4x10 S.D.C., can leap 15 feet (4.6 m), swim at 50% faster than running speed, hold breath for 1D6 minutes, and +2 to Horror Factor. Bite attack does 1D6 damage.

71-80% Amphibian Centauroid: The Nightbane has the upper torso of a humanoid shaped frog, toad or salamander, and the lower body of a salamander, including four legs and a long tail. **Bonuses:** +4 to P.S., +1 to P.P., +2 to P.E., and +2D6x10 S.D.C. Swimming speed is double running speed, can also hold his breath underwater for 2D4 minutes, and +1D4 to Horror Factor. Bite damage does 2D4, and most creatures have a long, prehensile tongue that can reach targets up to 10 feet (3 m) away. There is a 10% chance that the Nightbane will have poisonous glands that cover his skin with a contact poison. Exposure to the poison (touch with bare skin) inflicts a red rash and does 2D6 S.D.C. damage (to human and supernatural characters) unless a save versus lethal poison is successful. A good save means a small rash and only 1D4 damage.

81-00% Amphibian Head: A normal looking human with the head of a frog, toad or salamander! **Bonuses:** Bite inflicts 3D6 damage. The Nightbane has a long, prehensile tongue that can reach targets up to 15 feet (4.6 m) away, can hold breath underwater for 1D4 minutes and +1 to Horror Factor.

Biomechanical Table II

Players of Biomechanical characters can roll on the original table as presented in the **Nightbane® RPG,** page 105, or may roll on this one, or make selections from both. In most cases, Disguise, Seduction and Undercover Ops skills are impossible.

01-15% Screen Face: The face of the Nightbane is shaped normally, but the front of the face is a television or monitor screen instead of normal facial features. The screen images are controlled by the Nightbane; some flash written messages instead of talking, others have an animated or computer generated, cartoon image of a normal face, some show test patterns and others show electronic snow. The images may be changed to reflect the character's moods, or at random. **Bonus:** +1D4 to Horror Factor.

16-30% Speakers: Sound speakers are built into the head or body of the Nightbane. The actual location is determined by the player; some Nightbane have speakers instead of mouths, eyes, or ears, while others have them built into their torsos. The Nightbane can produce frightening human, animal and/or electronic sounds (but not specific voices). These sounds add to the Horror Factor of the Nightbane and can be used to intimidate. **Bonuses:** +1D4 to M.A., and +3 to Horror Factor. A frightened or intimidated victim (failed to save vs Horror Factor or intimidation factor) is -2 on initiative and -5% on all skill performance. Range for the sound transmission is roughly 100 feet (30.5 m).

31-45% Tool Hands: Any type of handheld tool, from hedge clippers and scissors to screwdrivers, drills and pliers replaced one or both hands of the character. If both hands are replaced with tools, any skill requiring delicate finger control is at -30%. **Bonuses:** The tools do +3D6 damage in addition to Supernatural P.S. punch damage, +1 to parry, and +1D4 to Horror Factor.

46-60% Monitor Eyes: The eyes of the character are replaced by two digital monitors or camera-like lenses. Some act like a hospital's life sign monitors, with a line that jumps at every heartbeat flashing through the monitors, some wave and jump in reaction to the character's voice or emotions, while others project psychedelic light shows, or simply flash with artificial green or violet light. **Bonuses:** The eyes raise the character's Nightvision to 2000 feet (610 m) and +2 to Horror Factor.

61-75% Chainsaw Arms: One or both of the Nightbane's forearms are replaced by a chainsaw. This lethal weapon does 4D6 S.D.C. in addition to Supernatural P.S. punch damage. **Bonuses:** +1 to parry, +1D4 to Horror Factor. **Note:** Nothing can be held by the chainsaw arms and characters with two such arms will be at a great disadvantage in performing skills (-70%).

76-90% Computer Creature: A home computer is built into the body of the Nightbane. The screen may be in the head, face, eyes, or built into the chest or belly. The keyboard is often grown onto a forearm, and connected by a cable(s) to the body, and the processor is usually in the upper or lower torso or hip. The computer will actually work, and will read information from disks, thumb drives and other computers. Retractable interface cables

are included. **Bonuses:** +15% on Computer Operations and Programming skills, +5% for Computer Hacking when he uses his "personal" computer, and +2 to Horror Factor.

91-00% Projectile Limbs: The hand, forearm or entire arm or arms of the character can be "fired" at a target. The hands act like flying fists, returning to the character after they strike. These projectile limbs have a range of 300 feet (91.4 m) and are +2 to strike. They inflict normal punch damage for the character, plus any claws or weapon damage that may be part of the hands.

Stigmata Table II

When determining stigmata features, the player can roll on the original table as presented in the **Nightbane® RPG**, page 101, or he may roll on this one, or make selections from both. -20% to skills such as Disguise, Seduction and Undercover Ops, unless stated otherwise.

01-20% Inside-Out Creature: The Nightbane's body has been literally turned inside out; his/her organs are on the outside of the body, resulting in the most grotesque image possible. Not even other Nightbane will feel comfortable around such a creature. Add 1D6x10 to S.D.C. and +1D4+2 to Horror Factor. **Note:** Disguise, Seduction and Undercover Ops are impossible.

21-40% Translucent Skin: The character's skin has a translucent, semi-transparent quality, reminiscent of a thin plastic or rubber membrane, allowing muscle tissue and organs to be semi-visible. **Bonuses:** +4D6 to S.D.C. and +1D4 to Horror Factor.

41-60% Body Faces: 1D6 Small faces and heads dot the character's body! These heads can be as small as a thumb or as large as a grapefruit. Some Nightbane can speak through these faces; others cannot stop the faces from screaming, laughing, gibbering, or mouthing expressions. The mouths of each face may also bite any enemy that gets within grappling distance; each can inflict 1D4 points of damage per bite. Bonuses: +4D6 to S.D.C. and +1D6 to Horror Factor.

61-75% Withered Flesh: The Nightbane's flesh is dried and mummy-like, making the character look like a desiccated corpse. Add 3D6 to S.D.C. and +1 to Horror Factor.

76-90% Gut Tentacles: A pair of tentacles covered in purple and blue blood vessels or that resemble intestines, can extend out of the body from the belly and grapple, whip or strike at one's opponents! These disgusting limbs inflict 2D6 damage with a whipping attack, 1D6 with a strike/punch, and can grapple enemies with the same strength as the Nightbane, with a maximum range of 6 feet (1.8 m). Adds one extra attack per melee, +2D6 S.D.C. and +2 to Horror Factor.

91-00% Shifting Body: The Nightbane's Morphus is always shifting uncontrollably, with characteristics from both stigmata tables appearing at random. So, for example, a tiny head might appear in the character's chest, linger for 1D6 minutes, and then disappear, replaced by open wounds, protruding nails or similarly disgusting traits. The new feature stays on for 1D6 minutes (1-

50%) or 1D4 hours (51-00%), and then is replaced by something else. Also roll or select a new stigmata every time the character switches to the Facade and then back to Morphus; roll randomly to see what new feature appears on his body. However, the character does *not* gain any of the bonuses that normally accompany those stigmata, except for the Horror Factor. **Bonuses:** Instead the character gets +1D4x10 S.D.C., +1 on Perception Rolls, and +1 on initiative. Horror Factor is determined by the stigmata of the moment.

Morphus Tables from Nightlands™ Sourcebook

Mineral Table

Although *rare*, some Nightbane have shapes that appear to be made from inorganic materials such as solid stone, metals or minerals; either crudely fashioned or life-like as if carefully sculpted. In other cases, the mineral aspects are only part of the body and can include large crystal formations, stone, crystal or metal spikes and/or horns, or limbs made of stone or metal. In most cases, Disguise, Undercover Ops and Swimming skills are impossible, and skills like Acrobatics, Gymnastics, Prowl, and others suffer a penalty of -40%.

01-20% Rough Metal Body: The Nightbane looks as if he was made from lumps/clusters of metal or molten metal that cooled in lumps and streams like the surface of a partially melted candle. Or he may look like crude, unprocessed metal ore with a rough surface dotted with tiny crystals and discoloration. The body is roughly human shaped, but large and heavy set. **Bonuses:** +4D6x10 to S.D.C. and +6 to P.S. and P.E., impervious to cold (no damage) but takes double damage from fire, and +1D4 to Horror Factor. **Note:** Reduce speed by 6 points and weight is increased by 400 pounds (180 kg).

21-35% Metal Statue: The Nightbane is shaped like a well-sculpted, metallic humanoid (this form, unless marred with a deformity, will mark the Nightbane as a "Ken or Barbie"). The form is not unattractive, but unsettling and inhuman. Since the Nightbane (unless other characteristics change this) has a basically humanoid size and shape, he can hide his appearance under clothing and a hood or hat. **Bonuses:** +3D6x10 to S.D.C., +3 to P.S. and P.E., impervious to cold (no damage) but takes double damage form fire, and +1 to Horror Factor. **Note:** Reduce speed by 4 points and weight is increased by 300 pounds (135 kg).

36-50% Rough Stone Body: As above, but the Nightbane looks like he is made of roughly hewn blocks of stone. **Bonuses:** +3D6x10 to S.D.C., +4 to P.S. and P.E., resistant to fire and cold (takes half damage), and +1D4 to Horror Factor. **Note:** Reduce speed by 4 and weight is increased by 300 pounds (135 kg).

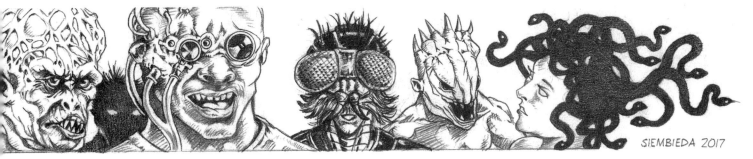

SIEMBIEDA 2017

51-65% Living Statue: A finely sculpted and detailed humanoid figure that looks normal except it's made of inorganic material (crystal, marble, ebony or stone). Since the Nightbane (unless other characteristics change this) has a basically humanoid size and shape, he can hide his appearance under clothing with a hood or a hat. Weight is increased by 200 pounds (90 kg). **Bonuses:** +2D6x10 to S.D.C., +2 to P.S. and P.E., resistant to fire and cold (takes half damage), and +1 to the Horror Factor. **Note:** Reduce speed by 2 points.

66-75% Part Inorganic: The character has hands and arms or his chest and head made of stone, crystal or metal, rough or highly polished. In the alternative, large patches all over the body are made of crystals, stone or metal and look as if they are protruding through a thin covering of skin. **Bonuses:** +2 to P.S., +4D6x2 to S.D.C. and +1 to Horror Factor.

76-85% Part Inorganic with Weapons: The Nightbane's forearms and hands turn into stone, crystal or metal, with a hand that is a sword or axe-like weapon or a hand that has long, inorganic claws or knuckle spikes. **Bonuses:** +2D6 to damage in additional to Supernatural P.S. punch damage, and +1 to Horror Factor. In addition, the hands are resistant to cold, heat and fire (take half damage).

86-90% Horns, Spines or Spikes: The character's spine is covered in thick spines or spikes made of inorganic material, or has a crown of inorganic horns/spikes, or has 3D4 small spikes or spines all over. **Bonuses:** +5D6 to S.D.C., +1 to Horror Factor and an additional 1D6 damage when used as a weapon/in combat.

91-00% Crystalline Body: The body looks like it is made of crystal. The shape is not unattractive but very inhuman. The crystalline body has many sharp edges, and will tear through clothing after a few hours of wear and tear. **Bonuses:** +2D4x10 to S.D.C., +1 to Horror Factor, laser resistant (half damage), and the crystalline hands and fingers act like claws, inflicting an additional 1D6 points of damage in addition to the Supernatural P.S. punch/kick damage. **Note:** The hands are not as articulated and have trouble holding on to things, -10% on all skills that require the use of hands.

Plant Life Table

Note: In all cases, fire does double damage to plant-life, but the Nightbane is resistant to cold (does half damage). In most cases, Disguise, Seduction and Undercover Ops skills are impossible.

01-20% Humanoid Tree: The Nightbane looks like a tree that has come to life. The strength and resilience of the character is incredible, but he is very slow and cumbersome. He has a tree trunk instead of a torso and two long branches with leaves instead of arms (if an Unnatural Limbs characteristic, adding extra limbs is also taken, the tree shape would have additional branches). His head is sunken at the top of the trunk and between the two arms/branches. It is leaf-covered and misshapen. Instead of legs, several root-like limbs allow some very slow movement. The character could pass for a strangely-shaped tree if he does not move; he can even make his "roots" sink into the ground, completing the illusion.

Add 3D4x10 to S.D.C., +6 to P.S., +1D4 to Horror Factor, can heal 2D6 S.D.C./Hit Points every 24 hours, but reduce speed by half, and reduce skill performance by 75%.

21-30% Cactus Skin: The character looks normal except his skin is green and covered with long, white needle-like cactus spines six inches (0.15 m) long. Add +4D6x2 to S.D.C., 1D4 to hand to hand damage, attackers cannot grab or wrestle with the character without taking 2D6 damage per each attack/grab. +2 to Horror Factor.

31-40% Thorn Skin: The character's skin is dark brown and his body is coiled in brown vines covered with thorns! **Bonuses:** +5D6x3 to S.D.C., 1D6 to damage in addition to Supernatural P.S. punches, attackers cannot grab or wrestle with the character without taking 3D6 damage per each attack/grab, and +3 to Horror Factor.

41-60% Living Mannequin: The Nightbane looks as if he is a giant, unfinished puppet or mannequin with a body made of polished wood but with the wood grain still showing. **Bonuses:** 2D4x10 to S.D.C., 1D4 to damage and +1 to Horror Factor.

61-70% Tree Features: The character's hair is replaced with green vines, or leaves or a cluster of tiny, thin branches; his fingers and nose are long and gnarled (branch-like in appearance), body hair becomes a fine, light green moss, and his skin a bit wrinkled (not like bark exactly, more like a 90 year old) and has a grayish green color. **Bonuses:** +4D6 to S.D.C. and +2 to Horror Factor.

71-80% Flower Child: The character seems radiant, with a bright smile, sparkling eyes and a pleasant, fresh clean, light flower aroma. The hair is long and flowing and literally filled with flowers of all kinds. Likewise, the skin is healthy but seems to have dozens of small, colorful flowers glued to it. Insects, even monstrous ones, will not attack this character (note that spiders and scorpions are not insects, they are arachnids and will attack). **Bonuses:** +1D6 to S.D.C., +1D6 to M.A. and +3D4 to P.B., strangely attractive and alluring!

81-90% Bark Skin: The character's skin is hard and looks and feels like rough tree bark. **Bonuses:** +4D6x20 to S.D.C., +1 to A.R. and +2 to Horror Factor.

91-00% Stink Weed: The character's skin is a pale green and he is covered by fine vines with 1D4x10 small, bulb-like clusters covering his body. One or two clusters can be opened at will (counts as one melee attack). Opening one cluster releases a repugnant, sweet odor. Anybody within 10 feet (3 m) must roll to save vs non-lethal poison (16 or higher) and a failed roll means the person gags, feels nauseous and is -3 on initiative, -1 to strike, parry and dodge, and -10% on skill performance; distracted by the terrible smell. Opening two will double the range and penalties. The smell lasts for one minute per level of the character and

radiates around him like a flower, so it goes where he goes. Once a cluster has been used/opened it cannot be used again for 24 hours. A successful save means the character is only -1 on initiative and -5% on skill performance. Smashing or cutting open a cluster will have the same effect. **Bonuses:** +3D6 to S.D.C. and +1 to Horror Factor.

Appendix Talents

For your convenience, we have reprinted the Morphus Tables from the **Nightbane® RPG** and select sourcebooks.

Talent Manifestations

Talents are unlike any other ability in Palladium's role-playing games. While powered by P.P.E., they are not spells. Nor are they psionic powers or super abilities. Talents are more akin to tangible expressions of will on the behalf of the Nightbane (and Shadow Mages).

As such, they tend to manifest in different ways for different Nightbane. What this means for players and Game Masters is that the mechanics of the powers are always the same, but visually they can be quite different.

For example, Stony Lonesome, a Nightbane with rock-like skin covered in razor wire, has the *Darkwhip Talent*. So does Crosswire, a Nightbane with a camera-like head and a robotic body. For both individuals, the Darkwhip Talent works the same way. However, Stony's Darkwhip comes out as a long, deadly strand of barbed wire, and Crosswire's Darkwhip flashes out as a bundle of seemingly animated electrical wiring. Such variations and effects do not add damage or functionality, but reflect aspects of personality and individuality to each Nightbane character.

It also means that other Nightbane sometimes have to guess at what Talents a Nightbane is using. When you see a holographic image overlay Crosswire's Facade, making him look like someone else, did he just use *Reshape Facade* or is it something else? The observers are not 100% certain.

And there's the fun.

A group of player characters may see Stony embrace with a badly injured woman and appear to vomit liquid concrete into her. He may be using *Infectious Control* or he might be using the *Sharing the Flesh* ability. If they attack and take the woman from him, they may save her life . . . or they may prevent him from healing her, and the shock could cause her to die.

Likewise, when special lenses drop over Crosswire's camera-like eyes, did he just use *See Truth* or is he peering at that mirror on the wall and using *Mirror Sight*?

The manifestation of Talents usually have some connection or similarity to the Nightbane's Morphus or personality. For example, *Darksong* may be a long, blood-curdling howl for a Nightbane with wolf-like attributes in Morphus, but a strange, unearthly choir begins singing whenever a Nightbane with an Angel Morphus uses the same Talent. Gloppy the Kid, a Nightbane with a plasmoid, shapeless body, oozes into his computer through the disc drive or DVD-ROM slot when he uses Lightning Rider, but Crosswire streams into his screen as a series of glowing "1"s and "0"s.

The only limit to the different *Talent manifestations* is your imagination. Just remember, the manifestations are only *cosmetic* visual variations. They do NOT provide any tangible benefit to the actual Talent; the Talent always functions the same, does the same damage and has the same effect, duration and range, it may just look different.

SIEMBIEDA 2017

Common Talents from Nightbane® RPG

Anti-Arcane
Borrow Morphus
Darksong
Darkwhip
Doorway
Infectious Control
Lightening Rider
Mirror Sight
Mirror Search
Nightbringer
Premonition
Reshape Facade
See Truth
Shadow Blast
Shadow Shield
Sharing the Flesh
The Shroud
Shadow Slide
Soul Shield
Splittin' Image
Stone Maker

Anti-Arcane

When activating this Talent, the Nightbane is surrounded by an aura of black light (easily confused with the Shadow Shield described below). While this aura is in effect, the Nightbane is utterly invulnerable to the effects of magic! Any magical spell that can be resisted by a save against magic will have *no effect* on the character. Spells that must be dodged, or have no saving throw, will work normally. The Anti-Arcane will last one minute (4 melees), at which time it must be reactivated.

Limitations: Usable only by the Morphus. Not available until the character has reached fifth level.

Cost: Fifteen P.P.E. are permanently spent to acquire it and 20 are needed every time to activate it.

Borrow Morphus

This rare power allows a Nightbane to assume the Morphus of another of his kind! The "other" Nightbane whose likeness is being copied suffers no ill effect other than the shock of seeing his double. The character gains the shape, all physical attributes, S.D.C. and Hit Points of the "borrowed" shape. He can also use any of the Talents possessed by the Nightbane he is imitating, but only abilities that the borrowing character knew the other possessed. Furthermore, the borrowing Nightbane cannot use his own Talents until he resumes his true form. He also uses his own combat skills (modified by the borrowed form's attribute bonuses) and his normal skills – the Talent borrows only the other person's physical body and does NOT include the character's memories, knowledge, or insanities. The transformation lasts 4 melee rounds (one minute).

Limitations: Usable by the Morphus only. Not available until fifth level.

Cost: Fifteen P.P.E. permanent; 15 to activate, plus 15 P.P.E. for each additional minute the borrowed Morphus is kept.

Darksong

The Nightbane can emit a piercing, deafening sound; it can be an inhuman howl, a mighty roar, an ultrasonic keening, or even electronic feedback, depending on the Nightbane's Morphus. Targets must make a roll to save (P.E. bonuses apply); if they roll under a 10, they are stunned for 1D4 melee rounds. The attacker can raise the number needed to save by expending additional P.P.E.: +1 point per 3 P.P.E. The Darksong can be used against an area (60 feet/18.3 m radius); in that case, everyone in the area, friend or foe, must make a save, but they are at +4 to resist.

Limitations: Usable by the Morphus only.

Cost: Seven P.P.E. are permanently spent to acquire it; 5 P.P.E. are needed to activate it (+3 to raise the save number by +1).

Darkwhip

Creates tendrils of darkness that inflict *supernatural damage* with a P.S. equal to the amount of P.P.E. spent on creating them. Lasts for 4 melee rounds (one minute), after which they must be recreated. Range is 60 feet (18.3 m). The tendrils can have any shape, not limited to whips and tentacles, although those are the most common. The Darkwhip can be used to strike and also to entangle or disarm, provided those skills are known to the wielder.

Limitations: Usable by the Morphus only.

Cost: Eight permanent to acquire; 4 to activate (additional P.P.E. increases the amount of damage the whip inflicts with each strike).

Doorway

Creates a door of dark energy that leads to a specific location desired by the creator of it. Takes one melee round (15 seconds) of concentration. Range: To a location up to 1 mile (1.6 km) per 2 P.P.E. spent. The Nightbane must have been to the destination point at least once in his life, or he must have line of sight.

Limitations: Usable by the Morphus only. Not available until reaching 5th level.

Cost: Fifteen P.P.E. to permanently acquire it, and a minimum of 2 P.P.E. to activate (see above). This power can also open a

doorway to the Nightlands or back, but this costs 40 P.P.E., plus 5 P.P.E. per mile.

Infectious Control

This often-repulsive Talent allows the Nightbane to take over a person by "infecting" him with a portion of his body. The manifestations of this power are varied. Some Nightbane shoot spines or needless that, when they pierce the flesh of the target, enable them to take over. Others create little "parasites" that burrow into the victim's body. Biomechanicals often drill or shoot wires or microchips into the victim. Some Stigmata-sufferers actually force-feed the victim some of their blood to infect them.

Once the infection is complete (usually takes one melee round from the time the piece of the Nightbane has entered the body of the victim), the subject is controlled by the Nightbane for one melee round (15 seconds). At the end of the round, the victim can try to resist (save vs magic); if he fails the save, he is under the control of the Nightbane for 30 minutes. New saves are allowed every 10 minutes.

While in control, the Nightbane can see, hear and experience everything his victim does while he acts as puppeteer, controlling every word and movement of the victim. The main drawback is that the Nightbane has to split his concentration and attention between his own body and that of his victim. Thus, his attacks/actions per melee round are divided evenly between the two bodies, he has no initiative bonus, and combat bonuses and skill performance is reduced by half, unless he relinquishes his control over his puppet.

The "infection" also allows the Nightbane to search the memories of his victim; one piece of information can be extracted by spending an additional 5 P.P.E. (and the victim gets a separate save to resist against the intrusion; this save is against psionic attack rather than magic). Each "memory search" takes 1D6 minutes and is limited to one small bit of information at a time.

Limitations: Usable only in Morphus form and is not available until 6th level.

Cost: Twenty P.P.E. are permanently spent to acquire it; 20 P.P.E. to activate, plus 20 P.P.E. every additional half hour. The memory of the victim can be searched for an additional 5 P.P.E. per piece of information.

Note: Victims who have an M.E. of 7 or less are controlled for an hour at a time rather than the usual half an hour.

Lightning Rider

The Nightbane becomes a being of pure electrical energy! Unless a great deal of P.P.E. is spent, the electrical charge is weak and does not inflict damage. However, while in electrical form, the Nightbane can travel through conductive materials at enormous speeds. When the power is activated, the Nightbane disappears in a flash of electricity and "leaps" onto the nearest conductive material (metal and exposed wires works best). If no such material is around, the Nightbane appears to become a small pool of sparks, or a small, crackling lightning ball that crawls around at a speed of 8.

With the invention of the telephone and electrical wires, this Talent came into its own and enables Nightbane to travel from one corner of the world to the next in a matter of minutes through them. Some Nightbane become extremely proficient in navigating through telephone exchanges. The easiest way, of course, was to call the place one wished to travel to and then travel through the phone lines and jump out of the receiver! With the advent of computers and the Internet, this power has become even more influential. A character with Computer Operations can understand the information superhighway and hitch rides on modem calls. A character with Computer Programming can become the ultimate hacker!

Limitations: Usable by the Morphus only.

Cost: Fifteen P.P.E. to permanently acquire it; 10 to activate per minute (it takes one melee round of concentration to activate). The Nightbane can increase the voltage to inflict damage: 1D6 S.D.C. per 5 P.P.E., per each attack **Note:** Eight points of damage will fry most electronics like radios, computers, etc. Specially shielded and hardened systems survive as much as 40 points of damage before being disabled.

Mirror Sight

This and other mirror related talents and natural abilities give the archaic name of "looking glass" great new significance when dealing with the Nightbane and the Nightlords. This Talent enables the Nightbane to see the other side of a mirror, into the Nightlands, and vice versa, as if it were a window. A mirror or any highly reflective surface (glass, polished metal, a quiet body of water) must be available. The character can only see what the mirror image faces in the Nightlands, and vice versa. Some Nightlands creatures may sense they are being "looked at" and could cross over to confront or attack the "peeper" (see the **Nightlands Section** for more information).

Limitations: Requires a mirror; can be used by both Morphus and Facade.

Duration: 10 minutes per level of the character's experience.

Cost: Five P.P.E. for permanent acquisition; 2 to activate.

Mirror Search

Prerequisite: Mirror Sight.

The Nightbane is able to see through the mirror closest to the person or object he seeks. This is an area effect Talent that effectively scans a 10 mile (16 km) radius (more if additional P.P.E. are expended) in search of the person or item sought. This does not mean that the nearest mirror will reveal the target of the search, but the closest area and mirror to it. For example: Search-

SIEMBIEDA 2017

ing for a kidnapped friend, the mirror search may reveal the image of a bathroom in a hotel. The name of the hotel is visible from the hanging towels, which may be enough to figure out, at least roughly, where the person is. Or there may actually be a mirror in the hotel room (there usually is) that shows the Nightbane's friend bound to a chair and being interrogated by two thugs and a Hound.

Limitations: Usable by the Morphus only.

Cost: Ten P.P.E. to acquire permanently; 15 to activate for a 10 mile (16 km) area, +5 P.P.E. per additional 10 miles (16 km).

Note: Both mirror sight and mirror search show only images, not sound – it is like looking through the glass of a closed window into the room or area that the mirror is located (which may show parts of other rooms or a hallway, things outside the windows in that room, etc.).

Covering a mirror with a blanket, towel, or other covering will prevent a character from effectively using mirror sight and mirror search, because all the mirror will show is that it is covered. However, it does not prevent a Nightlord or other so empowered being from traveling and entering that room through the covered mirror, even if wrapped snugly – the monster tears right through the cloth or tarp. However, painting the mirror will prevent such passage as well as use of the mirror as a window.

Nightbringer

Absorbs light around the Nightbane, creating an area of darkness equal to 10 feet (3 m) in diameter per every 2 P.P.E. spent. The power also absorbs energy attacks, except Shadow Blast, Dark Whip and other darkness-based attacks and magic. People caught in the unnatural darkness are at -6 to strike, parry and dodge, and -4 on their Perception Rolls (penalties are half for creatures with nightvision).

Limitations: Usable by the Morphus only.

Cost: Five P.P.E. to acquire permanently; 2 minimum to activate. Each additional 2 P.P.E. increases the diameter of the darkness by 10 feet (3 m).

Premonition

Gives the character feelings and visions about the future, often at unexpected times (ultimately, when the Game Master decides the character should get a vision, he does) or at moments of crisis. For the most part, "feelings" of premonition will give the character a feeling that something good, bad or dangerous is going to happen soon, or at some particular place, or to some particular person. These feelings are just that, and do not come with any dreams or images.

"Visions" on the other hand, are usually images and/or short dream sequences that are accompanied by "feelings." These images are often symbolic omens and can be cryptic (but G.M.s, not too cryptic) and may give some hints of things to come. For

example: The Nightbane may have a reoccurring vision about a man or Nightlord, or minion slaughtering innocent people, his friends or even himself. The murderous figure is always in shadow so his features cannot be seen, but the vision always ends with the image of a stylized eagle. Then one day, the Nightbane meets a person with a tattoo of that eagle, indicating that this person is the culprit, but not always. The tattoo could be the symbol of a gang or cult worn by all its members in one fashion or another. Or it could be the logo for a corporation, or a bar, or the emblem for a special police squad, the hilt of a magic sword, a statue, the cover of a book, and so on. At any rate, it gives our hero some warning about danger and who or what might be involved.

Limitations: Usable by the Morphus only. A premonition can happen spontaneously, or when the Nightbane actively attempts to sense the future.

Cost: Two P.P.E. to acquire it permanently; 2 to activate and 2 when a spontaneous occurrence happens.

Reshape Facade

Although contemptuously called the Facade, the Nightbane's human form is as unique and real to him or her as the superhuman Morphus. Nightbane with this Talent can *temporarily* alter the shape of the Facade, changing the features, hair color and even the size of their human form. The more extensive the change, the more P.P.E. the transformation will cost. Imitating a particular person is possible, but very difficult to get it right (20% plus I.Q. bonus, plus 3% per level of experience).

Limitations: Usable by the Facade only. Not available until the 3rd level.

Cost: Twelve P.P.E. to acquire it permanently, 6 to activate plus 4 per additional hour the disguise is desired.

See Truth

Every time this power is activated, the Nightbane is able to see the true nature of one person or object. This includes actually seeing a Nightbane's Facade and Morphus forms, superimposed one over the other. The alignment of the target can also be seen; applicable to humans and Nightbane (in the latter case, it counts as a separate use of this Talent). Furthermore, See Truth also reveals strong emanations of magic, the undead/vampires, serious illness, and strong emotions (hatred when the person is smiling and being nice, etc.); all these things are considered aspects of the soul and/or personality of the target being examined via this Talent.

The subject saves against magic (12 or higher) to resist revealing the truth. The Nightbane can increase the difficulty of the save by expending more P.P.E.: every additional 4 P.P.E. raises the save number by +1 (maximum of 18, for 24 P.P.E.).

Limitations:

Range: line of sight up to 300 feet (91 m) away.

Cost: Three permanent, 2 points to activate, +4 to increase save number by one.

Shadow Blast

Fires a black energy bolt that does 1D4 S.D.C. for every point of P.P.E. spent on it, so 10 P.P.E. would result in a 1D4x10 S.D.C. bolt, and so on.

Limitations: Usable by the Morphus only. The Nightbane can only spend 4 P.P.E. per level of experience.

<u>Range:</u> 500 feet/152 m.

Cost: Five P.P.E. to permanently acquire it; one P.P.E. per every 1D4 points of damage.

Shadow Shield

Creates a force field of dark energy around the Nightbane, providing 20 S.D.C. per 2 P.P.E. spent (P.P.E. spent cannot exceed 4 per level of experience). The Shadow Shield completely surrounds the character, protecting him from toxic gases, disease, punches, bullets, heat, fire, and similar dangers as long as it remains in force; it is the shield that takes the damage inflicted by such attacks.

Duration: 30 minutes per level of experience or until all the S.D.C. of the shadow shield is used up.

Limitations: Usable by the Morphus only. Maximum of 40 S.D.C. per level of experience.

Cost: Seven P.P.E. to acquire it permanently; two P.P.E. to activate Shadow Shield with 20 S.D.C., plus 2 P.P.E. for each additional 20 S.D.C. Cannot exceed 40 S.D.C. per level of experience.

Sharing the Flesh

This is a strange and horrific healing spell. The Nightbane touches an injured person to magically transfer the other person's wounds, injury and pain to himself. The person being healed falls into a coma or sleep that lasts 1D4 melee rounds and then awakens completely well. The effect if often gruesome, with nasty wounds spontaneously appearing on the Nightbane as the subject is being healed. The Nightbane can transfer as much damage as he or she can tolerate, which may be a little amount to all. This is actually a painful sacrifice on the part of the Nightbane as he/she heals as normal – fortunately, these creature heal rapidly compared to humans.

Limitations: Usable only while in the Morphus form and the Nightbane must perform this act of sacrifice of his own free will. Healing critically injured/comatose characters requires the Nightbane to temporarily expend 24 P.P.E. points and 100 of his S.D.C. and/or Hit Points to stabilize the injured person and heal the most serious injuries (brings the character up to 2D6 Hit Points). However, the pain and shock to his system will put the Nightbane in a coma for 2D4x10 minutes. A Nightbane with less than 100 S.D.C./Hit Points available at the time can perform the same healing but will die in the process.

Cost: Two P.P.E. to acquire it permanently; 8 to activate (see above for coma cases).

The Shroud

This powerful Talent enables a Nightbane to become invisible and noiseless to normal vision and senses as well as to electronic devices like cameras, motion detectors, heat sensors, etc. This ability can be used selectively, enabling some people to see the character while others can't. Vengeful Nightbane have been known to drive a human insane by pursuing him in plain sight, invisible to everyone else. The victim's cries for help would be useless, for nobody else can see the monsters threatening him!

The power is very expensive to maintain for long periods of time (10 P.P.E. per minute). Also, the moment the Nightbane attacks anybody (he can threaten, scream or make gestures all he wants), the Talent stops working and he becomes visible for all to see. Likewise, a Nightbane actively engaged in combat or other activity, or standing in plain sight, cannot activate this Talent to disappear. First, he must get out of sight.

Limitations: Usable only by the Morphus.

Cost: Twelve P.P.E. to acquire it permanently; 10 P.P.E. to activate per each minute in effect.

Shadow Slide

The Nightbane must be in Morphus form for this power to work. The character becomes an insubstantial shadow, or, more accurately, like one of those mirages you can see on a paved road during a sunny day – a flickering shadow that seems to sink into the earth and fades away as if it never was. While in this two-dimensional form, the Nightbane can slither along walls or across the ground, virtually invisible and able to slide through any opening, no matter how narrow (only air-tight containers will prevent the shadow-slider from coming through). The Nightbane's clothing and small personal effects are transformed automatically; additionally, he can carry objects at an additional P.P.E. cost (2 P.P.E. per pound/0.45 kg of weight).

Limitations: Usable by the Morphus only.

Cost: Eight P.P.E. to acquire it permanently; 10 points to activate and 10 per each minute the Talent is maintained.

Soul Shield

Protects against mental attacks/probes and the See Truth Talent. The Soul Shield acts like a psychic mind block, preventing most means of magical or psionic probes from intruding into the Nightbane's mind. More importantly, while the Soul Shield is up, any spell or power that tries to control or dominate the Nightbane's mind will automatically fail.

SIEMBIEDA 2017

Those who attempt to read the protected character's mind will see only a pool of utter darkness. The mind reader/psychic will find it very difficult to pry himself from that darkness (a save versus psionics is necessary; roll every melee round), and until he does, he will be unable to do anything other than stare vacantly into space.

Limitations: Usable by the Morphus only.

<u>Duration</u>: One hour.

Cost: Six P.P.E. to acquire it permanently; 4 to activate.

Splittin' Image

This powerful ability enables the Nightbane to separate his Facade and Morphus forms and act normally in both of them! The Nightbane in effect becomes two people. The character is aware of what both sides are doing, but his consciousness must be focused on one form or the other (he can switch viewpoints at will). The form where his consciousness is focused on acts normally; the other appears to lapse into a trance-like state and is at -2 to all combat and Perception Rolls, has half the normal attacks per melee round, and is at -40% to perform any skills.

Limitations: Usable only by the Morphus only. Not available until 5th level.

<u>Duration</u>: One or more hours depending on the amount of P.P.E. expended. The character can merge back into one body at will.

Cost: Fifteen P.P.E. to acquire it permanently; 20 to activate it for one hour and 10 P.P.E. per each additional hour (can spend the P.P.E. "up front" or as needed).

Storm Maker

This powerful talent enables the Nightbane to control the weather. Rain, winds and the temperature can be altered. The more extreme the changes and the greater the area affected, the more P.P.E. the character must spend. This talent is particularly powerful because two or more Nightbane who know it can combine their efforts (and P.P.E.) to produce an even more powerful effect. There are legends of ancient Nightbane groups sending hurricanes and tornadoes against people who offended or injured them.

The P.P.E. cost varies; the effects take 1D6x10 minutes to manifest, and then lasts one hour. At the end of the hour, the same amount of P.P.E. must be spent to keep it going or it fades away. Some guidelines are given below:

A minor change in existing weather conditions like raising the wind by up to 5 mph (8 km), increasing or decreasing cloudiness, intensifying already existing rain, raising or lowering overall temperature by 4 degrees Fahrenheit: 5 P.P.E.

A moderate change of weather conditions like starting rain on an overcast day, turning a downpour into a storm or vice versa, raising or lowering overall temperature by 10 degrees Fahrenheit: 10 P.P.E.

Sudden, major change in weather like starting rain during a clear, sunny day, stopping a downpour, or creating a major thunder or electrical storm during a rainy day, raising or lowering overall temperature by 20 degrees Fahrenheit: 20 P.P.E.

Extreme changes in weather like creating a fog, or starting a hailstorm or electrical storm during a clear, sunny day – or turning a storm into a sunny day, turning a thunderstorm into a tropical storm with near-hurricane winds (70 mph/112 km), raising or lowering overall temperature by 30 degrees Fahrenheit: 40 P.P.E.

Total upheaval in weather such as starting a hurricane or tornado from scratch (90+ mph/144 km winds), create a blinding snowstorm, dissipating a hurricane or terrible storm, raising or lowering overall temperature by 50 degrees Fahrenheit: 80 P.P.E.

The base area affected has a radius of one mile (1.6 km). Each additional mile of radius doubles the previous P.P.E. cost. For example: causing a moderate change in the weather costs 10 P.P.E. for one mile/1.6 km, 20 P.P.E. for two miles (3.2 km), 40 P.P.E. for three miles/4.8 km, and 80 P.P.E. for a four (mile/6.4 km) radius.

Limitations: Usable only by the Morphus. Not available until reaching 5th level.

Cost: Twenty P.P.E. to acquire it permanently; P.P.E. cost varies as described above.

Elite Talents from Nightbane® RPG

Bloodbath
Deus Ex Machina
Lord/Lady of the Wild
Swarm Self

These powers have certain prerequisites. For instance, animal control abilities apply only to Nightbane who have some elements of those animals in their Morphus.

Elite Talents seem to be an extension of the Nightbane's self-conception, i.e. a machine-man might see himself capable of controlling other machines, but not animals. On the other hand, a Biomechanical-animal Nightbane would have access to both types of powers.

Bloodbath

This grotesque power allows the Nightbane to use his own blood to suffocate victims. A stream of blood pours from the character (this inflicts 1D6 points of damage to the character activating the Talent). The Nightbane is at +3 to strike with it. On a successful hit, the blood will rush into the victim's nose and

throat, and cause him to choke! While drowning in blood, the victim is at -2 to all combat actions and is unable to use spells, Talents or any skill that requires concentration. The blood remains alive for 1D4 melee rounds, inflicting 2D6 points of damage at the end of each melee round. A successful save versus non-lethal poison will avoid damage for that round, but the penalties remain. Additionally, a victim unfamiliar with that attack must save versus a Horror Factor of 12 to avoid panicking. If panicked, the penalties for the victim are doubled.

Prerequisite: At least one characteristic from the Stigmata Table.

Limitations: Usable only by the Morphus. Not available until the 3rd level.

Duration: 1D4 melee rounds.

Cost: Fifteen P.P.E. for permanent acquisition; 8 to activate plus it inflicts 1D6 points of damage on the user.

Deus Ex Machina (Machine Control)

The Nightbane can control machines from cars to microwaves, to lamps or weapons. One device can be controlled for every three points of I.Q. he has (thus, a Nightbane with an I.Q. 13 could control 4 machines). The machines can then be made to do anything within their capabilities. For example, a lamp can turn itself on or off, but nothing else. A car or a motorcycle could start its motor and ride off (until it left the range of the effect). While the Nightbane can control several machines, only one of them can be directly controlled on an action-by-action basis. The remaining mechanisms can be given a general order for the rest of the round.

Example: The aforementioned Nightbane is trapped in a house by a number of NSB agents. Trying to create a diversion, he activates Deus Ex Machina and takes control of four machines, including a desktop computer, a laser printer, a lawn mower just outside the house, and a lamp on the desk. He first orders the office machines to start the diversion, the lamp will turn itself on and off for a melee round, the computer will start making noise at the top of its Soundblaster speakers, and the laser printer will start spitting blank pieces of paper. As the NSB are distracted by the noises coming from the office, the Nightbane takes full control of the lawn mower and sends it roaring into their midst! As the agents shoot the hapless machine to pieces, the Nightbane quietly slips out the back. In a pinch, the character can also seize control of guns and even explosive devices to prevent them from firing (or detonating) or to shoot (explode) whether the user wants them to or not.

Prerequisite: At least one Biomechanical characteristic.

Limitations: Usable by the Morphus only. Not available until the third level.

Duration of Control: One minute.

Range: 300 feet (91.4 m).

Cost: Twelve P.P.E. to acquire permanently; 4 to activate plus 6 for each additional minute of control or 20 for an additional 100 foot (30.5 m) radius of control.

Lord/Lady of the Wild (Animal Control)

The Nightbane gains mastery over any animal species he/she is associated with; thus, a wolf-life Nightbane will be able to control wolves and any canine animal, while a bird-like character would gain powers over all birds. The power has variable range and effects, depending on the amount of P.P.E. the Nightbane spends. Simple commands like "Come here," "Attack this man," "Go," or "Make a lot of noise" will be readily heeded. A character with this power can also make animals behave in unnatural ways, like attacking armed men, something most animals will never do, dance in circles, leap through a wall of fire, etc., but this will cost more P.P.E. Some guidelines are described below:

Calling animals: Any animals of the appropriate species will come from up to a one mile (1.6 km) radius per level of experience: Costs 2 P.P.E. Once they get there, the animals will revert to normal unless new commands are given.

Minor, non-dangerous actions: Like making noise, hiding, fluttering about, or acting in fairly normal ways: Costs 1 P.P.E. per large animal or per group of up to ten small animals (rat/pigeon-sized or smaller).

Dangerous actions: Threatening humans, bite/attack, leap at, block or otherwise hindering armed humans, or behavior that goes against the animal's normal behavior (asking a nocturnal animal to operate in the daytime, etc.): Costs 5 P.P.E. per large animal or per group of up to ten small animals.

Suicidal actions: Recklessly attacking humans or supernatural beings, intercepting vehicles (a flock of birds can bring down a plane by flying into its engines), fight to the death, and other suicidal or utterly unnatural acts: Costs 10 P.P.E. per large animal or per group of up to ten small animals.

Prerequisite: At least one characteristic from the Animal Form Table.

Limitations: Usable by the Morphus only. Not available until fourth level. Control is limited to the appropriate species.

Range: One mile (1.6 km) to summon, 500 feet (152 m) to control/command.

Duration: 15 minutes.

Cost: Fifteen P.P.E. to acquire permanently; activation varies as described above.

Swarm Self

Causes the Nightbane's body to separate into 2D4x10 tiny animals of the same animal type as the character (see prerequisites, below). The Nightbane controls this swarm and is aware of everything they do or see. Each swam member has 5 S.D.C. and 1

Hit Point. In combat, they do 1 point of S.D.C. damage individually or 5D6 S.D.C. from a group or swarm of 10 or more every melee round (all 10 attack one target; several groups of 10 can attack different targets).

The swarmlings have the same combat bonuses as the Nightbane when attacking individually; they are small targets, requiring a called shot at -5 to hit! If attacking as a group, each group of 10 will automatically swarm over a target in 3-5 seconds (equivalent to a melee attack/action) and inflict the damage at the end of each melee round. Attacks on the swarm have no modifiers to hit; a swarm of 10 critters will have 50 S.D.C. and 10 Hit Points. If the swarm takes more than half its S.D.C. damage, it means that half of the critters are dead, damage is reduced to 2D6. When all the S.D.C. is depleted, this means that only two swarmlings remain, and they attack and defend normally (see above).

The Hit Point (not S.D.C.) damage taken by the swarm carries over to the Nightbane's Hit Points after the swarm is destroyed or recalled. The swarmlings do not regenerate damage and the character must switch back to his normal Morphus form and limp away. At least two of the swarmlings must be present for the Nightbane to rebuild himself, but most retreat and reform when reduced to 10 or 15. If all are destroyed then the Nightbane is slain.

Prerequisite: At least one characteristic from the Animal or Insect Form Table. The creatures will be small versions of the animal. For example: A character with avian characteristics will be able to separate into a swarm of birds, a rodent into a swarm of rats or mice, arachnid into spiders or scorpions, insect into wasps/bees or biting flies and so on.

Limitations: Usable by the Morphus only.

Range: Self; once a swarm is created the range is unrestricted.

Cost: Fifteen P.P.E. to acquire permanently; 10 to activate for the first two minutes and an additional 10 points for each additional two minutes.

Talents from Between the Shadows™

Air Grab
Astral Self
Darkwave
Dervish Dance
Dreamer
Piece Work

Air Grab

The Nightbane can "grab" somebody up to 50 feet (15.2 m) away +10 feet (3 m) per additional level by making a grabbing gesture in the direction of the target. The grab simply *holds* a person for two melee actions, or roughly 5 seconds, during which time he cannot move or physically attack. The captive of an air grab can break free with one, flexing, melee action of his own, but only if his strength is equal to or greater than the Nightbane's.

An "air squeeze" does Supernatural P.S. punch damage; use the Nightbane's P.S. minus five points and counts as two melee attacks.

The Nightbane can also use the power to grab and bring/pull the victim to him in one melee action (2 seconds). The captive of an air grab and pull can break free or resist being pulled only if his own P.S. is equal to or greater than the Nightbane. Instead of pulling the grabbed character to him, the Nightbane can throw him up to 10 feet (3 m) away. Unless the victim makes a successful roll with fall/impact, he takes 1D6 S.D.C. damage and loses two melee actions/attacks and initiative.

Victims must know they are being targeted with this power to avoid it, and even then they need to roll a 16 or higher to dodge.

Limitations: Usable by the Morphus only. Each action or attack costs 8 P.P.E.

Cost: Ten P.P.E. to acquire it permanently; 8 P.P.E. per grabbing action.

Astral Self

The Nightbane becomes an astral being with no physical body. In astral form, the character has all the abilities and limitations of an astral projection (see **Nightbane® RPG**, page 70), but without a silver cord, or leaving his physical body behind. The S.D.C. of the astral-self is equal to the combined S.D.C. and Hit Points of the Nightbane, times two! While in astral form, the character can enter the Astral Plane, affect insubstantial creatures and other astral beings, and visit astral domains or kingdoms (see the Astral Plane section for more information). Once transformed, the Nightbane can stay in astral form indefinitely, although changing back will use up P.P.E.

Limitations: Usable by the Morphus form only.

Cost: Eight P.P.E. to acquire permanently. 8 P.P.E. to activate, and 8 P.P.E. to return to physical form (the character must have returned to the physical world, either Earth or the Nightlands, to return to his normal state).

Darkwave

The Nightbane becomes an engulfing, semi-liquid mass of pure darkness that can engulf and suffocate opponents. An engulf counts as a normal melee attack. An intended victim can try to dodge but does so with a -4 penalty. Once engulfed, the victim is either helplessly confined in absolute darkness, or confined and made to suffer 2D6 S.D.C. per melee round locked inside the Darkwave. This damage cannot be regenerated until the victim is free of the darkness. While trapped, the victim loses half his

attacks/actions per melee round, and all combat bonuses. The use of spells and psionics are impossible.

The size of the Darkwave is determined by the level of the Nightbane. At levels one and two, the character can engulf one victim, two victims at level three, three at level six, and one additional victim at levels nine, twelve and fifteen. Multiple victims get a dodge defense against the Nightbane's single attack roll without penalty.

While in this state, the Nightbane takes half damage from physical attacks directed at the darkness, and double damage from energy and magical attacks from those not trapped inside. Furthermore, strong light will inflict damage: no damage from streetlights, 1D6 from a pen light (range: 5 feet/1.5 m), 3D6 from a commercial flashlight (range 10 feet/3 m), 5D6 from a high-powered or police flashlight, and 1D6x10 from a spotlight or magic light or Guardian. This damage can be inflicted once per melee round per light wielder. The power cannot be used during the day, or the Nightbane will take 1D6x10 points of damage at the end of every melee round.

Limitations: Usable by the Morphus only, vulnerable to light, and not advisable in daylight.

Cost: Twelve P.P.E. to acquire permanently; 6 P.P.E. per 30 seconds (two melee rounds).

Dervish Dance

The Nightbane can move in a circular pattern and make spinning attacks with incredible speed. Basically, the character becomes a blur, as he spins at blurring speeds in a large circle – a circular area 10 feet (3 m) in diameter. All opponents within, or who enter, the 10 foot (3 m) diameter of the dance zone gets attacked as if the Nightbane had made an attack roll of 10 +1 per level of Nightbane (maximum 19). Everybody in the dance circle is attacked again if anyone in the zone tries to attack the Nightbane dervish dancer. Opponents can try to dodge the dervish attack as normal, parry at -6, or try to roll with the punch, fall or impact after being struck. The Nightbane also uses the attack roll number (10 +1 per level of experience) to automatic parry all incoming attacks, even bullets, arrows and similar missile attacks (but not energy attacks – they strike and damage as normal).

The dervish dance lasts one entire melee round (15 seconds), must be the Nightbane's first attack of that melee round, and counts as all the character's melee attacks for that round. Example: Sargon the Uncanny, 6th level Nightbane, attacks a group of three Hounds with his Dervish Dance. All fall within the diameter of his attack (10 feet/3 m). He activates the power and wades into the group, striking at each one with a 16 to hit (no die roll is necessary). Each Hounds tries to dodge; rolls are a 10, a 15, and a 3, all fail, so each takes damage as if Sargon had punched them individually. The Hounds then all attack back; their attack rolls must exceed a 16 to harm Sargon; only one attack roll in the entire melee round does so, lightly injuring Sargon. Because they

retaliated, Sargon's dervish dance enables him to strike again, this time the Hounds roll a 14, a 16 and a 19 respectively. Only the 14 suffers damage. The 16 ties, so the dodge was successful and the 19 dodged with ease (but all attempting the dodge use up one melee attack/action). Now, if none of the Hounds attack again, Sargon cannot strike again, but if even one Hound attacks, Sargon parries with a 16 (17 or higher hits) and all three are attacked again. Of course, any Hound that runs away is likely to get outside the diameter of the dance and is safe from any further attacks. However, looking in at the blur of action he can try to strike the whirling Nightbane but still must roll a 17 or higher to hit him. At the end of the melee round, the Nightbane stops and prepares to fight them normally. If he had wanted to keep the power going, he would have had to spend an additional 20 P.P.E.

Limitations: Only usable in the Morphus.

Range: Limited to a 10 foot (3 m) diameter striking range.

Cost: Fifteen P.P.E. to acquire permanently; 20 P.P.E. per melee round.

Dreamer

With this power the Nightbane can enter the Dreamstream body and soul. While in the Dreamstream, the Nightbane has a "psychic S.D.C." equal to his normal S.D.C. and Hit Points combined. The character can use his other talents normally, and can enter the Dream Pools of other people. Although Nightbane cannot manipulate dreamstuff to terrorize dreamers, their mere shape and appearance are often enough to create nightmares. See the *Dreamstream section* for more information.

Limitations: Usable by the Morphus only. If all psychic S.D.C. are reduced to below zero, the character is slain and vanishes as if he never existed.

Cost: Ten to permanently acquire, and 10 to enter, or leave the Dreamstream. Once there, the Nightbane can stay indefinitely.

Piece Work

By using this power, the Nightbane can remove a part of his own flesh; some actually remove an eye, ear, or other sensory body parts, but a finger or toe will do just as well. The body part will be able to hear, see and feel everything around it, although it may limited by where it has been placed and cannot move or communicate. The Nightbane cannot learn anything from the detached appendage until he reattaches it. When the piece is reattached to the Nightbane, the character *remembers* everything experienced by the piece, as if he had been there himself. Each piece has 10 S.D.C. and 4 Hit Points (these cannot be regenerated until the piece is destroyed or reattached).

Limitations: Usable by the Morphus only.

Cost: Ten to permanently acquire, and 8 to activate it. Every hour after the first, the Nightbane must spend an additional 6 P.P.E. or the missing piece will disappear. This allows the char-

SIEMBIEDA 2017

acter to regenerate the damage and the item, but he loses any information it might have gained. If the body part or piece of flesh is burned, eaten or otherwise destroyed, it ceases to exist, with the same effects.

Common Talents from Nightbane® Survival Guide

Air Swim
Fire Breather
Heal Facade
Severance
Shadow Pockets
Shadow Weapon
Speed Darkling

Air Swim

This Talent enables the Nightbane to *swim* through the air the same as if it were water. A Nightbane does not suffer penalties from drying out or breathing air when using this Talent when his Morphus is of an aquatic nature.

Limitations: Maximum height above the ground is 15 feet (4.6 m) per level of experience. Speed is the same as Swimming.

Cost: Seven P.P.E. to permanently acquire; 5 P.P.E. to activate for the first minute and 2 P.P.E. for each minute after that.

Fire Breather

The Nightbane is able to exhale a powerful jet of flames, similar to that of a flamethrower. The gout of fire inflicts 5D6 damage to anything caught in its path, unless stopped by a wall, vehicle or large object (including a large Nightbane), otherwise the flames continue to their full range, burning everything they touch. The 'Bane is impervious to his own flames, as well as natural fire and heat when this Talent is active (which is only the one melee round the fire breath is used). However, the character takes full damage from magical fire or the breath attacks of other Nightbane.

Limitations: Can only be used in Morphus form and only once per melee round (15 seconds), but counts as an *extra* melee attack.

<u>Range:</u> 30 feet (9.1 m) +5 feet (1.5 m) per experience level.

Cost: Eight P.P.E. to acquire permanently; 10 P.P.E. per melee round of use.

Heal Facade

This Talent enables a Nightbane to extend the superhuman regeneration rate of his Morphus to his Facade for a limited amount of time. When activated, the Facade form heals 1D6+4 S.D.C./ Hit Points per melee round!

Limitations: Healing is applicable only to the Facade.
<u>Duration:</u> One melee round per level of experience.
Cost: Ten P.P.E. to permanently acquire; 10 P.P.E. to activate for the first melee round, and 5 P.P.E. for each subsequent melee round.

Severance

The Nightbane is able to temporarily shut down his *supernatural aura*, making himself undetectable to other Nightbane, psychics, mages and supernatural creatures who can sense and track the supernatural aura of Nightbane and other paranormal beings. It can prevent detection by *Hounds, Hunters, Great Hounds,* and *Soul Trackers,* as well as defeat the "Sense Nightbane" ability inherent to other *Nightbane.* Furthermore, it makes the character's aura appear to be that of an ordinary human.

However, using the Severance Talent comes at a cost. As long as the Severance is in place and the supernatural aura is *suppressed,* the 'Bane can *not* use any of his other Talents nor cast any magic if the Nightbane is a Mystic or Sorcerer. Furthermore, the Nightbane feels cut-off from the metaphysical world, and the sensation of alienation can be unsettling, particularly for Mystics, who tend to feel the most attuned with the supernatural world.

Limitations: Not available until 4th level.
<u>Range:</u> Self, only.
<u>Duration:</u> One minute (4 melee rounds) per level of experience.
Cost: Fifteen P.P.E. to acquire permanently; 10 P.P.E. to activate.

Shadow Pockets

This Talent enables the Nightbane to access a mini-dimension suitable for storing small objects. Though it can be used in both the Facade and Morphus, P.P.E. must be spent for each item brought into or out of the pocket. The Shadow Pocket may hold up to five pounds (2.25 kg) per level of experience, but no single object may weigh more than 15 pounds (6.75 kg). Placing an object into or retrieving an object from the pocket takes one melee attack/action.

There are many different ways this Talent can appear to function. One is for the Nightbane to actually reach into the pockets of his clothing and another is to put his hand into a shadow and seem to remove an item from it like a sleight of hand trick.

While inside the pocket, objects are held in a state of limbo, and can only be brought back by the Nightbane who put them there. The objects can remain in the pocket indefinitely without ill effect, even if the Nightbane is sleeping or knocked unconscious. If the character is *killed* in Morphus form, his Morphus vanishes and all the objects in the Shadow Pocket appear where he last stood. If the character is killed in Facade form, the objects in the

Shadow Pocket remain in the shadow dimension and are presumably lost forever.

Limitations: Not available until 5th level.

Cost: Sixteen P.P.E. to acquire permanently; 8 P.P.E. to place or retrieve one object.

Shadow Weapon

A Nightbane with this Talent can create a melee weapon made of dark energy. The weapon can look like any type of one piece melee weapon, such as a sword, knife, axe, pole arm, pick, mace, morning star, etc., but not bows or modern weapons with moving parts. The character can only create one type of weapon and must decide what the weapon will look like when he first gains this Talent. From that point forward, his Shadow Weapon is always the same. Regardless of the weapon type, it inflicts 3D6 damage +1D6 additional damage at levels 6, 9, 12 and 15 – and does 50% greater damage to Night Princes and Nightlords! W.P. skill bonuses are applicable if the Shadow Weapon fits the Weapon Proficiency. The weapon is substantial and can be used to parry, but can NOT be thrown; the weapon disappears if it leaves the Nightbane's hands.

Limitations: Usable in Morphus form only; not available until 3rd level.

Cost: Fifteen P.P.E. to acquire permanently. 10 P.P.E. to activate for the first melee round and 5 P.P.E. for each melee round of subsequent use.

Speed Darkling

This Talent gives the Nightbane incredible speed. Take the Spd attribute number x10 mph (16 km). Thus if the character has a Spd of 9, he can now run 90 mph (144 km), if he had a Spd of 96 he can now run 960 mph (1,536 km), and so on. Speed Bonuses: +1 attack per melee, +1 on initiative, +4 to automatic dodge (the act of dodging does not use up a melee attack/action). Speed Penalty: When the duration of the enhanced speed ends, the character feels spent, his normal Spd is half, and he is -1 attack per melee, no initiative (is the last to attack) and is -2 to strike, parry and dodge for 1D6 melee rounds.

Limitations: Usable only in Morphus form and lasts for one minute per level of experience.

Cost: Twenty P.P.E. to permanently acquire it; 15 P.P.E. per melee to activate for the first minute and 5 P.P.E. for each minute of additional use.

Elite Talents from Nightbane® Survival Guide

A Face in the Crowd
Abduction
Commanding Presence
Forbidding Woods
Gorgon's Touch
Guardian Angel
Kill Switch
Lend a Hand

Nightshade
Spelljack
The Taint
True Reflection
Vicious Cycle
Voice of the Beast
Zombie Master

A Face in the Crowd

This powerful and useful Talent enables the Nightbane to temporarily conceal his inhuman appearance under the guise of a very average looking human being. The specific appearance of the human disguise automatically varies to fit the situation – i.e. attire will match the occasion, sex is that of the Nightbane, ethnicity mimics the local population, etc. – which also prevents the 'Bane from being recognized from use to use. When this Talent is in effect, the Nightbane temporarily loses all Morphus abilities (flight, weapon limbs, claws, horns, and Horror Factor). However, his attributes, P.P.E., S.D.C., Hit Points, and the like remain unchanged. Physical Beauty of the false appearance is 1D4+8.

Prerequisites: At least one monstrous or alien trait/feature from any appropriate table. This talent will not work on "Kens" and "Barbies" or other attractive or completely human looking Nightbane.

Limitations: Can be used only in Morphus form and not available until 4th level. The Talent does *not* mask the supernatural nature/aura of the Nightbane, meaning beings like Hounds and Hunters will recognize them for what they really are and are easily able to hunt those using this Talent!

Cost: Fifteen P.P.E. to permanently acquire; 10 P.P.E. to activate plus 5 for each minute of continued duration.

Abduction

Upon the activation of this Talent, a single target is whisked away by dark energies to a limbo-like pocket dimension. These energies can take the shape of a swirling vortex, sweeping portal, or even a beam of darkness that strikes the target from above. No harm comes to the target, but unless they can dimensionally teleport, they are stuck in limbo until the Talent's duration expires.

Prerequisites: One or more characteristics from the Alien Shape or Extraterrestrial Table.

Limitations: Usable in Morphus only. The target can attempt to save by rolling a 15 or better on a D20 with P.E. bonuses included.

Range: 90 feet (27 m) +10 feet (3 m) per level of experience.

Duration: One melee round (15 seconds) per level of experience.

Cost: Twenty P.P.E. to acquire permanently; 6 P.P.E to activate with a one melee round duration, +6 P.P.E. for each additional melee round.

Commanding Presence

When activated, a Nightbane with this Talent has his Mental Affinity temporarily increased by six points, with a minimum M.A. of 22. On a successful Trust/Intimidate roll, any person who sees the 'Bane will be affected by his charisma and supernatural charm. The subject(s) of the charm must roll under their M.E. attribute number to save vs the Nightbane's Trust/Intimidate or become completely swayed by the 'Bane. Those who fail to save will do nearly anything, short of endangering themselves or a loved one, to please the Nightbane. Even if the save is successful, others will still view the 'Bane with awe and reverence. This ability is cumulative with *Animal Magnetism* if the Nightbane possesses that trait, but Nightbane and other supernatural creatures are +3 to save against this Talent.

Prerequisites: Only Nightbane with an Unearthly Beauty or Angel trait may take this Talent.

Limitations: Usable only in the Morphus form and not available until 3rd level.

Cost: Twenty P.P.E. to acquire permanently; 12 P.P.E. to activate for the first two minutes, and an additional 6 P.P.E. for each two minutes thereafter.

Forbidding Woods

The Nightbane radiates an aura of fear and confusion over a large area of woodland. This can be a forest, city park, jungle, bamboo forest or anywhere with moderate to dense stands of living trees of any variety. For every 5 P.P.E. spent, the Nightbane transforms a 100 foot (30.5 m) radius of forest into a haunted wood. Shadows deepen, the trees become threatening and seem to sway with no apparent breeze, and there is the overwhelming sensation of being watched, followed, or stalked like prey. Those inside the area of effect who do not save vs a Horror Factor of 16, immediately attempt to flee the area in fear. Such frightened individuals are confused and disoriented, and are likely to get lost (must make a *Land Navigation* or *Navigation* roll at -50%), stumbling around the haunted grove terrified until the Talent elapses. Those who make their save vs Horror Factor are jumpy and nervous, but keep their wits about them.

Prerequisite: At least one Plant Life characteristic.

Limitations: Usable only in Morphus and not available until 3rd level.

Duration: 30 seconds (2 melee rounds) per level of experience.

Cost: Fifteen P.P.E. to acquire permanently. Activation costs 7 P.P.E. per 100 foot (30.5 m) radius of woods affected.

Gorgon's Touch

The Nightbane's physical touch turns the target temporarily into stone! Physical contact is necessary and the victim must roll a save of 14 or better (P.E. bonuses apply). A successful save prevents the character from turning to stone, but the P.P., P.E. and Spd attributes are (temporarily) reduced by 20% as he feels his joints and muscles stiffen. The effects of the touch are cumulative and any attribute bonuses from a high P.P. or P.E. disappear when reduced (adjust accordingly). Once the intended victim fails to save, or his P.P. and P.E. numbers are reduced to one, the victim is turned completely into stone. While stone, the victim is completely immobile and feels as cold and as hard as rock. There are no life signs (breathing, heartbeat, or even brain activity) whatsoever and the victim could be confused for an amazingly lifelike mannequin as items on the victim's body (clothes, weapons, etc.) are not turned to stone.

The Gorgon's Touch penetrates clothing and most armor, but will not penetrate modern full body armor unless the Nightbane's attack roll beats the Armor Rating (A.R.). The penalties and the stone form last one minute (4 melee rounds) per level of the Nightbane's experience. All the usual bonuses to strike apply when pressing the Gorgon's Touch attack, but does not inflict any punch, claw or P.S. damage since it is only a touch. The intended victim can either dodge or try to parry with something other than his or her own body, like a sword, piece of wood or gun.

Prerequisite: At least one characteristic from the Mineral Table.

Limitations: Usable only in Morphus. Not available until third level.

Duration: The victim remains stone for one minute per experience level of his attacker. The 'Bane possesses the Gorgon's Touch for one melee round or until his intended victim is turned to stone, whichever comes first.

Cost: Fifteen P.P.E. for permanent acquisition; 10 P.P.E. to activate for one full melee round in which the 'Bane's touch can turn a target to stone.

Note: The petrified individual's weight is doubled, but if he can be transported, he can be placed inside a jail cell, the trunk or back seat of a car, surrounded, stripped of his weapons and gear, but cannot be destroyed. Furthermore, the petrified victim is NOT aware of what transpires while he is turned to stone. It is as if he experienced a blackout.

Guardian Angel

A character with this Talent has a great desire to protect others even at his own expense. When the Talent is activated, a single target is selected for the Nightbane's mystical protection. This creates a ghostly image of the 'Bane superimposed over the protected individual. As long as the Guardian Angel Talent is activated and in place over the person it is to protect, any damage directed at him is transferred to his Nightbane Guardian Angel – the protected person remains unharmed, all damage comes off his

Nightbane Guardian Angel, first from S.D.C. then his Hit Points. When the 'Bane is down to 15 Hit Points of his own, the protective aura vanishes and damage directed at the innocent person will again hurt that person. This Talent is used by heroic and kind-hearted 'Bane to keep friends, allies, and innocent bystanders from being injured in a fray and can be cast upon as many as two people per level of the hero's experience.

Prerequisites: Useable only in Morphus form and only by characters with an Aberrant, Unprincipled, Scrupulous or Principled alignment.

Limitations: Not available until 2nd level.

Range: Line of sight.

Duration: Until the hero who cast it chooses to cancel the Talent or until his own S.D.C. is depleted to zero and Hit Points are reduced to 15.

Cost: Eight P.P.E. to acquire permanently; 4 P.P.E. to activate.

Kill Switch

This powerful ability mimics the effects of an electromagnetic pulse, temporarily shutting down all unprotected electronic devices (computers, cell phones, walkie-talkies, GPS devices, digital cameras, video cameras, surveillance bugs, flashlights and any small battery operated device, and even has a 01-40% chance of knocking out the electrical system of most automobiles and trucks) within the area of effect. The Talent temporarily overloads such devices, rendering them momentarily inoperable. This Talent also erases electronic data if stored on an unprotected hard drive or computer disk/CD/DVD as well as magnetic tape.

Prerequisites: At least one Biomechanical characteristic.

Limitations: Usable in Morphus form only and not available until 3rd level. Any high-tech systems with *hardened circuits* (such as most military electronics, sophisticated alarms and surveillance systems) are unaffected by a shut-down attempt, and continue to operate.

Range: 100 foot (30.5 m) radius around the Nightbane (his own gear is not affected).

Duration: Shuts down electronics for 1D6+1 minutes.

Cost: Fourteen P.P.E. to permanently acquire; 12 P.P.E. to activate with instant results.

Lend a Hand

This power allows the Nightbane to temporarily lend his Unnatural or Weapon Limb to another character, whether that other person is a human or Nightbane. The 'Bane does not lose his own Morphus characteristic or limbs, but can make an exact duplicate of one of his limbs appear on another character. The recipient of the Nightbane "special limb" sees his own arm turn into a copy of the Nightbane's, complete with claws, blades, tentacles or whatever, or one additional Nightbane appendage temporarily appears

as a third arm/limb with the special Nightbane features that come with it. The lent limb has all the characteristics and abilities of the Nightbane lending it, such as Supernatural Strength, claws, tentacles, etc. This Talent does NOT transfer spell casting abilities, Talents or any other ability except those associated with that one limb. Typically limited to the arms and hands, tails, or an extra limb.

Prerequisites: At least one Unnatural Limb or Biomechanical Morphus feature.

Limitations: Usable only in Morphus form and not available until 2nd level. Does not work on supernatural beings, must be a mortal or fellow Nightbane.

Cost: Twelve P.P.E. to acquire this Talent permanently; 6 P.P.E. to activate this Talent for a single melee round, and 3 P.P.E. more for every additional melee round.

Nightshade

Upon activation, the Talent releases a chemical scent into the air that has debilitating effects on everyone who inhales it. Characters get to save vs Non-Lethal Poison (16 or higher to save). Those who fail their saving throw fall into a deep sleep, remaining comatose for up to 2D4+2 minutes. Victims who successfully save are still affected, losing one attack per melee, -2 on all combat rolls, and -10% to all skills.

Prerequisites: At least one Plant or Extraterrestrial characteristic.

Limitations: Can only be used in Morphus form and is not available until 5th level. If someone under the effects of this Talent is attacked, he immediately awakens and can defend against the attack with full bonuses.

Range: 20 foot (6 m) radius around the Nightbane, +5 feet (1.5 m) per level of experience.

Cost: Fifteen P.P.E. to permanently acquire; 11 P.P.E. to activate with immediate effect.

Spelljack

This powerful Talent enables the Nightbane using it to hijack control of a spell cast either by someone near him or on an area, object, or person within his range! Once in control of the magic spell, the Nightbane may immediately cancel it, keep it in effect, reduce the duration or range/area of effect, or seize control of those affected by it. In order to affect spells with instant durations, the Nightbane must roll against the spell caster's initiative (though he gets to include his own initiative bonus to that roll). If the 'Bane wins the initiative, he seized control of the spell cast. If the mage wins initiative he casts his spell before the 'Bane can seize it, and it has the intended effect on the intended target (range, duration, level, and effects of the spell remain unchanged).

Another way this Talent can be used involves *Living Spells*. These enigmatic beings fall under the complete control of a

SIEMBIEDA 2017

Nightbane using the Spelljack Talent when they fail a save of 15. If Spelljacked, the Living Spell is forced to do anything the 'Bane commands for a duration of 1D4 minutes per experience level of the Nightbane, but is likely to feel very threatened and/or angry with the user of the Talent as soon as this duration elapses.

Prerequisites: At least one feature from the Fantasy Table or Infernal Table.

Limitations: Usable only by the Morphus form and not available until 4th level. Only effective against spell magic; cannot affect rituals, wards, circles, runes, magic weapons, and so on.

Range: The caster or target of the spell must be within 25 feet (7.6 m) of the 'Bane, +5 feet (1.5 m) per level of experience.

Cost: Twenty P.P.E. to permanently acquire; one quarter the P.P.E. the spell cost (rounded up) is needed to gain control of it.

The Taint

When this vicious Talent is used, anything the Nightbane *touches* seems to decay. Metal rusts where it is touched, cloth tatters, wood and plaster crack and splinter, rubber rots, and plants wither. Living creatures who fall prey to this Talent feel dark energy spread through them like ice water through their veins, wracking them with chilling cold and pain. Damage inflicted by the Taint is equal to 1D6 damage per every 2 P.P.E. spent, so 8 P.P.E. would result in 4D6 damage.

Furthermore, this damage causes a kind of magical necrosis, as it actually decays the tissue around the area touched. This effect inflicts a -20% penalty to any skill used to try and repair an object damaged by the Talent. Living beings recover lost S.D.C. and Hit Points at half the usual amount and it takes twice as long to recover. Medical skills used to try and treat this damage are performed at -20%, and even magical and psionic healing is *half* as effective. For supernatural beings like Nightbane and Wampyrs, Natural A.R. does not protect them. If touched they are damaged.

Since this is a touch-attack, it can be dodged or parried. However, any object used to parry it will take the damage instead, so using one's own limb to parry inflicts damage to the character, while parrying with a weapon sees damage done to the weapon. Victims of this devastating attack are more horrified if the attack continues, adding +2 to their attacker's Horror Factor. Any victim dropped below zero Hit Points by this power is -10% to Save vs Coma/Death.

Prerequisites: At least one Undead or Victim Table characteristic.

Limitations: Usable only by the Morphus form and not available until 3rd level. Can only spend 6 P.P.E. per level of experience on this attack. If the victim successfully saves vs magic, he suffers only one third damage.

Range: Touch.

Duration: Taint touch lasts for one melee round per activation.

Cost: Eighteen P.P.E. to acquire permanently; 9 P.P.E. to activate +2 P.P.E. = 1D6 damage. Up to 6 P.P.E. (3D6 damage) per level of experience can be spent on the amount to be inflicted. This Talent does 30% more damage to Night Princes and Nightlords. The P.P.E. is spent even if the attack fails to connect.

True Reflection

The use of this Talent temporarily imbues a mirror of any size with supernatural power. The mirror shows the "true" face of anyone reflected in it. Any shape-changing creatures are shown in their true form, Nightbane in Facade are shown in their Morphus (but the Facade is not revealed when a Nightbane in Morphus looks into it), and individuals under the effects of illusion or metamorphosis magic are revealed. Possessed individuals are shown with their true face as well as the ghostly image of the possessing being surrounding them.

This power is also alignment-based, allowing anyone who sees the person's reflection to be able to gauge the true alignment of the individual in front of the mirror. It is important to note that, in general, the average individual does not usually know what "alignment" they are. Some people can tell you that they are generally a good, selfish, or evil person, but most have no idea of their true selves.

Principled and Scrupulous individuals are shown as handsome, inspiring figures (Principled characters virtually glow) that radiate trust and surety. Those who see this in themselves in the mirror take heart as their beliefs are reinforced. The first time a Principled or Scrupulous person sees his reflection in a True Reflection mirror he receives a +2 to save vs Horror Factor and magic for 1D4 days. This bonus cannot be received again no matter how many times they look into a mirror affected by this Talent in the future.

Unprincipled characters see themselves generally as good-looking, but with several unsightly blemishes that they do not like, marring what would otherwise be a handsome or beautiful face. Still, there is beauty there enough to make them feel generally good about themselves and they are +1 to save vs Horror Factor for 1D4 days.

Anarchist characters see themselves as they are, but every little blemish, scar, and imperfection is enhanced greatly, dominating their faces.

Diabolic and Miscreant characters see twisted, monstrous visages of themselves that may horrify them. They must make a save vs Horror Factor of 14, or else they recoil from the mirror in fear or shame, losing an attack and initiative, and will attempt to flee the presence of all who may have seen their true face. The fear or shame lasts for 1D6 minutes until they regain their composure, but they will be shaken and unsure of their actions for 1D4 days, suffering a -2 to initiative as they second-guess every action. The fear occurs every time they look into a mirror affected by this Talent, but the uncertainty only happens the first time they see their true reflection.

Aberrant characters also have monstrous reflections in the mirror, but there is a sense of nobility and a spark of something

hopeful there, reflecting a chance for redemption if they want it. Aberrant characters must make a save vs a Horror Factor of 10 or suffer the same effects as a Miscreant or Diabolic character.

This Talent is a great opportunity for a character to undergo or finalize an alignment-shift, generally toward a more virtuous alignment. Aberrant and Anarchist characters are particularly affected by this Talent, as they are the most likely individuals to have an unrealistic view of their morals. Reaction over time to what they saw will vary from individual to individual. Some will later dismiss the mirror as a simple magic trick. Others may re-examine their lives, and some may grimly (or perhaps happily) accept what they saw as their real self and press on with the full knowledge that they are what they are, sinner or saint.

Supernaturally evil creatures are revealed in the mirror, but not affected by what they see. This includes the Nightlords and Night Princes who, although once human, have been permanently transformed into supernatural monsters. Vampires cast no reflection in a mirror affected by this Talent, giving their nature away. Humans, Wampyrs, Guardians, awakened Doppelgangers, and Nightbane, no matter what their alignment, are fully affected by this Talent.

Various uses. The Talent may also be used covertly, such as using a small compact to scan a group of people while pretending to fix your makeup. It can also be used very overtly by casting it upon a mirrored wall in a crowded ballroom, causing chaos. Some Nightbane within the Lightbringer organization have used this Talent to "screen" new recruits for both their true nature and moral fiber.

Prerequisites: Must have at least one Artificial or Unusual Facial Feature characteristic.

Limitations: Not usable until 3rd level.

Range: Touch and up to 50 feet away.

Duration: 5 minutes.

Cost: Twenty P.P.E. to acquire permanently; 5 P.P.E. for use on small pocket-mirrors, 10 P.P.E. for use on medium-sized mirrors (the size of someone's head to half-torso length), 15 P.P.E. for full-body and larger mirrors, 20 P.P.E. for massive mirrors like the length of a wall or ceiling up to 100 feet (30.5 m) long.

Vicious Cycle

This Talent represents the tragic irony that often plays out in cases of abuse and neglect, that of the victim later becoming the abuser. When this power is engaged the Nightbane becomes more physically imposing and aggressive, boosting his P.S. and S.D.C. by 20%, and gains +1 attack per melee round.

Prerequisites: One or more traits from the Victim or Disproportional Table.

Limitations: Not usable until 3rd level. Cannot affect the Facade form.

Range: Self.

Duration: One melee round per level of experience.

Cost: Ten P.P.E. to permanently acquire; 5 P.P.E. to activate.

Voice of the Beast

A Nightbane with this Talent must have an Animal Appearance. It allows the Nightbane to communicate with the type of animal or animals whose traits he bears. To use this Talent, the Nightbane can communicate through a means similar to Telepathy by making eye contact with the animal, or by hissing, growling or buzzing, whatever is appropriate, but the method of communication must be chosen when the Talent is acquired. Though the Nightbane cannot command the animal in any way, he can ask it questions or request its help. The animal will consider the Nightbane a friendly member of the same species and listen to what he has to say, but it is the animal itself which decides if it helps, answers any questions or declines (G.M.'s discretion).

Prerequisite: At least one Animal characteristic.

Limitations: Usable only by the Morphus form.

Duration: Will remain active as long as the Nightbane communicates with the animal only; if the Nightbane says anything to anyone other than the animal, he will need to reactivate the Talent.

Note: Keep in mind that animals retain their animal level of intelligence and perspective. This means they are only able to provide answers to simple questions that pertain to their nature and experience. Again, G.M.s, use your best discretion.

Cost: Ten P.P.E. to acquire it permanently; 5 P.P.E. to activate.

Zombie Master

Though not nearly as powerful as Necromantic magic, this Talent enables the character to animate and control the dead. The dead animated by this Talent have the same statistics of dead animated by the *Create Zombie* ritual (**Through the Glass Darkly**, page 59). Even if the 'Bane is incapacitated or killed, his animated dead minions continue to act on their last order until destroyed or the duration of the Talent elapses.

Prerequisite: Only Nightbane with an Infernal or Undead Morphus may acquire this Talent.

Limitations: Usable only by the Morphus form and not available until 3rd level. Can only animate one corpse (human or animal) per level of experience and only the dead bodies of mortals, not supernatural beings, though this does extend to Nightbane who died in their human Facade.

Range: All animated dead must stay within 300 feet (91.4 m) of the 'Bane.

Duration: 5 minutes per experience level of the Nightbane.

Cost: Twenty P.P.E. to acquire permanently; 11 P.P.E. to activate, animating one dead creature. One additional dead may be animated per level of experience, each costing 11 P.P.E., but they may all be animated in the same action.

Explore the Palladium Megaverse®

The Palladium "Fantasy" Role-Playing Game®

A world of epic fantasy, incredible magic and amazing beings including the shape-changing Changeling, ferocious Wolfen, monstrous Melech, dragons, giants, trolls, dragons and creatures that defy description. Players can create scores of human and inhuman characters.

Combat is fast and fun.

Magic is different! There is spell casting wizardry, the wards of the Diabolist, the circles of the Summoner, and the powers of Druidism. Plus the mind-powers of the Mind Mage, elemental magic, the enchantments of the Alchemists, the blessings of the priest, the dark magic of the witch and magic items and creatures galore.

Sourcebooks define the world, offer new types of player characters, different player races and monsters, adventures and/or adventure ideas. This line is currently Palladium's second best seller (behind *Rifts®* and just edging out *Heroes Unlimited™*). • $26.95 — 336 pages.

Rifts® Ultimate Edition

Dimensional *Rifts* are tears in the very fabric of space and time. Portals to other worlds. Doorways that allow the incredible, monstrous and magical to invade our world. Reshaping it into an alien landscape that is both frightening and wondrous, alien and yet strangely familiar.

Super-science, bionics, power armor and robots collide with the forces of magic, Techno-Wizardry, dragons and demons from the Rifts. Humankind struggles on the brink of extinction, and the possibilities are endless.

Discover a world where anything is possible and you are limited only by your imagination. • $39.95 – 376 page hardcover RPG.

Heroes Unlimited™ RPG, 2nd Ed.

Create any type of superhuman hero you can imagine.

Aliens, mutants, robots, cyborgs, super-soldiers, psychics, super-sleuths, martial arts masters, gun-toting vigilantes, super-geniuses, masters of magic, demigods, Mega-Heroes and more!

Over 100 super abilities, plus scores of sub-powers and 40+ psionic powers. Over 100 magic spells, plus enchanted weapons and objects.

Everything one needs to play other than dice and friends are in this complete role-playing game. Cover by Jim Steranko. Written by Kevin Siembieda • $26.95 — 352 pages.

After the Bomb® RPG

Discover the world of mutant animals. Play it as a stand-alone game environment or combine it with *Heroes Unlimited™*, but check it out.

Mutant animal creation rules that make building your mutant characters fast, fun and challenging. Over 100 mutant animals presented. More than 40 animal powers and psionics; many more if you include weird abilities exclusive to certain animal species. • $24.95 — 224 pages.

Ninjas & Superspies™ RPG

Over 40 different types of martial arts, oriental mysticism, and superhuman abilities combined with spies, gizmos, super-vehicles, cybernetic implants and disguises, and more to create the ultimate spy and combat game. A complete role-playing game with everything you need to play. A complete game in itself as well as completely interchangeable with *Heroes Unlimited™*. Written by Erick Wujcik. • $20.95 – 176 pages.

Nightbane® RPG

The world has never been the same since Dark Day. Some say the world governments have been supplanted, taken over by ... god only knows what. That dopplegangers can steal one's identity and life, and that demons and monsters lurk in the shadows. Creatures of evil who serve the Nightlords.

But the lords of shadow are not unopposed. There are creatures of light as well as creatures born from darkness but champion the light. These are the Nightbane. Ordinary people, many teenagers, able to shed their human facade and assume a supernatural alter ego. A monstrous, inhuman visage imbued with superhuman power and the stuff of magic. Written by C.J. Carella. • $24.95 – 240 pages.

Beyond the Supernatural™ RPG
A game of horror, mystery, & dark secrets

BTS-2™ is a stark, plausible reality where ghosts, demons, psychics, and magic are real, yet remain unknown to the world at large. Player characters are part of the secrets, part of the problems, and humanity's only true hope of dealing with the unexplained. Truly unique characters that will challenge and excite those who play them. New P.C.C.s include the Psychic Medium (and Spirit Guide), the Diviner and Autistic Psychic Savant, all with new and unique abilities. Characters like the Psychic Sensitive, Nega-Psychic and other original P.C.C.s get a face lift, new powers, and more details. The secrets of the supernatural, ESP, and magic revealed. • $24.95 – 256 pages. Written by Kevin Siembieda and Randy McCall.

Splicers® RPG

Splicers® is a new science fiction RPG set on a devastated world where machines rule, and human beings are vermin who are hunted and exterminated. The human struggle is complicated by a nano-virus that instantly turns metal objects touched by human flesh into killing machines. Consequently, humans have been forced to turn to organic technology to battle the world-dominating machines if they hope to reclaim any portion of their planet for themselves. Mega-Damage System – compatible with *Rifts®*, *Phase World®*, *Chaos Earth™* and *Mechanoid Space™*. • $23.95 – 224 pages. Written by Carmen Bellaire.

Palladium Books Inc.
39074 Webb Court
Westland, MI 48185

www.palladiumbooks.com

The Rifter® Subscription

The Rifter® **is your doorway to unlimited imagination** and numerous Palladium role-playing worlds. It offers new heroes, powers, weapons, magic and adventure for your games. It presents new villains, monsters and dangers to battle, and new ideas to consider.

It helps you unlock your imagination by showing you what gamers, just like *you*, have created. That's right, many of the articles and source material are written by ordinary gamers and fans like *you*. Other articles are by freelance writers and staff.

The Rifter® is made for *you*, our fans. Each issue presents unofficial (and sometimes official) source material, adventures, characters, monsters, villains, powers, weapons, equipment, ideas and fiction for **Rifts®, Chaos Earth®, Splicers®, Beyond the Supernatural™, Heroes Unlimited™, Ninjas & Superspies™, Palladium Fantasy RPG®, Nightbane®,** and/or any variety of other Palladium games and world settings. It's also a place where we test new ideas, and showcase new games, like *Dead Reign®* and the upcoming *Mechanoids® Space*.

It is also a way to get the latest news, coming attractions, and sneak previews of upcoming Palladium products, events and secret projects.

Sourcebook

As a sourcebook, each issue of **The Rifter®** presents optional and/or official source material for a variety of Palladium's role-playing settings – **Rifts®, Phase World®, Palladium Fantasy RPG®, Heroes Unlimited™, Nightbane®, Beyond the Supernatural™**, and other titles such as **After the Bomb®, Ninjas & Superspies™, Rifts® Chaos Earth®, Splicers®,** and others. Every issue includes material for 3-6 different Palladium RPG lines.

Magazine

As a magazine, each issue includes the latest news and goings on at Palladium Books, information on new product, our schedule of releases, convention appearances, special offers, and even sneak previews and extra "official" material for new Palladium games or sourcebooks.

Talent Show

The Rifter is unlike anything on the market because it is a way for *you*, the fan, the unpublished writer and hopeful young artist to get published and break into the industry.

No other game company does that, so take advantage of the opportunity to see *your* work and *your* name in print! You'll get a small payment (about $10 per printed page of text), four free copies of the issue your work appears in, and bragging rights to all your friends. Best of all, you get to share your ideas with thousands of other Palladium gamers.

Think it can't happen to you? Think again. Many of Palladium's artists and writers got started in **The Rifter®**, including *Apollo Okamura, Brian Manning, Mike Mumah, Carl Gleba, Todd Yoho, Brandon Aten, Taylor White, Jason Richards,* and *many others*.

Palladium is always looking for written material for **Rifts®, Chaos Earth®, Beyond the Supernatural™, Nightbane®, Palladium Fantasy RPG®, Heroes Unlimited™, Ninjas & Superspies™, After the Bomb®,** and all our game lines. We'd also like to see cartoons and comic strips.

Send your "article/source material" (5-30 pages) or art samples (photocopies, never original art), to *The Rifter® Submissions Dept, 39074 Webb Court, Westland, MI 48185.*

Subscribe Today

Lock in the current price and discount

The price of **The Rifter®** is $13.95 retail (a steal for 96 pages of RPG source material and adventures), but a subscription saves you even more money, and you have the convenience of delivery right to your door. All prices are in U.S. dollars.

- **$39.80 – that's only $9.95 each,** a savings of $16, and Palladium picks up the shipping cost. **Note:** This rate is *limited* to subscribers in the USA only.
- **$61.80 – Canada.** Our apologies, but Palladium Books can no longer cover the increased cost of postage to other countries. We hope you understand.
- **$75.80 – Overseas:** Overseas subscriptions *are* charged an additional fee for overseas shipping costs. Sorry. We are only passing along the additional postage costs, but it is hefty. Our apologies.
- **Free Shipping anywhere in the USA.**
- **Great Savings.**
- **A Megaverse® of adventure and fun.**
- **How to order.** *Send mail orders* with a check or money order payable to *Palladium Books* (for *$39.80 in the USA*) to:

Palladium Books®

39074 Webb Court

Westland, MI 48185

Credit Card Orders: Can be made on our web site *(www.palladiumbooks.com)* or by telephone 734-271-2903 (this is an order line *only*).

Check or Money Orders: Send them to the address above with a note indicating which issue number you want your subscription to start.

Please indicate what issue number you'd like your subscription to *start* (i.e., last issue, current issue, next issue, or when your current subscription ends).

This offer is good till December 31, 2017.

www.palladiumbooks.com

The Rifter® Series
___ 175 The Rifter® #75 – $13.95
___ 176 The Rifter® #76 – $13.95
___ 177 The Rifter® #77 – $13.95
___ 178 The Rifter® #78 – $13.95 (Spring)
___ 179 The Rifter® #79 – $13.95 (Summer)

Splicers® Note: Sourcebooks coming soon.
___ 200 Splicers® RPG – $23.95

Dead Reign®
___ 230 Dead Reign® RPG – $22.95
___ 231 SB 1: Civilization Gone™ – $12.95
___ 232 SB 2: Dark Places™ – $12.95
___ 233 SB 3: Endless Dead™ – $16.95
___ 234 SB 4: Fear the Reaper™ – $12.95
___ 235 SB 5: Graveyard Earth™ – $12.95
___ 236 SB 6: Hell Followed™ – $20.95
___ 237 SB 7: In the Face of Death™ (coming)

Rifts® Novels
___ 301 Sonic Boom™ – $9.95
___ 302 Deception's Web™ – $9.95
___ 303 Treacherous Awakenings™ – $9.95
___ 304 Tales of the Chi-Town 'Burbs™ – $12.95
___ 305 Rifts® Path of the Storm™ – $12.95

Weapons Books
___ 401 Weapons and Armor™ – $8.95
___ 402 Weapons and Castles™ – $8.95
___ 403 Weapons and Assassins™ – $9.95
___ 404 Weapons & Castles of the Orient™ – $9.95
___ 409 Exotic Weapons™ – $9.95
___ 410 European Castles™ – $9.95

Palladium Fantasy RPG®
___ 450 The Palladium Fantasy RPG® – $26.95
___ 4500HC Palladium Fantasy RPG® 30th Anniversary Hardcover – $50.00
___ 451 Dragons & Gods™ – $24.95
___ 453 Old Ones™ 2nd Ed. – $24.95
___ 454 Monsters & Animals™ 2nd Ed. – $24.95
___ 455 Adventures on the High Seas™ – $24.95
___ 458 Island at the Edge of the World™ – $20.95
___ 459 Yin-Sloth Jungles™ – $20.95
___ 462 Western Empire™ – $24.95
___ 463 Baalgor Wastelands™ – $24.95
___ 464 Mount Nimro™ – $20.95
___ 465 Eastern Territory™ – $24.95
___ 466 Library of Bletherad™ – $20.95
___ 467 Northern Hinterlands™ – $24.95
___ 468 Land/Damned 1: Chaos Lands™ – $24.95
___ 469 LoD 2: Eternal Torment™ – $24.95
___ 470 LoD 3: The Citadel – $24.95 (coming)
___ 471 Wolfen Empire™ – $20.95
___ 472 Mysteries of Magic™ One: Heart of Magic – $16.95
___ 474 Bizantium/Northern Islands™ – $20.95
___ 475 Garden of the Gods™ – $16.95 (coming)

Heroes Unlimited™ / After the Bomb®
___ 500-2 Heroes Unlimited™, 2nd Ed. – $26.95
___ 5000HC Heroes Unlimited™ 30th Anniversary Hardcover – $50.00
___ 501 Villains Unlimited™ Revised – $24.95
___ 503 After the Bomb® RPG – $24.95
___ 505 Road Hogs™ (After the Bomb® II) – $9.95
___ 507 Mutants Down Under™ (AB III) – $9.95
___ 511 Mutants of the Yucatan™ (AB IV) – $9.95
___ 513 Mutants in Avalon™ (AB V) – $16.95
___ 514 Mutants in Orbit™ (AB VI) – $16.95
___ 515 Aliens Unlimited™ – $24.95
___ 516 Heroes Unlimited™ G.M.'s Guide – $24.95
___ 517 Century Station™ – $24.95
___ 518 Gramercy Island™ – $24.95
___ 519 Aliens Unlimited Galaxy Guide™ – $24.95
___ 520 Mutant Underground™ – $16.95
___ 521 Powers Unlimited® One – $16.95
___ 522 Powers Unlimited® Two – $16.95
___ 523 Powers Unlimited® Three – $16.95
___ 525 Revised Ninjas & Superspies™ – $20.95
___ 526 Mystic China™ – $24.95
___ 527 Armageddon Unlimited™ – $20.95

Robotech® RPG
___ 550 Robotech® The Shadow Chronicles® RPG (manga size) – $16.95
___ 550HC Robotech® The Shadow Chronicles® Deluxe Hardcover RPG – $30.95
___ 5500HC Robotech® The Shadow Chronicles® Gold Ed. Hardcover RPG – $70.00
___ 551 Robotech® Macross® Saga Sourcebook – $16.95
___ 552 Robotech® The Masters Saga™ Sourcebook (NEW in 8½ x 11) – $20.95
___ 553 Robotech®: Expeditionary Force Marines Sourcebook – $20.95
___ 554 Robotech® The New Generation™ Sourcebook – $16.95
___ 555 Robotech® Genesis Pits Sourcebook – $16.95

Robotech® RPG Tactics™ (New!)
___ 55100 Robotech® RPG Tactics™ – $99.95
___ 55105 Robotech® RPG Tactics™ Rulebook – $20.00
___ 55101 UEDF Dice Pack – $12.00
___ 55102 Zentraedi Dice Pack – $12.00
___ 55201 UEDF Valkyrie Wing – $36.95
___ 55202 UEDF Destroid Pack – $32.95
___ 55203 UEDF Spartan Pack – $32.95
___ 55401 Zentraedi Regult Battlepods – $36.95
___ 55402 Zentraedi Artillery Battlepods – $36.95
___ 55403 Zentraedi Glaug Command – $36.95

Rifts® Chaos Earth®
___ 660 Rifts® Chaos Earth® RPG – $20.95
___ 661 Rifts® CE Creatures of Chaos™ – $12.95
___ 662 Rifts® CE The Rise of Magic™ – $12.95
___ 665 Rifts® Chaos Earth® First Responders™ – $16.95 (coming)
___ 666 Rifts® Chaos Earth® Resurrection™ – $20.95

Beyond the Supernatural™
___ 700 Beyond the Supernatural™, 2nd Ed. – $24.95
___ 702 Tome Grotesque™ – $20.95 (coming)
___ 703 Beyond Arcanum™ – $24.95 (coming)

Nightbane®
___ 730 Nightbane® RPG – $24.95
___ 731 Nightbane®: Between the Shadows™ – $20.95
___ 732 Nightbane®: Nightlands™ – $20.95
___ 733 Nightbane®: Through the Glass Darkly™ – $20.95
___ 735 Nightbane® Survival Guide™ – $20.95
___ 736 Nightbane® Dark Designs™ – $20.95

Rifts®
___ 800HC Rifts® RPG Ultimate Edition – $39.95
___ 801 Rifts® Sourcebook One Revised – $20.95
___ 802-E Rifts® World Book 1: Vampire Kingdoms™, Revised – $24.95
___ 803 Rifts® Conversion Book One™ – $24.95
___ 804 Rifts® WB 2: Atlantis™ – $20.95
___ 805 Rifts® Sourcebook 2: Mechanoids™ – $16.95
___ 807 Rifts® WB 3: England™ – $20.95
___ 808 Rifts® WB 4: Africa™ – $20.95
___ 809 Rifts® Dimension Book 1: Wormwood™ – $20.95
___ 810 Rifts® WB 5: Triax™ – $24.95
___ 811 Rifts® Pantheons of the Megaverse® – $24.95
___ 812 Rifts® Sourcebook 3: Mindwerks™ – $16.95
___ 813 Rifts® Mercenaries™ – $20.95
___ 814 Rifts® WB 6: South America – $20.95
___ 815 Rifts® WB 7: Underseas™ – $24.95
___ 816 Rifts® DB 2: Phase World® – $24.95
___ 817 Rifts® DB 3: Phase World® Sourcebook – $16.95
___ 818 Rifts® WB 8: Rifts® Japan™ – $24.95
___ 819 Rifts® WB 9: South America Two™ – $24.95
___ 820 Rifts® WB 10: Juicer Uprising™ – $20.95
___ 821 Rifts® WB 11: Coalition War Campaign™ – $24.95
___ 822 Rifts® WB 12: Psyscape™ – $20.95
___ 825 Rifts® WB 13: Lone Star™ – $20.95

___ 826 Rifts® WB 14: New West™ – $24.95
___ 827 Rifts® WB 15: Spirit West™ – $24.95
___ 828 Rifts® Sourcebook 4: Coalition Navy™ – $16.95
___ 829 Rifts® WB 16: Federation of Magic™ – $20.95
___ 830 Rifts® DB 4: Skraypers™ – $20.95
___ 831 Rifts® Index Volume Two™ – $16.95
___ 832 Rifts® WB 17: Warlords of Russia™ – $24.95
___ 833 Rifts® WB 18: Mystic Russia™ – $20.95
___ 834 Rifts® WB 19: Australia – $24.95
___ 835 Rifts® WB 20: Canada™ – $24.95
___ 836 Rifts® WB 21: Splynn Dimensional Market™ – $24.95
___ 837 Rifts® WB 22: Free Quebec™ – $24.95
___ 838 Rifts® WB 23: Xiticix Invasion™ – $20.95
___ 839 Rifts® Coalition Wars®: Sedition™ – $20.95
___ 840 Rifts® Coalition Wars®: Coalition Overkill™ – $16.95
___ 841 Rifts® Coalition Wars®: Sorcerers' Revenge™ – $16.95
___ 842 Rifts® Coalition Wars®: Cyber-Knights™ – $16.95
___ 843 Rifts® Coalition Wars®: Shadows of Evil™ – $16.95
___ 844 Rifts® Coalition Wars®: Final Siege™ – $24.95
___ 845 Rifts® Game Master Guide™ – $26.95
___ 846 Rifts® Aftermath™ – $24.95
___ 847 Rifts® DB5: Anvil Galaxy™ – $20.95
___ 848 Rifts® Book of Magic™ – $26.95
___ 849 Rifts® Adventure Guide™ – $24.95
___ 850 Rifts® Bionics Sourcebook™ – $16.95
___ 851 Rifts® DB 6: Three Galaxies™ – $20.95
___ 852 Rifts® Dark Conversions™ – $24.95
___ 853 Rifts® Chi-Town 'Burbs™ – $9.95
___ 854 Rifts® The Tolkeen Crisis™ – $12.95
___ 855 Rifts® The Black Vault™ – $9.95
___ 856 Rifts® The Vanguard™ – $9.95
___ 857 Rifts® WB 24: China One™ – $20.95
___ 858 Rifts® WB 25: China Two™ – $20.95
___ 859 Rifts® DB 7: Megaverse Builder™ – $16.95
___ 860 Rifts® DB 8: Naruni Wave 2™ – $16.95
___ 862 Rifts® WB 26: Dinosaur Swamp™ – $20.95
___ 863 Rifts® MercTown™ – $20.95
___ 865 Rifts® Merc Ops™ – $20.95
___ 866 Rifts® WB 27: Adventures in Dinosaur Swamp™ – $20.95
___ 867 Rifts® Mercenary Adventure Sourcebook – $12.95
___ 868 Rifts® WB 28: Arzno™ – $20.95
___ 869 Rifts® WB 29: Madhaven™ – $16.95
___ 870 Rifts® John Zeleznik Coloring Book – $5.95
___ 871 Rifts® Machinations of Doom™ – $18.95
___ 872 Rifts® DB 10: Hades™ – $24.95
___ 873 Rifts® DB 11: Dyval™ – $24.95
___ 874 Rifts® WB 30: D-Bees of North America™ – $24.95
___ 875 Rifts® DB12: Dimensional Outbreak – $24.95

___ 876 Rifts® Megaverse® in Flames™ – $24.95
___ 876HC Rifts® Megaverse® in Flames™ Gold Hardcover Edition – $50.00
___ 877 Rifts® Heroes of the Megaverse® – $16.95
___ 878 Rifts® Sourcebook: Shemarrian Nation™ – $16.95
___ 880 Phase World®: Fleets of the Three Galaxies™ – $16.95
___ 881 Rifts® WB 31: Triax™ Two – $24.95
___ 883 Rifts® DB 14: Thundercloud Galaxy™ – $20.95
___ 884 Rifts® Vampires Sourcebook™ – $20.95
___ 885 Rifts® WB 32: Lemuria™ – $24.95
___ 886 Rifts® Black Market™ – $24.95
___ 886HC Rifts® Black Market™ Hardcover Gold Edition – $60.00
___ 887 Rifts® WB 33: Northern Gun™ One – $24.95
___ 888 Rifts® WB 34: Northern Gun™ Two – $26.95
___ 889 Rifts® Sourcebook: Coalition States, Heroes of Humanity™ – $20.95
___ 890 Rifts® Dimension Book 15: Secrets of the Atlanteans™ – $24.95
___ 890HC Rifts® DB 15: Secrets of the Atlanteans™ Gold Edition – $50.00
___ 891 Rifts® World Book: Sovietski™ – $24.95 (coming)
___ 892 Rifts® Sourcebook: The Disavowed™ – $16.95 (coming)
___ 893 Rifts® CS: Heroes of Humanity™ Arsenal Sourcebook – $16.95 (coming)
___ 894 Rifts® Haunted Tech™ – $16.95 (coming)
___ 895 Rifts® Living Nowhere™ – $16.95 (coming)
___ 2510 Rifts® & The Megaverse® Art Book – $22.95
___ 2510-HC Rifts® & The Megaverse® Art Book, Hardcover – $50.00
___ 2510-CML Rifts® & The Megaverse® Art Book, Collector's Masterwork – $125.00

Miscellaneous Products
___ 600 Deluxe Revised RECON® RPG – $22.95
___ 2537 Gamer Coffee Mug – $10.00
___ 2545 Dead Reign™ Coffee Mug – $10.00
___ 2554 Palladium Bookmarks, Set One – $5.00
___ 2555 Palladium Bookmarks, Set Two – $5.00
___ 2561 Property of Chi-Town Library Pencil – $0.50 each
___ 2562 Future Visions™ – The Artistry of Charles Walton II – $13.95
___ 2566 Glitter Boy Mouse Pad – $9.95
___ 2567 Old Ones Mouse Pad – $9.95
___ 2568 Zombie Graveyard Mouse Pad – $9.95
___ 2575 Rifts Poker Cards 1 (full color) – $11.99
___ 2576 Rifts Poker Cards 2 (line art) – $11.99

Note: T-shirts and other products can be found online: www.palladiumbooks.com

Rifts® Miniatures
___ MI8002 Xiticix Pack – $18.00
___ MI8004 Coalition Dog Pack – $18.00
___ MI8005 Men of Magic Pack #1 – $18.00

___ MI8006 Cyborgs Pack #1 – $18.00
___ MI8007 Simvan & Ostrosaurus Pack – $18.00
___ MI8008 Coalition Skelebots Pack #1 – $18.00
___ MI8009 Coalition SAMAS Pack #1 – $22.00
___ MI8010 Coalition Sky Cycle Pack – $22.00
___ MI8011 Coalition Dog Pack #2 – $18.00
___ MI8015 Damaged Skelebots Pack #1 – $12.00
___ MI8016 Cyber-Adventurers Pack – $18.00
___ MI8017 Rogues & Scout Pack #1 – $18.00
___ MI8018 Brodkil & Witchling Pack – $18.00
___ MI8019 Damaged Skelebots Pack #2 – $18.00
___ MI8020 Psi-Stalkers & Scouts Pack #1 – $18.00
___ MI8021 Shadow Beast – $12.00
___ MI8022 Mystic Knight – $6.00
___ MI8023 Lord Magus – $6.00
___ MI8024 High Magus – $6.00
___ MI8025 Coalition Psi-Stalker – $6.00
___ MI8026 Coalition Dog Boy in DPM-D1 Armor – $6.00
___ MI8027 Coalition Dog Boy #2 – $6.00
___ MI8028 Coalition Dog Boy #3 – $6.00
___ MI8029 Coalition Dog Boy #4 – $6.00
___ MI8030 Coalition Dog Boy #5 – $6.00
___ MI8031 Glitter Boy – $20.00
___ MI8032 Glitter Boy Pilot – $6.00
___ MI8033 Kydian Overlord – $20.00
___ MI8034 Dragonsaurus – $10.00
___ MI8035 Slaver and Slave (Atlantis) Set – $10.00
___ MI8036 Crazy – $6.00
___ MI8037 Juicer #1 – $6.00
___ MI8038 Juicer #2 – $6.00
___ MI8039 Cyborg #1 – $12.00
___ MI8040 Cyborg #2 – $12.00
___ MI8041 Cyborg #3 – $6.00
___ MI8042 Coalition Officer – $6.00
___ MI8043 Coalition Grunt #1 – $6.00
___ MI8044 Coalition Grunt #2 – $6.00
___ MI8045 Coalition Grunt #3 – $6.00

www.palladiumbooks.com